MW00574185

Free Time

Free Time

THE HISTORY OF AN ELUSIVE IDEAL

Gary S. Cross

NEW YORK UNIVERSITY PRESS
New York

NEW YORK UNIVERSITY PRESS
New York
www.nyupress.org

Library of Congress Cataloging-in-Publication Data
Names: Cross, Gary S., author.
Title: Free time : the history of an elusive ideal / Gary S. Cross.
Description: New York : New York University Press, [2024] |
Includes bibliographical references and index.
Identifiers: LCCN 2023003746 | ISBN 9781479813070 (hardback ; alk. paper) |
ISBN 9781479813087 (ebook) | ISBN 9781479813094 (ebook other)
Subjects: LCSH: Leisure—History. | Labor—History. | Work-life balance—History.
Classification: LCC HD4904.7 .C76 2024 | DDC 306.4/812—dc23/eng/20230201
LC record available at https://lccn.loc.gov/2023003746

This book is printed on acid-free paper, and its binding materials are chosen for strength and durability. We strive to use environmentally responsible suppliers and materials to the greatest extent possible in publishing our books.

Manufactured in the United States of America

10 9 8 7 6 5 4 3 2 1

Also available as an ebook

Contents

1

The Trouble with Time Today

Day to day, we experience time in blocks of work and freedom—periods of obligation (with or without pay) and durations of choice. Sleep is necessary down time. Periodically, we become conscious of these blocks, especially when they seem unbalanced or disrupted. Despite living in a society that heavily prioritizes work, many feel overworked and seek (however impractically) a better balance between obliged and free time. Others experience a surfeit of "play" time due to unemployment, retirement, and crises like the COVID-19 pandemic, which led to layoffs and shutdowns of schools. Such "free" time seems deprived of the social and personal meanings as well as the economic advantages of work time. Time grows tedious when unstructured and many ultimately find the technological delivery of pleasure to be satiating, ultimately even boring. Yet this is a daily experience for many of the jobless and retired.

Especially during the lengthy shutdown of "Covid times" all the worst aspects of our dealing with time came to the fore: both kids and grandparents, forcibly cut off from friends in school or senior centers, experienced loneliness. An extended vacation from school lost any appeal and the freedom from work of the retired grew stale. The "sheltering in place" and "social distancing" of the pandemic was especially stressful, depriving many of accustomed social interaction and obliging them to fall back unsatisfactorily on their personal "play" resources. Yet for many others the pandemic heightened still another feature of modern life—overwork. For some, this was long hours of overtime (increasingly without bonus pay rates) in hospitals, Amazon "fulfillment centers" (where twenty minutes of rest on ten-hour workdays became common), and delivery services.[1]

The stress of scarce free time during Covid times often took on another, relatively recent form—the problem of finding time for family and child care when both parents worked full-time. The COVID-19 pandemic accentuated the stress of the two-income household that sometimes has left personal and domestic care compromised. COVID-19 ramped up this pressure as school children were forced to stay at home, adding to the chores of parents (especially mothers) deprived of the services of teachers, coaches, and others. The lines between work time/space and personal time/space were also blurred as employees worked at home. While some businesses during the pandemic found advantages in remote work from home, for many workers this arrangement turned the fixed workday into work through the day . . . and into the night. Free time disappeared.[2]

But the problem of time scarcity had been building for years. This has been hard to detect: at least since the 2008 recession, professionals and office workers have become less secure in their jobs, increasingly reluctant to take even earned time off. The 24/7 work ethic remains, despite repeated studies that show the negative impact on productivity of long workdays. Burnout from overwork has been repeatedly reported among medical doctors (42 percent in a 2018 survey). Resistance to long hours and inflexible schedules seems especially pronounced among younger employees, the millennials, who, it is claimed, face older bosses who do not share the family-work conflicts of their underlings and assume productivity comes only with long office time.[3]

American business lags behind others in recognizing the needs of employees for free time for family or themselves. One estimate is that only 9 percent of American companies provided paid maternity leave in 2014. While other nations have offered generous paid parental leave for years, only in 1993 did the US Congress pass the "Family and Medical Leave Act," sanctioning twelve weeks of *unpaid* leave for baby, parent, or spouse care, but only for employees on the job for a year and in companies with more than fifty workers. The wealthy have progressively turned to paid child and home care. No one expects Congress to restrict employer rights to email or phone workers at home (as instituted in France in 2017) or for many business to consider a four-day workweek (as has happened in some workplaces in Spain on an experimental basic in 2021 and Britain in 2022).[4]

Beyond all this is the oft-noted disparity between the work year of Americans as compared to Europeans: in 2021, employed Americans worked an average of 1,767 hours per year compared to 1,354 hours for employees in Germany (much due to paid vacations at thirty-five days per year compared to an average of thirteen in the US, though many Americans do not take all of their vacation time). Americans work even more than the workaholic Japanese with 1,738. With no legal rights to holidays (paid or otherwise) as compared to Europeans, Americans' recognition of the right to a private life has been largely limited to the employers' goodwill and desire to retain the loyalty of the worker. With stagnation in wages over decades, as one scholar notes, "Americans simply can't afford to work less."[5] Very telling is the study of Valerie Ramsey and Neville Francis that found that Americans (over age fourteen) in 2005 enjoyed a mere four hours more per week of leisure (free from home and market work) as compared to 1910.[6]

The COVID-19 pandemic accentuated existing problems of time scarcity but also time disappointment. While free time for some was extended when schools and retail and entertainment venues were closed to scotch the epidemic, the pleasures of the plethora of electronic media could satisfy only to a degree. To be sure, the digital revolution with internet social media, interaction gaming, and even smart TV streaming has mitigated the loneliness of the quarantine. But even all that choice eventually became boring. Moreover, that revolution furthered a contemporary trend—the substitution of virtual interaction for the real (be it social, sensual, sexual, or whatever). One prominent sign of this substitution is the decrease in hours per week that Americans spend with friends, dropping from a stable 6 ½ hours between 2000 and 2013 to 2 ¾ in 2021, according to the Census Bureau's American Time Use Survey. The decline began not with COVID-19 but when the smartphone reached a majority of Americans.[7] In any case, surprise and often disappointment with what is done with free time remains.

With the question of free-time use comes the question of culture. Broadly, free time raises the question of what kind of culture to make in it. Free-time culture relates fundamentally to two issues: a search for personal expression and autonomy and a quest for worldly engagement. For the sake of simplification, I will concentrate on the social aspect of that "world." The individual and the social dimensions of free time have often been in conflict, but both are essential to any definition of happiness. Contemporary free-time culture offers seemingly limitless personal choices (hundreds of channels of electronic entertainment with a global reach) and access to apparently boundless opportunities for interacting with others (as in near universal automobility and internet social media). Nevertheless, our daily dose of pleasure does not seem to measure up to expectations for personal and social achievement that are part of the promise of modernity.

In both the question of time scarcity and time use, there is a sense of loss—insufficient free time and free time that is unfulfilling. And that loss is not there just during exceptional situations like the COVID-19 crisis, but, for many, it is an unexplained and often unrecognized condition of twenty-first-century daily life in America and much of the industrial world. For two hundred and fifty years, industrialization has meant labor- and thus time-saving innovation; and there have been periodic efforts to expand time free from labor. Yet, work time has scarcely declined over the past nearly eighty years in the US. And, even with more free time, the expectation that free time would bring greater cultural enrichment and happiness has often been disappointed. Winning and making satisfying free time has eluded America especially. Explaining how we have addressed these abiding issues is this book's mission.

Coping Today with Free-Time Scarcity and Disappointment

The "imbalance" of work and life across the day is the most noted form of this surprising scarcity of free time. Understandably, remedies for time imbalance are continually offered in a long-established American tradition—self-help books.[8] Many are found on airport newsstands and publicized by the appearance of their authors on TV talk shows and online blogs. While scholars and human resources professionals measure the costs and benefits of flextime, special leaves, and other accommodations to the stresses and conflicts between work and family,[9] these self-help books focus on the attitudes and actions of individual workers. An edited survey of this approach is the *Harvard Business Review*'s *Guide to Work-Life Balance*, where experts encourage a "full life" made possible by thoughtful planning designed to reduce personal stress in the balancing act of career success and fulfilling family life. Such planning requires distinguishing between necessary and optional uses of time in both work and life and learning to be "present" in both essential periods.[10] Rather than address the actual problem of too many hours at work and too few at home, most "work-life balance" writers focus on training readers to manage work time more efficiently: reducing meetings, using remote work options, and setting limits to what can be expected at work.[11] Matthew Kelly (among others) even calls the work-life balance a myth (denying there was a conflict and suggesting that the term suggests that "life" is more important than work). Instead, employees need to develop a "strategy, daily attention, self-awareness and discipline" to improve satisfaction in both work and life.[12]

Inevitably, the work-life balance literature tends to devolve into heroic stories of achievers. A common theme is the profile of Chris O'Neil, a male executive, who rises at 5:30 a.m. to meditate before he drops the kids at school and then goes to the club for more exercise before a full day of focused business. Many of these books follow Tony Schwartz's *Power of Full Engagement: Managing Energy, Not Time* (2003), with his stress on maximizing personal energy (with exercise) rather than attempting to increase time free from work.[13] An interesting variation is the books geared for the female reader and the debate about whether life and work can be reconciled. A prominent group argues that career women must "lean in" to work and make "life" (or family) time secondary in order to prove their commitment to the job.[14]

It sometimes is not obvious that these self-help writers have actually considered time in the work-life balance question. But time is a real, if often complex, problem: How much flextime is needed for family? Is giving more free time to workers with dependents really fair to those without such needs? These books seldom address the emergence of a "gig economy," where flextime is less an issue and where unpredictable working hours are often more the problem. Note that in 2015 only a quarter of Walmart workers had a regular work schedule. Work-life books generally ignore the problems of all but the professional elite. This literature also seldom addresses the right or value of free time for personally attained happiness, only conceding the need (perhaps) of family care. In any case, its main thrust is to maximize personal efficiency, turning work and life into modernized versions of the old time-and-motion studies of early twentieth-century efficiency experts.[15]

Still, the fact that this literature exists at all points to the dilemma of many Americans—that they have little control over their time at work or home. The answer to this dilemma is mostly to adapt psychologically. And this "solution" suggests that the division between work and life is a personal choice, even though many wage earners have no choice in their working hours if they want a job. Even where there is a choice (as in taking on after-hours work), the laggard growth in income among the low waged has forced many to work more hours than the well paid.[16] In sum, the self-help literature hardly provides answers to the elusive problem of time scarcity and the historic lag in the reduction of work time.

Beyond the pressing problem of free time are frustrations over how free time is used. Here too there is a lot of advice about causes and especially remedies for this disappointment in free-time culture. One thoughtful response is to focus on the dilemmas of our highly commercialized free-time culture, especially consumer spending based on competing with others (or emulation) and unpurposive accumulation or cluttering of goods. The answer here often is "minimalism," a rejection of consumerism in free time. A vast literature and popular documentaries offer guidance on living with less consumption: two dozen videos on the subject were available on Amazon Prime Video in the Spring of 2021. Joshua Fields Millburn and Ryan Nicodemus created websites, podcasts, and a Netflix documentary (*Minimalism: A Documentary About the Important Things*) to advocate eliminating the distraction of accumulated stuff (and working so much to amass it). These sources argue that fewer possessions can lead to more meaningful relationships with others and nature. If we were to eliminate clutter in closets, perhaps even move into a "tiny house" or take to the road in a minimalist van or truck, we would be "living more deliberately." Our possessions would all serve an essential purpose.[17]

Minimalists share much with ancient Christian ascetics, but the minimalists claim also to address modern issues: the false, ready-made identities in consumer goods created in advertising, the treadmill of fashion, and the absurdity of oversized houses that are scarcely used. Minimalists deny that we necessarily have to define ourselves and our relationships with others through goods. Rather, they argue, consumer goods impede self-realization and social and worldly engagement. In support of this approach is Juliet Schor's insight that consumer materialism short-circuits the need for an aesthetic relationship with things. Consumerism encourages a superficial engagement with consumer goods because so many are accumulated to keep up with the Joneses.[18] Though a lot of this thinking is abstract, even mystical, minimalist advice can be very practical. For example, Project 333 counsels us to limit the number of clothes in our closets to thirty-three items for three months, carefully selected for personal meaning and utility. Minimalists argue that (with finesse and compromise) reduced consumerism can even become a family way of life, freeing children as well as parents from the irrational desires and demands foisted them by advertising and peer pressure.[19]

Despite these insights and efforts to mainstream minimalism, inevitably this approach appeals to a minority. Its ideas are occasionally noted in the press, but with little social impact. Minimalist advice is often mocked as part of a geeky elitism that ignores the real world of the majority, who supposedly lack the security and self-confidence to find "meaning" without the latest fashion or gadget.[20]

A second challenge to the culture of free time argues that happiness requires not just less consumption but a new set of free-time activities based on the findings of science. Especially important here is "positive psychology," which is focused on creating conditions for "happiness" through purposive play and an "experience economy" based on encounters and activities rather than goods.[21] In this vein, Benjamin K. Hunnicutt argues that private enterprise can provide alternatives to consumer culture's disappointments, built on an understanding of what experiences create happiness.[22] This is part of a longer tradition, often associated with Mihaly Csikszentmihalyi and his theory of the "flow," where an activity (a game, sport, or even social interaction) is designed to challenge but not frustrate the "flow" of the participant, resulting in the individual's playful immersion.[23]

The experience economy draws on positive psychology to identify behaviors and experiences that meet complex and even contradictory needs (for the sensual, but also the cognitive; for the interactive, but also the autonomous). The object is to facilitate independence and self-initiation (rather than the typical passivity of consumerism) but also foster relatedness to others and new things. The experience economy aims to create mental and emotional complexity in a fearless encounter with the new and even the liminal. But it also is supposed to bring intellectual and emotional integration (once called refinement). All this is to provide an alternative to the disappointment of passive, repetitive, and satiating free-time culture—and, presumably, it can be provided in the market.[24]

This happiness literature offers biologically based claims about how to create positive experiences and does not require a withdrawal from contemporary society (as the minimalists seem to). This perspective offers promise, but it faces major obstacles. Capitalism seems not to be leading (on its own) to a "higher civilization," as Simon Patten predicted in 1907, and the experience economy is still vague and unformed, with as yet few signs of realizing "liberating" and self-directed "experience" as the happiness literature advocates.[25] This is not to denigrate these proposals or to reject efforts to clarify them but to recognize the enormity of the problem of change.

This rough-and-ready review of contemporary responses to the twin problems of time scarcity and cultural disappointment points to important aspects of these issues, but the responses themselves are also problematic. The advice literature for coping with work-life dilemmas and those around free-time culture comes up short. Advocates of a work-life balance underestimate the constraints and limited choices, especially of working people, often offering little more than advocating that we "lean in" to the competitive game. More subtly, suggestions for improving free-time culture with spending constraints or more fulfilling "experiences" than are provided by modern consumerism sometimes underestimate the pressures and appeals of consumerism and the power of the market to commoditize even well-meaning "happiness" activities. Both paths for coping with the modern problems of time and culture address only part of the story. They ignore the fact that the work-time dilemma is inextricably tied to the dilemma of free-time culture. Some, but not all, analysts lack a historical understanding of the time and culture problem—the legacy of past ideas and social institutions as well as past expectations and disappointments. I argue that our present quandary is rooted in past decisions and trends—political, social, cultural, and even technological—that shape and limit our present attitudes and choices. To understand and then address these dilemmas of time and culture, we must go back in history and search for the big picture. So, let us dig a little deeper.

Bigger Questions: A Historical Approach

Our understanding of time and its uses is rooted in the past, in our biological/evolutionary inheritance, but especially in a cultural heritage where our ancestors adjusted to and transformed how they divided time between work and leisure and how they constructed their culture in free time. Some of these patterns continue to shape contemporary choices; others have disappeared and cannot (or should not) be recovered. Both inform and are useful to us today. Moreover, past expectations about time and culture are as enlightening as their disappointments.

Since agriculture and craft production appeared about ten thousand years ago, time free from work for most people has been episodic and seasonal, with festival periods being the most common and certainly most meaningful form of free time. Festival free time has had an abiding appeal to modern readers, sometimes with suggestions that at least parts of festival culture might be revived.[26] Over centuries, elites emerged (as warriors and administrators but also priests and intellectuals) who, by definition, were unburdened by daily obligations of labor. They enjoyed not only more free time than the vast majority but opportunities for very different uses of it (often displaying their wealth and power). A very few, however, devoted free time to personal contemplation/cultivation or to free social engagement separate from vocational or other practical/prudential matters. This combination defined an ideal meaning of leisure- or free-time culture that survives to the present (as in the modern happiness literature noted above).[27] There has been a tendency to glorify this "leisure" culture (usually identified with classical Greek philosophy, especially Aristotle) and to suggest that it might be recovered and used as a model. However, it cannot be extricated from its historical and social nexus: aristocratic leisure resting on slave or otherwise dependent labor. This should make us wary of finding in it the solution to contemporary problems. But this ideal remains part of the cultural furniture of our lives.[28]

These premodern patterns, however, are primarily background to the revolution of industrialization that is deeply significant in explaining time and culture today. The key was the complex development of capitalism with its roots in the fifteenth century in Western Europe but taking off only late in the eighteenth century. Broadly understood, capitalism challenged popular forms of free time by reducing the role of seasonal festivals and imposing regularity in work and eliminating intermittent leisure. But, for the privileged, historically free from work on the farm and in the shop, capitalism also eroded the leisure ethic of the traditional aristocracy, replacing it with a work ethic championed by merchants and industrialists. This created, as we shall see, the foundation of modern work obsessions and the expectation of limitless growth.

This is well known (if oversimplified), but capitalism also produced new ideals of free-time culture. By the end of the seventeenth century, a genteel culture had emerged, creating new forms of personal cultivation and sociability in such forms as private reading, restrained music and dance, and rule-restricted games and sports. Despite modern rejection of many aspects of this bourgeois tradition, with its formality and restraint, it survives and, for some, is still the solution to the culture question.

But the legacy of early capitalism went further. By the nineteenth century, along with its increased time discipline and new forms of genteel leisure, capitalism produced both wealth and distress that led to new expectations for time and culture. Workers, but also enlightened sections of the elite, demanded the reduction of work time for relief from labor, as well as for a democratic extension of cultural fulfillment in free time. Though seldom acknowledged by historians, a central tenet of the eighteenth-century Enlightenment was to mobilize human creativity and happiness by liberating time from work and creating a life-affirming culture in free time. By the middle of the nineteenth century, this idea took the form of John S. Mill's expectation of the "stationary state" economy, where production became sufficient to meet human needs and further progress could be devoted to the cultivation of self and community in time free from the market.[29]

Along with a belief in the progressive liberation of time from labor came the conviction that prosperity would lead to the end of barbaric pleasures, replacing them with "rational recreation"—adult education, healthy exercise, and family activities, for example—modeled on genteel practices and developed by an emerging bourgeoisie. More free time for all presumably would make the leisure ideals of the ancient Greeks available for everyone by replacing exhausting and boring labor with machines, and thus eliminating slavery and dependent labor. Technology and science would liberate humanity from toil and life-draining want and disease. As we shall see, communities of religious contemplation and immersive practice as well as warrior and court elites had long basked in free time. To progressives, however, industrialism was to liberate everyone from endless toil, "enslaving" the machine rather than the human, and making (with training) the life of leisure of the monk, aristocrat, and bourgeois available for all.

From the end of the eighteenth century, the expectation of expanded free time and belief in the inevitability of its "improvement" and "democratization" were inseparable, at least to the progressive elite. Even if technology and science were to bring more goods, some economists believed that material needs were *satiable*—their satisfaction would be reached. With this, people would choose more time free from work and the market rather than still more goods. With the end of scarcity in view, thinkers began to predict an era of expanding free time and promoted its cultivated use (often modeled on classical ideals of leisure). Obviously, these assumptions today have largely been forgotten or denied.

About a century ago learned and respected people believed that a revolution in industrial productivity, marked by Ford's assembly lines and the munitions factories of World War I, would soon lead to the accomplishment of a historic dream—the satiation of human physical needs and the realization of Mill's stationary state economy. This, in turn, would necessarily lead to greater time free from work and create new opportunities for organizing personal and public leisure. Advocates of reduced work time won a share of this increase in productivity through successful movements for an eight-hour workday (an international standard in most industrial countries after World War I) and paid holiday leaves (at the national level). Some went on to propose a progressive disengagement from the pains of work for a society built around personal autonomy and renewed social solidarities in leisure. All this came out of the dream of the benefits of industrialization in the nineteenth and early twentieth centuries, even if unrealized today.

Time and Culture Today: Explaining the Unexpected

Questions immediately arise: Why has there not been a progressive liberation of time from obligation? Why has increased productivity led to increased consumption but not decreased work time as economists once expected? Closely related is the question of the fate of earlier expectations of an enhanced free-time culture. Why this historical failure? Answering these questions returns us to the dilemmas of time and culture today.

There are many possible explanations. Perhaps the most common comes from much of modern economics—that contemporary work-time and free-time use are the result of consumer choices. This has produced a general preference for income from work instead of time free from work. Meanwhile, the content of free-time culture, many economists have argued, is a matter of personal taste (recalling the famous dictum "There is no disputing taste"). This can be a complicated argument when economists try to explain why consumers do not try to optimize both income and free time. But I argue that this approach unfairly minimizes the lack of choice about work time (often determined by employers and the market) and ignores how past reductions of work have placed political and social constraints on future reductions. Most Americans work around forty hours a week in large part because of a 1938 law that has become a fixed standard ever since. Likewise, the character of our free-time culture is shaped by forces (technological, cultural, and social) that make the claims of individual choice seem naive at best.

Other explanations that go beyond presumed "choice" are rather more sophisticated, seeking to explain our modern frustration with time scarcity. Many emphasize how relatively recent shifts in economic power explain the persistence of long work time. For example, Jamie McCallum's *Worked Over: How Round-the-Clock Work is Killing the American Dream* (2020) finds that since 1970 the expansion of corporate political power, the rise of digital technologies' control over work, and the decline of unions explain the increased pressure to work longer and accept more intense and more regulated hours. The accompanying lag in real income among low-paid employees has reduced any incentive to decrease work time or for employees to challenge controls or intensification. According to McCallum, all this has led to a rise in the average American work year—from 1,664 to 1,883 hours—from 1975 to 2016 (figures often disputed). These trends have "prohibited our wealth from translating into free time."[30] Beyond this relatively short-term analysis of the shifts in economic (or class) power, McCallum finds that neoliberalism since the late 1970s has reinforced the American work ethic. Office professionals, trained in the values of productivity and careerism, have adopted the work ethic with a vengeance. Congress's demand, starting in 1996, that welfare benefits for families require wage work has reinforced the priority of work.[31]

A second explanation of our time frustrations focuses on the question of free-time culture. Instead of emphasizing recent political and economic change, it draws on biological/evolutionary determinants along with American "Puritanism" to explain the disappointment with how we use free time in consumption. Two examples are Tibor Scitovsky's classic, The *Joyless Economy: The Psychology of Human Satisfaction*, and Peter Whybrow's *American Mania: When More is Not Enough*.[32] Scitovsky is critical of conventional neoclassical economics and the assumption that consumer choice is based on the rational maximization of "utility." Instead, based on the ambiguous biological roots of human "drives," he argues that consumer frustration (in a "joyless economy") is inevitable. The ease of modern access to biologically driven stimuli has led to addiction and merchandiser manipulation rather than self-interested choice in modern consumer society. He notes that it is easy to achieve "comfort" in consumption, but this leads to passivity and manipulation. By contrast, cultivated enjoyment in free time is more difficult. Perhaps reflecting his European and genteel background, Scitovsky insists that Puritan American culture, with its denigration of "training" for leisure and its glorification of work and condemnation of "wasting time," has ill prepared this society for refined pleasure, as opposed to immediate or routine enjoyment. Evidence of this is the shift of education (especially higher education) from classic aristocratic training for leisure to the modern "democratic" emphasis upon job training. The result is the perpetual dominance of an entertainment industry in free time that offers compensatory "comfort" requiring no skill or refinement—and which ultimately is "joyless."[33]

Whybrow's argument is similar but draws instead from his psychiatric training. Beginning with a recognition of our instinctual and aggressive striving for "more" stimulation, he argues that American culture (partially a result of immigrants motivated by a drive for material success) has a pronounced "appetite for life." This cultural accentuation of our biological aggressiveness has produced an individualism that has trumped the "social learning" (and constraint) that prevails in other historic cultures. In the past, this has produced a dynamic and growth-oriented America. In recent years, however, this "imbalance" between individual striving and social responsibility has been radically extended with the increasing dominance of capitalist-materialist values and the heightened ease of obtaining stimulation (via information technology). What had worked on the old frontier and in the early period of industrialization to foster economic growth has produced an "American mania" of stress resulting from an overload of stimuli and the failure to recognize limits. For Whybrow, our biological capacity to cope with intermittent stress has been swamped by overstimulation in the contemporary consumer economy. The problem with our use of free time is the problem of this "mania."[34]

Though I do not discount these arguments, I think that they are incomplete and do not explain fully either the issue of time scarcity or free-time culture. These theories overemphasize both recent changes as well as the determining impact of biology and culture. We need to consider the longer historical trajectory of the trend toward endless work and disappointing free time. As noted above, this trend has roots dating back several hundred years and cannot be reduced either to events since 1970 or to cultural lag with the persistence of our "Puritan Ghosts" (according to Scitovsky), much less to biological inheritance. And there is no reason to assume that today's outcomes are necessarily inevitable. While the stress on "natural" and evolved "drives" cannot be ignored, this approach tends to lead to deterministic and immobilizing conclusions.

First, the problem of time scarcity is rooted in a longer history than the procapitalist turn of the past fifty years that McCallum and others stress. Basically, the shortage of free time is a consequence of a failure to balance free time with consumption and to adopt an alternative to the work-driven and passive and intense consumer culture of today. Explaining that failure requires us to look closer at the beginning of the twentieth century. The standard economist's argument about the consumer's quest for "utility" certainly does not explain it.

What is missing from all these analyses is the role of politics and broad social and cultural trends in defining work time (as well as consumer culture). Beginning in the nineteenth century and culminating in the early twentieth century, political and social movements led to work-time reductions (notable especially in the international eight-hour day around 1919) but not to the progressive diminution of labor. I argue that in the United States the Great Depression led to a standard workweek at forty hours, but that this period also prioritized income (and work) over further time reductions. After World War II, despite anticipating a wave of productivity and material progress, Americans (and others) stopped expanding and cultivating free time. Rather, the goal became to distribute growing affluence by promoting mass marketing and state-sanctioned income redistribution in hopes of creating endless economic growth and full employment based on at least a forty-hour workweek. This was to be a guarantor of social stability within the unstable dynamic of capitalism.

At the root of this "choice" was the unrelenting resistance of capital to slowing down the inextricably linked twins—growth and profit. Moreover, the increasing dominance of capital over state (and international) regulation reduced the possibilities of alternatives—such as extending the legal rights of workers to more time. By the mid-twentieth century, this pressure had marginalized earlier hopes for a progressive reduction of work. From the 1970s, this led in many cases to an increase in work time and a still deeper devotion to the work ethic. This was not merely a conspiracy of capitalists and their political allies but a result of broader social and cultural trends. There were a lot of reasons for people to "choose" (however unconsciously) more stuff over more free time, many of which we will consider in the following pages.

Concerning the second issue—the disappointing free-time culture—the tendency to blame consumer taste, aggressive individualism, or the "Puritan Ghost" distorts a much more complex cultural legacy and ultimately denies us a more serious understanding of the origins of today's consumer culture. By taking a more nuanced historical view, we will see that today's free-time culture is rooted in the history of contested free-time cultures that culminated in the nineteenth century: expectations of genteel (and working-class) reformers for cultural "uplift" failed. Despite the spread of urban museums, public education, and parks, earlier forms of leisure (especially carnival/festival culture) persisted, but increasingly in the commercialized form of amusement parks, professional sports, and mass media. At the same time, large sections of the emerging middle class rejected the austerity and refinement of genteel culture along with the disruptive excitement of the festival culture of the masses. Instead of the values of either the elite or masses, many in the middle class opted for fun and sentiment in the secure confines of the home and conventionality. Added to the clash of free-time cultures was emulative aspiration, a quest for keeping up with the Joneses that, as Schor and others note, has ramped up consumerism.

The result was a constantly contested free-time culture divided in three parts: 1) genteel culture that sometimes shaded into high modernism with its goals of restrained social and personal refinement (no doubt favored by Scitovsky and others); 2) midcult cultural conservatism, but open to accessible delight and emotion (much popular music, radio and TV sitcoms, cartoons, etc.); and 3) a commercialized carnival culture of the "masses" that often challenged the sobriety and sentimentality of midcult, but which today has invaded mainstream middle-class culture, especially in movies, video games, and the recreational drug culture. To a large degree, the "disappointment" of free-time culture is a manifestation of different attitudes (partially based on class, partially on generation and other factors). Most notable, of course, is how genteel elites critique contemporary consumerist forms of that culture without offering plausible alternatives.

This is where many might end this investigation. There is a lot here: not just a limitless desire for goods but also a political settlement of the forty-hour week along with a capitalist rejection of any assault on a growth- and profit-based economy help explain the persistence of long working hours. The clash of free-time cultures and the failure of critics to abandon their prejudices and provide alternatives to the free-time consumer culture acceptable to the broad population explain a lot of the disappointment in how free time is used today. But I think there is more.

I argue that a closer look at the history of modern consumer culture shows how changes in consumption since 1900 have exacerbated the failed expectations of time and culture. Early twentieth-century innovations in mass production and electronic media defined much of modern consumer culture. These technologies altered liberated time just as it was becoming more available with the eight-hour day and the weekend. Mass production not only accelerated output and distribution, it also began the process of fast consumer capitalism: this meant the turnover of goods at an accelerated rate, but also goods that were both packaged and more sensually "packed," producing more convenience and an intensified consumer experience. Fast consumer capitalism increased the incentive to purchase more goods, encouraging longer (paid) work time to obtain these goods.

Moreover, that consumption ultimately shaped our views of free time and its culture. While often exciting and alluring, the ever-faster flow of more and more sensually intense goods and commercial experiences displaced slower and less commercial forms of leisure. Fast capitalism made free time that was "slow" less valuable and increased the incentive to work for and consume fast goods, making work time more valuable than "empty" free time with "slow" goods and experiences.

Twentieth-century consumer capitalism was more than fast. Parts of it became "funneled." Automobiles and especially modern media technologies transformed free-time culture by isolating the individual and "globalizing" the social. This revolutionized the personal and societal dimensions of free time that had been so central to genteel ideals of leisure. Personalized access to new media partially replaced time-consuming self-cultivation (like hobbies or book reading) with more immediate individual gratifications (like hit songs) and replaced many socially interactive activities (like communal singing) with an abstracted sharing of pleasures (as in mass, but passive, engagement with movie stars). Modern media offers isolated personal access to the global, i.e., funneled free-time culture. And this is a substitute for the old ideal of self-cultivation and social (and real-world) engagement. It began with the home phonograph shortly before the twentieth century and culminated in the smartphone at the opening of the twenty-first, with nearly infinite individual choice to join virtual, rather than real, global communities.

Funneled consumption became a radically new form of free-time culture. Mostly, we are delighted as the smartphone gives us personal and instant access to worlds we never even imagined visiting. Moreover, there is no turning back to an idealized world of Victorian gentility, with its slow virtues of the cultivated self and social engagement. But funneled, like fast, capitalism has compounded our bias against more "slow" free time and against cultivated and social uses of that free time. It has created a free-time culture that often disappoints.

Retrospection: A Historian's Approach to the Present

Before we can understand our current situation or consider alternatives, we need to think about both time and culture as they have come down to us from the past. Such an exercise will help us sort out what is "natural" and perhaps difficult to change from historical decisions rooted in situations that are no longer valid and thus needlessly survive today. A historical perspective gives us a way to reconsider what we have inherited from the past. I will draw on a wide range of sources, some of which are recent and others older and often seminal, depending on the topic.

I begin with an unavoidably brief analysis of time and culture in precapitalist societies and how capitalism impacted all this. Over these centuries, work and free time were very different from today, offering us a perspective for comparing our experience, behavior, and values with the past. I will try to present a baseline that highlights how modern approaches to time and culture compare with what came before the "great transformation" of industrial capitalism. In greater detail, I will focus on the coming of capitalism in the seventeenth and eighteenth centuries and how it gave birth to our work-driven values as well as to genteel forms of free-time culture that continue to abide in various ways in modern psyches.

My primary goal, however, is to understand the present through retrospection. Thus, the remaining chapters will focus on the past 250 years (especially the last century), when capitalism shaped time and culture. I offer two organizing principles for presenting this complex history. First, I focus on movements for free time and free-time culture and their often disappointing fates. I will consider a wide range of political, technological, economic, and cultural factors that explain these movements and their expectations. My point is not to advocate a return to the past.

However, in explaining why work-time reduction stopped and free-time culture was disappointing, we can understand more fully the limits of our choices regarding time and culture. Second, I consider changes in time and culture as they relate to the emergence of consumer culture since about 1900 around the themes of fast capitalism and funneled free time, each manifested in new technologies that shaped our attitudes toward time and culture.

This is not a story of declension, of a lost golden age, or a lament about sidetracked historical ideals that we should admire and possibly recover. That would be silly and reactionary. Moreover, elite values rooted in historical privilege and snobbery should not be a standard for a critique of contemporary culture. Nor is this a story of unalterable, deterministic trends in technology or political power. In some measure, the consumption bias regarding free time was a historic choice (or better, a sociohistorical shift) that seldom was consciously made by individuals, even though it set the path that led to the present, limiting our choices today. It still behooves us to recognize the alternatives not chosen. In the process, we can consider whether those choices made sense in the past, and more important, whether they make sense today.

A moment for a few other disclaimers: despite my concern about the scarcity of work-free time, I do not suggest that time liberated from work is either possible or desirable. Work is obviously not only necessary for survival and improvement in life but key to dignity and an essential means of participating in a prosperous society. Nor do I argue that much leisure is or can be completely detached from consumer spending. Though free-time culture disappoints in many ways, many people are satisfied with it and aspire to enjoy more of it. A major point of this book is to reflect on why and how consumer culture is embraced by so many against the values and proposals of cultural critiques and improvers. I recognize much time free from the market is still "obliged time," as in housework and child care, though these uncompensated periods sometimes can be "leisurely" and akin to free time in their character of being personally fulfilling and socially engaging. I acknowledge this "gray area." However, I am primarily interested here in time and culture that is not routine domestic and child-care work. And by "culture," I mean activities and meanings that create an integral and cultivated self that is enriched through social engagement and interaction with the broader world, for example, of nature. This is a broad understanding that deliberately avoids judgements, such as privileging "high" culture or for that matter glorifying "low" culture. Free-time culture includes gardening and woodworking as well as opera appreciation and book club membership. Instead, I analyze when and how that quest for time for culture has produced diversity and conflict, which have often made difficult any consensus or mutual toleration in how free time is used.

My approach is primarily political, cultural, and technological rather than psychological or biological: where others might see personal and natural drives and insecurities, I see production systems, markets, and classes shaping behavior and attitudes. I do not mean to discount the psychological and biological factors and will from time to time acknowledge them. But, like most historians, I focus on how people's lives are shaped by events, institutions, and changing cultures. Moreover, my approach is not primarily economic. It insists on the centrality of political power, cultural influence, and technological trends.[35]

In a book I wrote long ago, I argued that the twentieth century brought the victory of "money" over "time," a shorthand for saying that with economic growth and advanced productivity came more consumption rather than more free time. Some readers suggested that this formulation made the lure of consumer goods rather than the power of capital over labor the cause of modern overwork. A second critique claimed that I argued that free time had nothing to do with consumption. The critique was based on the fact that free time inevitably is also consumption time.[36]

In this book, I offer a nuanced revision. I do not think now (if I ever did) that the only or even primary cause of overwork is consumer drive. Instead, I now think the lack of time free from work despite increased productivity is in large part explained by the power shift to capital over labor. This turns us to politics, but there are also other social and cultural factors. The problem of free time is more complex than consumption time displacing "real leisure." In fact, little leisure is free of consumption. Still, the transformation of consumption, especially through the creation of "fast" consumption and new media, has profoundly impacted free-time culture. All this will be laid out in this book.

Necessarily, in a book intended for a general audience with limited time, I must limit the scope and detail of my history. It will focus on that part of the world that led global industrialization (primarily the US but with some European references). The US offers a somewhat unique story of time and culture. Yet it is only a variation of what has happened in other advanced industrial countries. My account explores a wide range of institutions, ideas, events, and trends—from factories and struggles over the length of the workday to the meaning of festivals and even video games. I make no specific proposals about work time or how to use free time. Mostly this book is about how we became who we are in our daily lives—how we came to work forty hours a week or more, how we learned to spend so much free time in front of screens shopping—and, in modest measure, how we might change.

2

Two Traditional Cultures and the Capitalist Revolution

Between the appearance of agriculture and the introduction of capitalist industry, the worlds of work and free time were radically unlike ours. At the core of these differences was the simple fact that for millennia productivity grew little and frequently was reversed by war, disease, and climate change. This conundrum produced a basic division of most pre-capitalist societies into vast majorities of dependent and poor producers and tiny elites free from manual labor. There was little incentive for either group to innovate. For the vast majority, the result was a work-life division dominated by the growing seasons (within which were free-time events—festivals) and erratic periods of work and leisure. The elite sometimes produced art and even cultivated conversation (which later would be the foundation for ideals of leisure), even if these activities depended on the labor of others. Yet, more often elite free time was consumed in displays of exclusivity (sometimes wasteful) and competition (often violent). This is grossly oversimplified, of course, but it is an important starting point for our topic.

The Gordian knot of low productivity was eventually cut by capitalism. Entrepreneurs raised output by gaining control over and intensifying the work process (supply) and by introducing goods that partially overcame workers' resistance to innovation and work (demand). They also revolutionized the work-life division. Despite a slow and often chaotic process, work and free time became less seasonal and less intermittent. Labor often increased and became more constant. As work was removed from the domicile to the factory and office, labor often became more intense, less relieved by sporadic times for family care and rest. This led to the dominance of the work ethic, but the new division of work and life also created new ideas and opportunities for free time. This division set the stage for our modern world of work and leisure.

This admittedly generalized summary of thousands of years of history before and at the beginning of modern capitalism is a necessary abbreviation. This chapter will elaborate, but my objective is primarily to provide benchmarks from which I can illuminate how things changed (or stayed the same) thereafter.

Conundrum of Civilization: Low Productivity until Recent Centuries

The Neolithic revolution, beginning nearly twelve thousand years ago in the Middle East, launched the long process of fixed farming, replacing migratory hunting and gathering. This ultimately led to cities and "civilization." Despite important innovations that accompanied the coming of agriculture, these Neolithic advances dominated human societies with relatively minor changes until the equally monumental industrial revolution of the eighteenth and nineteenth centuries in Europe and the US. This observation especially holds true for our central theme—free time and its culture.[1]

The Neolithic revolution did two fundamental things: First, it radically changed and often reduced the time and trouble of searching for food, through the cultivation of renewable crops on settled land and the domestication of animal resources. Second, cultivation centered on hard grains that did not quickly decay and could be milled into flour for bread. These innovations encouraged accumulating and preserving surpluses. Closely related innovations followed (plows to cultivate, baskets, ceramics, glass containers to contain and preserve food, and metal refining for tools and especially for weapons to protect or confiscate food surpluses).[2] The ability to produce a preservable surplus allowed a division of labor—the possibility of specialized craftspeople and merchants (for trade), but also the creation of an elite, free from physical labor. This included warriors and rulers to protect and extend the surplus and priests to manage the anxieties of people coping with the insecurities of the food supply. Simply put, only after the agricultural revolution was there a "stable surplus and that means a hierarchy based on poverty and wealth," as historian David Smail notes.[3] The result was two cultures. Most people worked in fields or tended herds, while a few fought wars and tended temples, mostly free from agricultural work. This is reductionist and ignores a wealth of diversity, but compared to modern society, it broadly holds true.

As Marshall Stahlins famously notes, this long transition from hunting-gathering to sedentary cultivation ultimately revolutionized expectations. As mobile people in search of food, hunter-gatherers neither accumulated goods nor had many needs. Compared to Neolithic and later "civilized" people, they had much free time after immediate needs were met. By contrast, an agricultural surplus and the advantage of holding land and other resources created inheritance and social class, the humiliation of poverty, and the necessity of armed power to maintain inequality. This surplus made possible the vast expansion of needs and, with it, work—but also a more complex free-time culture, especially for the privileged.[4]

Yet for millennia innovation was minimal and the possibilities of making free time were limited. Angus Maddison estimates per capita annual income in the Roman Empire at a mere $400 (in 1990 dollars), and it dropped in Western Europe during the early Middle Ages. From 1000 to 1820 (when industrialization began to take hold) global per capita income grew about 50 percent, but that was over a very long period and most of it was based on extending cultivated land. Maddison estimates that per capita income growth rates in Europe between 1000 and 1500 were only 0.13 percent per annum and were uneven for the next three centuries. Only with industrialization starting around 1820 did growth take off and continue. Because of improved productivity of labor and land, by 1998 per capita income had increased 8.5-fold over 1820 (until recently largely benefiting the West).[5] These contrasts strikingly illustrate just how unproductive humanity has been until relatively recently.

Until industrialization, the crop and animal basis of civilization remained largely constant: in the West, grain crops were inefficient, and in the East, access to animal power and protein was limited. Wheat yields in England from 1250 to 1500 ranged from 6.3 to 8.3 bushels per acre. They rose to 25.3 bushels by 1850–1899. Today, yields per acre can reach sixty bushels.[6] There were craftspeople and merchants for trade, but exchange and specialization were severely limited by costly and slow transportation (especially over land). It is no accident that the Roman Empire surrounded the Mediterranean Sea. Costly and slow transportation meant that most goods were local, and craftspeople had to rely on custom orders from local buyers (or on sales of luxury goods to elites) and were often restricted by trade associations (such as guilds).[7]

This meant little or no economic growth over centuries except through conquest and limited reclamation of land for cultivation. War and warrior classes dominated, leading to the ebb and flow of city-states, some becoming empires, linking cities and agricultural zones. In turn, empires and kingdoms were repeatedly invaded by "barbarians," often attacking centers of agricultural surplus. War and conquests also led to large groups of enslaved people as well as landless and impoverished laborers, further accentuating the gap between the two cultures.

That division is another factor in explaining the low productivity before industrial capitalism. As often noted, elite reliance on slave labor discouraged mechanization, even when the basic principles of mechanization were understood (such as in the ancient Roman knowledge of water wheels and even steam power). The essential disconnect between productive workers and the elite led to a ruling class that generally denigrated work to the benefit of glory or leisure. Even though the privileged often possessed the capital, time, and potential skills to introduce economic innovations, few were forthcoming. Enslaved people and dependent field workers had no incentive to work longer or harder than they were forced to. Moreover, artisan income remained low, offering little opportunity for investment. Even merchant-manufacturers were seldom innovative in this long preindustrial period: profit rarely came from improved productivity but from successful risk-taking (or monopolies), especially in luxury-goods trade. In any case, low agricultural productivity limited any craft or trade expansion.[8]

To be sure, the Middle Ages saw important innovations (the famous stirrup, heavy plough, horse collar, and water mill from the seventh century; the windmill and vertical loom from the twelfth century; and printing and iron blast furnaces in the fifteenth century). But such innovations had a limited impact on the work lives of the majority whose days were tied to the hand tools and draught animals of farming.[9]

For Most: Hard Work, but Seasonal and Intermittent Free Time

Stagnant productivity meant that working hours for most stretched from sunup to sundown with little time for leisure. Neolithic people and those who followed worked more hours than their hunter-gatherer ancestors. Up to 90 percent of income was spent on food, any surplus beyond subsistence was siphoned off one way or another by the ruling class. And work time was time at the disposal of demanding, often bullying bosses, even if a worker were not a slave. The work was often heavy, repetitious, and dangerous. There was no or little wealth for retirement or for allowing the young a work-free childhood. This meant that work time extended from early youth to early death (the mean age of death in medieval Europe was fifty for those who reached twenty years of age).[10] None of this is surprising, though it is easy to forget.

Work time, however, was not necessarily incessant or unyielding. First, work varied much by the time of year and sunlight, especially in northern Europe. The workday was interrupted by several meal and rest breaks (often including time for breakfast because work started so early). Technological stagnation meant that variations in nature, especially the seasonal availability of crops to plant and harvest, governed the ebb and flow of work time. The pace of life was not dictated by the speed of the machine or the incessant flow of goods and services as it is in today's market. Long days at farm labor were common from early spring planting to autumn harvests, but fewer and shorter workdays were required in winter.[11]

Most work was done "to task" until the job was completed. The mechanical clock emerged only in the fourteenth century to set work time in urban areas, though bells to regulate work time were used earlier. Moreover, because of the seasonality of agriculture, farm labor was often supplemented with craft work like gardening, spinning yarn, or brewing beer (especially by women), often for family use. This made farm work intermittent. In addition, women's productive work was frequently "interrupted" by childbearing and care.[12]

Artisans often shared this seasonal and intermittent pattern because of irregular delivery of work materials (often dependent on the agricultural season for raw materials) as well as uncertain and episodic markets for finished goods. Because of slow transportation and uncertain supply chains, craft workers often found themselves with "free time" (though usually unpaid), often whole days. Because they were paid by the piece or the variable workday (or even year), laborers generally did not contest working hours. Because goods were produced on order rather than to maximum output potential, except in seasonally busy times, work sometimes took a leisurely tempo, frequently interrupted by informal conversation and other forms of play. Craftspeople often worked as family units, complicating any efforts of the master to increase output of family members. Often there was little difference between servants (who frequently lived with the family) and working family members. For many craftspeople, work and family/leisure time were intertwined (as they were for farm families). Still, for employees, this often meant little time free from the master's control. To our modern eyes, the premodern relationship between laborer and boss seems confused because it contrasts with our relatively sharp division of work time and place from free time and personal life.[13]

While seasonality and intermittency explain much of the pace and productivity of preindustrial work, also important was the separation of much work from elites (if not from shop masters). This sometimes left work groups with autonomy, but it also led to inefficient extraction of wealth from labor. Aristocratic elites usually resisted direct participation in the production process and disdained even the relatively clean work of the merchant. This, and the decentralized character of work on the farm and in family-based workshops (in contrast to factories) allowed some workers to maintain a relatively slow and often erratic pace of work.[14]

There were efforts to increase productivity before industrialization. Sixteenth-century English textile merchants attempted to lower labor costs by tapping underutilized (and cheap) rural labor, sidelining expensive and relatively independent urban artisans. Still, they did not manage the work process. Merchants supplied rural yarn spinners and weavers with raw materials, but these textile producers worked at home on their own time, often only as a supplement to farm work. Merchants had little direct control over the pace or methods of work, and the laborers had little incentive to produce more than necessary to survive because there were few affordable consumer goods.

So how did these work- and free-time patterns impact how preindustrial people used their own time? First, and most important, seasonal work produced multiday festivals. Though often identified with religion or the state, most festivals also coincided with the annual weather cycle that determined the planting and harvesting of crops. In the temperate zones of Europe and North America, the spring festivals of Easter, Whitsuntide (or Pentecost), and May Day fell during planting and amid hopes for a "fertile" growing season. Late autumn and early winter festivals, especially Christmas, corresponded with harvests and the need to slaughter livestock where costs of winter feeding were prohibitive.[15] The seasonality of festivals was also linked to the annual movement of the sun—high or low in the sky—and to the attendant religious ideas that emerged from the encounter with these annual cycles of light and warmth. Many cultures segmented their year by the solstices and equinoxes. These agricultural and solar holidays, usually with pagan roots, were Christianized by the early Church (most notably the winter solstice feast days became the twelve days of Christmas, and the summer solstice became St. John's Eve of June 23–24, in remembrance of John the Baptist).[16] As Roger Caillois famously remarked, preindustrial people lived "in remembrance of one festival and in expectation of the next."[17]

Unlike modern holidays, which tend to be organized around small groups, especially the nuclear family and children, traditional festivals preeminently served to bond communities—an outgrowth of the collective sharing of food after a successful hunt in the days before agriculture. Often festivals were sponsored by elites—from the king down to the local gentry—who supplied food, drink, and even entertainment. They often doubled as trade festivals (St. Bartholomew's Fair in August) and hiring events (St. John's Eve) and even served as occasions for courtship and its collective oversight (in sharp contrast to the individualistic modern "date" or "hookup").[18]

These were societies where communities had outsized roles in individual lives. Villages, for example, often provided support for needy widows and orphans when families failed as they frequently did because of early and unexpected deaths. Festivals were occasions for sporting contests between villages (or their champions). The purpose was usually to build group loyalty. Most festivals were local as were their participants. In a world where almost no one lived alone, an individualistic outlook was not only discouraged but rarely developed. Few had any privacy and most lived in lodgings of one or two rooms. Letting off steam often required space outside of home and the family such as in the collective area of the alehouse (especially in the colder climates) or the town square (especially during festivals). Inns and taverns were dominated by males, while women's collective leisure was often confined to work spaces or joint work-leisure events for sewing or candle making, for example. Individuality had little space to develop, and conformity was expected. In fact, festivals were times for the collective marking and mocking of nonconformist behavior. Sometimes, this took the form of a charivari, involving a crowd surrounding and ridiculing a social outcaste with song, bells, and banging of pots. Among the crowd's targets were adulterers or husbands who were beaten and abused by their wives.[19]

Festivals also released social tension in celebrations usually referred to as saturnalia. This term was taken from the ancient Roman festival of mid-December honoring the god Saturn, where Romans enjoyed a week of pleasurable release from drudgery, subordination to masters, and daily routine. The saturnalian character of the preindustrial European festival was best expressed in the winter carnival, a celebration of excess that introduced Lent, a period of religious restraint. Carnival culminated in Mardi Gras (Shrove Tuesday in Britain.) The festival was more elaborate and public in the comparatively warmer zones of southern Europe. Carnival involved indulgence in food and drink, of course, but also, as the word *carne* (meat) suggests, it involved flesh and sex (as noted in the uptick of premarital pregnancies initiated during carnival). Even more, carnival was a time for release from the constraints of a hierarchal and socially oppressive everyday life. Carnival revelers had limited permission to mock bishops, dukes, and other authorities in plays, processions, and songs. Sometimes, they even appointed one of their own as lord or bishop for the day. Carnival crowds abandoned temporarily the rules of civil behavior by throwing flour, eggs, and even stones at each other. Sex roles were transgressed as men sometimes wore women's clothes and vice versa.[20]

These saturnalian behaviors of carnival were echoed in other festivals and for the same reasons: note the British tradition of "mumming," where revelers went door to door begging or demanding food and drink on All Souls' Day and during the twelve days of Christmas. Sometimes mummers at least pretended to threaten homeowners (even the rich and powerful) if "treats" were not offered—a custom bowdlerized in the modern, predominately American practice of children trick-or-treating on Halloween.[21]

If festivals turned the "world upside down," they did so within the strict confines of space and time set by tradition (even though they occasionally broke these boundaries in riots). At least until the early modern period, the authorities tolerated saturnalia such as carnival, knowing that Lent, or the expected return to normality, followed. The carnival (both the pre-Lenten celebration and the general festival outburst) served as a safety valve, periodically reducing the pent-up social tension of a hierarchical society.[22]

The saturnalian festival was more than indulgence and a constrained release of social tension. As Mikhail Bakhtin emphasizes (alongside many followers), carnival was a celebration of the body, not the godly or spiritual; and that fleshly form had nothing to do with the Greek idea of physical beauty. Rather, carnival celebrated the outlandish, even monstrous, body.[23] It is not surprising that freakish bodies were on display at festivals and that these became part of circus sideshows by the late nineteenth century.[24]

Even more characteristic of the festival was its celebration of aggression and violence, especially in the prevalence of rough team sports. Festival games lacked the rules, characteristic of modern competitive sports, that reduced violence and injury. A common game dating from the Middle Ages was "camp ball." One variation was played until the 1830s on Shrove Tuesday afternoon in Derby, England. It was essentially a free-for-all between hundreds of the male youths of the town, driving a ball across town and disrupting local business. This was a far cry from modern association football (or soccer), with its rules-filled play on a standardized field.[25]

At festivals (and other times and places, especially alehouses) violent contests and "blood sports" were also common. Duels of bodily power (and daring) included cudgeling: equipped with broad sticks or cudgels, two competitors fought, frequently aiming for the head. Boisterous crowds and gambling usually accompanied these events. Even more typical of this celebration was the untethered violence of games of cruelty involving animals. Perhaps most common was cockfighting: two roosters were brought to an open place, fitted with spurs, and set upon each other while the crowd placed bets and cheered their choice. The roosters pecked each other, usually until one cut open the other's abdomen, and often ending with the victor crowing over the victim. A variant of this drama was bullbaiting, where a trained dog tried to grasp the bull's underbelly and gonads while the bull (fastened to a leash) used its legs and horns to shake the dog off. Perhaps, the crowd enjoyed rooting for the "underdog" attacking this marker of male fertility. Whatever may be the case, this custom—along with other variants like badger-baiting or bear-baiting—baffles the modern sensibility with its violence, even though it has a faint echo in modern professional wrestling.[26]

Cockfighting found a home in eighteenth-century Virginia and even cudgeling was practiced in Puritan Boston on "training days." Chaotic if less violent games like greased pig chasing were common to American fairs and other festive occasions during the colonial period and later. These rough, even cruel, sports had a tenacious appeal to all classes. But long after elites abandoned them, the common people, especially in rural areas, held on to these festival games of violence. A moderated saturnalia has survived today in festivals as diverse as the modern Mardi Gras (of New Orleans), spring break bashes of college students in Florida, and outdoor concerts of various sorts (especially from the 1960s on). More subtly, saturnalia's anarchistic and transgressive spirit prevails in much of modern popular culture.[27]

Seasonal festivals were the most characteristic form of free time, but intermittent daily work also had its parallel in free time. Work breaks were often spread through the day as free time was frequently devoted to recuperation: eating, drinking, and periodic thrills to break the work routine. This was particularly common in urban trades, where paid work was not regular and could vary from day to day. Examples are dock and construction labor in early modern Europe and America. The slow pace of technological change meant that work and leisure customs were passed on from one generation to another. From the High Middle Ages, urban workers took holidays celebrating the patron saint of their trades. Sometimes new holidays were added to old. Though varying much by time and region, 115 annual days off (some due to bad weather) would be a good estimate. That seems like a lot, but then modern Americans generally receive two-day weekends and an average of 17.4 days of vacation, reaching about 121 days. The point is that premodern people, despite low productivity, took a surprising amount of time off work, some of it for leisure.[28]

An oft-cited example of this "leisure ethic" is the custom of Saint Monday. Though most often associated with early modern urban crafts of England and Paris, Saint Monday survived into the nineteenth century in various parts of Europe. In brief, it involved laborers skipping work on Monday mornings, if not the whole day. It was mostly a male custom; the women working, for example, in lacemaking and laundry were too poorly paid, had domestic chores, and lacked the organization necessary to participate. Monday was chosen not only because it extended the traditional Christian Sunday holiday but because it dovetailed with preindustrial work patterns. Necessary work materials often did not arrive until Monday afternoon or later, and orders often did not have to be completed until Saturday morning; thus, work early in the week was impossible or less pressing.[29] These patterns of intermittent free time had little in common with the modern weekend or paid vacation. The frequent breaks and irregular "holidays" of the preindustrial system were ultimately rooted in the low-output economy that preceded industrialization.

Low productivity and the lack of modern consumer goods explain another curiosity of this long era—the seeming preference of low-wage workers for leisure over more money. One might expect the opposite: if more work could have brought higher monthly wages, why would they not work as many hours as possible? First, few worked by the hour, but rather by the day or even season. So, there was no incentive to work longer in a day or even week. Additional work had little prospect of raising the standard of living significantly because of a shortage of consumer goods beyond the basics. Even if wages went up, there was little incentive to work more. Some might have worked less. A low-growth economy led people to expect a fixed level of consumption. Even when working more hours would have provided higher income, many possessed a stronger leisure than work ethic. As late as 1771 the English economist Arthur Young wrote: "everyone but an idiot knows that the lower classes must be kept poor, or they will never be industrious."[30] Only the threat of starvation would make them work longer. This is the self-serving perspective of employers, but it sometimes reflected the worker's preference for free time, especially when increased consumption was not an option. Perhaps even beyond the lack of consumer goods was the simple loyalty to the custom of the festival calendar.[31]

For the Elite: Continuous, Mostly Exclusive, Extravagant, and Often Violent Free Time

Very different was the free-time culture of the tiny elite that preindustrial societies could support with their limited surplus. Because this group was free from most obliged time, especially at physical labor, their free time was neither seasonal nor intermittent, nor was it recuperative or rebellious, even though it could often be anarchistic and violent. Ruling elites, often with origins in conquest, perpetuated their power through the physical intimidation of their subjects and enemies, especially in the early Middle Ages, when bureaucratic state power was weak. In such times, aristocratic male leisure was dominated by physical training for combat and hunting. At first, tournaments consisted of young knights competing in mock battles in hopes of unhorsing and seizing the property of rivals. Gradually, the tournament became a series of athletic and quasi-military contests, the most famous of which was the joust, a regulated dual between two mounted knights who charged each other with lances. Until modern times, hunting was the exclusive right of the aristocracy in most of Europe, despite widespread poaching. Hunting was an expression of power, a substitute and preparation for war.[32]

The American economist Thorstein Veblen claimed in 1899 that predatory elites have historically affirmed their social status by the conspicuous and even wasteful display of wealth and their freedom from work in leisure. Though perhaps exaggerating, Veblen identified an important motivation of traditional landed aristocracies for their luxurious displays of wealth in food and in decorous spaces like palaces and gardens.[33]

Elite banquets seem to have originated in the Neolithic period when a few took control over communal food supplies and displayed their power and wealth in banquets reserved for their own clan and sometimes used to impress potential allies. The rulers and priests of ancient city-states and empires like those of Greece and Rome continued to make the banquet and its rituals hallmarks of their superior status and high culture.[34] Still, Roman authorities were sometimes willing to offer ordinary citizens a share of the pleasure in gladiator games (from the third century BCE). Probably more popular were the chariot races and the often daily visits to the public baths, which combined hygiene and casual leisure.[35]

While Christians generally opposed the sensual indulgence (and violent games) of the Roman Empire, medieval aristocrats returned to the ancient love of rich foods and embraced roasted game for their large midday meals and occasional banquets. They revived the ancient taste for perfumes and pungent flavors after the Crusaders rediscovered them in the Middle East. Later, these elites expanded their taste for luxury with sugar and coffee from the East. But the nobility also supported the traditions of the "strolling" singer or minstrel, who performed in their great halls during banquets. Quieter leisure time was devoted to dice as well as other board games like backgammon, but especially to chess (an obvious derivative of warfare). From the fourteenth century CE, the leisure activity of cards (imported from Muslim India) came to the aristocracy. Much of this was popularized and survives today.[36]

Another common form of aristocratic leisure time was centered on private landscaped spaces. These sites date back at least to the hunting preserves of the kings of Assyria in the thirteenth century BCE. The Roman elite also built zoological parks for hunting and observing exotic animals, imitated by medieval European aristocrats with their hunting preserves. In addition, elites created sites of pure (though again largely exclusive) aesthetic enjoyment. Consider the famous Hanging Gardens of Babylon (circa 604 BCE), with their irrigated terraces and walls bedecked in exuberantly flowering plants and trees. Wealthy Athenians of ancient Greece retreated from the urban throngs into private parks. Sometimes these landscaped places were open to the public (as in ancient Rome), but most were exclusive. Imperial and aristocratic palaces in Rome were often surrounded by private gardens that featured artificial ponds. Later, they served as models for Renaissance Italian princes and French aristocrats and kings. Louis XIV of France went to extremes with ordered landscaping at Versailles in the 1680s, while the English aristocratic garden was more romantic, with grottoes, manufactured ruins, and artificial streams. The English gardens especially anticipated modern theme parks that invite visitors to walk though rather than merely look upon an image of a fantasy.[37]

In its measured violence, hedonism, aesthetic grandeur, and exclusivity, aristocratic free time stood apart in preindustrial society. Yet, elite and popular leisure coexisted and sometimes overlapped. Notably, the powerful made little effort to "reform" popular pleasures (unlike later). At least until the seventeenth century, popular leisure was enjoyed by both the rich and poor. Even kings and aristocrats joined in the festivals: they sometimes wrestled with their peasants during such events; and clerics, especially young ones, joined the fun, despite the general irreverence of the festivals. As late as the seventeenth century, "parliament men" as well as apprentices gathered to cheer and bet at cockfights in London. By the eighteenth century, aristocratic chivalric tales were reprinted in the cheap "blue" or "chap" books affordable to a growing community of artisans. As noted above, elite tolerance of the festival tradition was often linked to a desire to diffuse social tension. Even in the American South before the Civil War, slave owners sometimes tolerated, even encouraged, enslaved people taking a traditional work break for festivities between Christmas and New Year's Day, hoping, it seems, to pacify them.[38]

Of course, some members of the preindustrial elite tried to control and repress pleasure taking in the masses and even to regulate pleasure among themselves. There was sometimes an economic imperative for such controls: food was often in short supply; and, during such periods, elites wanted to reduce social unrest and suffering by regulating excessive consumption. A wide range of such authorities—from Hebrew prophets and early Christian ascetics to Protestant Puritans and Catholic Jesuits—attempted to rein in the hedonism into which the privileged so often fell in their unlimited free time. These ascetic moralities, upon which so much of traditional religion is based, helped preindustrial people ration uncertain surplus and put a break on the excesses of the rich and powerful. This was one of the reasons that medieval authorities forbade the eating of meat on fast days. Gluttony along with lust was a deadly sin. Gluttony, however, was clearly the transgression of the privileged few. Of course, many of these calls for restraint came from authorities who wanted to control the excesses of the poor rather than the rich. Perhaps it was necessary for Edward III of England to ration the diet of servants during the food shortages following the Black Death of 1348. Other times, however, such regulations, often called "sumptuary laws," simply repressed social "upstarts" seeking to imitate the lifestyle of the aristocracy.[39]

Of course, there are many examples of ancient philosophers and religious champions who sought spiritual goals when they called for the denial of the senses. Yet these groups almost always also looked askance at the "freedom" in the free time of the common people. These elites were concerned that any hours without the discipline of work or the control of elites (presumably trained in self-denial) would be spent in self-destructive sensuality. The old saying "idle hands are the devil's workshop" sums up this perspective.[40]

Another group agreed that free time was "dangerous" but offered a more positive view of free time, especially for a trained elite. Commonly, this perspective is identified with Aristotle (384–322 BCE), though it resembles the admonitions of the still more ancient Confucius (551–479 BCE). For Aristotle, leisure was freedom from the need to work; it could not be merely a compensation for work. Instead, free time should be devoted to self-cultivating activity without any utilitarian purpose. As Sebastian de Grazia famously remarks, the Greek aristocratic ideal was "the hearing of noble music and noble poetry, intercourse with friends chosen for their own worth, and above all the exercise, alone or in company, of the speculative faculty."[41] However, both the disdain for socially useful work and reliance on enslaved people to do that work should make us wary of finding in Aristotelian leisure the solution to contemporary problems. But these ideals remain part of our cultural furniture. With all its elitism and narrowness of perspective, it still called for free time to make culture in self-cultivation and community enrichment.

For most preindustrial people, however, free time and its culture were shaped by the limits of technology and how the two cultures limited productivity. The everyday world of the majority was set by long hours of physical drudgery and often humiliating dependence on an overlord. Still, these conditions were mollified by the seasonal nature of much work, ultimately linked to the slow maturation of nature's bounty and its infrequent payoffs (harvest, for example). This meant opportunities for irregular periods of free time: breaks in the day and week and extended periods for festivals. It also produced a particular culture of free time that is radically unlike our own: irregular days off, Saint Monday, multiple rest breaks, and local festivals set by the movement of the sun and the growing season—not our often fixed workweeks, weekends, and vacations (sometimes with pay and travel). Despite appealing aspects of popular and elite free-time culture in traditional society, there is no reason to romanticize it. The intermittent breaks and festivals of the masses were largely periods of recuperation from labor. They usually denied opportunities for personal expression and choice of social engagement. Moreover, elite leisure was based on the unfreedom of others, practiced exclusion, and often displayed violence and crudity.

As we shall see, the central role of saturnalia and the carnivalesque in the preindustrial festival shaped modern popular culture in unexpected ways. Still, the festival with its violence, anarchy (even if contained), and most of all its communal values reflected a world of preindustrial work and life that is alien to our own. While the free time of the traditional elite brought us many cultural practices (hunting, the banquet, the park, and especially a set of ideals about leisure), it too was based on a world very different from our own, where the elite was often free from work and largely disdained it. What intervened to make us so different from these ancestors, of course, was the development of capitalism and its accompanying cultural change. Let us briefly explore how capitalism shaped work and changed free time.

Capitalism Transforms Work and Time

Challenging both these popular and elite patterns of free time was capitalism and a rising "middle class." Though having ancient roots and expanding in the fifteenth century, capitalism took off only late in the eighteenth century. It involved investing in materials and labor to produce goods and services for a competitive market for profit. Unlike traditional self-provisioning or production to supply a parasitical elite, market production was dynamic, responsive to price changes reflecting supply and demand. This may not have always meant that the "invisible hand" maximized the allocation of capital, labor, and materials. But capitalism did expand production, and with new technology, often prompted by potential profit, it led to unprecedented growth.

But here I want to focus on how this system impacted free time. Competition between suppliers of goods and services encouraged efforts to increase productivity and thus often affected the working time of laborers. More subtly, the extension of the market beyond local customers (caused by aggressive competition, freer trade, and improved transportation) pushed profit-seeking capitalists to replace intermittent and irregular production with steady output. This often reduced the seasonal character of production and sped up the cycle of production and consumption, resulting, in principle, in a faster turnover of capital and greater profit. All this challenged the precapitalist system of production that was largely driven by agricultural cycles, localized markets, few innovations, and limited incentives to increase productivity. Steady and uninterrupted wage work became the norm. Working hours increased and work time intensified, while seasonality and intermittency gradually declined. Also, the intertwining of work and family/leisure was gradually replaced with regulated workplaces like factories and offices, separate from family and home. The old patterns of work and free time were largely eliminated—though over a long period.

As we all know, industrialization brought the factory, beginning mostly in England in the mid-eighteenth century. While it impacted only a minority of workers for a century after it first appeared, the factory was at the cutting edge of a revolution in productivity and eventually set the standard for daily work. As a place controlled by the employer, containing materials and tools as well as workers, the factory solved a problem that had long bedeviled merchants who outsourced raw materials for fabrication by rural workers in their own cottages. The factory gave managers control over the methods and hours of work, separating labor from domestic duties (like farming or child care). In the factory, management determined hours of work as a condition of employment and overseers continuously monitored work to assure a regular and constant attention to the job.[42]

Karl Marx famously argued that the factory created the involuntary workday wherein the competitive capitalist extracted "surplus labor time" from the worker beyond the "necessary labor time" required for the upkeep and reproduction of workers. Thus, the capitalist, as opposed to the merely parasitical landed aristocrat, created more wealth or capital. As Marx wrote, "Capital is dead labour, that vampire-like only lives by sucking living labor, and lives the more, the more labour it sucks."[43]

Lashing workers to machines added to the loss of the old autonomy. The uptick began with the introduction of spinning and weaving machines between the 1760s and 1780s, which were harnessed to James Watt's steam engine as well as to the traditional water wheel. These machines aided the entrepreneur's desire to control production through centralization: steam engines (and water wheels) were efficient only when linked to many spinning and weaving machines and when supplies of coal (and water) were available nearby.[44] Machines set the pace of work. They were seldom stopped to allow workers to tend to personal needs or even to take a break. This newfound power over labor helped manufacturers lower production costs and undercut competition.

The key to this power was the employers' control of workers' time. And regulating it ultimately depended on measuring it. That required the clock, a machine perhaps as important as the steam engine in the industrialization of work. It gave the capitalist a way to quantify, control, and eventually intensify the pace of work. The nineteenth-century factory clock—often perched high in its ornate copula over the factory door or gate—regulated when work began and ended. Those failing to pass underneath it before it showed 6:00 a.m. were subject to a fine and even discharge. When the cheap standardized watch emerged in the middle of the nineteenth century, time accounting became mobile, a means of monitoring the rate of activity or output for the overseer, but it also regulated the time-anxious employee.[45]

Though intensifying and regularizing work was the main objective, lengthening the workday was also a goal of time discipline. Early nineteenth-century mill owners had many economic incentives to extend the workweek: competition had driven down the price of cotton goods, and owners were also anxious to recover the costs of machinery before it became obsolete. This sometimes meant increasing the daily hours of machine operation—and lengthening work time. By 1810, daily work in cotton textile mills in both England and New England extended to 12 or even 13 ½ hours, six days a week. Moreover, factory workers were powerless to challenge these conditions. Unlike skilled workers in traditional crafts (construction, for example), the early factory workers lacked organizations or customary expectations about work and conditions. Most were also women or children, who were expected to be docile temporary workers. In 1836, for example, 85 percent of workers employed in a Massachusetts textile company were women, of which 80 percent were between fifteen and thirty years old.[46]

The New World slave plantation was another site that broke from traditional work patterns. For example, the French sugar works in the early nineteenth century had a rigorous system of time management with steam engines, division of labor, and strict work discipline, producing a work regime even more severe than in the cotton mills of England and Massachusetts. The expansion and consolidation of slavery in early eighteenth-century Virginia resulted in a dramatic increase in work time for Black enslaved people but also for White workers, as holidays were reduced to three per year.[47]

Work-time changes also came from another direction—the transformation of the consumer market and the household economy. According to Jan de Vries, by the eighteenth century, Western Europe was beginning to change from "leisure rich, but oppressive societies," where the surplus was funneled into the "old luxury" of a parasitical aristocracy. A new, positive, and potentially more popular understanding of luxury was advanced by intellectuals like Daniel Defoe, David Hume, and especially Adam Smith. While traditional Christian authorities were hostile to or at least concerned about elite opulence (and low-class debauchery), these intellectuals embraced luxury, no longer viewing it as vice but as a means of developing refinement, encouraging saving, and especially promoting disciplined work among the masses as luxuries became more accessible to them. For de Vries, this cultural revolution made possible a new society, where "workers became more productive" as "new luxury" products could be had by them. Examples were domestic refinements like crockery and tea. This new consumer economy encouraged working families (even before factories) to abandon the traditional leisure preference of their ancestors. Such workers even accepted wage labor (over traditional crafts). This meant that working families adopted a work ethic and accepted innovation in order to partake in the new luxury economy. De Vries even suggests that "factory discipline forced workers to do what they wanted to do but could not unaided," and evidently that was to work more to get more.[48]

Of course, Marx (and classical economists like Smith) stressed instead the emergence of investing, competing, and profit-making capitalists. Gradually, these entrepreneurs replaced the traditional parasitical aristocrat and imposed more and more intense work time. De Vries's "demand side" arguments inevitably were challenged by historians doubtful that access to consumer goods in this early period was sufficient to explain a "choice" of working longer. A better explanation, according to critics, was the decline in wages in early industrialization, legal controls, and employer supervision.[49] I tend to think each argument explains part of what happened. However, in the early period, I suspect the driving force was economic need and the imposition of more work rather than the choice of work for consumption.

Further light on this question is provided by Hans-Joachim Voth. In 1500, Western Europeans worked about 250–260 days per year. From 1500 until the mid-nineteenth century, the work year seems to have increased. Much of it occurred during early industrialization. Voth finds that, at least in parts of England, the work year rose between 1760 and 1831 an average of about six hundred hours (to 3,300 per year). Voth claims that no one in Europe worked more than the English between 1800 and 1830. This was the price of their early introduction of industrial capitalism. Increased work time rather than saving or even mechanization was "at the heart of economic growth" in England in this period. Interestingly, Voth finds that work time grew primarily because of the reduction of holidays (including Saint Monday) rather than extended workdays; and this affected both factory and the more numerous traditional workers.[50]

Historians correctly criticize Marxism for overemphasizing the role of mechanization and the factory in the modern revolution of productivity and time. Until late in the nineteenth century, craft workers (e.g., tailors, shoemakers, and furniture makers) continued to labor with little power machinery, sometimes in isolated garrets or cottages. As late as 1851, even in Britain, workers in nonmechanized industries outnumbered those in mechanized trades by three to one. Yet, the bigger point is that working conditions for artisans declined. Increasingly the old path from journeyman to master was blocked, as workers remained in dead-end positions in large and impersonal workrooms, where jobs were broken into less complex and less satisfying, but more cost-efficient, tasks. Even when employers did not set working time, reduced piece rates drove up the days and hours of labor.[51]

In the US, matters were rather different: urban craftspeople in colonial times and into the nineteenth century often expected to work long hours as apprentices and journeyman, hoping to move up to master status, becoming an autonomous householder, or, with saving, to purchase land to become an independent farmer. There is little evidence for collective traditions like Saint Monday migrating across the Atlantic. However, expanding capitalist competition, mechanization, and consolidation of workshops gradually eroded these expectations of eventual freedom from wage labor; and journeymen became merely low-wage entry workers. In both the US and Europe, the traditional domestic worker and craftsperson often were replaced by the factory and the machine tender whose work time was set by management.[52] Even those who worked in unsupervised conditions of garret or cottage experienced a speedup in the nineteenth century with increased competition. So-called sweated artisans were forced to work up to sixteen hours a day during the rush season to compensate for months of unemployment.[53]

Of course, in some industries (like construction and metal goods), where skilled and often organized males dominated, the traditional ten-hour workday did not increase during the nineteenth century. In England, for example, the workday and workweek were often "irregular" because skilled artisans worked by the piece, taking pride in "controlling the product" until they delivered it to the merchant. And their traditional values of taking pleasure when available and habits of rough games, gambling, and drinking made many reluctant to embrace the work ethic of de Vries's worker-consumers. Unsurprisingly, Saint Monday remained sacred in many places.[54]

Yet, even for the skilled and proud artisan, the long and regular workday gradually prevailed. As Voth notes, in London, Saint Monday had largely disappeared by 1800. By midcentury, it was gone in most trades elsewhere in Britain as it became associated with debauchery and imprudence (even to some labor leaders). In the end, the pressure of competition and the growing power of masters turned into modern capitalists led to the suppression of these holidays and with them the "leisure preference" of many workers.[55]

The Great Transformation: Repressing the Carnival and Affirming the Work Ethic

Early industrialization brought more than longer and more intense workdays, and changes came from religious and cultural sources as well as economic. A broader attack on the traditional culture of free time led to a gradual decline of holidays and seasonal festivals. While a muted form of this process occurred in North America, the festival tradition was never strong there; so, I will focus on Europe.

In Western Europe, between the sixteenth and nineteenth centuries, powerful economic and religious figures challenged the annual cycle of collective festivals with their saturnalian rituals. In the long run, the festival cycle was replaced by a few national holidays, the weekend, and personal vacations. This meant a synchronized work year conforming to the needs of a capitalist economy for a predictable and continuous flow of business. It corresponded also to a gradual shift from rural life, linked to the seasons, to urban life tied to the regularity of emerging markets.

But this challenge to the local, seasonal, and frequent festival holiday was hardly a direct result of capitalist pressure. It was a product of a far broader cultural upheaval. Peter Burke describes it as the victory of habits of "diligence, gravity, modesty, orderliness, prudence, reason, self-control, sobriety, and thrift" over an older culture of "generosity and spontaneity and a greater tolerance of disorder." Ronald Hutton describes the change in England in religious terms: the triumph of a

Protestant movement that rejected "works" religion (based on ritual and the sacraments) for a simple Biblical faith. This presumably meant that a consistent and rigorous religious sobriety replaced a village-based festival culture of ritualized Catholicism.[56]

Long before modern capitalism, some English farmers, artisans, and merchants rejected the old festivals and even the love of sport, gaming, and drink as they embraced an all-inclusive seriousness, expressed in the gospel of work. This is commonly associated with the Protestant Reformation of the sixteenth century and with the Puritans who prevailed for a time in seventeenth-century England (and who founded New England). They advanced the famous "Protestant ethic" of Max Weber, which, he argued, created the modern "spirit of capitalism" (though a similar ethos emerged in Catholic countries with advanced commercial economies). Especially for the Calvinist Puritans, the guiding belief behind the work ethic was that salvation came not from religious ritual or "good deeds" but as a "gift" from God. This doctrine, however, led to an uncertainty among Protestant believers about whether they were "elected" for salvation, causing them to prove to themselves and others their divine selection. This required living a life of consistent godliness, not in ritual or in monastic withdrawal from the world (as Catholics presumably preferred) but in daily and constant work as well as virtue. Steady labor was an end in itself, a rejection of the intermittent and inconsistent work of medieval society in favor of systematic and disciplined work. As a New England Puritan pastor insisted, "God sent you not into this world as into a Play-house, but a Work-house." This made the festival with its frivolity and irreverence intolerable.[57]

Puritans also believed they had to "sanctify" the world by abolishing the abomination of the festival. Puritan distress over the chaos and violence of the festival led them to prohibit bearbaiting, cudgeling, and other violent sports. The festival in parts of England was a target for more than a century after the 1540s, culminating in the 1640s when all festive holidays were abolished and Sundays were reserved for worship and rest. Leaders of the Puritan-dominated Massachusetts Bay Colony celebrated no holidays except the weekly Sabbath and even banned Christmas celebrations in 1659, viewing the holiday as a pagan Catholic holdover.[58]

These views were not unique to radical Protestants. The Catholic Reformation of the mid-sixteenth century not only reaffirmed traditional doctrine, but it also tried to revitalize the Church by driving irreverence from communal celebrations. The Council of Trent of 1562 denounced the use of saint's days for irreverent and drunken festivities. By the mid-seventeenth century, "this-worldly asceticism," as Weber called this ethic, was almost as common in Catholic as in Protestant Europe.[59]

This attack on festival and carnival culture extended far beyond religious reform. A major illustration is the withdrawal of both aristocrats and modern capitalists from the carnival. While, in 1515, Henry VIII of England joined the May Day Robin Hood plays and dances, in 1661, his Stuart successor, Charles II, went to Hyde Park on May Day for an exclusive celebration that included a procession of "rich coaches." Some English gentry retained the old paternalism by supporting cross-class rituals during holidays (at least by paying for some of the festivities). However, the English gentry after about 1780 began to withdraw financial support for communal festivals and instead joined private and more sedate celebrations with family and close friends. Gradually, the communal Christmas festival, sometimes featuring a village banquet hosted by the local leading family, was replaced by a child-centered event at home around yule logs and Christmas trees, such as was celebrated by Charles Dickens in his *Christmas Carol* of 1843.[60] Sometimes ruling authorities took more direct action as when London authorities banned the Bartholomew Fair in 1854. These campaigns against festival activities reveal a growing unwillingness of elites to share in popular culture (or even to allow it) and a desire of the affluent to define themselves against that culture (see chapter 3). Both goals survive today.[61]

Of course, there was much resistance to this assault on custom. The Puritans' banning of festivals and sport was evaded in mid-seventeenth century England, and part of the old ritual calendar was restored when these religious radicals fell from power in 1660. And the Puritan hold on New England had declined by the end of the seventeenth century. Carnival traditions survived, even thrived, in rural England, for example, until the mid-nineteenth century. But only remnants remained after 1900. The old carnival culture ceased to mark time, even if, as we shall see, it survived in popular consumer culture. Instead, the clock and the regularity of the weekend ordered modern life, bringing a bias toward work rather than freedom from it. These changes met the economic interests and religious beliefs of the rich and powerful in early modern England especially. This bias toward work prevailed through the Enlightenment even as religious belief waned. The attack on carnival culture continued.[62]

An even more important legacy of the early modern period has survived—the "Protestant" work ethic. It flourished in secularizing bourgeois culture but also reached down (via religion especially) into the working classes. An emerging entrepreneurial class in eighteenth-century England defined itself against the presumed sloth and indulgence of the working masses. But that class went further by rejecting the aristocratic view that labor was degrading, suitable only for enslaved people, peasants, and craftspeople. Rather, this rising bourgeoisie saw methodical work as its own reward and also as a promise of future benefits, spiritual but especially material. These values became the bedrock of the modern genteel values of rationality, deferred gratification, and material progress, as we shall see in the next chapter.

For many, including Weber, the best example of all this is the eighteenth-century artisan turned businessman-statesman, Benjamin Franklin of Philadelphia. Although a child of New England Puritans, in adult life he found the subtleties of religious doctrine unintelligible. Still, he followed the Protestant work ethic without the theological underpinning, advising readers in his *Poor Richard's Almanack*: "Sloth like Rust, consumes faster than Labour wears. . . . Do not squander Time, for that's the stuff Life is made of. . . . There will be sleeping enough in the Grave."[63] As a young apprentice, he was appalled by his workmates' convivial work breaks, when ale was drunk. His focus on hard and steady work in youth gave him the means to retire early at forty-two (a common goal of many an entrepreneur and professional from Franklin's time onward). He famously equated time with money, valuable primarily for accumulating wealth rather than enjoying life. As Franklin wrote, "He that is prodigal of his time, is, in effect, a Squanderer of Money. . . . Time is Money."[64]

Still, the religious impetus for the work ethic survived during the Enlightenment epoch of Franklin. Especially in the Anglo-American world, Protestant churches with their work ethic sometimes appealed to the working classes and the poor when the bourgeois ethos of the Enlightenment bypassed them. E. P. Thompson famously noted the impact of the Protestant Methodist Church, with its emotional mass meetings and informal worship in chapels, on miners, factory workers, and farmers during early industrialization. Methodism promoted the systematic pursuit of self-control and hard work, deemed essential to avoid the temptations of gambling, drinking, and other sins that threatened the ultimate goal of salvation. Many working-class believers rejected the carnival culture of their ancestors, even as these spirited evangelists perpetuated carnival passions with the emotionality of their revivals and hymn singing. This culture has survived to the present in waves of religious fervor, especially in the US.[65]

In effect, efforts to instill work discipline in the factory were reinforced in evangelical churches. Sunday schools taught the virtues of hard work and punctuality. But then so did schools and penitentiaries, poorhouses, and insane asylums that appeared in the first half of the nineteenth century. Through such ubiquitous indoctrination, the work ethic for many workers was self-imposed (or imposed outside the workplace). It hardly required the slave-driving factory overseer (or the allure of consumer goods). Moreover, the internalized work ethic promised (and sometimes realized) upward mobility. It, at least, provided respectability, an alternative to the carnival culture.[66] As we shall see, these genteel ideals never eradicated carnival, especially in the working classes. But they extended beyond the interests of capitalists and continue to shape the lives of many today.

Crowning Change: Separating Work from Free Time

Capitalism (and its cultural allies) extended and intensified work and discredited old values of carnival and leisure. But capitalism also relocated work time, separating it from the space of free time. This was essential for the success of the new work regime, but this division also led to new expectations for using time free from market work. In many cases, work time could not be expanded and disciplined until it was removed from workers' cottages and families. Ending the traditional intertwining of work and life made for greater efficiency in work time in a place controlled by the capitalist and free from the "distractions" of family and personal activities. Separating wage work from the home also liberated free time from work discipline and the rigors of the employment relationship. *Ideally*, this allowed the cultivation of pleasure, comfort, and affection in the domestic/family setting. Domesticity often replaced the communal festival culture of the past.

Yet, this system radically disrupted traditional time and space, causing stress and difficulties in resolving problems that remain with us today. The worker's day became segmented into hours of work and hours of leisure, each conducted in different, sometimes distant places (requiring a commute), whereas formerly the place of both activities was often the same and the time of each was often indistinguishable. This had many implications, but none so important as its impact on the family and the roles of its members. Parents and children who had frequently labored together or near each other increasingly spent work time in different places, often determined by age or gender. Women were increasingly isolated in domestic places as homemakers and men in public places as breadwinners, with children in between (first at home and later at work or school). We all know this, but this division of time/space was profound and had subtle consequences. It set the stage for modern daily life, with which we still contend.

This time/space division had many implications, especially for working-class families. These are familiar to some readers but worth reviewing here:

1. Work and free time would increasingly be experienced as radical opposites, rather than as complementary, even indistinguishable, activities. Work was something people went to in a place where their freedom was relinquished for a set time, as the price of deferred freedom. In turn, pleasure was located in different (often private) places "after hours." Gradually working people expected less satisfaction at jobs and instead sought increased money for work and more time free from it.
2. While work space no longer allowed personal freedom, within the home most market work disappeared. The domestic shelter became a "haven from a heartless world" of increasingly impersonal labor and economic competition. Thus, a cult of domestic pleasures emerged, set against the world of business and labor. Of course, this was an idealized picture. Domestic harmony and happiness were hardly givens in the home free from wage work but where male dominance and sometimes oppression were common.[67]
3. The early industrial system also often separated the daily lives of women from men. While men increasingly became distant "outside" breadwinners, many women (excluding, of course, the poor) gradually lost contact with the world of business and labor; they remained in the home, conducting nonmarket family activities. Women at home, free from the regularized and intense pace of clocked work time experienced by many men, sometimes retained a more traditional "task-oriented" work culture, allowing them to intersperse work and leisure across the day. But women in the industrial era did not have the clear division of

work time and space that made possible the "after hours" leisure of many working men. During these periods of freedom from obligation, men sometimes expected to be treated as "lords of the castle" at home. As a result, female work was often "never done" and certainly not limited to fixed hours. Of course, the working-class female during this period of early industrialization might well have taken a job in a mill (or more often as a servant in the new households of the industrial well-to-do). But this sometimes ended upon marriage and childbearing, especially where women's industrial employment was rare. It was difficult (and often taboo) for women with children to combine income with family work in the age of the factory.

4. This division was refined and reinforced with the Victorian ideology of the "women's sphere," which particularly impacted middle-class families. Women (at first, the more affluent) also developed innovative approaches to the traditional time and space of labor in the home. While the male sought to increase productivity or income on the job, the women in the home attempted to save time from domestic tasks and child-rearing, shifting time and domestic space to new forms of leisure. Domestic space was gradually shorn of productive activities in favor of comfort and family leisure use. In some measure, women embraced a new domestic leisure built around "togetherness" (such as in the celebration of holidays) and favored the abandonment of saturnalian community activities of the past, including Saint Monday and blood sports.[68]

The result of this separation of work time and place from free time and place has been profound, creating problems, but also possibilities, with which we are still grappling. Not the least of those dilemmas is the ongoing dissatisfaction over the gender division of work and life and conflicts over home/family care and economic work. Still, that division has created the foundation, for better or worse, for our modern notions of work and leisure that many still do not want to lose. This includes defined periods of freedom from obligation, domestic spaces usually unimpeded by market work, and the possibility of special relationships devoted to family and personally chosen activities.

The capitalist revolution in work time and free time also led to new forms of leisure that emerged fully in the nineteenth century. Although some may find this hard to accept, that new culture of leisure was created in large part (but hardly exclusively) by some of the same people that promoted capitalist work time, the emerging middle class. This new, ultimately modern, culture changed, if not eradicated, the old aristocratic and popular cultures. The nineteenth century produced many of the familiar characteristics of the world we still live in, even models for the use of free time that remain ideals, albeit unrealized. And yet, the nineteenth century also witnessed resistance to the intensified and extended work time imposed by industrial capitalism. This led to movements for the reduction of work time that resulted in the twentieth century in the eight-hour day and forty-hour week. How the era of modern capitalism transformed and increased free time will occupy us in the next two chapters.

3

Modernizing Free Time

THE OTHER SIDE OF THE CAPITALIST REVOLUTION

Early capitalism not only revolutionized work but also brought new cultures of free time. Along with the bourgeois work ethic and self-discipline came both a partial rejection of the traditional leisure culture of the aristocracy and the abandonment of the popular carnival culture. A new culture emerged, one between and against the old upper and lower classes. We commonly, if simplistically, associate it with the "middle class" or bourgeoisie. This challenge to the old free-time cultures of the rich and poor went beyond rejection. It led to the creation of a new culture of free time built around new ideas about self-development and social and worldly engagement that continue to shape the lives of many today. The result was two broad elements of genteel free-time culture: expressions of individuality and privacy, especially in the home, and new patterns of restrained, but refined, public culture, both of which emerged in the seventeenth and eighteenth centuries in the West.

This genteel culture radically modified the traditional elite leisure of the landed aristocracy. It consisted of new forms of personal cultivation and sociability while challenging older aristocratic practices of emotional and even violent individualism as well as tribal bonding. This came with the "taming" of the old warrior class of the Middle Ages in Renaissance court society, but also with the melding of old and new elites and the gradual shift from an aristocratic to bourgeois ruling class.

Accompanying this shift was the new elite's withdrawal from the popular communal festival. And with it was a new stress on privacy and new forms of social exclusivity. These changes led to a new emphasis on intimacy in domestic space and family togetherness, but also to new solo activities in a radical rearrangement of the house. An emerging propertied class also adopted personally restrained manners and habits (including the keeping of house pets). These genteel behaviors fostered self-awareness and private pleasure, especially in solo activities like reading (which led to modern magazines, newspapers, novels, etc.). All this brought the wide world of fashion and innovation to the private experience of the individual, even as this culture was shared by a broad, even international, community of consumers. This consumer trend began a distinctly modern phenomenon: the merging of the private and the public/universal, culminating today in our smartphone culture.

The new rich also adopted new standards of physical comfort and convenience in heating, lighting, and domestic furnishings, unknown to the medieval aristocracy. Genteel elites purchased goods and services to decorate their homes and entertain guests, creating a new domestic culture. This led to a private world of convenience and immediate gratification. Displays of wealth became more diverse but also more private in an emerging consumer culture. All this became the standard of the good life that extended far beyond the ranks of the rich. It is still with us.

The great withdrawal from carnival culture went beyond the abandonment of the old, sometimes emotional, communal pleasures for private and subdued ones. The withdrawal also took social or worldly expression in restrained forms of dancing, music, sport, and games, as well as in clubs, societies, travel, and a new appreciation of nature. Audiences were increasingly silent before active performers. Elite social leisure involved not only a withdrawal from the festival but a retreat from increasingly crowded and industrial cities to the exclusive, relatively controlled spaces of spas, pleasure gardens, and weekend or summer homes, often limited to family and close friends. But clubs and societies were also important for promoting conversation and learning.[1] This genteel culture radically modified old practices of aristocratic leisure that continue to define "good" free time today, even if elements of the aristocratic past survived.

These trends may have challenged older forms of ecstatic enjoyment but did not eliminate them. In fact, traditional mood-altering consumption of alcohol and other drugs dramatically expanded in this period with global exploration. But these ecstatic experiences occurred increasingly outside the festival structure of old. Like the emerging genteel standard, the psychotropic revolution of the seventeenth and eighteenth centuries was increasingly individualistic. While elites sometimes attempted to control popular use of these drugs (such as gin in the eighteenth century), the emerging bourgeoisie cultivated its own psychotropic cultures around coffee, sugar, and tobacco (as well as selected alcoholic drinks). Arguably, even the craze for novels provided a pleasure like that of drugs. These contradictions, fully exposed in the eighteenth century, remain today in many ways. Genteel culture was fraught with paradoxes that shape our continued confusion and ambivalence about free time.

These broad trends trickled down the social ladder in the industrial era of the nineteenth century. Free-time cultural reforms culminated in two broad nineteenth-century trends: 1) a home-based consumer culture built around homemaking women, escape-seeking men, and the sheltered and cultivated child; and 2) a public culture of free time that restricted pockets of carnival while promoting "rational recreation." These "respectable" public recreations included regulated sports, parks, and museums intended both to offer "improving" alternatives to carnival (and commercial) pleasures and to foster social harmony. Still, traditional forms of elite leisure like hunting survived and took new forms as in the time-consuming game of golf, which few but the privileged could enjoy.

Though rooted in the bourgeois elite, the emerging genteel culture was sometimes shared with the nonprivileged. This gave rise to hopes of a progressive, cross-class, and democratic culture. Still, the carnival survived, often in new commercialized forms such as amusement parks, laying the groundwork for the conflicting free-time cultures that prevail today. Again, necessarily, my treatment of this topic will be in broad strokes, setting benchmarks for what follows.

"Civilizing" the Aristocracy and Creating Genteel Standards

Genteel culture did not have its roots directly in capitalism. Rather, its origins are found in the aristocratic court society of the late Middle Ages and Renaissance of Western Europe. With the emergence of more centralized states, some aristocrats abandoned the individualistic and emotionally charged training of the male nobility that had been appropriate for hand-to-hand combat, replacing it with the training in restrained manners and social accommodation valuable for membership in court society. This "civilizing process," as Norbert Elias describes it with some exaggeration, transformed the nobility's impulsivity and violence-prone behavior into traits of self-control and calculating "politeness," which were required in that more complex and hierarchical court society. In place of the exuberance of medieval banqueting and familiarity, and in place of crudity in matters of sex and the toilet, the nobility learned table manners and modesty in sexual and bodily affairs.[2]

A famous illustration of this transition is in Baldassare Castiglione's *The Book of the Courtier* (1528), one of the first self-help books. It offers advice on how to become a gentleman in the Renaissance courts of sixteenth-century Europe. Castiglione wrote only for the traditional aristocracy, "since this luster of nobility does not shine forth in the deeds of the lowly born." The aristocrat must continue to be skilled in "arms and . . . be known . . . as bold, energetic, and faithful to whomever he serves." But, breaking from medieval expectations, the new-style noble gentleman must also have "that certain grace which we call an 'air,' which shall make him at first sight pleasing and lovable to all who see him." He must "make whatever is done or said appear to be without effort and almost without any thought about it." This nonchalance should be shown in his horsemanship and musical skill but also in his knowledge of "the poets, as well as the orators and historians." The gentleman should "honor his lady . . . and love in her the beauty of her mind no less than that of her body." Women, at least, were to be a part of the "civilizing process." The gentleman also should dance, but with dignity. Most of all, "the gentleman must do all this to obtain the favor and praise of others." Castiglione's advice conforms with Elias's notion of the "civilizing process." But, no less important, Castiglione advocated withdrawing from the exuberance of the "vulgar herd" in activities like wrestling, running, and jumping.[3]

These ideas greatly influenced modern notions of correct behavior and the cultivated individual, even if medieval entertainments like jousting survived the rise of centralized armies and bureaucratic war waged with gunpowder weapons.[4] More important, these behaviors set the standard for a rising elite that included merchants, landed gentry, state officials, professionals, and eventually industrialists. Even so, many from the aristocracy embraced these values. Together, we can call them the genteel.[5]

This diverse group enjoyed freedom from physical work and usually had significant free time at some period of life to create a new culture of gentility, transferring elements of court culture to new private places. This process necessarily required a flight from the carnival of the masses, as noted by Peter Burke, Robert Malcolmson, and others.[6] As we have seen, this withdrawal had roots in religious reform, the rejection of the profanation of the sacred in the festival, and godless celebration of the flesh. However, there were often social motives as well, including the desire of an emerging bourgeoisie to withdraw from this saturnalian culture to the isolation of their homes and families. That rising elite desired to replace the boisterous, public, and communal carnival with free time that was quiet, private, and individualistic.

A Retreat to Privacy and its Pleasures

All this took form with revolutionary changes in domestic space and its new role as the center for elite free time. In part, this tilt to the private replaced the public site of the palace banquet hall or village square. That transformation, again, began with the aristocracy. It also involved greater roles for women. This process can be seen clearly in the transformation of the lodgings of medieval kings and high aristocrats. To us, there was a surprising disregard for privacy and comfort in the medieval castle. This is revealed in the hall, an undifferentiated space used for dining, holding court, and even sleeping. The main thing that differentiated castle halls from peasants' interior space in their one- or two-room cottages was the fact that the castle hall was large enough for the lord to display power and wealth in decorations and in unequal relationships marked spatially. For example, in banquets the lord was seated at the high end of the hall, orchestrating rituals of display and the presentation of food for his admiring retainers. However, beginning slowly from the fifteenth century, country houses replaced the fortress domiciles of the elite, especially in northern Italy. Space became differentiated as the hall turned into an entrance separated from the grand chamber (used for entertaining), and it was eventually further divided with side withdrawing rooms with more defined functions (for sitting, sleeping, display of curiosities, and study). First introduced in Renaissance Italy, the corridor, running from the entrance through the house, allowed servants and others to move from one room to another without disturbing the privacy of members of the family. Bed chambers that formerly doubled as rooms for greeting visitors gradually became more private. The trend was not only to specialize space but for the masters of the dwelling and their families to separate themselves from servants and, at times, even from other family members. Specialized rooms for women and men appeared. All this is common today, making the intermingling of medieval housing appear to us as "uncivilized." Obviously, specialized space was not possible for the poor of early modern times, who continued to lack domestic privacy. Often the peasant or crafts family had only two rooms, only one heated with fire and sometimes shared with farm animals. However, by the seventeenth century, the more prosperous yeomen farmers and tradespeople in England had houses that separated work from living space, removing animals and servants from the family.[7]

This was a slow process. As late as 1750, only one in ten households in Paris had specialized bedchambers. Still, by the mid-eighteenth century, even the comparatively backward colonists in North America were beginning to build larger houses with more differentiated rooms. Enslaved people, however, were relegated to one-room cottages, often without windows or chimneys. Especially on larger plantations, these cabins were usually allotted for women and children, while men were housed in barracks. For the elite and upwardly mobile, public and private/personal space was becoming clearly differentiated as privacy became a central value and goal. This made free time the opposite of public and market time. This division, as Keith Thomas notes, "reflects the tendency of modern men and women to withdraw into their own small family unit for their greatest emotional satisfactions." The quest for privacy and individual cultivation fundamentally defines us as moderns. Separation of public and domestic space, and further division within the elite home, were critical for the development of modern ideas of privacy and self-creation as a unique individual. A room of one's own makes modern individualism possible. And free time became when we escaped into our "true" selves.[8]

This separation of private from public space (and time) also introduced four other distinctly modern developments that shaped personal free time: 1) cultivation of new, relatively restrained activities in the confines of domestic space; 2) promotion of domestic comfort and convenience; 3) self-definition through domestic consumer goods; and, more subtly, 4) new attitudes toward nature and violence.

First, from the seventeenth century, the "great houses" that featured a variety of relatively small rooms fostered intimacy and restrained individualism. Specialized dining rooms not only facilitated closer and more intimate ties with family and friends but minimized interaction with servants (especially with the introduction of dumbwaiters that delivered food from basement kitchens to dining rooms). Intimate parties in other rooms might have also included amateur plays and card games like loo and whist. The increasing privacy of the bedroom may have increased sexual activity. Among the specialized rooms was the man's library (used more for billiards, drinks, and smoking with other men than reading) and the woman's sitting room or boudoir for meeting friends and pursuing female skills like embroidery.[9]

Increased privacy was accompanied by increased literacy, which rose from one-third to one-half of men in Western Europe between 1650 and 1800. But pleasure reading among women was especially notable. Cheaper printing and increased literacy coincided with the rise of silent reading (replacing listening to others reading aloud). Early English epistolary novels, which were linked to learning the art of letter writing, offered the genteel reader compelling stories as well as models for conduct and relationships. Later novels also became part of an emerging culture of entertainment, sometimes replacing books of instruction, advice, or religious uplift. Novels offered stories that evoked feelings that reached especially a female audience. Many were romantic, but exotic and even mystery and terror themes were popular too. Gothic novels became particularly popular in the nineteenth century. Although often condemned by moralists, some novels gained aesthetic and literary legitimacy. The range of imagination and sensuality increased as a result. Newspapers offered a similar, if more reality-based, experience. By 1790, there were already fourteen morning papers in London. These novels and newspapers shared much with later media culture. They were forms of entertainment that were ephemeral and shared by a broad public, but in private. A plethora of constantly changing entertainment and information options, chosen and enjoyed individually, contrasted with a traditional culture based on repetitive common rituals (like festivals and church services). This was the beginning of a media culture that introduced fads and fashions, and which dominates free time today.[10]

This quest for privacy took another form: the English enthusiasm for a retreat to the "cottage" in the country. This withdrawal from town and the social demands of the great house to the picturesque dwelling (not always small) was to offer free time close to nature and its peaceful delights (like fishing and hiking). The "escape to the country" remains an ideal (as shown by the long-lasting popularity of a reality TV show by that name in Britain).[11]

Second, added to this cultivation of private space and time was a revolution in expectations of comfort and convenience. John Crowley shows how a traditional indifference to or tolerance for physical discomfort in heating, lighting, and furnishing homes was gradually replaced by the expectation of easy comfort. This process began when the open fire in the center of the house (with an open roof for smoke) was replaced with chimneys and fireplaces (and eventually stoves). Similarly, shutters (or no openings) gave way to glass windows. For the well-off, dark interiors were illuminated with complex candle settings, behind which were mirrors that magnified candlelight and filled nighttime rooms with light. These innovations, which revolutionized standards of comfort, took place over centuries, starting in the late Middle Ages and eventually reaching the broad public by the nineteenth century. Multiple fireplaces made possible specialized living space and chandeliers of candles allowed night theater, parties, and dining (setting the stage for modern nocturnal leisure). Even so, ideals of comfort lagged in parlor furniture, which often remained formal and stiff (though the affluent replaced wooden benches with upholstery), and in clothing that, through the Victorian era, favored presentation and decorum over comfort. Today, we have taken comfort in furnishings, temperature, and clothing to extremes.[12]

A third change that shaped modernity was the shift of luxury from communal display (as in royal banquets or patronized festivals) to personal consumer goods for the home. Though this had roots in the Italian Renaissance, domestic consumerism became an essential part of the industrious revolution in the eighteenth century. The luxury of the old aristocracy was based on ephemeral (often public) display and on tradition, as in banquets. By contrast, the new luxury was more an expression of personal delight, practical use, fast-changing fashion, and novelty. In part, these individual goals replaced or at least supplemented status and tradition. This change may be understood as still another expression of Elias's civilizing process. The most common example is the adoption of elaborate crockery and eating utensils (especially the popularization of forks). But as Maxine Berg notes, the new luxury also included "rich dresses, comfortable houses, and precious jewels." Even so, the market for many of these objects extended down to the "middling sort" of tradespeople and local professionals, even if on a modest scale. These consumer goods were embraced by men perhaps as much as women. Luxury had long been denounced as wasteful and a threat to economic and social stability (especially by the church and traditional moralists). However, as noted in chapter 2, by the mid-eighteenth century thinkers like David Hume and Adam Smith no longer worried that luxury was a vice, depriving the poor of sustenance and promoting the sin of avarice. Instead, they recognized that the emerging middle-class consumer culture stimulated work and economic growth. Moreover, Hume recognized this indulgence as a "great refinement in the gratification of the senses," which, in moderation, constituted the good life.[13]

Members of the rising upper middle class were advanced proponents of using free time to acquire and enjoy a plethora of domestic consumer goods. But this consumer culture was often expected to be restrained—sometimes in contrast to modern consumerism. In genteel culture, spending money and accumulating consumer goods were supposed to be checked by ideals of polite society: goods were to be useful to one's family (as were luxuries like tea urns and Wedgewood porcelains); they were also needed to bring "civilization" to the home. These goods presumably also "revealed polite people's sensitivity to style and aesthetics—which set them aside from the uncouth laboring masses—and at the same time facilitated sociability and conversation," as Frank Trentmann notes.[14] The use of refined sets of dinnerware and furnishings required self-control and good manners. Such goods and the rituals surrounding them (such as afternoon tea) contrasted with the indulgence and exuberance of the festival and the medieval aristocratic banquet or, for that matter, with modern commercialized street life.

While these goods were modern, novel, and sensually delightful, they were not meant to be ephemeral (like the aristocrat's banquet). These commodities were expected to be well made, in good taste, and even transferable to the next generation. As Berg notes, the genteel English of the eighteenth century "embraced the new civility and manners," believing that along with such civility "the great adornment of middling class domestic interiors and dress" was required. This, of course, created a demand for self-help manuals that linked the new luxury in domestic goods with the culture of politeness. This meant, too, that the genteel had to pair luxury with learning and refinement (as in cultured reading, travel, and even attending university to obtain a refined understanding and appreciation for luxury). Ultimately, as Jon Stobart and Mark Rothery note, "Refinement of taste and the codes of politeness were a means of tempering the excesses of both fashion and luxury." This refinement of personal culture separated the genteel from the lower classes and the unlettered nouveaux riches. It also distinguished the rising middle class from aristocratic frivolity and extravagance. And all this promoted attention to, and even appreciation and knowledge about, the arts, theater, opera, and symphonic music, without which these highbrow cultures would not have existed.[15]

Fourth and finally, personal genteel culture included new attitudes toward nature and violence. Gentility, of course, shares origins with the word "gentle," and it encompassed acceptance of "men of feeling" (from about 1660 in England). This represented a revolution in expectations in emotional life. As an alternative to valuing assertiveness and daring, and with them a disdain for biological inferiors, there emerged an appreciation of nature, a new sensitivity toward the suffering of others, and a disapproval of wanton cruelty toward humans or animals. In part, this embrace of the "gentle" was part of the domestication trend, a move away from the culture of personal conflict with the Other "out there," be it vegetable, animal, or human. Gentle men and women learned to cultivate flowers, plant trees, and especially care for and breed house pets. A portion of the natural world was invited "in" to share in genteel culture. This led to garden clubs and organizations like the Society for the Prevention of Cruelty to Animals, founded in 1824 in Britain. However, gentility also defined more sharply the division between the civilized and the bestial in animals and also humans. This meant insisting that humans not behave like monkeys or dogs, certainly not in the front parlor. It also justified the oppression of peoples deemed to be animal-like, such as non-Europeans that lacked family homes and certainly were not to be invited into genteel ones.[16] These ideals were fraught with tension that later would produce rebellion from within the broad middle class itself.

A New Sociability

The genteel withdrew from festival exuberance and violence in favor of the restrained, refined, and private pleasures of domestic comfort, consumption, and "feeling." Still, they hardly abandoned public life. Rather they found new ways of sharing with others their cultivated self-control. For example, tennis, a game noted for its confined playing court, fixed rules, and limited physicality, became popular in France among the urbanizing aristocracy in the fifteenth century. It spread to England, where the young Henry VIII was a devotee. It was a "civilized" alternative to the joust among the aristocracy, though that sport was also patronized by Henry. Cricket, a rural village sport taken over by the English gentry in the eighteenth century, set the standard for "sportsmanship" and courtesy. Its leisurely pace of multiday contests added to its gentility. The sport would play an important role in modern ideas of amateurism (the code that contrasted with presumably mercenary professional athletes, whose lack of time and money as compared to the wealthy amateur required they be paid to play). Dancing too, especially its ecstatic expression in festival gatherings, was left behind by the new elite. Early modern European explorers associated peasant dance with the wild movements of "possessed natives" whom they encountered in Africa and the Americas. In the privacy of their great houses, the dance was transformed, marked with distinct rules, emotional restrain, and decorum.[17]

The emerging genteel elite of England and the continent, who had the funds and time to travel, also developed a taste for the seaside and especially the inland spas like Bath that offered new opportunities for social engagement and positive encounters with nature. At these places, daily routines of bathing and the drinking of healing waters were combined with rounds of socializing, music, and dancing, often in "assembly rooms." From about 1660, wealthy young English gentlemen found time and resources for a lengthy European tour, especially to the Renaissance centers of northern Italy, lasting several months or even years. Often accompanied by a tutor, the grand tour, as these journeys came to be known, was supposed to be a cultural rite of passage for these privileged but presumably serious youths to experience, firsthand, famous sites of classical antiquity. For some, the grand tour was an essential prerequisite for participating in upper-class society. By 1750, other wealthy young men from Europe and even North America joined what had become a ritualized trek, expected of those aspiring to gentility.[18]

Still others pursued an "imaged countryside" in hikes across rural trails and touring picturesque villages in England, for example. As Malcolm Andrews notes, "One of the chief excitements for the Picturesque tourist was the recognition and tracing of resemblances between art and nature." These refined tourists were often familiar with landscape paintings and had read in literary accounts of travelers before they sought on their own treks the "pleasing melancholy" of castle ruins or the beauty or sublimity of the craggy ravine or waterfall viewed from a high perch.[19]

The emergence of pleasure parks perhaps best illustrates the genteel shift in socializing and exploring nature. Especially notable are the ways that these sites differed from the traditional royal or aristocratic garden and hunting ground. As noted in chapter 2, aristocratic gardens had roots in the ancient Near East that were perpetuated in the Roman Empire and were adopted in the Middle Ages and Renaissance Italy. Royal and aristocratic gardens were places for the display of wealth and power over both nature and other people. On special occasions, they featured parades, theatrical performances, and dancing. Extending from them also were landscaped hunting parks that offered the quasi-militarized elite exclusive opportunities to pursue prey.

With the growth of the bourgeoisie in seventeenth-century England, however, a new type of pleasure park appeared. Like its aristocratic predecessors, it was an escape from the throng and shared an aesthetic of refined and cultivated nature. But the new pleasure park no longer required connections to royalty or high nobility. Instead, it was open to the paying public. Along with rural mineral wells and later the seaside resort,[20] this new type of pleasure garden offered city dwellers a refuge from crowded city streets while being located near or within cities like London. These commercialized, but genteel, sites of sociability offered convenient urban settings for sedate encounters with nature and peers. Still, they retained some festive-like features (though now cut off from the village and the agricultural cycle). In time, the pleasure garden gave in to the carnivalesque taste of the shopkeeper and artisan to attract paying crowds sufficient for survival.[21]

The best illustrations are the gardens of late seventeenth- and eighteenth-century London—especially Ranelagh, Marylebone, and Vauxhall. Upon entering their gated entrances, customers found gardens, clipped hedges, fountains, and statues along graveled paths. Grassy surfaces for lawn bowling and cricket as well as swings and carousels were common, as were open-air sites for concerts in the evenings. All this was consistent with the "civilizing process." But the entertainment was sometimes less genteel—including jugglers, tightrope walkers, and popular music, which later would be standard fare in the modern circus. To be profitable, Vauxhall's owners had to go down-market. Eventually, this meant alienating wealthy patrons. Spectacles included the 1827 reenactment of the Battle of Waterloo, complete with a cavalry charge. Inevitably, this clash of tastes and the urban decay surrounding the gardens led to the closing of Vauxhall in 1859. The dilemma of maintaining genteel standards and accommodating a broad, even "mass," audience has long bedeviled impresarios of pleasure sites. That need to accommodate a carnivalesque crowd survives today in commercial pleasure spots like theme and amusement parks.[22]

Similar sites for the affluent (and the aspiring crowd beneath them) appeared in New York City in the nineteenth century, including five called Vauxhall Gardens. These pleasure gardens attracted crowds with an ever-changing array of music and special events—including balloon ascensions, tightrope walkers, and historical reenactments. Military victories were especially popular. An example is the reenactment of the American defeat of the Barbary pirates in 1805, involving mechanical models, painted scenes, and fireworks. By midcentury, these pleasure gardens were in decline, losing their upper-class patrons and becoming associated with the increasingly down-market neighborhood, known as the Bowery. In response, the New York genteel embraced the setting of the planned landscape farther north at Central Park (opened in 1859).[23]

This pattern of elite withdrawal after commercialization was often repeated. In the United States, many sublime sites of nature like Niagara Falls that first attracted the elite became commercial spectacles in the second half of the nineteenth century with cheaper transportation. The romantic and dramatic vista of the Falls first brought genteel crowds, but soon also it attracted the carnival crowd with daredevil tightrope walkers and even freak shows. While the genteel found this deplorable (and still do) and retreated to more exclusive play sites, these commercial spectacles, like the festival once had, offered a wider range of sensuality beyond what even the majesty of the Falls offered. Today, the descendants of the Victorians escape to "purer" sites of natural sublimity in exotic resorts, away from the carnival crowd.[24]

Psychotropics: Challenging and Affirming Genteel Culture

While a rising class of the rich in early modern times withdrew to the privacy of their drawing rooms and to social engagements in their pleasure gardens, a very different world was being constructed in the emerging market for psychotropic goods. The global expansion of

European capitalism produced chattel slavery in the Americas and cotton imports that fueled early industrialization in Europe. But early global capitalism also resulted in new ways of altering human consciousness through more intense sensuality in alcoholic drink, nicotine, opioids, and even caffeine. These psychotropics posed real threats to the emerging culture of sobriety and self-control. This was true even as a portion of the genteel grew rich in supplying a mass market with these products. These mind-altering drugs impacted all classes but affected especially the poor and laboring classes, for whom the quickest escape from work or the factory (as Engels famously noted) was through alcohol. Though many of these drugs challenged genteel culture, they still reinforced the trend toward privatization.

Historians of psychotropics stress their ancient roots: beer was invented along with the domestication of barley and opium was widely used by prehistoric peoples. These authorities also emphasize the global commercialization of these products with sixteenth-century and seventeenth-century world trade. In particular, new psychotropics entered Europe and its colonies from the Americas (tobacco, sugarcane, and chocolate). They were accompanied by others from Asia (coffee, tea, opium, and cannabis). Tobacco and especially sugar cultivation for European and White colonial markets led to the enslavement of millions of Africans in the Americas: 60–70 percent of all enslaved African people were forced into sugar plantation production. The seventeenth century also saw the intensification of traditional alcohol use with the widespread distillation of wine into brandy, grains into hard liquor (whiskey and vodka), sugar into rum, juniper berries into gin, and fruit into hard apple cider. A striking example is gin, consumed widely in England by the early eighteenth century. Consumption rose from half a million liters in 1684 to five million in 1737. Often first used as medicine, distilled drinks, by the end of the eighteenth century, were replacing beer, with alcohol content frequently ten times that of the barley beverage. Distilled drink shipped more easily than wine and beer, partially explaining the marketing impulse to push it. But, of course, it packed a much bigger and faster punch. Interestingly, this psychotropic revolution of the seventeenth and eighteenth centuries occurred during the rise of the cult of gentility.[25]

It is obvious that humans had a natural proclivity toward these substances. Some reduced fatigue and tension, and they stimulated neural pleasure circuits. Especially in the modern world, these drugs have become shortcuts for pleasure, substitutes for other forms (religious ecstasy, contemplation, the arts, sports and exercise, and even cultivated conversation) that required time, will, and training.[26] Daniel Smail argues that psychotropics in effect replaced more social activities, including festivals, pageants, and church rituals that religious and secular authorities had long used to shape the moods and behaviors of subservient populations. These traditional forms of euphoria declined with the social disruptions of capitalism. They were replaced by the self-dispensed ecstasy found in the bottle (or later the syringe or pill). In a largely unregulated market, capitalists found the best market was one where individual consumers were addicted to or dependent on their product. This was especially true in activities like solo drinking that were believed to plague early nineteenth-century America.[27]

Inevitably, the authorities attempted to regulate these often private ministrations of euphoria, as negatively documented by the famous illustrator William Hogarth in eighteenth-century England. Notably, a tax was imposed on gin consumption in England in 1736, followed by new licensing requirements of gin shops in 1751. This, of course, was only the beginning, as psychotropics have been repeatedly targeted for regulation and abolition ever since.[28]

However, controls over these drugs were always highly selective and varied in time. By the eighteenth century, tobacco use was common (in snuff and cigars by the elite, in pipes for the poor, and then from the latter half of the nineteenth century by all classes in fast and efficient cigarettes). Caffeine reached near universal acceptance in the eighteenth century (though with class and regional differences in the use of chocolate, coffee, and tea). Tobacco was often deemed acceptable as its immediate effects were moderate; and caffeine was recognized as a positive alternative to the depressant, alcohol, especially as a stimulant that enhanced mental and physical labor. These exceptions to the genteel abhorrence to psychotropics were often hypocritical and self-serving. In any case, all of these drugs were another side to the trend toward privatization and commodity consumption.[29]

Consolidating Genteel Culture: Industrial-Era Domesticity

While early modern elites challenged the traditional aristocracy and popular carnival, and went on to establish many of hallmarks of genteel free-time culture, it was only in the nineteenth century that this culture expanded beyond a narrow cast of the privileged. With industrialization, gentility took on a modern look and was extended socially. As John Kasson notes, in the US the civilizing process was barely underway by the American Revolution (when admonitions against spitting at table were still common). However, in the following decades, the rather fixed social hierarchy that had produced a measure of toleration for the carnival and the violent culture of the lowborn gradually declined. In its place, Kasson identifies a rising class of merchants and industrialists who were more insecure than their patrician predecessors and thus more sensitive to practicing "correct" manners and personally upholding genteel standards of dress, decoration, and much else. This meant that they abandoned the flashy clothing (especially by men) of the eighteenth century. They also opposed the male dandy and the "painted" lady, who aggressively displayed themselves and their appearance. Instead, these middling Americans showed restraint in emotional expression (condemning exhibits of anger, weeping, and even laughter). They were also more insistent than their predecessors that their manners and values should be practiced broadly across society (and should even be a requirement of a successful democracy). In time, this meant attempts to marginalize or even abolish such popular practices as gawking at freak shows and participating in the bawdy culture of song, dance, and drink at the saloon. Both in the US and Britain this genteel culture was often closely linked to the revival of evangelical religion.[30]

There was obviously much continuity between early modern gentility and its nineteenth-century expression. But perhaps the biggest change was that the genteel Victorian more thoroughly rejected the traditional elite's disdain for work and instead glorified the work ethic. The new gentility adopted the private leisure world of the eighteenth-century country house but modified it as the urban industrial bourgeoisie grew in influence. The contradiction between new attitudes toward work and traditional values in leisure time was managed by separating public work, primarily of men, from home activities, orchestrated mostly by women.

This division became "naturalized" in the famous doctrine of the separate spheres of public men and private women. This change was rooted in a changing economy. With the rise of the factory and office, work that once had been done in or adjacent to the home moved to commercial and industrial districts. Meanwhile, the home became the center of free-time culture, devoid of "work" at least for men. At its heart was the "traditional" homemaker, in many ways an invention of the industrial era, whose job was to create a domestic haven from market time for the husband and a shelter from a dangerous world for children. This analysis may be familiar, but it is a useful backdrop to understanding the dynamics of a free-time culture that still haunts many of us today.

As noted in chapter 2, while male employers in nineteenth-century factories and offices sought to increase business productivity or profit, their wives in the home shifted their time from onerous domestic work to organizing leisure in the family. Beginning with the more affluent, homemakers reduced the toil of cleaning and food preparation by hiring servants where possible and later adopting domestic technology. Across the nineteenth century, childbearing was halved in America, a pattern that also spread west to east across Europe, starting first with the more capitalistic regions. The domestic work of female homemakers shifted to cultural activities—decoration and organizing family rites and holidays and more elaborate cooking. Time saved with the reduction of births made possible more engaged child-rearing, often resulting in children becoming the center of the family. Women became the focal point for new domestic leisure built around "togetherness" and gentility rather than the traditional and often rough community pleasures of peasant society. Much work was required of wives and mothers to both maintain and "improve" family life (even with servants). In time, many women rejected this role or economically were not able to assume it. Despite a great paring down of domestic duties, the assumption that household duties are women's responsibilities haunts us still.[31]

While the Victorian home was a workplace for women, it became the place of free time for men as the home became radically separated from work site and time. Manliness was presumably found in the public world of action, impersonal risk-taking, and business relations, as well as in formal organizations—ranging from educational, political, and charitable to commercial. Women attempted also to find space for social engagement, especially in churches and charity. Yet the home was a retreat from the market for the man, the setting where "his deepest needs were met," as noted by John Tosh. The home was to be much more than a physical witness to male success, where the wife and children displayed wealth vicariously for the male breadwinner (as observed by Thorstein Veblen). Even successful bourgeois men sought escape from the cash nexus to take up domestic hobbies. Some were even personally engaged with children, especially sons (sometimes in play). However, this domestication was limited: men often sought refuge from domesticity in the homosocial world of clubs and sports. Sometimes they had to be lured back to the home with their wives' encouraging the "male domesticity" of do-it-yourself or other home-based activities.[32]

The withdrawal of the early modern gentry to their big country houses took on a new form in the nineteenth century—the suburbs. This setting, both accessible to business but distant from it, facilitated an attempt to balance male work and leisure. From as early as the 1790s, merchant families withdrew from the town houses of London to create suburban neighborhoods free both from the rowdy poor on the street and the self-indulgent aristocracy. Yet, they were close enough to the business districts of the city for a daily commute to work. By the mid-nineteenth century, the affluent American businessmen of New York, Chicago, and Philadelphia had also begun to flee the city to suburbs to provide their families a detached home with yard or garden, sometimes built along winding lanes. An ideal emerged that remains today: the home should be set back but visible from the street, enveloped by an expansive lawn, fences, and gardens. This escape to the suburban country developed earlier in the Anglo-American world than in French and other European centers like Paris and Berlin, where the nineteenth-century bourgeoisie retained a leisure style based in luxurious apartments along tree-lined boulevards near restaurants and shops.[33]

Victorian suburban domestic space, however, was more than an escape. The home was supposed to be a sacred place, almost a domestic chapel, where rites of passage were acknowledged in rituals and holidays. Affluent women devoted much time to home decoration and furnishings not only to display their taste and cultivation but to create a morally uplifting setting, where visitors and family were expected to be respectful, well groomed, and well spoken. Like the country houses of earlier generations of gentry, Victorian suburban homes were divided into specialized functions: for example, front parlors with fine furniture and displays of family heritage and talent were distinct from less formal sitting rooms toward the back of the house, intended for intimate family gatherings. Rooms devoted to male and female activities were eventually supplemented by a new idea, nurseries for children's play.[34] Even more innovative were times and places for "fun"—not the exuberance of the traditional festival but singing around a piano, or board and lawn games like croquet and badminton. Such fun was supposed to build family bonds.

Domesticated Holidays, Childhood, and Consumption

This inward trend toward domestic or family time/space culminated in the nineteenth-century reorganization of holidays. As John Gillis notes, the shift from communal to family holidays was part of a social transformation that gave rise to the nuclear family, which prevailed over notions of local community and replaced the household that included live-in workers. Anniversaries, graduations, and eventually birthdays and homecomings of family members displaced communal festivals, and linear as opposed to cyclical time came to dominate. Public squares and other special spaces of the community gave way to domestic hearths and parlors as centers of celebratory life.[35]

The domestication of holidays is best expressed in the family Christmas. The new holiday replaced the traditional communal Christmas festival and its remnants (as well as the noncelebration of Christmas in Puritan New England). A variety of essentially modern institutions included the yule log, the Christmas tree and cookies, and the exchange of Christmas gifts and cards. Together, they were supposed to enhance familial bonding. The old themes of saturnalia and social reconciliation were replaced by a new festival aesthetic—the delight and intimacy of family. Emblematic of this change was the new emphasis on the nativity story that corresponded with a new cultural focus on the innocent child and the loving family. Gone was the traditional gift-giving of Christmas boxes bestowed on servants by gentry masters to affirm the myth of social harmony. In its place were parents showering their own children with all manner of gifts, which were to evoke innocent delight from children and display loving care from adults. Even more characteristic of this change was the Victorian invention of the jolly and benevolent Santa Claus (replacing various other images of Saint Nicholas, often as a harsh judge). The Saint Nick that emerged gradually from Clement Moore's 1822 poem—famously beginning "'Twas the night before Christmas"—both affirmed a delighted and delightful innocence in the young child and disguised the parental excess and commercial origin of the presents under the tree.[36]

Gradually, most holidays, especially in the US, lost their bacchanalian character as they became family and child centered. Americans, who in the early nineteenth century had celebrated July Fourth as if it were Mardi Gras, with heavy drinking, made it into a family picnic by the 1850s. The American Thanksgiving honoring the Pilgrims became a tradition of family reunion. In the early twentieth century, Halloween, which once was an occasion for youthful mischief, became by the 1940s an evening of celebrating childish innocence (as kids dressed up in costumes and masks) and indulging kids with undeserved candy. Similarly, birthdays became occasions for celebrating children's individuality. Even the vacation trip, which had been largely an event for adults, became a time of parent-child bonding, something Walt Disney understood very well when he opened Disneyland in 1955.[37]

Along with and essential to this inward cultural turn was the focus on the sheltered and cultivated child, especially from the nineteenth century onward. Previous practices of integrating very young children into the daily work of adults are well known. The glorification of the precocious child (e.g., Wolfgang Amadeus Mozart) was merely a celebrated example of this. Training was often early and harsh, intent on fostering obedience and driving out "original sin." But children were also included in the leisure of adults (as in the failure to isolate the young and "innocent" from adult behavior, including drinking and sex). This, however, began to change in late seventeenth-century England. John Locke's view of humanity as a product of the environment undermined the common Christian belief that children were born willfully disobedient or were irrational animals who had to be "broken." Instead, the idea that children were products of their surroundings (rather than inheritors of original sin) led middle-class parents to shelter children from the presumed disorder and criminality of the lower classes. This led to boarding schools and suburbs, both far from the "danger" of city streets. Jean-Jacques Rousseau in the 1760s held that small children were angelic innocents whose naive simplicity and spontaneity should be guarded by an education that encouraged individual expression. All this reinforced an emerging trend, the extension of the years of childhood isolated from adults and spent with others in their own age group. Purposeful play facilitated these goals. As Rousseau put it, "Nature wants children to be children before they are men. If we deliberately pervert this order, we shall get premature fruits which are neither ripe nor well-flavoured, and which soon decay."[38]

Genteel women, in charge of domestic affairs, were largely responsible for protecting and cultivating the child. This was still another reason to withdraw from the community. In this case, an example was pulling offspring away from street play of the local "gang" while substituting such play with closely monitored and manipulated distractions at home. There is nothing new about today's helicopter parent. The greater involvement of middle-class mothers became possible with the progressive reduction of the size of their families. The reasons for this are obvious: the drift from the farm meant less need for children as laborers, and the aspiring middle class incurred extended child-rearing costs due to increased educational standards. In contrast to working-class kids, few middle-class children contributed to the family's income, and their domestic chores tended to be a means of building character and responsibility rather than a requirement for family upkeep. Not only did smaller families give middle-class mothers more time for each child, but this reduction allowed for less harsh—more permissive and tolerant—child-rearing. This even meant encouraging children to play. Some of these class differences still pertain.[39]

More intense and personal child-rearing, of course, impacted children in many ways, but here I want to stress the dramatic change in the child's playtime. Mothers not only sheltered the child from adults but from older children who might threaten their "innocence." This encouraged both age-graded schools and greater parental sensitivity to developmental stages of youth, including in the selection of children's literature and the creation of specialized children's magazines and books. Typical were stories that discouraged cruelty to animals on the assumption that this would reduce the chance that the child would become a violent or aggressive adult. Such books presumably trained the child in genteel "feeling." These stories appealed to the child's conscience rather than to the fear of punishment or the demand for obedience.[40]

This change encouraged a much-expanded role for children's games and toys. Before the nineteenth century, most toys were made by children out of materials readily available (the famous hoop and stick); or they were passed down from adults for special occasions (toy soldiers or Noah's Ark miniatures, for example). Across the nineteenth century, however, toys and games became part of the moral and educational training of middle-class children. Time spent with playthings introducing gender roles, especially dolls and miniature kitchens for girls and small work tools and vehicles for boys, became a substitute for children's domestic work. Board and card games taught children the essential virtues of thrift and sobriety (such as the board game The Mansion of Happiness) and trained them in the names and faces of literary notables (as did the card game Authors). Playthings not only served as substitutes for learning through work but also gave parents an indirect way of manipulating "character development" and controlling children's time.[41]

By the end of the nineteenth century, however, middle-class parents were becoming far more indulgent in children's playthings as well as in family recreation. This reflected what I discuss elsewhere as the parental "discovery" of the active wonder and the "cute" in children; and this partially replaced the earlier values of sheltering the "innocent" child and imposing moral standards. Finding the cute in children meant a more permissive understanding of the desires and willfulness of young children. Parents began seeing children's spontaneous behavior as natural and as expressions of wonder and delight rather than as ignorance or sin. Even more, the change reflects a desire on the part of adults to share in that delight. This took many forms—from the celebration of the impulsiveness of youth that appeared in Mark Twain's *Huckleberry Finn* and Thomas Aldrich's *The Story of a Bad Boy* to parents' giving their children teddy bears and later Barbie toys. The abandonment of Victorian didacticism for modern indulgence prompted endless confusion about children's play and what should occupy their free time.[42]

A final point about Victorian domesticity that still haunts us is that, while it was presumably driven by standards of behavior and values, it was also shaped by consumer goods. While values of civility, domestic order, and happiness prevailed, such ideals were still expressed through goods. This sometimes meant that gentility could be purchased and recognized as a particular "standard of living." Like the cult of good manners, that standard was presumably attainable in time by the many (especially in the US). Obtaining a particular basket of goods (a parlor piano, a house with carpets, etc.) made you genteel. The sacred, as Leigh Schmidt notes, also became accessible through consumer goods, as in the commercial trappings of Christmas, Easter, and other family holidays. The genteel class learned to appreciate and understand grand opera and classical music (after about 1900, displayed and heard on phonograph records), and some purchased family portraits and other markers of refinement and tradition. All of this set those claiming genteel status above the masses. The advantage to the aspiring genteel was that most of these tokens of gentility were purchased, rather than inherited, and thus did not require "ancestry." This elite often railed against materialism, but it still found in its consumerism markers of spirituality and decency, especially when they were used to enhance family life. But genteel culture all too easily morphed into a consumer culture where those refined values were incidental and even disappeared.[43]

The Public Face of Gentility: Restrictions and Rational Recreation

Despite these contradictions, genteel elites in the nineteenth century confidently tried to impose their values on the rest of society. They attempted to root out pockets of carnival and new commercial expressions of plebian pleasure while promoting institutions like museums, regulated sport, and parks as "improving" alternatives. Under the banner of "rational recreation," these institutions and activities were intended to foster social harmony. The restrictive impulse was partially driven by middle-class fear of the "dangerous classes" from the slums of London, New York, and other cities, where crime and even more disrespect of social "betters" was common. This was like the anxiety that White suburbanites show toward inner-city Blacks and immigrants in modern America and Britain.

Given the upsurge of conservative Christianity in the nineteenth century, a major thrust of "reform" was the effort to restrict "dangerous" activities on the Christian Sabbath. As in Puritan England of the seventeenth century, Victorian Sabbatarians sought to eliminate Sunday amusement by closing all businesses and even museums and other venues of social uplift. The British Museum and National Gallery in London were shut on Sundays until 1896. In the US, Sabbatarian restrictions were set by the states, led by New England's blue laws. These regulations were expanded in the 1820s. Sunday was to be the day of worship but also moral training in Sunday school for children. Beginning in England in the 1780s, the Sunday school spread to the US in the 1820s.[44]

Another battle for public purification was the campaign to control or even ban drinking (temperance and prohibition). Given the explosion of distilled drink and other drugs from the late seventeenth and eighteenth centuries, this was hardly surprising. In Britain, temperance advocates first favored only voluntary abstinence from distilled spirits, even encouraging beer as a more benign substitute in the 1830s. Frustrated by their failure to reduce drinking, a faction (including some working-class reformed alcoholics) called for voluntary teetotalism, and some even advocated legal prohibition. Their American cousins were far more strident. Serious problems of binge and solo drinking accompanied the uprooting of working people (especially single men) in this unsettled country. This led to popular support for outlawing alcohol. By the 1850s, temperance groups had won restrictions on alcohol use in thirteen states and territories. They were especially prominent with women who saw the saloon as a threat to the economic and social security of the family. "To relieve the distressed mother and helpless children is our aim," claimed one American prohibitionist. Founded in 1874, the Women's Christian Temperance Union helped to win national prohibition in 1920 by constitutional amendment.[45]

Another oft-cited example of restriction was the British movement to enclose common lands, close public foot paths, and prohibit public bathing in the late eighteenth and early nineteenth centuries. Much of this was done to extend and protect the property rights of major landowners. Paternalistic concern that working people were being deprived access to wholesome exercise and recreation (as an alternative to the pub) led to legislation in 1836 to exempt enclosing some common land near towns. Still, land set aside for recreation accounted for only 0.28 percent of the common land enclosed for private use between 1845 and 1869.[46]

Concern for working-class alternatives to drinking and gambling was not always lackluster or hypocritical. In fact, concern over public leisure frequently took less rigid and prohibitionary forms in the second half of the nineteenth century. By then, reformers had become more aware of the social costs of industrialization. They observed the breakdown of traditional religion and its moral controls, the decline of festivals with their meliorative effects, and the loss of patriarchal authority in families. Replacing them were the commercialized diversions of the pub and saloon, the thrills of the popular theater, and cheap books. Reformers looked for positive alternatives. Their goal was to instill bourgeois ideals of order and constraint as substitutes for the ecstatic ethos of the commercialized carnival, but to do so in an appealing way. They advocated "rational recreation" for physical, intellectual, and moral improvement (rather than the "mere" release of tension) in the hope of creating social harmony across the widening class divide. Of course, these goals were hardly met, but they were shared by an important portion of the rising ruling class that believed that more was required than "work discipline" and restriction on free-time amusement.[47]

The most obvious expression of this movement was the reform of sports and provision for parks. Exercise, physical competition, and physical assertion remained from the carnivalesque past, but the accompanying violence and disorder of carnival games was to be eliminated with rules and values of "fair play" in modern sport. For example, instead of the anarchy and saturnalia of the bull run, recreation reformers at Stamford, England, in the 1830s favored the racetrack, which confined sport to a defined area with set rules and made it possible to regulate gambling. Replacing the day-long mass "football" contests were new ball games with defined playing fields, strict timing, and rules of action controlled by impartial referees. Sport moved from the pub (eliminating blood and animal sports) and the village green to the school and eventually to the regulated and designated playing field and stadium. Notably, between 1840 and 1860, elite English schools substituted disorderly unsupervised games, animal torture, and the ritual of older students bullying younger students with enthusiastic support for organized sport. Instead of violence and often cruelty, the contained competition in modern sports would presumably build character (in boys). In the 1830s and 1840s, the elite English public school modernized the rough peasant game of football. As it expanded to urban clubs, a national set of rules was adopted in 1863 in the Football Association (soccer). About the same time, variations on this story occurred with other team sports (baseball, American football, English rugby, and Australian Rules football). Modern sports, in the US as well as Britain and elsewhere, participated in the "civilizing process" (as did the decline of dueling). But the idea was not the restraint of courtly politeness but energetic physical competition that was regulated by rules limiting injury and violence, and which demanded "fair play." Rule changes encouraged individual skill and cooperative team play rather than the melee of past festival games and the violence that they engendered. Individual achievement was paramount and systematically recorded, allowing for competition through comparing scores. Athletes also were encouraged to specialize and train to maximize their natural ability to meet the increasingly keener competition. This paralleled trends in business. In time, the vaunted values of the "amateur" made way for the paying spectator and professional player.[48]

The park and playground movement were other manifestations of rational recreation. From 1833, a British effort to create urban parks was largely dedicated to fostering genteel values of sublimity and family togetherness. Royal parks were sometimes opened to the public. They offered walkways and pleasure garden–type vistas but often banned games and sports.[49] In admiration of grand European parks in capital cities, Americans built large parks in their increasingly crowded cities. Most famous was Frederick Olmsted's Central Park in New York, opened in 1859, a park large enough, he boasted, "to completely shut out the city." The expectation was that these green spaces, with their meandering walkways and natural vistas, would foster "courtesy, self-control, and temperance" in an otherwise rushed and heartless city of machines and commerce. Though often touted as solutions to the degradation of the working classes, they were frequently located in the business district, far from the neighborhoods of working-class children, and were patronized mostly by the middle class.[50]

Rather different were playgrounds, especially common in the US beginning in the 1890s. They were smaller than the grand parks and located in residential neighborhoods often inhabited by immigrants. Playgrounds were supposed to provide an alternative to the street, where unsupervised children, frequently dominated by youth gangs, gathered to play their sometimes violent games. These playgrounds were designed for children, not adults, safe from traffic and routinely managed by trained staff. These sites offered dedicated playing fields and play areas. A major player in this movement in the US was the Playground Association (founded in 1906 and later renamed the National Recreation Association). Its leaders insisted that games and play areas should separate children by age and that the sexes should be kept apart to protect the young from being dominated by older children and to teach conventional sex roles.[51]

Rational recreation also meant new urban services like swimming pools, libraries, and zoos. Museums had even earlier origins but similar "rational" purposes. As early as 1757, with the founding of the British

Museum, enlightened elites tried to separate the collection and observation of nature from the carnival crowd's quest for shock and sensation in the extraordinary (as in freak shows). A century later, in 1856, the US Congress chartered the Smithsonian Institution, which over time created a series of museums for uplift. These museums also challenged the spectacle of the circus and freak show. By 1840, London had an arboretum with the careful and orderly display of trees. While appealing especially to the middle classes, rational recreation reached wider audiences. For example, the promotion of music reading led to massive working-class choirs, some of which were attracted to the choral music of Handel, evident in the thousands who joined mass gatherings at London's Crystal Palace to sing the *Messiah*. By midcentury, the British parliament had begun to sponsor public baths, museums, and libraries. About fifty years later, the American steel tycoon Andrew Carnegie constructed hundreds of neoclassical buildings that housed the Carnegie Public Libraries in the US and Britain. In the 1890s, the newly rich built cultural complexes to house art and natural history museums in cities such as Chicago and Pittsburgh in order to raise the tone of leisure and bring harmony to industrial centers.[52]

Directors of natural history and other museums expected their institutions to attract orderly and respectful crowds and to uplift the masses. Some benefactors of such institutions believed that a "mingling between the social classes" at the museum would make it "an agency for better citizenship and for more stability of civic conditions."[53] This and other expectations of attracting and bettering working-class crowds were no doubt illusory, but these hopes reflected the common view in the late nineteenth century that educational recreation could reduce the class strife caused by industrialization.

This optimism seems quaint or hypocritical today, but it permeated the public culture of genteel classes in the late nineteenth century. It was grandly displayed in the exhibitions of 1851 at London's Crystal Palace and imitated by the Chicago world's fair exhibition of 1893. These world's fairs offered cultural uplift (and entertainment) that was expected to reach a broad public. The prevailing assumption of these reformers was that progress would lead to the universal embrace of the values of cultivated and subdued individuality and social harmony.[54]

Aristocratic Holdovers and Working-Class Converts in the Genteel Age

The genteel ideal for free time was obviously not victorious. Some conservatives today believe that this was a tragedy. But here I want to note that not only did this culture fail to win many of the carnival crowd of the working class (a theme for chapter 6) but elements of traditional aristocratic leisure survived and were even embraced by the supposedly genteel bourgeoisie. Landed elites and their control over politics and the military survived deep into "capitalist" times, especially in Europe. Status defined by links with heritage and by freedom from work and money concerns (at least in theory) defined the old aristocracy. And even if these values seemed to contradict the progressivism and work ethic of the rising elite, they retained appeal in part because they were markers of status.

Let me briefly consider the cases of hunting and horse racing. We know that hunting was an elite pastime through the ages. Long associated with ownership of land and the ability to coerce and demonstrate power as well as to possess weapons, it was sometimes an exclusive right of the European aristocracy. By the seventeenth century in Europe, the recreation of kings and aristocrats had been passed down to the gentry. Only in 1831 were undemocratic laws privileging aristocratic and wealthy hunters repealed in relatively democratic England. But even there, land devoted to hunting in the Scottish Highlands greatly expanded in the nineteenth century. The use of firearms in hunting came rather slowly with the flintlock musket's introduction in the late seventeenth century. Gradually in the eighteenth century, the gentry adopted the sport of fox hunting, which was more difficult and costly than the common sport of hare hunting and required specially trained horses and dogs. The fox hunt helped to extend the prestige of a class in decline. By the late 1840s, fox hunting became a complex ritual, drawing in the nouveaux riches. The event was accompanied by an aura of ritual and ceremony—the early morning breakfasts, the horn calls, and fox hunting fashion. Deer (like fox) hunting was often a contrived affair with the stag being carted to the field for a chase.[55] Hunting was "democratized" in the American colonies, as was gun ownership and, with it, a unique problem of gun violence that plagues the US today.[56] Still, hunting remained associated with the nobility in most of the West.

Horse racing too remained predominately an aristocratic activity, linked with land holdings and costly thoroughbred horses. In the seventeenth and eighteenth centuries, the landed English elite bet on private races but also developed a complex culture of sporting clubs around racing. In England, the center of this society was the Newmarket horse track, opened in 1667. It was inaccessible to all but those with carriages and horses, from which the races were usually watched. Gambling was closely associated with horse racing, as it was with boxing, both patronized early by the aristocracy. It is not surprising that southern American planters, seeking the status of European aristocrats, modeled their horse racing at colonial Williamsburg on Newmarket. Colonists imported English thoroughbred horses for racing and founded jockey clubs. Southern wannabe nobles even undertook a "revival" of the chivalric tournament in the 1830s. Yachting, an activity dating from seventeenth-century England, was revived in mid-nineteenth-century America, serving the longing of the nouveaux riches to imitate the aristocracy with an expensive hobby.[57]

Golf is another obvious example of the genteel classes adopting an aristocratic sport. Like hunting, this sport required extensive use of increasingly expensive land. By the late nineteenth century, golf became popular in both Britain and the US. This property was often taken from farms near emerging suburbs. Golfers also needed hours per outing to play, time seldom available to clerks, craftspeople, or shopkeepers. Though sometimes touted in the US as "democratic" (as compared to the cost of yachting), the game appealed to the American merchant and industrialist for its "royal and ancient origins" and its association with a rural past. It was the perfect escape from industrial modernity for those who often took advantage of it.[58]

Hunting, horse racing, golf, and more harked back to the traditional aristocracy and to values that often contradicted the bourgeoisie of the industrial age. These included the violence of the hunt, the gambling of the horse race, and the leisure ethic of golf. Yet the new business elite, ever insecure and responsive to an aristocratic culture that still retained prestige, often jumped to join it. As Peter Borsay notes, "throughout the period from 1500 to the present day, the elite used sport and the arts to define and defend its position in the social order."[59]

Rational Recreation and its Legacy

The free-time culture of the old elite certainly survived, and bourgeois expectations of "rational recreation" were naive and probably presumptuous. Yet, many of the private and public values of the rising genteel middle class survive today. Part of the reason is that a portion of the working class embraced the cult of domesticity and public betterment. Most of these people were aspiring to middle-class status and had exposure to genteel values (for example, as servants or clerks). By the second half of the nineteenth century, families in the upper working class were devoting a large share of scarce living space to dining rooms and parlors, often never used except for the formal visit of guests. Even factory workers, for example, from Lancashire, England, were famous for their insistence on privacy. Wives carefully washed and cleaned the white and yellow stone porches of their modest terrace houses to display their respectability. But often none but family—not even old mates from the pub and work—ever entered. In Britain, servants were cheap enough for some skilled workers to employ one. By 1850, wives of skilled British workers supported the switch from Saint Monday to the half-Saturday because it promoted family and home life as opposed to Monday drinking and gambling. Especially in the US, decades before long-term mortgages became available, home ownership was a key marker of status and a symbol of family happiness to many working families. By 1900, relatively inexpensive homes built from pattern books with balloon (stick) construction often brought relatively spacious housing to the working and lower-middle strata as they strived to move out of the industrial and tenement districts. By then, union outings were increasingly set in parks for family togetherness, often replacing the saloons. In both countries, songs performed in working-class music halls were sentimental, focusing on home and family, not class struggle or consciousness.[60]

Workers' adoption of the domestic ethic of the middle class was not merely a sign of striving for genteel status. It helped to justify the workers' demand for reducing working hours for the sake of family time (discussed in chapter 4). Even radicals like Friedrich Engels reinforced the ideal of domesticity when he claimed that women's factory employment was a threat to female-orchestrated domestic felicity: "When women work in factories, the most important result is the dissolution of family ties."[61] The ideal of the female homemaker and male provider may have been launched by the rising bourgeoisie, but with higher wages (and union successes) it trickled down to the working classes. Today, these gender divisions survive, even though they are on the decline, in conservative working-class families as markers of status and even more as a cultural ideal. In the nineteenth century, however, the problem for most wage earners was lack of time for genteel domesticity.

As often noted, working-class leaders frequently endorsed the public culture of rational recreation. However, in the past, historians have made too much of initiatives like the British mechanics' institutes and their quest for "improvement" in free time or in the adult education movements of the late nineteenth century that some unions supported. After all, attendees were less artisans and workers than young clerks on the make, whose descendants probably earned BAs in literature and science. The Working Men's Social Clubs (from the 1850s), which claimed to offer both entertainment (taprooms for card playing) and education, were more successful. But even these clubs hardly competed with the neighborhood pub. As W. Scott Haine has noted, the bar and café remained the central sites of working-class leisure across Europe and the US until at least the end of the nineteenth century. The home with its cramped and crowded space (as discussed in chapter 6) was hardly a viable competitor.[62]

More important, perhaps, was the chasm between working-class and genteel aesthetics. Richard Hoggart's famous description of mid-twentieth-century English working-class free-time life was an exaggeration, but it is not wrong: "a rough, raucous, earthy, concrete, anti-intellectual, instinctive world of heavy drinking and sports; oral communication, tradition, and superstition; and pleasure in the gaudy and effusive."[63] There was always a cultural gap that could not be bridged with patronizing institutions.

An emerging middle-class program of free time rejected the preindustrial duo of the popular carnival and aristocratic pleasure for a privatized and improving culture. Though rooted in capitalist wealth and power, this new model offered an escape from the industrial and commercial worlds that capitalism created. Still, it adapted free time to capitalist ideals of the work ethic, self-control, and individualism. That program finally pioneered aspects of a consumer culture that increasingly drove capitalism. Yet, in some quarters, this genteel ideal seemed to be a bourgeois resurrection of the ancient Greek idea of leisure—cultivated, controlled, and even anti-materialistic. And this is not so different from the goals of some modern advocates of anticommercial leisure.

Still, there were differences between the classical ideal of leisure and the industrial-era culture of gentility. In particular, the Victorians tried to create a personal leisure culture around the home and nuclear family with improvements orchestrated by wives and mothers, not primarily by a band of cultivated men. Most (except in the antebellum South of the US) did not rely (at least directly) on the enslaved as did the ancients
[illegible] condemned as useless the life completely

devoted to leisure. At the same time, some of them sought to build a public culture that claimed to be inclusive by enveloping all classes in the improving project. With some exceptions, this differed from the exclusivity of the classical ideal of Aristotle and his followers. We need to recognize that the modernizing genteel opened new possibilities for personal life and new opportunities to engage with the wider social and natural worlds. Technological breakthroughs in production and transportation and capitalist market expansion, along with the enlightened ideals of modernity, made for a far richer culture of free time than was previously available.

However, this was not simply progress over the classical definition of leisure. This Victorian ideal was also problematic. The private side of this free-time culture served the capitalist goal of efficiency by separating work and free time (at least it seemed that way to contemporaries). But this required a gender divide that many women (and men) ultimately rejected. This domestic ideal also proved to be difficult to sustain, dependent as it was on the male breadwinner (who, too often, was unprepared or unwilling to perform the task). This is especially true in the last fifty years given the economic decline of the middle class and the growing demands of consumption. The decline of the homemaker and of the culture of the Victorian domestic/gender divide is at the heart of the modern free-time famine, especially as many of us have not yet worked out an adequate replacement for the old arrangement. Men today often do not fully share the work of domestic leisure and life. And particularly in the US, there remains a lack of public assistance for family time, with minimal support for family leaves, daycare, and paid vacations.

The public side of the genteel cultural project has been even more problematic. The majority never much embraced rational recreation beyond organized sports. As we shall see, carnivalesque and middlebrow alternatives to the rigors of improvement survived and even prevailed in the commercialization of free time. And the consumer culture that the Victorian middle class embraced was eventually shorn of its genteel gloss. Still, genteel values, coming out of the capitalist revolution in time, remain with us, shaping our expectations, critiques, and certainties about our current dilemmas of time and culture. With their appeal to self-development and social (and real-world) engagement, genteel values remain central to any challenge to the ephemerality and alienation of modern consumer culture.

A major problem with this genteel culture in both the past and today has been that it required free time to express it; and the demands of early industrialization and the work ethic frustrated this need for time, especially for the working classes. Any chance for a democratization of this culture required a major reduction of work in people's lives. As we shall see, this reduction came not as a natural economic change or a shift in workers' preference for free time. It came because of a movement and political struggle. This is our next topic.

4

Time Struggles and the Settlements of the Twentieth Century

As we are often told, in the long run, industrialization brought less work and more free time for personal life. The average hours per week committed to the labor market have declined in the US from 69.1 hours in manufacturing in 1830 to the 41.7 weekly hours for full-time workers in the prime working age of 25–54 in 2020.[1] The work life of the average individual has also decreased as education and new child-rearing ideals have delayed entry into full-time work. Retirement time has been extended, made possible by pensions and savings as well as longer life expectancy. Industrialization also produced major changes in the uses and meaning of time free from work. The separation of work and home weakened the economic links between family members, but it also made the home a place for leisure. The home became the focus of family-based recreation centered around the child and often organized by the mother. Capitalism eliminated many seasonal community festivals; yet it also created new, more personal choice in free time and new, more regular blocks of free time (as in longer evenings, two-day weekends, and paid vacations). No one should want to return to preindustrial work and life.

But how did these benefits occur? Economists often assume that this change is a direct result of rising productivity and the choice of employees for more free time over more income. But this neglects another factor—social and political struggles over time. These conflicts directly resulted in reduced work time as workers fought for shorter hours, found allies to support them, and made compromises in the face of often intransigent employers. That struggle has abated in recent years, perhaps explaining contemporary disinterest in the subject. But it is worth revisiting this story of struggle, if only briefly, because it is an essential part of the story of free time.

Along with the history of increased labor productivity is the political and social demand for time free from that productivity. In its early stages in the nineteenth century, competitive pressures and new technologies displaced manual labor and intensified (sometimes lengthened) work, often lowering wages and raising periodic unemployment. Working-class leaders believed that these hardships could be reversed by reducing work time. Freedom from market time was not the only or often even the most important objective of short-hours movements, but the right to free time to compensate for the many consequences of increased productivity was central to European and American labor for a century before the 1940s. That demand was resisted by employers and the state, despite productivity gains. Tables showing gradual reductions in average work time obscure these facts and just how discontinuous were the reductions for the actual regular workforce. These data provide averages of part-time and seasonal work as well as work reductions due to recessions, for example. All this is important, but these averages fail to recognize standards of "full-time" work that set the expectation of employment.

In the past, leftist historians have often dismissed short-hour movements as mere "reformism," as opposed to "revolutionary" calls for workers' control of production or full socialism. However, this ignores the fact that hour demands have often been at the cutting edge of labor or socialist movements. Liberating time from work was resisted by early industrialists, often more than raised pay. Demands for free time fundamentally challenged capitalism. Reduced work time meant a drag on growth and profit, obviously strongly resisted by employers in the past (and now). Nineteenth-century employers with investments in machinery did not want their equipment to be idle, especially when less innovative businesses that they competed with relied on the long hours of their employees rather than increased productivity through technology. In increasingly competitive markets across regions and countries, employers often sought an edge by keeping hours long, even if slowing the "arms race" of long hours was socially, even economically, beneficial to the nation. This made reductions at the enterprise or even national level difficult. In the second half of the nineteenth century, this led to the demand for an international eight-hour day by unions and the Socialist Internationals. Legal regulation of "labor standards" in hours, pay, and conditions of work were like arms control treaties, forcing competitive enterprises to do what they were reluctant to do on their own. They may have prevented a "race to the bottom" in terms of hours, wages, and working conditions. Recognizing this, progressives who otherwise supported capitalism sometimes coalesced with the labor left over the issue of work time.

In fact, these calls for reduced work were often consistent with the long-term growth of capitalism. Fewer hours encouraged employers to introduce machines and new management methods. Reduced workdays might force employers to hire more workers and raise wages, leading to reduced profits, but less work also meant more time and money for more wage earners to consume. Growth and profit would follow.

Most advocates of free time also hoped for "uplifting" activities of personal cultivation and social (and real-world) engagement rather than a return to the festival culture of the past. This was largely a call to democratize genteel ideas about "improved time," despite their middle-class origins. More free time for everyone would make the leisure ideals of the ancient Greeks available for all—with the time free from work made possible by machines rather than slavery. Middle-class reformers, even from the ranks of business, sometimes approved of these ideas.

Increased societal wealth persuaded thinkers like John Stuart Mill (and later John Maynard Keynes) that material needs for comfort and convenience would gradually be met, and thus that less time in the market would be required. The imperative for continuous economic growth would be reduced and possibilities increased for the cultivation of culture in expanded free time. This assumption that wealth and time for culture were to be the dividends of technology and economic rationality persisted through the early twentieth century, broadening support for free time. This was especially the case when these ideas about the benefits of free time were paired with concerns over the psychological and physical costs of overwork. The question of work time was central to the very meaning of progress.

Almost a century of struggle culminated in 1919 in the broad adoption of the eight-hour day (on a six-day workweek, with gaps in adoption in the US). Today, the eight-hour day remains the standard throughout the industrial world. It was a product of an extraordinary confluence of international factors: labor mobilization following World War I, an active and well-placed force of progressive bureaucrats, and a temporary weakening of business opposition. Many thought that this unique international conjuncture was only the first step. But, as we shall see in chapter 5, this expectation proved to be disappointing. The unique opportunity (such as in 1919) for an international labor standard has remained elusive. As before, I will focus on American and British history (with some reference to the European continent).

Early Industrialization and Short-Time Movements, 1818–1848

The idea of a right to a set time for work and leisure did not come naturally. In colonial America and the early US, work both on the farm and in the shop was often from "sunup to sundown," encompassing fourteen hours or more (but with rest and meal breaks of up to three hours). This of course meant that outdoor work varied greatly by season. Yet, even in winter, indoor work might extend by candlelight until eight o'clock in the evening. This often was tolerable because, as noted earlier, young artisans expected to become masters in a few years. Work time depended on seasonal agriculture and materials, weather, and the vastly changing market for finished goods across the year; sometimes pay was by the day or year, other times by the piece, but almost never by the hour. All this made the idea of a standard workday irrelevant. Only when wage work became lifelong and methodical—through a division of labor and intensification, with an obvious effort on the part of the employer to squeeze out more work per day—did the issue of work time become a major point of contention between workers and their employers. As early as 1791, Philadelphia carpenters petitioned for a fixed ten-hour day (replacing the customary sunup-to-sundown regime). But that was in an industry with an advanced division of labor, which was increasingly paying workers by time rather than piece. Early factory work demanded long hours, but employees were powerless women and children. In many cases, they expected to leave the factory for family or self-employment after a few years. Early protests over work hours in 1824 in American cotton textile mills were against violations of customary breaks (like shortening time for meals) rather than for a fixed workday.[2]

Gradually, however, short-hour movements emerged. Perhaps the earliest in Britain was the Manchester Cotton Spinners' Association of 1818. While it failed to gain a ten-hour day, the movement was revived in 1831. Craft journeymen in Philadelphia and Boston in the 1820s also began demanding a fixed day of ten hours as prospects for becoming independent artisans declined and work intensified. As one worker noted in 1834, "To the man whose dependence is solely on his labor, time is everything." In the early 1830s, women textile workers around Lowell, Massachusetts, joined a ten-hour movement that called for free time for religion and self-development. The depression of 1837 stilled these struggles; but again, in the mid-1840s, short-time committees sprang up in the industrial regions of both countries.[3]

The question of what motivated these movements is complex and controversial. One obvious goal was to reduce daily fatigue. Another was to force employers to hire more people as mechanization displaced craft workers, since shorter workdays often required more workers to maintain output and increased demand for labor might also raise wages. In particular, the ten- and eventually eight-hour movements captured the imagination of workers long before vacations, retirement, or even an extended childhood. The immediate concern with daily wages naturally loomed larger. Longer and life-stage doses of leisure were far more popular with the elite, who had the resources to take a vacation as well as to defer work until maturity and abandon it years before death. The middle and upper classes also had a well-developed desire to protect and train their young and to cultivate their own retirement. While these goals were unattainable to laborers, in an era of expanding political rights free time was more than a daily release from toil or a way of preventing layoffs and raising wages. Time away from work was an expression of personal liberty, a tangible marker of citizenship. From the 1830s, workers in both countries equated long factory hours with slavery. In the US, free time was associated with the "republican" heritage, dating from the Revolution, and with the tradition of the independence of artisans. A circular of 1835 by Boston artisans called for a ten-hour day as a "natural right to dispose of our own time in such quantities as we deem and believe to be most conducive to our own happiness and the welfare of all those engaged in manual labor."[4]

In England, the ten-hour day was linked to the Chartist movement for manhood suffrage. Free time sometimes meant freedom from the authoritarian environment of the modern factory or office. For example, retail clerks and shop assistants strove to end the "living in" system—wherein the employee was lodged at the workplace and was often expected to be on call at all hours. These store workers attempted to create a sharper division between the masters' time and space and their own. The ideal was not merely shorter workdays but the sharing of blocks with the family, regaining family time lost when work and home were separated. These ideas were well entrenched by the twentieth century. Until recently, wage-earners often resisted multiple shift work or "unnatural" working hours as a threat to shared family time.[5]

Yet what were the results of these movements? Work-time reductions came slowly, very sporadically, and were often compromised by exceptions and poor enforcement; they were not correlated with improved productivity. In the nineteenth century, unions were weak and government was dominated by the propertied, who, for economic and ideological reasons, resisted regulation of business space and usually opposed any constraints on the presumed freedom to work however long the worker and employer "agreed to." This served business interests, of course, but it also conformed to the prevailing laissez-faire doctrine, embraced by judges and legislators. When hour laws were passed in the United States, for example, they appeared in piecemeal fashion at the state level and were frequently reversed by the courts. For example, in 1840, Congress passed a ten-hour law that applied only to manual workers in government employment—and it was not even enforced. In Britain such changes in work time likewise came very slowly and were long limited to children and women, whom Parliament deemed in need of protection. These groups lacked the presumed "free agency" of men (who, in any case, the ruling class assumed, could not be relied on to spend their free time "profitably" or for the benefit of their families).[6]

Bourgeois attitudes toward free time, however, were not entirely negative. Beyond the economic self-interest of employers, that class (as we have seen) introduced an ideology of gender spheres, domesticity, and childhood innocence that shaped not only middle-class understanding of the work-time issue but that of many workers. Thus, in 1819, the British Parliament (with no labor representation) reduced hours for children under sixteen years old in cotton textile factories to twelve hours per day. This was necessary because children working in factories were presumably no longer protected by parents in the traditional domestic economy. The government, Parliament reasoned, had to assume this role, especially when parents often had an incentive to push their offspring into factories to help support families. Rough discipline and immoral environments in factories reminded observers of brothels. This led to an 1833 act restricting young children to eight hours of factory work per day, even though parents in need of additional income often evaded it, especially when parents themselves worked longer hours. The public in both countries was increasingly aware that children needed formal education.[7]

Still, in Europe, political upheaval was required for any substantial reduction in work time. In 1847, a massive petition (the "Charter") for universal manhood suffrage in Britain and, in 1848, a revolution on the continent were required for a broader concession of shorter work time. Nevertheless, the scope of the first short-hours movement was limited: in Britain, the Ten-Hours Act in 1847 applied only to women and children in textile factories. It was sold under the cover of rescuing women for domesticity and child care (conforming to bourgeois expectations of the "normal" family). The law, however, was supported by male spinners as a means of increasing their own leisure because the ten-hour day often also had to be granted to men who worked closely with women in the factory. Following the midcentury crisis, there gradually emerged a broad consensus in Europe that child and female workers should be protected from overwork.[8]

Universal White male suffrage brought male workers more political power in the USA. Moreover, skilled "mechanics" won the ten-hour day in New England in the 1850s through bargaining. Still, economic interests prevailed over concessions of free time to factory children and women. The Massachusetts legislature rejected a ten-hour law for women in 1846, largely because it might make the state uncompetitive nationally and abroad, where there was no control over work time. While children under twelve were prohibited from working in Massachusetts as early as 1842, this standard was only slowly adopted by other states. Only after nearly thirty years of agitation in New England did women and children factory workers win meaningful work-time legislation, coming in industrial Massachusetts in a ten-hour law for children in 1867, which was extended, in 1874, to women. The fact that Americans faced no parallel political crisis in the late 1840s may help explain the slower evolution of hours legislation in the United States.[9]

Short-Time Movements after 1850: Ideological Concessions and Radicalism

The midcentury political upheaval in Europe was quickly quashed. Still, British textile employers found that they could flourish with a ten-hour day, leading to the gradual extension of this work regime across major industries by the late 1870s. However, the ten-hour standard only copied what skilled workers had often already won through bargaining. The American political upheaval came during and after the Civil War, when short-time committees sprang up in many industrial towns, producing the first demands for the eight-hour day. Eight states introduced the eight-hour day in government work after the war, as did the federal government in 1868. Again, these laws were riddled with loopholes and often not enforced.[10]

In both the US and Europe, hour reductions were painfully and unevenly achieved. Frequent depressions and unstable workforces repeatedly led to the failure of short-hour movements and strikes. Especially in Britain, some conservative union leaders saw statutory limits to work time for men as "grandmotherly legislation" and a threat to the power of labor organizations to negotiate in collective bargaining. Divisions between skilled and unskilled workers made the task doubly hard. In the US, racial prejudice and nativism added to divisions that weakened collective action. For example, in California, late nineteenth-century labor groups subordinated the national goal of the eight-hour day to curbing the employment of Chinese, whom White workers blamed for strike breaking and keeping wages low. In 1900, while one-seventh of the US population were immigrants, 36 percent of workers in manufacturing and 45 percent in mining were non-native, many of whom knew little English. And while in the 1920s immigration from southern and eastern Europe was largely cut off, Black migration from the American South flowed into manual and urban jobs. Divisions between White and Black workers became even sharper. This caused both divisions and instability that made organizing unions difficult. All this contributed to a less "idealistic" approach to work time beginning in the late nineteenth century.[11]

Labor historians have frequently argued that work time was less important to workers than wages or working conditions, and that hour reductions were only a way of getting a raise. There is some truth to this. As noted already, a common argument was that shorter working hours would shift wealth from capital to labor as demand for workers would increase, thus forcing employers to raise wages and give workers a larger share of their productivity. A second theory challenged the claim that reduced work time inevitably meant economic stagnation and loss of markets to long-hour countries. Instead, reformers claimed that hour reductions would force management to introduce innovation to increase productivity, eliminating enterprises that relied on inefficient (and time-consuming) work methods and sweated labor. These arguments did not claim the political or moral right to more free time, as was common earlier in the nineteenth century. Instead, they asserted that shorter hours would raise wages and advance further efficiency. Even though these two ideas challenged economic orthodoxy, neither was revolutionary and both could have won support from progressive employers.[12]

An equally important claim made by Victorian American and British labor leaders was that shorter hours would stimulate consumption because fewer hours provided workers more time to develop the desires so amply expressed by the bourgeoisie. George Gunton of the American Federation of Labor argued in *Wealth and Progress* (1887) for what today might be called a "demand-side economy." He claimed that economic growth depended on consumption rather than investment. Increased consumer spending required higher wages and the "social opportunities" (more free time) for the "most expensive" (skilled) workers to consume. The democratization of consumption would create in workers "such a conscious need for an object that its absence will cause sufficient pain to induce the effort and sacrifice necessary to its attainment." In other words, consumption-driven laborers would work harder to get stuff, even if they worked less time. This combination of higher wages and more free time would increase markets for popular goods and services (and perhaps reduce the luxury economy) while, as an added benefit, creating new jobs in the retail and service sectors.[13] All this was supposed to appeal to business. But it also promised working people access to a consumer culture enjoyed by the affluent as the prize of more free time.

Labor leaders offered still another apparent concession to the dominant culture of capitalism by linking middle-class ideals of the male breadwinner and female homemaker to their wage and hour demands. Repeatedly, male labor leaders pushed for a "family wage"—an income sufficient for the husband to support his family without his wife or even children having to work outside the home. A corollary to this call for higher wages, especially for men, was the demand for more time for men's family life. In various ways, many male workers accepted the demise of the old long but "porous" workday in exchange for a shorter, more compact one, often with fewer breaks. Despite the loss of a sociable work culture in which workers had frequent breaks in a long day to meet with workmates, a shorter, if more intense, workday promised more family life off the job. The labor movement in effect accepted the bourgeois demarcation of time and thus the separation of family from work.[14] Was this an embrace of bourgeois values or a reasonable response to new, irreversible conditions? Probably both.

In any case, the path to a reduced workday was always a challenge. In a laissez-faire world, any legislation that went beyond protecting women and children was anathema to employers who universally embraced the doctrine of the free labor contract. Robert Giffen of the British Board of Trade in 1893 made a common economic argument—that hour reductions were the natural and inevitable by-product of increased productivity. This process, Giffen reasoned, was distorted by premature legal action to reduce work time, which would only lead to labor shortages, lower wages, and capital flight. Few employers believed that mechanization or a more rested worker could compensate for lost production with reduced hours. Not many would imitate Henry Ford in 1914 when he reduced production workers' hours to eight after he had introduced the assembly line.[15]

An 1883 survey of American businesses found that the average workweek was still sixty hours. The manipulation of clocks to add minutes to the workday was common, as was the employment of women and children for sixty or more hours per week. By the 1880s, American businesses had organized to fight unions and reduced work time. The National Association of Manufacturers (NAM), originally created to lobby on trade issues, also focused after 1902 on stopping the eight-hour day. Their French counterparts were surprised at the willingness of American employers to use state militia and detective agencies to break up strikes.[16]

It is within the constraints of labor ambivalence and employer opposition that we should understand the seemingly narrow economic focus of the movement for reduced work time in the late nineteenth century. Advocates did not simply abandon the moral vision of earlier supporters of reduced work time. Rather, they addressed the practical question of winning labor and public support for a radical reform within the political constraints of governments hostile to labor goals and committed to laissez-faire. In this context, embracing economic, family, or legal arguments for free time was perhaps inevitable. But that did not make the movement any less radical.

By the 1880s, the eight-hour day had become the central demand of labor across the Atlantic World. This standard, so "normal" to us today, was a radical idea 150 years ago. Beyond the often-stated economic goals of the eight-hour day were issues particular to workers. For them, the eight-hour day was often a solution to the irregularity of seasonal work where annual fluctuations in supplies of work materials and demand for finished goods often led to periods of overwork and under- or unemployment. Employers reduced costs by demanding exhaustingly long hours in rush periods while laying off or reducing work time in lulls. This, of course, produced economic and psychological hardship for workers. The eight-hour day would stretch jobs out over longer busy seasons and reduce periods of unemployment. Moreover, the eight-hour day would create regular blocks of leisure time. As noted above, hour reductions would eliminate workdays that stretched across fourteen hours or more. Instead, working over a nine-hour span with an hour for lunch made for longer periods free from work, especially in the evening. The eight-hour goal went further. It made the then outrageous claim that hours of work and leisure should be equal (with the final third of the day devoted to rest), in effect challenging the work ethic. It also included the democratic idea of a standard workday for all, no matter how productive or exhausting the work was. The idea was that everyone deserved the same time liberated from the unfreedom of work. Some workers no longer felt the need to justify their leisure on family, moral, or even economic grounds. An American labor song of the 1880s fully expresses this sentiment:

> We mean to make things over, we are tired of toil for naught,
> With but bare enough to live upon, and never an hour for thought,
> We want to feel the sunshine, and we want to smell the flowers,
> We are sure that God has will'd it, and we mean to have eight hours.
> We're summoning our forces from the shipyard, shop, and mill:
> Eight hours for work, eight hours for rest, eight hours for what we will![17]

The song made clear that leisure was a right that required no rationale. Challenging genteel standards, it implied that free time did not have to be "rational recreation." Paul Lafargue's *The Right to Be Lazy* of 1883 fully embraced this with its mocking of the bourgeois obsession with work and his praise of "laziness" or leisure.[18]

Still, this claim of a "right" to free time has been a tough sell, even today. Of course, most labor leaders were from the skilled and often better educated section of the working class. They might concede the carnival culture of dog fights to their members, but they shared much with the cultural goals of the middle class (as noted in chapter 3). The words of the American union leader Samuel Gompers were hardly exceptions: workers should have time "for going to the parks, of having better homes, of reading books, of creating more desires."[19]

Despite these differences, the demand of most free-time advocates for a common workday was radical. They argued that time at work should not be tethered to economic or moral arguments nor determined by age or sex. This was essentially a cultural extension of the right of citizenship that in Britain followed the expansion of male suffrage in the 1880s. Both the unskilled laborer who worked up to eighty-four hours per week and the skilled tradesman whose workweek was no more than sixty-four hours should have the same leisure based on an eight-hour day (forty-eight hours). By the 1890s, British unions rejected the employers' claim that labor time should vary with the intensity of work or the degree of fatigue. It was a demand for a universal standard, linked neither to the productivity of any industry, nor isolated to a particularly well-organized trade.[20]

The quest for time was more than an attempt to raise wages, reduce unemployment, or expand a democratic consumer economy. People of vastly different occupations sought the same opportunity for "social time" outside of work. With the eight-hour-day movement, we see a shift from a traditional to a modern leisure ethic. No longer was the goal simply to forgo income for leisure time (often irregular) free from work once income expectations were met. Instead, workers sought uniform and universal periods of work, compressed into as few hours as possible, allowing for the longest and most predictable blocks of time for family and leisure. It is instructive how this ideal has largely been forgotten today.

Finally, after 1850, labor unions and socialist parties developed a new strategy for winning free time. They recognized that international competition increasingly made national or state laws (or factory- or industry-wide work contracts) inadequate. Such local and national arrangements were perpetually threatened by long-hour employers abroad. Some saw the need for international solutions, culminating in the demand for the eight-hour day to be adapted across nations. In fact, the eight-hour movement arose in the now largely forgotten context of an international labor movement. From 1864, the eight-hour day was the dream of the visionaries of the International Workingmen's Association (First International), an amalgamation of European socialist and union groups, reaching perhaps eight million members at its peak. It was revived in 1889 as the Second International. The principle was simple: the reduction of hours in one country would result in an economic disadvantage in an increasingly international market. Therefore, a simultaneous reduction of hours on an international scale was necessary. What was needed in effect was an international economic disarmament treaty. The Second International grew with a wave of labor activism for the eight-hour day in Europe and the US between 1884 and 1891. This international movement coincided with a surge in unemployment in the long depression in the 1870s and 1880s. This broadened the appeal of the eight-hour day as a means of increasing wages and jobs. But this goal went beyond economics.[21]

In America, the eight-hour movement in the 1880s actually ran ahead of it in Europe, uniting labor divided between the Knights of Labor and the emerging American Federation of Labor. The movement culminated in a march of twenty thousand through Chicago on May Day in 1886 (discredited by the "Haymarket Massacre" three days later when a policeman and others were killed at a rally by a bomb). Still, the Second International adopted a plan proposed by the American Federation of Labor (AFL) for simultaneous demonstrations for the eight-hour day on May 1, 1890, to bring "leisure, that is, life, liberty and action for the working class." In Western Europe, the May Day 1890 demonstrations and strikes were on a scale unprecedented since the revolutions of 1848: Vienna, Berlin, Rome, and Paris, as well as hundreds of mining and manufacturing towns in Europe, witnessed massive turnouts.[22] The eight-hour day had become the unifying idea of both the reformists and radicals in 1890, under the banner of internationalism.

1890–1914: Reform as a Prelude to the Eight-Hour Day

All the talk of an eight-hour day in the nineteenth century, of course, was about an idea, not a real political possibility. The eight-hour demonstrations on May 1, 1890, were followed by annual May Day rituals, eventually becoming the "labor day" for most of the world. However, given the political and business resistance to this radical goal and internal divisions between supporters, only piecemeal efforts to reduce work time took place before World War I.

In 1900, the workweek in the US and western Europe ranged from fifty-two to sixty hours in most industries. At that time, most efforts to liberate time were focused on issues like weekly rest days, the Saturday half holiday, and the early closing of shops, some of which were joined by conservative and religious groups concerned about family stability. The AFL became increasingly conservative. The AFL mostly stuck to craft unions and "pure and simple" bargaining, avoiding politics and legislative solutions. Spokespeople for the American labor movement usually argued that the eight-hour day would increase productivity and consumer demand rather than raise wages or compensate for work. Seldom was it claimed simply to be a right of workers in an industrial democracy.[23]

Still, the popular desire for free time in the first two decades of the century was evident when employers complained of increased absenteeism and turnover. In the US, new immigrants from eastern and southern Europe reportedly sacrificed wages for time with family. Moreover, the eight-hour day was still advanced by the most militant sectors of labor, especially in Europe. The British engineers' (metal workers') strikes and lockouts of 1897–1898 temporarily led to an eight-hour regime. But, as elsewhere, employer organizations across industries were successful in frustrating even coordinated labor action. On the continent, the French call for a general strike on May Day of 1906 and the pledge to work no more than eight hours thereafter was ambitious, if futile. Radicals in the American International Workers of the World (IWW) copied the French demand for an eight-hour day in May 1912. Partially in response to their threat to unionize Ford's factory in Detroit, the automaker conceded the eight-hour (five-dollar) day in 1914. But again, this was an isolated case, made possible at Ford because of the adoption of the assembly line the preceding year and new controls over the lives of Ford workers.[24]

During this frustrating standoff between capital and labor, it is not surprising that new parties entered the fray. This included groups of progressive engineers, scientists, and social reformers who favored socioeconomic efficiency, in theory transcending the interests of either employers or labor. Still, these progressives legitimized reduced work, even the eight-hour day. This movement took three forms.

1. A new class of professional industrial engineers promoted a set of factory productivity innovations, usually called scientific management. Working for factory owners, they promised to eliminate worker inefficiency and "soldiering"—deliberate efforts to slow production to save workers' energy and extend jobs. Led by the American Frederick Taylor, scientific management tried to increase the pace and maximize employer control over work methods through time and motion studies, specialized supervisors, piece rates, and bonus pay systems designed to increase productivity. Scientific management isolated and divided laborers by privileging younger (or more money-seeking) workers over older and slower workers by strictly tying wages to individual output. Yet, some American (and European) workers saw scientific management positively as a means of forcing management to be more efficient and thus make possible hour reductions. In the 1920s, after the eight-hour day was won, union leaders and others argued that efficiency made it possible to preserve the shorter workday, despite employer attempts to restore longer hours. Scientific management promised to increase production and with it raise profit and reduce the autonomy of workers, but it also weakened the argument that shorter hours would lead to stagnation and reduced output.[25]
2. Another professional group promoted reduced labor through "work science." Less closely tied to management, this group addressed ways of reducing fatigue on the job, an old concern of workers, while promising not to compromise production. Beginning with Angelo Mosso in 1891, this group mostly adhered to laboratory studies. Work scientists calculated the capacity of the human body for work and the economic and biological costs of overwork. Though at first rigorously "objective," even skeptical of

the eight-hour day, some work scientists shortly before World War I claimed that long hours were manifestly inefficient, justifying their reduction. Some even cooperated with unions in Britain and on the continent. Work science findings also gained legitimacy in the reports of government labor inspectors. These studies confirmed that job fatigue not only reduced output but threatened the health and longevity of workers. These issues came to the fore during World War I in Britain and France, especially as governments attempted to optimize work efficiency in munitions plants. Even though efforts to reduce inefficient overwork were limited (in Britain leading only to a twelve-hour daily maximum for women in munitions manufacturing), this recognition of the costs of fatigue gave legitimacy to hour reform.[26]

3 A new generation of economists also helped set the stage for the eight-hour day, though only from a distance. In 1848, the English political economist John Stuart Mill set the stage. He predicted the coming of a "steady state" economy where growth and unlimited work would end when future mechanization created general abundance, thus fulfilling all essential and real needs. With this, a substantial expansion of free time would occur. Mill recognized that this would require full employment and population constraint as well as a general embrace of the value of cultural uplift and recreation over the work ethic and endless wealth accumulation. Mill was an optimist in the age of the dismal science of economics. But his challenge to the pessimistic view that toil could not be reduced had much earlier been advanced by Adam Smith in his classic *Wealth of Nations* (1776). Smith challenged the common eighteenth-century mercantilist doctrine that long hours of work and low wages were required to induce workers to produce at a high rate. Later in the nineteenth century, proponents of neoclassical economics, including Alfred Marshall and John Hobson, recognized that workers naturally sought to optimize the "goods" of both wages and free time. When economic needs were met, fu-

> ture benefits of growth would shift toward free time. Marshall even argued that in the future a workday of six hours (in two shifts) would be sufficient so that all could be "gentlemen," no matter their occupations.[27] Such thinking, later echoed by Keynes and others in the twentieth century, gave support to the idea that the end of capitalism was not ceaseless economic growth but abundance with time free for culture.

Drawing on the ideas of these engineers, scientists, and economists was an international group of reformers dedicated to the transnational amelioration of working conditions. By the early 1890s, a group of British professionals and academics, including John Rae, Thomas Munro, and Victorine Jeans, favored some form of hours regulation. In 1893, the Labour Department was established in London, staffed by bureaucrats at least somewhat sympathetic to unions and shorter hours. The 1906 victory of the Liberal Party led to government machinery that enabled some collective bargaining and the miners' Eight-Hour Act of 1908. American reformers, including Florence Kelley, Josephine Goldmark, and Louis Brandeis, along with organizations of American labor inspectors, shared similar ideas and activities. They promoted work reduction for efficiency and even supported scientific management as a way of justifying less work.[28] Political opposition was clearly softening in the years leading up to World War I.

However, anything but piecemeal reform required more, eventually an international labor standard guaranteed by conventions or treaties. Only this would prevent international competition from undermining the advanced hour (or other labor) standard of any country. More than the minority movements of socialists and trade unions were required for any international standard to be realized.

The early British socialist Robert Owen was the first to advocate international labor legislation in a letter to the Congress of Vienna in 1815. Yet, it was only in 1880, at an international conference in Brussels on public hygiene, that this idea again was taken up by government officials. The conference called for a moderate set of labor standards (weekly rest, prohibition of night work for women, and a "normal" workday). It was supported by social Catholics and conservative economists concerned about the deterioration of the family. The next year a group of Swiss textile manufacturers and reformers called for another international conference to reduce cutthroat competition by creating international labor norms. Emperor Wilhelm II of Germany even organized his own international conference in 1890, which led to recommendations for various standards to protect children and women and to assure all workers had one day of weekly rest. The conservative character of these recommendations (especially a rejection of any hour limits on male workers, assumed to be "free agents") is less important than the fact that these establishment figures favored international standards at all. In 1897, another international group met in Brussels, composed not of government officials but of intellectuals and activists, many from the work science movement. In 1900, they founded the International Association for Labor Legislation (IALL), which later included both liberal reformers and moderate trade unionists (as well as social Catholics). Though their accomplishments were few, by World War I there were fifteen national "sections" that supported international cooperation on labor legislation. The IALL notably became a setting for collaboration between labor and middle-class and professional reformers.[29] This loose amalgam of reformers and their ideas was an essential part of what follows.

1919—An International Breakthrough in Work Time

For most workers the eight-hour day came only in the aftermath of World War I, some thirty-three years after it was first seriously proposed. Only then was the political and ideological opposition to the eight-hour day overcome in an extraordinary confluence of trends and events.

During the last year of World War I, many of the constraints against reduction of the workday had broken down in Europe. Wartime munitions production had shown that new technology and work methods (including the assembly line and scientific management) could radically raise productivity, making feasible a postwar reduction of hours. In France, for example, the moderate socialist Albert Thomas was the head of the Ministry of Munitions, where he promoted innovation; after the war, he became a very credible advocate of the eight-hour day. British work science in government had made the case for the costs of overwork. The liberal international movement for labor legislation, which emerged between 1890 and 1919, legitimized the radical idea that a simultaneous international reduction of working hours could prevent any nation from gaining a competitive advantage.

Little would have come of this, however, if not for the international mobilization of labor and the left that began in the spring of 1917 and spread through the spring and summer of 1919 across the industrial world. The upheaval of the immediate postwar years created an exceptional break from the past: a combination on an international scale of end-of-war strikes and the threat of radical, even communist, political power from below, along with well-placed social and labor reformers in the power structure above, created a unique opportunity for the eight-hour day. Even in the US, the Democratic administration of Woodrow Wilson began a shift toward labor with the Adamson Act of 1917, which gave railroad workers the eight-hour day. This was the first move of the US national government to regulate working conditions of nongovernment labor.[30]

Yet, this extraordinary international trend to reduce work time has fallen in the cracks between social historians and historians of international politics. In the past, social historians have focused on labor and leftist insurgency and the struggle between reform and revolution in the post–World War I split dividing socialist and communist movements. This attention has obscured the interaction between radical international insurgency and moderate reformism in the coming of the eight-hour day. Diplomatic historians have concentrated on events surrounding the Paris Peace Conference of 1919 and its impact on the coming of World War II, showing little interest in issues like work time.

Yet one of the key demands of Vladimir Lenin's Bolsheviks in 1917 was the eight-hour day, a goal shared by the communist parties that rapidly emerged across Europe in 1918–1919. While Lenin's expectation of world revolution coming out of the war failed, the eight-hour day swept across Europe as governments and employers conceded this major reform. Beginning in the Bolshevik Revolution of 1917, the eight-hour day spread in 1918 to Finland and Norway and then to Germany immediately after the armistice and the overthrow of the monarchy in November 1918. By mid-December, the movement encompassed the newly independent countries of Eastern Europe, including Poland, Czechoslovakia, and Austria. By February 1919, the demand for eight hours reached Italy in a wave of strikes sweeping from the industrial north to the less developed south. In France, under threat of a general strike, on April 23, 1919, the new parliament passed an eight-hour law in a mere eight days (excluding only farm workers). Elsewhere eight-hour laws followed by November 1919. In the six months after the armistice, major British industries conceded the eight-hour day after a wave of strikes (though the British did not institute an eight-hour statute). While this new standard was generally established in a six-day week, for many it was treated as a just reward for the sacrifices of the war and a payoff for the improved productivity of the military mobilization. Yet it was also simply understood as a universal right no matter how arduous the day's work.[31]

These ideas were embraced by a transnational network of middle-class and professional reformers, many of whom were linked with the International Association for Labor Legislation. Players included George Barnes, once of the British Amalgamated Society of Engineers and active in the eight-hour movement since 1897. Especially important was Albert Thomas. Though denounced by the French far left for joining the government in the war and opposing the communists afterward, he became a critical advocate for the international eight-hour day in the 1920s, after he became director of the International Labor Office (ILO), which was affiliated with the League of Nations. As an alternative to cut-throat competition and class conflict, the ILO advocated international and interclass cooperation and endorsed the eight-hour day in 1919. Barnes expressed well this international reformist perspective, declaring that the advanced countries had to establish an "international standard" for labor because "capital has no country." The goal was to extend the peace settlement from issues of war and diplomacy to reducing excessive cross-state competition by creating an international labor standard. Hopefully, it would protect the free time of workers in the industrial north by extending that standard to the developing south.[32]

This new openness to reduced work time extended to the highest levels of government. David Lloyd George admitted late in 1919 that "it is not a question of whether the men can stand the strain of a longer day, but that the working class is entitled to the same sort of leisure as the middle class." During mass strikes for the eight-hour day at the beginning of 1919, officials at the Paris Peace Conference set up a Commission for International Labor Legislation, which led to the ILO later that year.[33] In November of 1919, the ILO held an international meeting in Washington, DC, to vote on an eight-hour convention. However, by that time the US Congress had abandoned support for international treaties (including, of course, the League of Nations itself), and British employers had again gained the upper hand, demanding to up three hundred hours of annual overtime beyond the eight-hour day/six-day week. As a result, the Washington eight-hour convention was limited in many ways: it applied only to industry and transport and allowed many exceptions (flexible workweeks in seasonal industries and longer workdays for developing countries at least temporarily). Though the ILO vote for the convention was 83–2, following the American and British example, many countries delayed ratification. Gradually however, the eight-hour standard prevailed. By 1922, 75 percent of British workers had it. With significant exceptions, the eight-hour day had become a "full day's work." Even in the US, participants in strikes rose from a third of a million in 1913 to 4.16 million in 1919. As a result, twenty-eight states passed hour legislation and 48.6 percent of industrial wage earners worked eight-hour days by the end of 1919 (an increase from 8 percent in 1910).[34]

This, of course, was not the end of shorter hours. Many continued to believe that with increased productivity and fulfillment of material needs, free time would grow. And there would be numerous occasions when work was reduced further, especially in the form of a five-day week and paid holidays. But the confluence of international trends seen in 1918–1919 would not occur again and the expectation that time would (or could) be chosen over more goods proved to be naive. In fact, expectations both for continued reduction of work and an enlightened (genteel) free-time culture were thwarted. These failures have contributed mightily to our contemporary frustrations. Explaining all this will be the subject of my next two chapters.

5

Why Free Time Stopped Growing

The most famous economist of the twentieth century, John Maynard Keynes, predicted in 1930 that within a century the normal workweek would decrease to fifteen hours. Yet in the US the nominal eight-hour day / forty-hour week has remained unchanged since 1938, despite great growth in productivity and consumption. In 2005, a group of prominent economists were asked to explain the failure of Keynes's prediction. Their answers were conventional economist responses: Work is preferred to leisure (especially as manual work has declined) because it offers "utility" in rising wages. Consumption has continued to rise because of emulative spending on "positional" goods (especially with rising inequality). There has been a progressive increase in consumer expectations. And the relative power of advertising (over other forms of learning) has produced new consumer desires that require more work. Earlier John Owen argued that Keynes was wrong because work had become less fatiguing and thus there was less urgency in its reduction. Moreover, rising costs of recreation and related goods created a demand for more money and thus work. Affluence, of course, made possible consumption of labor-intensive and costly services like advanced education and health care (creating a further incentive to increase work time and thus wages).[1]

Beyond all these explanations, it is easy to assume that an eight-hour workday is simply "natural" or "reasonable"—a third of the day, sharing the day equally with rest and leisure (as nineteenth-century advocates of the eight-hour day had demanded). We still might ask: what would we do with all the free time that Keynes anticipated? Even if technology and economic growth would offer comfort and advanced living standards for all with less work, as Keynes predicted, would not such a short workweek mean sacrificing further prosperity? However, we might ask such questions because we have internalized a preference for more goods (and a belief in the virtue of market work) over freedom from market work time; in short, many of us today assume that happiness requires limitless growth. These are expectations that were not yet hegemonic in 1930 when Keynes made his prediction.

The dominant, if often unstated, assumption of Keynes and others is that workers optimize their preferences for free time and wages. This was foundational to the neoclassical revolution in economics. And this idea was central to Keynes's expectation of progressive reduction in work time. He assumed that demand for higher wages was finite because consumer needs were limited. When needs for wage increases were met, given the onus of work, wage earners would favor free time. Both money and time would be optimized in a progressive decline of work time.

Of course, such rational expectations did not translate into demand for or success in winning freedom from work at any particular time. The experience of intense work and long hours, but also rising wages during World War I, may have led many to strive for more free time in 1919. As we have seen, that year was unusually favorable for winning such a demand. However, after the "reasonable" workday of eight hours was achieved (reduced later to a forty-hour week), presumably workers might prefer to "take their share" of improved productivity in higher wages and more goods rather than more free time. This might be the response especially when consumption of durable goods like cars and houses became available to the masses and when standards of higher education and health care rose, creating a need for more income. But this does not really explain the surprisingly stable work-time pattern long after those coveted goods became possible. Stephen Rosenberg notes that if even 10 percent of the increase in productivity between 1940 and 2007 had gone to free time instead of increased output, the average workweek would have been 28 hours. This is a long way from the 41.7 hours for American full-time workers in the prime working ages of 25 to 54 in 2020.[2] It is obvious that needs were not finite in the twentieth century. Advertising, planned obsolescence, and new, exciting (but costly) goods and services induced wage earners to work more (and certainly not less) for the money to buy them.

There is an even more sophisticated economic argument for stagnant free-time growth. As noted by Staffan Linder and others, the affluence that Keynes thought would lead to a fifteen-hour workweek had a very different impact: First, the opportunity cost of time away from work when wages per hour rose made increasing one's free time less economically appealing. Second and more subtly, greater efficiency (productivity) meant more goods per household, leading to a scarcity of time per good. That might suggest workers would want more free time to consume, but then time not working was time not earning money to buy those goods. In a consumption-saturated society, time spent neither producing nor consuming goods appeared as wasted time. Time free from work or shopping became boring and was often used in unmemorable hours watching TV or (today) "cruising the net." This made more free time less valuable for its own sake. Third, with more goods competing for free-time use, time-consuming activities (do-it-yourself, hobbies, walks in the country, and reading that often also required little money) could not compete with goods that offer quicker access to pleasure but are also costlier, like pickup trucks and weekend trips to a casino resort. And the time required to maintain and purchase these goods often increased. All this made free time more rushed—creating a "harried leisure class," in Linder's terms—and more dependent on consumer goods and experiences that cost more money (and thus required more time earning money at work). As a result, free time became less appealing and work time more attractive. Increased or steady hours of employment brought individuals more "fast" consumer goods. I will return to this theme in chapter 7.[3]

But these arguments still may not be enough. Many of them assume that worker-consumers made a "choice" of more goods or services over free time. But people work and consume in market structures over which they have very little personal control. The choice is not generally even considered. "Full time" is forty hours per week. Less is "part-time" and often without benefits. Most people have never been free to make a rational choice between time free from work and wage income (for consumption). Time especially has usually been far less negotiable than wages in employment, making talk of a choice between time and money often meaningless. A central fact was that management responded very differently to workers' demands for free time as compared to wages. Reduced employee work time increased training and benefit costs. Lowering work time could limit a business's ability to increase deliveries in response to the market without maintaining large and costly inventories or making capital improvements. Reduced work time also could enhance the worker's job options to the disadvantage of an employer. In contrast, when wages were increased, it was relatively easy to lower them with a changed market or through inflation. Finally, a worker's bias in favor of wages over free time often had little to do with the choice between money and time. Instead, workers who were seasonally employed and poorly paid had little choice but to work as long as possible when jobs were available.[4]

However, beyond these economic constraints on personal choice were other, probably more important, political, social, and cultural factors resulting in a societal predisposition toward endless economic growth rather than an optimization of work and free time. Central to this bias toward growth were key events—the culmination of a political struggle (rather than economic logic) that led to a handful of societal settlements around relatively fixed work time and unlimited economic expansion. That allocation of time and expanding consumption became baked into the political economy with only minor variation across the industrial world. Like all systemic transformations, these settlements proved difficult to change. I do not claim that politics alone dictates time and money. Economic explanations have their place: they suggest why these settlements were accepted or not challenged more vigorously, for example. But they do not explain the essential discontinuity of work-time regimes or why they have proven to be so imbalanced. And there are other factors that go beyond my political argument—social and cultural, especially—that need to be factored in. But I will begin with politics.

I argue that political settlements set the terms of future debates about time and money, even whether there would be a real debate. In Europe and elsewhere the adoption of the eight-hour standard in 1919–1920 is perhaps the most important settlement. In the US, probably more important is the social and political compromise favoring full-time work, full employment, and economic growth, which emerged out of the American New Deal. Instead of the leisure-expanding policy of a thirty-hour week to reduce Depression-era unemployment as proposed by the unions and some middle-class activists, the US adopted the forty-hour legal standard in 1938 with the Fair Labor Standards Act. It was followed by a national political consensus around unlimited economic growth as the primary path toward low joblessness.

This American settlement was a major achievement when initiated, creating a work regime that few Europeans would enjoy until well after World War II. In principle, at least, this settlement offered many Americans access to a democratized consumer economy that promised low unemployment. In the long run, however, this settlement frustrated further progress in freedom from work. As made clear in the debate over the 1938 law, full employment was to be achieved through growth, not a reduction of work. This preserved the fundamental drive of capitalism for unlimited growth and expansion of the market into all facets of life. This settlement offered most workers access to the goods and services that they collectively produced with jobs in an ever-expanding economy. The price, however, was no further societal reduction of the standard workweek and no law-sanctioned universal paid vacation (though employer-provided vacations increased). This compromise ultimately was based on the successful resistance of business, for whom the additional freedom from the market was a threat to growth and profit. The result was an "end of ideology"—an inability of any significant players in the political economy to advance or often even imagine any alternative to a work-and-spend culture.[5]

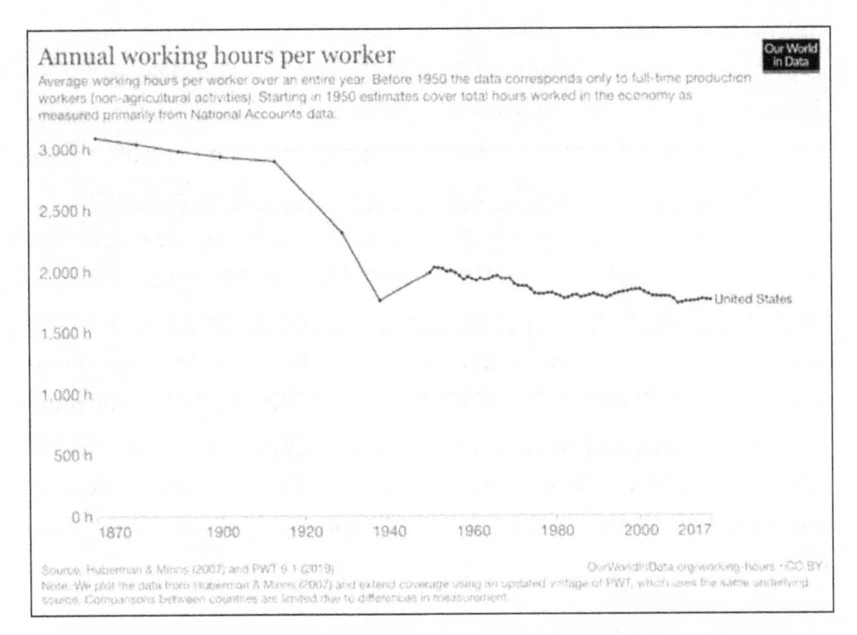

Although work-time data is complex and controversial, this graph shows how the dramatic downward trend in annual working hours in the US before 1940 reversed in the second half of the twentieth century, especially after about 1970. Source: Paul Krugman, "Happy Holidays. Now Get Back to Work," *New York Times*, December 20, 2022, www.nytimes.com.

The ultimate victory of a politics of growth explains much (especially in the US). But it occurred in the context of other historical forces, including an unchallenged and persistent culture of the work ethic.[6] However, I will focus on three of these historical trends: 1) the social and cultural allure of an expanding consumer culture; 2) the failure to create a positive alternative to a dominant consumer culture; and 3) the (temporary) persistence of a family culture built on male providers and female consumers. All three trends coincided with the consolidation of the full-time / full-employment settlement, especially in the events of the 1930s and 1940s.

There were further reductions of work time after 1945, especially in Europe (catching up to and surpassing the American standard, especially in the spread of the paid holiday). But after about 1970, even this ended. In fact, by the late twentieth century, with new business strategies in globalized markets and new digital technologies, the clear and fixed divisions between free and work time of the early twentieth century broke down and work time sometimes increased. Hours of labor varied much by age, gender, family situation, and class, and there is much debate about whether average work time actually has increased on average. However, the standard for full-time work has scarcely changed despite productivity gains even as many more households have two full-time workers. Work time certainly did not decrease for most in the age of employment as had been expected. And for practically all, life became more rushed. Time scarcity became the norm, limiting the range of cultural possibilities when off work. To make my case, I need to discuss further the international settlements of 1919 and especially the American settlement of 1938.

The Full-Time / Full-Employment / Growth Settlement in the US

The brief historical opening favorable for international hours reform closed quickly in the early 1920s as nationalism and business regained control. Labor leaders in Europe and the US continued to press for reduced work, especially the two-day weekend. However, outside especially egregious workplaces (like the steel industry in the US, which reduced the workday from twelve to eight hours in 1923), little changed until the Great Depression. Other forms of release from work, especially the paid vacation, were so rare for wage earners that it was scarcely proposed even by skilled and well-organized workers. Only 10 percent of American wage earners benefitted from a paid vacation in 1930 compared to 85 percent of salaried employees. Vacations were a mark of status and a reward for loyalty for white-collar employees. In 1929, 55.5 percent of America labor still worked over 48 hours per week and only 19 percent worked less.[7]

The Depression of the 1930s changed all this, setting off a debate about the causes and solutions to this economic collapse. That crisis again raised the question of work time. Especially important was the sharp rise in American unemployment, increasing from 1.55 million unemployed in 1929 (3.2 percent of the workforce) to over 12.8 million by 1933 (24.9 percent). Despite the New Deal, it never dropped below 7.7 million (14.3 percent) in the 1930s. Only Germany experienced such high levels of joblessness.[8] Employers blamed the crisis on high costs, especially of labor. Conservative economists and many employers expected that lower wages and prices would "clear markets" by creating demand for labor and goods, leading to cyclical recovery. Not surprisingly, businesses argued that shorter hours (especially without reduced pay rates) would simply produce inflation as supply would drop and demand would remain the same. Conventional economists like Lionel Robbins in 1937 condemned hours legislation for disrupting markets and interfering with the workers' choice to work longer.[9]

However, in the 1930s, many questioned the orthodox view that reduced wages and prices would eventually expand demand and consumption, thus eliminating any problem of overproduction and unemployment. While a group of "consumer engineers" called for new strategies to increase consumer spending, this hardly addressed the problem of wage decreases and high unemployment. Not surprisingly, trade unions and reformist allies had another solution: reduce daily work time of the employed to create additional jobs. This was not only an answer to the immediate unemployment crisis. For the Left, it was essential to balancing an economy out of kilter. They claimed that the increased productivity of the 1920s had not been balanced by either higher wages or a reduction in working hours. This led to underconsumption and massive unemployment. Simply put, technological growth reduced the demand for labor, both by replacing workers with machines and by making more goods than working consumers could buy. The solution for unions was to maintain wages and reduce weekly working hours, thus increasing both jobs and consumer spending. Even the conservative administration of Hubert Hoover talked of voluntary reduction of hours.[10]

While the American Federation of Labor's William Green called for hour reductions primarily to compensate for joblessness, allied intellectuals and a few in the labor movement were even more bold, insisting that in a mature economy, technology has produced a choice between fewer hours of work or more joblessness. As Louis Walker put it in 1932: "Now we face the necessity of substituting leisure for mass unemployment."[11] In effect, he resurrected Mill's old idea that disengaging from work was the logical consequence of a mature economy. All this set the stage for a new discussion of work time.

Across the industrial world, the crisis of the Depression led to the demand for the forty-hour week, a perhaps inevitable solution to the problem of mass unemployment. There was a second opportunity for an international settlement when, in 1933, the International Labor Office proposed an international forty-hour week (eight-hour days, five days per week) without wage reduction. But this was no easy task. Business groups denounced it as wealth redistribution. Moreover, this call for a forty-hour week was an extension of the international eight-hour convention of 1919; but in the 1930s, with rising nationalism and resistance to international cooperation, this idea had no chance of being realized as a new international standard.[12] Instead, the forty-hour week was taken up by the few countries that trended left in the 1930s, especially France and the US.

In 1935, the leftist coalition in France known as the Popular Front promoted the forty-hour week without wage cuts, along with rights of collective bargaining, to raise the purchasing power of the French masses and expand leisure. As happened in 1919, in May 1936, following the electoral victory of the Popular Front, a wave of strikes led to a law reducing working hours, this time to forty hours per week (and two weeks of vacation per year). This time, however, hours reduction failed. Capital flight and inflation in 1937 led to overtime work. The collapse of the Popular Front in May 1937 resulted in the virtual restoration of the forty-eight-hour, six-day workweek when France was forced to gear up for war. The fate of the French forty-hour week is instructive. The French forty-hour act was modeled on the eight-hour-day law of 1919. However, the 1936 law was passed in isolation, in contrast to the international adoption of the eight-hour day after World War I. Missing in 1936 was the transnational coalition of reformers and mass insurgency. A strong supporter of the international short-hours movement disappeared when the Nazis destroyed the German labor movement in May of 1933. British labor in 1936 was far less militant than 1919. The war and the reconstruction after 1945 delayed the forty-hour week in Europe until the 1960s.[13]

Ironically, the United States, which had abstained from the eight-hour convention of 1919, adopted a forty-hour law in 1938 rather like the law that had failed in France. This did not signify the success of the international movement for hours reform but the isolation of the US from those economic and military events engulfing Europe in 1938. Moreover, though progressive at the time, it became part of a settlement that basically closed the debate over the allocation of time and money in the United States. Let us see how.

The joblessness of the early 1930s was monumental in the US, so much so that the otherwise moderate AFL went further than the five-day, forty-hour week. In November 1932, it called for a thirty-hour week (six-hours for five days, though without a wage maintenance provision). Advocates assumed that a six-hour limit per day would reduce joblessness enough to raise or at least maintain current wages. The thirty-hour week gained notoriety when the W. K. Kellogg company, a widely known manufacturer of breakfast cereals, adopted the thirty-hour week in an experiment of industrial paternalism. Senator Hugo Black of Alabama (later a Supreme Court Justice) introduced a thirty-hour bill in December 1932. At the depth of the economic crisis, this bill actually passed the US Senate in April 1933 and initially won approval by the incoming Roosevelt administration as an emergency measure to reduce unemployment by work sharing.[14]

But almost immediately, both American business and the New Deal government backed away. As early as April 1933, key senators, cabinet officials, business leaders, and economists proposed public works and collective bargaining rights as an alternative to work sharing with a thirty-hour week. This alternative would not only raise working-class income but increase private-sector jobs and thereby increase mass purchasing power to reflate the American economy. Instead of supporting the thirty-hour bill, the White House pushed through the National Industrial Recovery Act (NIRA) in 1933, which promoted a forty-hour workweek in industry-wide agreements (even though actual hours were often lower). The objective was not to expand employment through job sharing but to eliminate excessive hours that gave an unfair competitive advantage to some companies. At the same time, the government introduced public works jobs. Subtly, these measures challenged the work-sharing idea behind the thirty-hour bill, with the promise of more work instead of shared work. When the NIRA was declared unconstitutional in 1935, Roosevelt embraced the Wagner Act to ease unionization and, through collective bargaining, to raise wages. This, plus public works employment and low interest rates, was to stimulate the economy on the demand side. Even the rationale for a dramatic increase in the progressivity of the income tax shifted from the idea that the rich should pay more to the ideologically neutral notion that progressive income taxes and government spending would foster growth. These measures, it was argued, would transfer income from savers and investors to spenders and wage earners, thus encouraging demand and job creation.[15] In the context of the 1937 recession, the goal became increased production. Along with this, the old ideal of reduced work as a response to technological growth largely disappeared. As M. S. Eccles at the Federal Reserve simply noted in the late 1930s, reduced hours posed the "danger that it may mean sharing poverty rather than sharing wealth."[16]

Instead of the thirty-hours bill, the Social Security Act of 1935 and Fair Labor Standards Act of 1938 became law. The former law provided a small stipend for the aged, hopefully opening jobs for the more productive young (another "growth" alternative to the thirty-hour week). The law of 1938 introduced the first national minimum wage (twenty-five cents per hour, about four dollars in 2020) and a standard forty-hour week (with delays and conditional provisions for overtime pay at one and a half times regular hourly wages). Though progressive (being a national regulation superior to European standards of the time), it was also quite watered down. There were exclusions and special provisions for farm and domestic workers, for example, reflecting the intense lobbying of business and conservative Democrats, especially from the South and rural areas. Moreover, the forty-hour week was the average workweek in industry at the time (and thus the law did not promote work sharing), nor did it encourage a shift to free time as the solution to unemployment. The justification for reducing working hours was humanitarian, setting limits on abuse. The solution to joblessness was not leisure, as Walker had advocated in 1932, but more production (and ultimately more work). Over time, the minimum wage has been raised and applied to more workers, but the forty-hour standard has not changed, and many salaried and professional employees have been excluded from overtime pay.[17]

Of course, we can legitimately ask: In the 1930s, was there any real support for more time as opposed to money and more production? The AFL's primary goal was always more jobs, not more leisure, and it was willing to separate the two. Their concerns were immediate, not focused on any idea about the "ultimate" fate of the economy. By 1937, pragmatic leaders of American unions had embraced Roosevelt's alternative to the thirty-hour week in a package of public works, minimum wage, and eventually a forty-hour maximum (with overtime pay). This was in many ways politically expedient—meeting the reality of the revival of business by the late 1930s and the limits of radical change. Some unions continued to call for the thirty-hour week until the war and then again briefly after victory. A few won paid holidays, but in general wages issues displaced time. In any case, even when addressed, free time was often bound to job and wage issues. Intellectuals, not workers, focused on maximizing free time in a "mature" economy. Moreover, labor was in no position to take the lead.[18]

The Gospel of Growth and Its Impact on Work Time

Leadership on the question of work time and jobs was taken up by Roosevelt's government and its technocratic supporters, and they had another way of creating jobs that went beyond the classic economic theories of laissez-faire: government action to stimulate economic growth.

A 1934, the influential Brookings Institution published a study, *America's Capacity to Consume*, that insisted that the unfulfilled desire for goods in the US is "large enough to absorb a productive output many times that achieved in the peak year 1929. . . . The trouble is clearly not lack of desire but lack of purchasing power. . . . [W]e have not as yet reached the age of abundance of which we all like to dream and that extensive leisure has not as yet been *forced upon us*" (my italics). The thirty-hour week plan would have meant a "compulsory reduction of the hours of work, which would freeze the possible volume of production below the level required to give all the people the abundance they desire." This view has prevailed ever since. There was no need for a balance of free time and goods; desire for goods was effectively unlimited and desire for time freed from the market was a threat to growth. A six-hour day / thirty-hour week would mean that workers would have to share the misery of scarcity. Expanded production and growth would meet the people's desires for more with no end in sight—and it would reduce unemployment.[19]

The other side of this gospel of growth was a disdain and perhaps even fear of free time. The words of Harold Ickes, Roosevelt's secretary of the interior, in 1935 are revealing: "Only during the past few years have we seen how closely bound together are happiness and work." In 1933, the New Deal intellectual Rexford Tugwell admitted that technology was eliminating work, but he did not see this as an opportunity for more free time. Instead, he argued that this technology could produce less routinized labor and introduce more work that could bring purpose and social meaning to people. Curiously, Tugwell could not imagine free time providing individual purpose and social interaction. The work ethic was thoroughly ingrained in his thinking.[20] At base, growth and work went together, creating "happiness," both by meeting "desire" for goods and assuring the psychological and social benefits of wage labor. In the Depression, when scarcity of both goods and work was a pressing reality, this thinking seemed perfectly sensible. Understood in this context, then, the forty-hour law constituted a full-time / full-employment / growth settlement.

Perhaps most important in understanding this settlement was the fact that in the late 1930s it was still progressive. It called on the government to promote growth and employment. We commonly associate state intervention to restore economic growth through consumption and full employment with John Maynard Keynes. Although Keynes's theory was controversial, his view was adopted by the New Deal economist Alvin Hansen. A policy of progressive taxation and government deficit spending had the advantage of encouraging job creation through increased consumption. It also promised to preserve the traditional work ethic. While Roosevelt reduced his deficit spending policy (leading to the 1937 recession), state-initiated growth would become orthodoxy. Meanwhile, work sharing and the broader idea of the progressive disengagement from work was discredited.

A consensus emerged after the war between government, labor, and business. Most factions agreed that to prevent a return of the Depression, the peace economy required mass consumption to make up for military spending during the war. In the context of the emerging Cold War, income redistribution and much government regulation were discredited as "socialist." Consumer-driven growth seemed to offer a multiclass solution—full employment and business profit with a standard forty-hour week. Even Walter Reuther, the left-wing leader of the United Auto Workers, abandoned his union's commitment to the thirty-hour week in 1945.[21] A solution to the crisis of the Depression became a postwar policy of unlimited growth as a guarantor of full employment.

To be sure, as Robert Collins documents, the policy of "more" was uneven after the war. Conservatives in the 1950s balked at full-throated fiscal Keynesianism, calling instead for minimizing inflation and government debt. The Democratic administrations of John F. Kennedy and Lyndon B. Johnson in the 1960s, however, were fully committed to government spending to assure full employment and growth sufficient to increase the economic pie for most Americans. But Republican Richard Nixon, too, shared this goal in the late 1960s and early 1970s. Moreover, there was disagreement among Democrats over whether growth should be pursued as an end in itself or more attention should be given to distribution of wealth and the quality of affluence (seen in debates between Leon Keyserling and John Kenneth Galbraith, for example). The rise of antimaterialist movements in the 1960s and 1970s around the environment and against consumer culture further challenged the gospel of growth. However, in the wake of the inflation and other crises of the late 1970s, Ronald Reagan won the presidency in 1980 partially because of Jimmy Carter's abandonment of the politics of growth. Though conservative, Reagan's solution was not traditional fiscal restraint but an "antistatist growthmanship" that encouraged private sector expansion (supply-side economics) and unrestrained consumption through tax and regulation reductions. The point of this policy was not conservative constraint (such as traditional "root-canal economics" in response to the inflation of the 1970s). As Collins notes, "The Reagan program was, at bottom, yet another expression of postwar growthmanship." In this little changed from the 1940s. Growth may have had disparate purposes (social peace, world power, reducing poverty, etc.), but, in the end, it was always built on increased consumption. The difference between liberals and conservatives was in degree, both worshiping at the shrine of growth; and only a small minority (in the 1950s, the beats, for example) questioned it. Growthmanship expressed a basic trend: the "convergence between the postwar political economy and the voracious postwar culture of consumption became ever more complete."[22]

The American bias for consumption over leisure, money over time, would define American capitalism in the second half of the twentieth century. But, as often noted, other countries never fully embraced the

American model. Even when Western Europeans were in an economic position to embrace American consumerism by the 1960s, they resisted the American pattern of rising personal consumer debt, shopping malls, and overstuffed closets. One measure of this is the fact that Western Europeans continued to reduce work after World War II. They not only joined the US with the forty-hour week but, even more, increased paid vacation time, lowered the retirement age, and introduced paid family leave. Americans relied on paid vacations achieved through collective bargaining and personal job contracts. The US remains the outlier on these issues. In 2020, the difference was dramatic: Americans worked an average of 1,767 hours per year compared with 1,435 hours worked by the French. The only countries higher than the US in an Organization for Economic Cooperation and Development study were Chile (1,825), Costa Rica (1,913), Korea (1,908), and Mexico (2,124). Even the workaholic Japanese worked fewer hours (1,738).[23] The American settlement was not an inevitable balance of time and money, but the fruit of a particular political configuration in the past. The full-time / full-employment / growth formula had a profound impact on the United States. Any debate over how to allocate the fruits of productivity was reduced to the struggle between profit and wages, supply and demand, in an ever-growing economy. Still, politics alone does not explain the consumption bias.

The American Consumerist Allure

Implicit in the 1938 settlement was a desire to foster American consumerism. As many have noted, America's consumerist bias was hardly born in the Depression. As Americans argued since George Gunton in the 1880s, free time was time to consume. By the late 1930s, this identity of leisure and consumption was key to achieving economic equilibrium in the age of mass production. Mass consumption balanced supply and demand, serving as a check on "overproduction" and helping to create jobs in the service and "leisure" sectors. This process was already well on its way by the 1920s. While real wages scarcely increased between 1900 and 1920, the following decade saw a 27 percent increase in purchasing power.[24]

That pattern returned after the Depression and World War II. According to Stephen Rosenberg, at least some workers saw that their wages were high enough to buy consumer durables, and that these purchases were sufficient to sacrifice time at work for the pleasure of consumption. This realization presumably explains the willingness of workers to accept no further reduction in free time after 1938. Earlier, especially before 1900, there were fewer enticing consumer goods to buy, and thus time was often as or more important than income. But thanks to the new regime of "Fordism," increased wages became more valuable to workers, not just as money but for what money could buy, as more goods became available to workers (including Model T Fords). This change, presumably, warranted the acceptance of sacrificed leisure time. This trade-off of time for (consumable) money was famously illustrated at Ford's factories in 1914 when Ford paid roughly double the common factory wage (at five dollars a day). There, workers accepted Ford's intense assembly line factory work in exchange for relatively high income in order to purchase goods that offered personal enhancement after work. Before the revolution in accessible consumer durables, time was a more likely preference. In the abstract language of Stephen Rosenberg, these durables (like cars and houses) represented "hypothetical durations of free activity," what consumers potentially could do with their free time and thus a fair exchange for giving up free time by working.[25]

This was not isolated to Ford, as illustrated by the relatively high wages and the democratization of car ownership in the US. In the period 1925–1929, real wages were about sixty percent higher in the US than in Britain and roughly two and one-half times those in France. In 1929, there was one car for every 5.4 Americans, but only one car for every 43 Britons and one for every 335 Italians.[26] Americans, including some manual workers, could participate in the consumer culture, even to buy the relatively costly durable of the car (especially with the advent of the installment plan).[27]

The fifteen years of the Great Depression and World War II were a significant, but still temporary, break in mass consumption. It was a return to and expansion of that period of growth in consumption that New Dealers sought in their rejection of the thirty-hour proposal of work sharing and their embrace of the 1938 settlement. The Depression and the New Deal set the stage for a consumer splurge that followed the war.

Moreover, advertisers and the government prepared Americans during the war with the message that they were fighting for the "glorious future" of "mass distribution and mass ownership." A powerful way of promoting this expectation was images of crystal balls with the promise "There's a Ford in Your Future" in magazine advertising in the last year of the war.[28] Postwar pent-up demand for consumer goods led to an extravagance of consumption: bigger cars with dramatic styling (tailfins, for example), an explosion of government-subsidized suburbs of ranch houses, garages full of power lawn mowers, and kitchens graced with colorful refrigerators.[29] In the 1930s, groups like Consumer Research had hoped to make consumer protection a force to check the power of corporations and advertisers to engage in price gouging and deception. However, after 1945 consumer rights were largely transformed into the duty of consumers to spend so that others might work. Advertisers, discredited in the crisis of the 1930s, regained popular support by presenting themselves as guardians of consumer "sovereignty," which government regulators, they claimed, often threatened with regulation. Postwar ads, by the 1950s on TV, promised that new appliances and homes offered women personal freedom.[30] In this context, workers abandoned the goal of shorter hours. A 1963 Gallup poll found only 42 percent of American union members supported reducing the workweek to thirty-five hours. Most apparently preferred higher wages. The simple fact was that "Fordism"—especially the workers' trade-off of arduous work time for consumer goods—sealed the deal for many.[31]

Still, it is easy to overstress the allure of "stuff." For many wage earners, work income has been compensation for effort, skill, the degradation of work, and the time lost during employment. Money, rather than meaning or recognition, was the main reward for work. But this did not make workers materialists. The long-held claim that working people deserved access to a fair share of the nation's productivity was essentially an egalitarian idea; and high wages were a very visible marker of that fairness, especially when they bought goods shared with others. Those goods brought more than a feeling of having kept up with the Joneses. They increasingly brought a sense of power and the vitality of living (such as in the purchase of a car). Wages became more than "getting a living," survival, or just getting by. The things that wages could buy represented "getting ahead." In the oft-noted words of Robert and Helen Lynd, "car ownership stands to [Middletowners] for a large share of the 'American Dream'; they cling to it as they cling to self-respect."[32] A rising wage brought more than stuff. It meant more life and a sense of belonging and dignity.

Nevertheless, by the end of the 1930s, spending had become a duty, according to political leaders and others, one required to create jobs and ensure national economic growth. Individuals, encountering an expanding array of products and services, "naturally" and without visible coercion accepted the discipline of steady work. For economist George Katona in 1964, American consumer society fulfilled the "dream of unlimited economic opportunities in a classless society." It seemed to promise a consensus: a "full" (and unchanging) day's work was a fair trade-off for money to share in an American standard of living that promised continual improvement. Put another way, the settlement provided the means for capital to accumulate profit and wealth and for consumer-workers to accumulate goods. We need to be reminded that, after World War II, workers were never so strong and organized that they could have demanded more free time. Instead, they accepted—or probably more accurately acquiesced—to the settlement. It was their best option at the time.[33]

The victory of the full-time / full-employment / growth formula went beyond identifying the good life with steady work and consumption. There are two other factors to consider. First, the bias toward consumption came also from the inability of American reformers to create alternative uses of free time that could challenge consumerism. This failure still haunts us as the descendants of those reformers continue to critique consumer culture but fail to reach the broad public with plausible alternatives that would persuade Americans to press for more free time. Second, and even more important, a bias toward consumption was baked into patterns of family life that date from at least the nineteenth century, when men mostly were breadwinners and women mostly were family consumers. The Depression era not only could not challenge this bias but actually reinforced this gender division. The 1930s also affirmed family consumption as the central meaning of free time. This gender division has been seriously challenged, especially since the 1960s, with the expansion of women in the labor force, but the pressures of consumption and the forty-hour standard remain.

Failures to Create Popular Alternatives to Free Time as Spending Time

People with lots of free time seem always to fear or misunderstand it in others, especially when the latter are poorer or less educated. This lies at the heart of a persistent gap between the two groups over free time and how to respond to the commercialization of leisure. In the heat of the debate over the eight-hour day and its early implementation, this fear and misunderstanding became obvious. Not just traditional moralists and business leaders but influential intellectuals fretted that unregulated leisure and consumption, as well as freedom from the constraints of tradition, would unleash the egoistic or atavistic drives in the masses. This disdain has contributed to the failure of reformers to win Americans to uses of free time other than consumerism.

The seminal text is Gustave Le Bon's *The Crowd* of 1895. He feared the recently urbanized masses (with leisure time) were easily turned into emotionally suggestible and violent mobs by unscrupulous demagogues. In *The Division of Labor in Society* in 1893, Émile Durkheim similarly concluded that the urban masses had become isolated individuals because of the decline of the social cohesion of small traditional groups. This made them malleable by elites and bureaucracies. Ferdinand Tönnies, with his famous distinction between the instrumentalist society of *Gesellschaft* and the presumed communal bonds of traditional *Gemeinschaft*, reinforced the view that modern urban life was socially unrestrained and alienating.[34] Sigmund Freud held similar views. His *Group Psychology* (1921) pictures the masses as children or even savages. In his *Civilization and Its Discontents* (1929), Freud asserts that the psychological war between self-control and indulgence only grew with consumer society, and that additional time free from constraints of work would only compound the conflict. Work alone could tie the average individual to reality. Such a person had to "undergo the renunciations upon which the existence of civilisation depends."[35] The free time of the masses was dangerous.

Perhaps even more influential was the Spanish intellectual José Ortega y Gasset. In his *Revolt of the Masses* (1929), Ortega argued that the emerging consumer and entertainment culture lured a newly economically empowered, but culturally untrained, public fresh from the village. In his rather grim assessment, the "masses," with higher wages and more free time, imposed their tastes on the cultured minority, driving out refinement. This claim that common pleasures and plebian aesthetics pushed cultivated tastes from the modern market became central to generations of authors whose cultural jeremiads dismissed "mass culture" and worried about the dangers of "mass leisure."[36]

These fears were hardly confined to an intellectual elite anxious about the barbarians at the gates of European high culture. Similar concerns can be found among early twentieth-century American Progressive reformers, who were as obsessed with the presumed inability of immigrant workers to control their desires as European elites were of "their" newly urbanized peasants. Along with other issues, George Beard expressed concern in 1881 about the "neurasthenia" of urban culture, in which the speed and alienation of industrial city life seemed to be turning Americans into emotional wrecks. By 1900, the rush of movies and consumer novelty seemed to have produced a mass "nervousness" that contrasted with the rationality and intentionality of business (which, of course, helped create this anxiety). More basically, bourgeois reformers chaffed at immigrants and the broader working class "wasting" scarce resources in communal events such as weddings, funerals, and christenings. Such traditions of "extravagance" meant less saving, fewer domestic durables, and reduced funds for family activities, all priorities of genteel elites. Elites of almost all stripes had little understanding of, or trust in, the free time of the masses.[37]

Desires that once were confined to rare and ritualized saturnalian festivals that served as safety valves to ward off discontent could now be satisfied practically anytime and anyplace. The constraints of the old festival culture were no more. The masses, it seemed, who elites assumed were incapable of self-control and required the restraints of supervised work and imposed moral codes, would be turned loose with free time. A related concern was the swamping of high culture by "low." In this regard, the presumed emotional impact of mass media on the general population particularly concerned elites. Some condemned the mass culture of radio in the 1930s for marginalizing the highbrow (and culturally diverse) minority with a preponderance of undifferentiated and passive commercialized entertainment, which seemed to attract the typical American. Authors of a series of books sponsored by the Payne Fund warned the public about the presumed emotional vulnerability of children who watched gangster and sexually suggestive romance movies in the early 1930s.[38]

According to Stuart Chase, writing in 1935, the threat of mechanized work to the psyche and health needed to be counteracted by recreation that offered a "balance that has been lost at work." The problem was that commercialized leisure did the opposite—making people more nervous. Others objected that free time had become too passive, failed to release unused energy, and gave rise to criminality. Just as the Depression economy required more "controls," even liberal elites believed, so did free time.[39] With the eight-hour day and an emerging consumer culture, the "regulation" of free time became even more urgent.

Especially in Europe, this urgency became a political issue as ideological tribes across the spectrum—socialist, communist, liberal, Catholic, conservative, and fascist—attempted to organize their adherents or prospects in their free time, and to win them to their respective social vision. Each saw individualistic consumption as a threat to the group. Recognizing the futility of overt indoctrination, these ideological organizations formed activities for youth and family in playful or entertaining settings beyond the rigors and seriousness of the workplace, party hall, or church—or the delights of the shopping mall. In the interwar years, vacations with pay became a form of free time that gained approval (in Europe) across the political spectrum. In one way or another, divergent groups agreed that vacations promised not only a release from the stress and routine of the workaday life but an opportunity for industrial urbanites to experience nature. For some it also offered the opportunity for the renewal of family life and possibly for forming bonds of understanding across occupation, region, and even class. All these groups in the 1930s seemed to agree that the impact of industrialization needed to be reversed; and the annual vacation (like the festival in the past) was a way of doing it—especially if that time freed from work life was organized by a knowing elite intent on challenging the commerce of instant and individual gratification.[40]

Of course, free time, especially when "organized," often was laden with ideological bias and intent. British schools introduced recreation and sports in the 1930s, for example. Despite themselves, these groups were often patronizing toward their participants. One group on the right, the Duke of York's Camp, brought (elite) public school and industrial schoolboys together to share sports, games, and presumably comradery. The idea was to soften class prejudices and conflicts, to the obvious advantage of the status quo. Italian and German fascists also found that leisure was an excellent vehicle for fostering political loyalty. *Dopolavaro* and *Kraft durch Freude* organized leisure tours and youth summer camps. Leftist groups shared much with the Right in this regard. Not only did unions and leftist parties organize their own separate leisure activities but, in doing so, they often shared the paternalistic perspective of the Right. Even so, most of the gatherings of workers and the Left took place in the pub and workers' clubs, where politics might be discussed but need hardly dominate.[41]

A different approach was taken by social democrats and liberals on both sides of the Atlantic. They attempted to create a nonpartisan but still "organized" and patronizing program of organized leisure. They sponsored an often professionally led system of holiday camps, playground programs, discussion groups, and sports clubs, in theory at least outside the manipulative environments of both ideological groups and commercialized leisure. In Europe, this movement was often called "democratic leisure." Advocates were responsive to popular desires for free time, rejecting both the fear of the crowd evidenced by Freud and company as well as political manipulation by the far Left and Right. In the 1930s, this idea was frequently linked to Albert Thomas of the ILO. Thomas favored leisure activities organized by local, self-managed bodies with limited involvement by either government or commerce. Still, he was an advocate of Victorian gentility, encouraging the organized use of free time in physical and social educational programs. Like his Victorian predecessors, he supported reduced commuting time and activities to improve family life, including workers' gardens and do-it-yourself, which would hopefully make home an alternative to bars located near worksites. Reformers like Thomas wanted more than "wholesome" leisure activities (though that was certainly a goal). They looked toward a public culture that somehow would bridge the chasm between their own genteel culture and that of the working classes. All this was certainly only a dream in 1936 as Europe careened into war. But it was a program that, at least, offered an alternative to consumerism.[42]

This approach also prevailed in the US during the Depression. It had roots in the recreation professionals who emerged out of the Playground Association (founded in 1907). Like Thomas, they shared the goal of "well-directed" free time. Municipal governments hired recreational staff to organize games and sports on public playgrounds in hopes of luring youth from the unsupervised street.[43] One unique American institution, the summer youth camp, often shared a similar ethos. In 1929, a million children yearly encountered nature in seven thousand camps organized by school, church, and youth institutions like the Scouts.[44] During the New Deal, these programs were vastly extended through public works projects that constructed public parks, golf courses, tennis courts, and swimming pools, as well as libraries and museums (see chapter 6).[45] In the interwar years, small groups opposed to urban life and consumerism sometimes joined rural communities or chose to do without the goods that others seemed to require. They advocated a gospel of the simple life in search of the peace of quiet places, routines of self-sustaining work, and reliable relationships, in harmony with nature and the seasons.[46]

As earnest and positive as these programs and ideas were, they had limited impact on the general population, especially in the US. This was in part because of the class bias of their planners, who both misunderstood and often despised popular desires. A common nostalgia for an idealized folk culture among the leisure planners was seldom shared by the working-class descendants of the "folk." Moreover, New Deal intellectuals often identified consumer leisure with women and male emasculation and instead glorified "male" work. The popular culture in radio and movies was "false consciousness."[47] Between this failed imposition of folk culture on a modern working class and this disdain for popular taste, there was only a narrow range of possibilities for an alternative to consumerism. The simple fact was that commercialized free time met the needs of most Americans, however inadequately.

It was all the more difficult to counteract the mass consumer culture in the US because of the very diversity of American cultural traditions. First, the US lacked even a semblance of a unified cultural elite, despite the pretensions of East Coast gentility. Plus, a popular tradition of distance from and disdain for that elite made impossible any claim of highbrow cultural hegemony. This stood in contrast with the semi-success of the BBC (British Broadcasting Corporation) in imposing elite-run public broadcasting on the British public. It is notable that there never has been a public media tradition in the US as in Europe and elsewhere. The lack of a national educational system prevented the kind of consensus over the meaning of national civilization that made the BBC work in Britain. Instead, the commercial networks that dominated American radio (and later TV) prevailed, offering an amalgam of mass entertainment appealing to the broad and predominately White middle and working classes. Moreover, high culture appeared snobbish and foreign (often urban and sometimes "Jewish"), alien to salt-of-the-earth Americans. The victorious formula was largely that of P. T. Barnum—a culture that appealed to middle America but accommodated aspiring immigrants and minorities with measured concessions to the carnival. The immigrant and African American experience produced a diverse folk culture that might have led to a wide-ranging free-time culture; and it did to a degree, when these groups contributed to both the mass culture and pockets of diversity. But the mass culture that so disturbed the elite prevailed. Moreover, social mobility and intermarriage reduced the lasting influence of ethnic and regional popular culture. Racial segregation and bias made the mass culture predominantly White and middle class. America did not become a "melting pot" in the early twentieth century. But a national media and name-brand consumer culture made immigrants into "Americans" and reduced, but hardly eliminated, the isolation of African Americans.[48]

As Susan Currell observes, "In many ways, recreation reform of the thirties was a last-ditch attempt . . . to create a better society outside the capitalist work ethic."[49] It was supposed to transcend class-bound work worlds in an equality of leisure. Yet, it was unable to transcend those class divisions and the conflicting cultures that they produced (a topic I will explore more fully in chapter 6). The genteel values of leisure reformers, even when supportive of diversity and when open to building bridges to the "masses," had little chance of forging ties to the "people" in an alternative to commercialized leisure. To many people, their program was little more than paternalism.

Instead of a "democratic leisure" society that effectively challenged commercialism, the winner was a commercialized leisure that exploited class difference (sometimes posing the down-to-earth popular culture against the pretentious elite). This meant a continued division between elite reformers and working-class consumers. Among other things, this division inhibited any challenge to the work-and-spend settlement of the late 1930s or a viable movement for a progressive reduction of work time.

The postwar rehabilitation of capitalism and its inherent drive to colonize all sectors of civic life (sports, holiday making, music, dance, even simple socializing) may have made the triumph of the commercial inevitable. But it is still important to recognize that democratic leisure failed to seriously challenge the work-and-spend regime. Reformers never fully understood this simple fact: commercialized free time met needs more quickly, directly, and with less stress than did public offerings with their demanding goals of uplift and improvement. Commercial leisure was (and is) far less threatening to often economically insecure (or just tired) people than were the intellectual's pleas that working people join study groups or holiday fellowships. From the 1930s on, these groups had extraordinary difficulties in winning people to free-time activities outside the consumer market. Ironically, voluntary, noncommercial organizations—from amateur singing societies to agate collectors' clubs—have been often less flexible than commercially organized groups in adjusting to their members' personal needs. Volunteer groups have often fallen into discord or stagnation precisely because they were organized by their core members. Unlike the staff who organized paying groups, members have had a personal interest in shaping the group's social dynamics. Core participants often formed cliques or drove out newcomers by their resistance to change. The modern recreation worker on a cruise line has an interest in keeping everyone involved and happy—individually secure in a welcomed group setting. Well-meaning proponents of hiking trails and library book clubs have seldom prevailed over commercial gyms and guided cruises. Volunteer organizations that also have centered on consumer goods, such as collectors' groups for old cars, illustrate this point. These collectors can talk about their own cars and share with others an enthusiasm for a type of car. But this led to narrow niche communities, often with a limited ability to share and perpetuate their enthusiasms. As a result, free time that was not commercialized (as promoted by advocates of democratic leisure) failed to win more than a fraction of the population. Noncommercial volunteer organizations often lacked the seemingly magical power of the consumer culture to give individuals a sense of self within a chosen group of spenders.[50] They failed to create an alternative to the values of work-and-spend and thus challenge the bias toward consumption within free-time culture.

Even more to the point, consumer goods and services have often become the most satisfying and reassuring way of expressing individuality and sociability. People less skilled at self-expression and less secure in disclosing themselves to others seemed to prefer to reveal themselves and "join" groups through their goods rather than through direct personal interaction. Consumer society accommodated that insecurity by giving people the cloak of goods to hide their insecurity and help them avoid risking self-disclosure in their interactions with other consumers. Once again, groups without the mediating role of consumer goods offered an alternative to only a minority, comfortable with direct personal disclosure.[51]

As we shall see more fully in chapter 6, the difficult task of uplifting mass culture was often frustrating. In time, many protectors of high culture gave up or did not even try. This often led them into self-imposed isolation and self-satisfying cultural criticism when they failed in their difficult task of winning the masses to their cause. This failure contributed to a split or at least persistent discord between genteel advocates of "democratic leisure" and the people they wanted to reach. The resulting cultural jeremiads pose the impossible choice between "true" leisure based on increasingly rarified principles and a presumably manipulated consumerism, while the practical possibilities of a broadly based cultural alternative to the market nearly disappeared—and with it the idea of a progressive expansion of free time.

After World War II, the only effective alternative to the jeremiads against mass culture were from the apologists of economic growth among economists, marketeers, and politicians. And, especially in the US, the dream of a democratic leisure beyond the market largely dropped out of sight. In effect, for both the pessimistic (and isolated) critics of consumerism and the optimistic (and often corporate-connected) apologists of consumption, the only future was the endless expansion of spending. The extension of free time was forgotten or seen merely as more consumption time. For the proponents of growth, free time served mostly to create consumer demand for more production; for the writers of jeremiads, free time of the masses was wasted in consumption or a threat to "civilization." As a result, the imbalance of time and money—a fixed eight-hour day and seemingly endless growth of consumption—was seen by almost all as natural or inevitable.

Perhaps the work-and-spend solution can be fully explained by the consumption bias and the failure to offer a plausible alternative to understanding free time. But I think that we still need to think a bit more about how ordinary people confronted free time and consumption in their family lives during the crisis of the 1930s. This may make this "decision" for money over time even more intelligible.

The Depression Family Reinforces the Consumption Bias

The failure of "democratic leisure" went beyond the disappointments of elite reform in an era of popular commercialism. The dilemma of the reformers was ultimately rooted in the domestic setting of most consumption. The question of family and the home was generally disregarded by the critics of the commercial; some saw it as pedestrian, even hopelessly bourgeois. By contrast, commercial interests learned very well how to appeal to the domestic world of husbands, wives, parents, and children. For many people, spending money on the home and for commercial holidays provided nearly ideal forms of self-expression and ways to meet social needs. We must go beyond the workplace and political and cultural centers to understand the success of the work-and-spend settlement and its culture. The dynamics of the interrelationships within the home help explain the modern bias toward money rather than time. Even though these relationships have dramatically changed in the last half century, their consequences for how we understand free time remain. This comes out clearly in the domestic crisis of the Depression.

Joblessness and reduced income disrupted family roles and life during the 1930s. In the US, the Depression seldom led to health-threatening misery, but it took a psychological toll. The economic crisis threatened a by then nearly universal gender division established first by the genteel elite of the nineteenth century, which had fundamentally shaped understandings of time and money. That division made the male the "provider" and the female the "homemaker." As we have seen, these roles separated male public from female domestic work space and time (even though many single and some married women worked for pay). Husbands often expected free time and domestic consumption to balance and be a reward for work time that provided wage money (and also gave them domestic power). Wives expected the time and sufficient money, mostly provided by husbands, to create that domestic leisure for the family through their housework and shopping throughout the day.

For many, this arrangement was disrupted by the Depression. Sociologists who observed the jobless in Western Europe and the US during the Depression found mostly jobless male workers with "time on their hands." Workless time, even with the dole, was humiliating in societies that valued paid labor, especially when the jobless compared themselves to the employed. As George Orwell saw it in England, "So long as Bert Jones across the stress is still at work, Alf Smith is bound to feel himself dishonoured and a failure. Hence the frightful feeling of impotence and despair which is almost worse than the demoralisation of enforced idleness."[52] Understandably, many of the unemployed withdrew from public life rather than engage in political protest. Male fixation on social status, almost always linked with work, became more intense. Perhaps even more problematic was the loss of wage income and what that money could buy. Work time became even more closely linked to consumption time. These losses reinforced the work ethic. As Robert and Helen Lynd observed in 1937 in their second local study of "Middletown," "enforced leisure drowned men with its once coveted abundance, and its taste became sour and brackish . . . It is this . . . sour background of too much leisure that prompts local workingmen to insist that they don't want relief, but jobs."[53]

The work ethic was reaffirmed. Work and wages, always central to the self-esteem and domestic authority of male workers, became more so, while free time without income and goods and the social meaning that they brought appeared empty (as Lynd notes), even humiliating. This was so in several ways.

First, unemployment in the Depression disrupted routines and made the free time of predominantly male wage earners seem "undeserved" because it was not compensation for work. Even more, joblessness made male leisure in the home problematic. Without work outside the home, men felt that they were breaking a contract with their wives and violating the "natural" gender division of time and space. The male felt he did not belong at home during "working hours" and had not earned his right to be there and take advantage of the domestic work of his wife. But men often felt even more mortified by the prospect of sharing domestic work or, when wives worked outside the home, becoming househusbands. And neither men nor women seemed to want that. A contemporary sociologist observed, "Apparently this shift of the husband to domestic duties is desired neither by the husband nor by the wife. She is conditioned as much as he is to the fact that the husband's business is to earn money and not to do the household tasks."[54] It was not just the absence of work that was disturbing but the disruption of expected sex roles, and with any reversal of those roles came a negative attitude toward free time, especially in the home for both men and women.

Unemployment in the Depression disrupted routines, especially the division between work time and the reward of domestic free time. According to contemporary sociologists, unemployed Britons were ill at ease without the day divided between public work and private leisure. Work gave structure to the day and week, both when on the job and off it. To alleviate this stress, some men tried to maintain the leisure schedule that they had known when working, like continuing to go to the movies on Saturday night, even when a weekday matinee was cheaper. On the American side, Eli Ginzberg observed in 1943: "We learn from contrast. We learn from unemployment the true significance of work. Work establishes the basic routine of modern living."[55]

The unemployed male's "invasion" of the traditional work space/time of the wife and frustration with unstructured time were only part of the disturbance of expected sex roles. A second disruption was the issue of money—who earned it and how much was available to spend—making money ultimately more important than time. The first thing to note is the obvious: the growing importance of money in the Depression. If freedom from work meant "empty" time in an "eventless" day and a problematic home life, it also meant that free time became associated with little income and minimal consumption—by the 1930s the expected content of free time. The Depression actually intensified the allure of consumption as many unemployed or underemployed experienced not just a decline in the comforts of spending but a loss in the social meaning of consumption. Idealists had hoped to win Americans to a less materialistic lifestyle with the coming of the Depression; but, as the American sociologist Glenn Elder notes, loss of income reinforced consumerism in the 1930s as families compared their lives with the prosperous 1920s.[56] We find signs of this discontent in how Depression-era people spent their diminished resources. "Luxury" spending often continued (tobacco, gambling, and the movies, for example); fashions kept changing and people tried to keep up with them; few gave up their cars (though they may have kept them longer or bought used models). Depression-era Americans also adopted innovations like the modern refrigerator and even the car trailer.[57] Prudential austerity may have been practical, but it was psychologically difficult.

Reduced family income impacted the roles of both male "providers" and female "spenders." The husband's provisioning function had given him power and authority over his family. But it also was a source of pride and self-worth. Without that income and the sacrifice of work, he was diminished. Free time was a reminder of that loss. And female consumers lacked the wherewithal to play their accustomed role as consumers who worked with goods to make a home. Like time, expectations of money were disrupted for both men and women.

The Depression sometimes led to a reversal of roles when married women earned wages while their husbands did not. As was the case with my grandparents, women in low-paying service jobs (in my grandmother's case as a housekeeper) sometimes found work while their husbands (my grandfather was a miner) in industry or commerce did not. Yet these job-holding women hardly gained the former status of their husbands. Instead, some experienced the double duty of being both a provider and homemaker. This situation did not change during World War II for many married women who worked outside the home. This disruption of accustomed gender roles was pleasing to few. As a result, sex roles did not reverse or change much due to the Depression or the war.[58]

Of course, for those who did not experience joblessness and income loss in the Depression, this did not apply. The Victorian sexual division between men as outside providers and women as domestic spenders remained even as it was increasingly challenged after World War II. Still, the Depression seems to have reaffirmed Victorian gender roles, at least for a time for many. While the Depression and especially the war might have led to a permanent transformation of gender roles, after 1945 many American women returned to or reaffirmed the security of the home to bear large families and to participate in the promise of domestic consumerism.

This gender system was perpetuated through "full-time employment" (often assumed primarily for men) and the growth economy (which provided the opportunity for female domestic consumption). It meant a forty-hour workweek for men who had a domestic partner providing family work and leisure preparation. This seemed conventionally reasonable to many after World War II, though many women, especially by the 1960s, chafed under this male-breadwinner model and sought meaningful work and income in the labor force. The forty-hour week brought mostly male workers structured work time and free time, while providing them income to justify domesticated free time. That arrangement also made possible for many women (but certainly not all) freedom from wage work and time and money for domestic refinement and participation in an expanding consumer society. Until the 1960s, many married American men and women conformed to this gender-based work-and-spend system, though they often modified it with female part-time, seasonal, and life-stage employment.

The recent change in that gender division of work and income is a good reason to reassess this arrangement. The rise of two-income, as well as single-parent, families based on the forty-hour standard of full-time work has changed the game. Even with time-saving domestic technology and smaller families, the new regime has reduced homemaking and family caring time and placed new pressure on households, leading to the famous imbalance of work and life. Yet, that new stress has not led to a mass movement for a reduction in "full-time" time, so powerful are the forces that maintain the established system. The cultural power of work time and consumption, reinforced in the Depression and after, remains.

All of these factors discussed in this chapter help explain why work time has not decreased with economic progress. It never made sense to think that working people would "rationally maximize" time and money with affluence, nor that they would adopt the "improving" values of "democratic leisure" intellectuals. But neither was it fair to say (as many cultural critics suggested) that wage earners simply succumbed to consumerism and disdained free time as they happily embraced overtime and moonlighting, all to obtain more stuff. Despite the vaunted influence and power of workaholics, given a chance most people today would work less.

However, openings for free time have been very brief; and the disciplinary power of the market and the inertia of past work-time settlements has made any alternative to the full-time / full-employment / growth model difficult to even image, much less realize. Depression-era material scarcity made the call for time without work and consumption meaningless, and despite the efforts of leisure reformers, relatively purposeless. People for whom identity and sociability were intertwined in working and spending could not easily find personal pride and social engagement in their free time. Postwar growth answered the problem of Depression-era scarcity as well as promised jobs. Moreover, unlike free time, growth not only did not threaten capitalism (based on the need for expanding profit) but in fact provided a compromise, combining capital accumulation, identity-creating work, and reasonably full employment. In the light of all this, it is not surprising that leisure reformers could not find a functional equivalent to consumerism and win the public to the idea of more free time. Their own inability to relate to or understand the common experience only added to the inevitability of this failure.

The settlement of 1938 offered a return to the social status quo that had been developing since the beginnings of industrialization: families based on full-time breadwinners and consuming breadgivers, the former reinforcing the work ethic, the latter the consumer culture, both leaving expanded free time behind.

But, as we shall see in the next chapter, the failed expectation of more free time was compounded by unexpected developments in the free-time culture itself that emerged in the twentieth century—leading to conflicts and ultimately disappointments in that culture, despite the hopes of progress coming out of the nineteenth century.

6

Why Free-Time Culture Frustrates

Expectations of a progressive reduction of work time a century ago seem a pipe dream today, ignorant of the dynamics of modern capitalism and the social and political order that it created—even though understanding that failure tells us much about what we have become. But there was a second expectation that proved equally disappointing: the transformation of mass free-time culture. Like the first expectation, the second came out of nineteenth-century dreams of progress. Today, Keynes's belief in 1930 that a fifteen-hour week would prevail in a century is a joke. But, in the same writing, he offered a second dream: after productivity had met real needs, we would "devote our further energies to non-economic purposes," when the human being "will be faced with his real, his permanent problem—how to use his freedom from pressing economic cares, how to occupy the leisure, which science and compound interest will have won for him, to live wisely and agreeably, and well." While Keynes does not elaborate on what that meant, he was sure that the important leaders of the future would no longer be the "money makers" but "those peoples, who can keep alive, and cultivate into fuller perfection, the art of life itself." This is a perfect expression of the genteel ideal of free time, not a surprising hope for a cultured economist like Keynes—a hope held doubtless by many others.[1]

Yet, like the time expectation, this hope for free-time culture disappointed idealists; and, across the twentieth century, this dream was mostly forgotten or marginalized. Instead of following Keynes's advice that we turn from "money makers" to those who "cultivate" the "art of life," today we honor the accumulators and navigate, largely unaided, through a complex and conflicted cultural landscape. This may not be surprising in our jaded times, but this confused culture has greatly impacted how we think about free time today, making it an arena of controversy and tension. Not only do we lack a consensus about what the "art of life" is beyond work, but we are wary of extending free time to our neighbors for fear of, or out of disdain for, how they would spend it. We saw this in the response of Freud, Ortega y Gasset, and others in the 1920s and 30s to the "threat" of the eight-hour workday. The story got much more complex and interesting as the century wore on.[2]

As we saw in chapter 3, Victorian-era activists both marginalized the carnival and promoted public uplift through rational recreation. The goal was to organize time freed from work. This project continued in the twentieth century, but with new complications. First, the carnival was thoroughly commercialized, becoming part of a vastly extended, dynamic, and profit-driven phenomenon that reached crowds far beyond the local villagers or working classes of the past—even including a rebellious (and often young) group, often with parentage in the genteel elite. Second, a large portion of an *expanding* middle class rejected the rigor of genteel uplift for a culture of kitsch and "fun." Against both of these challenges, an "improving" elite became largely an isolated group of Jeremiahs, marginalized in an emerging consumer culture—even as they still played a major role in the discussion about the ills and needs of free time. This was not, of course, what the genteel, exemplified in Keynes, had expected early in the twentieth century.

In his classic, *Highbrow/Lowbrow: The Emergence of Cultural Hierarchy in America*, Lawrence Levine describes the division of American culture in the late nineteenth century. On the one hand, a rising elite abandoned a multiclass culture for highbrow Italian opera and Shakespeare performed in their purity; on the other, a lowbrow popular culture retained many of the features of the traditional festival or carnival. The new elite made sharp distinctions, whereas their predecessors often accepted a blended culture, such as in "opera" houses that had combined bits of Rossini with burlesque. Moreover, this elite attempted to introduce values of refinement, restraint, and measured sublimity to the wider society and even to isolate and degrade what it defined as lowbrow.[3] Though occurring elsewhere too, such efforts by the elite were a particularly American trait. This agenda of cultural uplift was embraced by many in the broad middle class and even a portion of the aspiring working class, who abandoned their ancestor's devotion to carnival culture. Uplift was a major justification for extending free time.

However, in the twentieth century, instead of the victory of refinement, carnival/festival culture persisted—but in new commercial expressions. Some of these forms were adaptations of traditional carnival activities, such as bars and circuses or sideshows; others were new but perpetuated elements of the saturnalian ethos of the past, for example, amusement park rides and horror movies. At the same time, a growing mass of middle-class (but not elite) consumers rejected the austerity and refinement of gentility and highbrow culture (embodied in institutions like art museums, grand opera, and later in abstract art, modern literature, and other forms of cosmopolitanism). But this middlebrow sector also rejected the traditional carnival and its modern manifestations. Instead, these middling consumers opted for a midcult mix of domesticity, tradition, and sentimentality, building free time around the cult of the home, family, and child.

The result was a continuously contested culture divided largely in three parts: 1) a legacy of genteel culture in the high modernism and restrained social and personal refinement that today continues to define the cultural critique of consumer culture; 2) a modified carnival culture that is energized and expanded by commercial empresarios and has become a major part of mainstream culture, especially as it has been adopted by young middle-class rebels; and 3) a midcult conservatism that shares much of the criticism of carnival (and youth culture) with the high modernists but is also attracted to sentimental and romantic emotion and to the delight of children. All three, but especially the latter two, are intertwined in a work-driven consumer culture.

The result was a free-time culture that was and is richly diverse, though in constant tension. These conflicts have even defined generational and partisan political identities. Genteel ideals of progress, secularity, rational self-control, and self-determination clash with the nostalgic, pious, paternalistic, and familial values of the midcult, while the modern carnivalesque nips at the heels of both in the outrageous, the camp, and the ecstatic. This division of free-time culture tells us much about the persistence of class and sociocultural prejudice. But these different communities of pleasure have often interacted and fragmented, producing anything but an inevitable and coherent culture out of capitalist affluence. Most important, these differences led to misunderstandings and conflict between each free-time culture. For example, the persistence of carnival culture justifies elite rejection of or disinterest in further reductions of work time for the "unsophisticated plebs." Midcult people share this disdain of the "plebs," but they balk at elite refinement. And the carnival crowd rejects the other two. This cultural confusion continually shapes how we understand free time and its use, by us and by others.

Repressing the Commercial Carnival

Genteel withdrawal from the carnival and much aristocratic leisure has defined the modern bourgeoisie since the seventeenth century. While the bourgeoisie never abandoned aristocratic pleasures in toto, they continued to attack the carnival in its modern form as it shifted from the local and seasonal festival to become a national and eventually global phenomenon, experienced daily in commercialized form. Historians have described how an anxious elite confronted the boisterous sensuality of the bar, boxing ring, gambling den, and even youthful rebellion in dance halls, all of which manifested residues of the carnival. These assaults peaked early in the twentieth century as popular pleasures became part of a profit-driven consumer culture. Religious and bourgeois tastemakers desperately tried to impose refinement and defer gratification for a population of immigrants, African Americans, and the working class in general. Many among this population were still linked to the ecstatic carnival culture, often eager, in the stress of industrial life, to make exuberance a daily occurrence. Let me illustrate genteel efforts to prohibit, marginalize, and censor the commercial carnival culture with a few examples: the bar, the circus and amusement park, and the movie theater.

Drinking and other indulgences of the flesh were always part of the traditional carnival culture and part of why the middle class withdrew from it. But the temperance and prohibition movements that emerged in the nineteenth century confronted more than festival and sporadic drunkenness. With commercialization and the stresses of industry, these crusaders faced the expansion of the tavern and what appeared to be runaway intoxication. In fact, alcohol consumption seemed to increase for working people while declining for the aspiring middle class. Significantly, the US consumption of hard liquor had decreased from 9.5 to 1.8 gallons per capita between 1830 and 1920, but saloon beer drinking rose from 2.7 gallons at midcentury to 29.53 gallons per capita by 1911–1915. Beer was especially common in working-class districts where, by 1900, there was one beer distributor for every fifty men. The Anti-Saloon League made its understanding of the problem clear in 1914: "The vices of the cities have been the undoing of past empires and civilizations. . . . If our Republic is to be saved the liquor traffic must be destroyed."[4]

That traffic was temporarily and unevenly eliminated in 1920 with the Eighteenth Amendment to the Constitution (overturned in 1933). For prohibitionists, prevalent in middle-class sectors of small-town and rural America, alcohol use expressed the character flaw of others—especially working-class city dwellers, immigrants, and non-Anglo-Saxons, who succumbed to temptation (aided by aggressive commercialization), against which the weak needed the forceful hand of the virtuous. Among those who agreed with this were the American Medical Association and leading industrialists like Henry Ford. There is some truth to the common belief that prohibition was a spiteful effort of middle-class America to impose "morality" on the drinking outsider, and of industrialists to make a sometimes unreliable workforce sober, productive, and profitable. Yet prohibition was also an attempt to contain a threat to the family and public health in the marketing of a highly attractive, but potentially addictive, product that sometimes destroyed personal and family life. And arguably prohibition reduced drinking by a third or even half. However, prohibition did not work because large swaths of the public resisted and defied it, and because of the black market and crime that it promoted. Still, prohibition was part of a middle-class effort to reign in desire, unleashed by capitalism. The defeat of prohibition was part of the eclipse of a form of self-constraint that had long been a marker of middle-class respectability. In large measure, that ethos was replaced with the modern code of tolerance, the embrace of novelty, and measured self-indulgence, which became the norm for many in that middle class.[5]

As we have seen, America was largely exceptional in this attack on alcohol, though in Britain the more moderate aims of restricting pub hours (closing at ten or eleven o'clock in the evening) did have an impact. Public drinking in the UK decreased significantly as measured by the rise of adults per pub, increasing from 161 adults for each pub in 1831 to 316 by 1901 and 668 by 1961. This change may have reflected a shift of drinking from the pub to the home as much as a decline in imbibing. In any case, efforts to control psychotropic pleasures in free time remain an ambiguous legacy of the Victorian era.[6]

Another commercial extension of the carnival was the circus or freak show that emerged in full force in the second half of the nineteenth century. Supplementing it was the thrill site of the amusement park around 1900. Initially, both appealed to the "respectable" middling class as well as the plebs. Mid-nineteenth-century freak shows (such as those of the famous P. T. Barnum at his "dime museums") attempted to "normalize" midgets, bearded ladies, and conjoined twins, and to make them examples of bourgeois respectability, even as they also attracted mocking crowds of immigrants. Late nineteenth- and early twentieth-century sites of amusement parks at Coney Island, for example, drew broad swaths of New Yorkers to its mechanical rides and spectacles.[7]

However, by the early twentieth century, the middle class abandoned its earlier fascination with bodily anomalies, as science and medicine demystified freaks (making them pitiful victims of birth defects rather than fascinating exceptions to the normal). Moreover, rising standards of propriety made staring at freaks taboo. Zip (aka "What is It?"), a famed "pinhead" long touted in freak shows as the "missing link" between humans and apes, became in the twentieth century merely a microcephalic, a creature of low intelligence and short life expectancy due to an abnormal birth. No longer could the middle-class crowd express openly feelings of superiority over exotics from the tropics with elongated necks or "saucer lips." The "respectable" not only began to find the freaks frauds or pitiful; they were appalled by the sideshow audience, whom they considered both naive and boorishly insensitive. By the early twentieth century, freak shows were marginalized to tawdry carnivals and circus sideshows; and by the 1970s, freak shows had largely disappeared. Sometimes even the authorities intervened to ban or constrict this carnival holdover.[8]

The amusement parks at Coney Island (and elsewhere) gradually went down-market. Famously, Robert Moses, a New York City official who controlled parks and urban projects, crusaded against the raunchy frivolities of Coney Island in the 1930s. He tried to eliminate the sideshow from the beach with regulations and limited the hours of freak shows at the New York World's Fair of 1939.[9] Again, this moralistic attack on plebeian leisure was far less obvious in Europe. The famous seaside resort of Blackpool, in England, tolerated the "golden mile" of freak and fantasy spectacles on its shore; as a result, they lasted much longer than did those at Coney Island.[10]

Another target of middle-class reformers was the movies, especially when this entertainment challenged their moral code. The film industry had origins in an emerging working-class and youth consumer culture, attracting the same crowd as did the amusement parks and freak shows. Movies first appeared as coin-operated peep shows located in urban arcades in the mid-1890s, and as short films projected onto screens in crude storefront viewing rooms from 1905 (called nickelodeons in the US and the penny cinema in the UK). These movies offered frequent doses of escape and the thrills of prurience, violence, or fantasy, particularly for young working people lashed to the routines of industrial and office work. Though movie makers soon attempted to appeal to a wider middle-class audience (see chapter 8), moralists saw the cinema as a threat.[11]

And once again, the opponents of carnival culture opposed the movies just as they had working-class bars and sideshows. Around 1910, local and state governments began to ban or censor morally objectionable films. Even Progressive reformers like the social worker Jane Addams and intellectuals like the psychologist Hugo Münsterberg complained that movies fostered an emotional and illusory view of the world: they seduced working-class youth with irrational and unrealistic expectations. To deflect these threats to their businesses, the major players in the film industry set up their own review boards. This strategy culminated in 1922 with the famous "Hays Office," led by the conservative politician Will Hays with the support of the major studios. In 1930, it published a "Production Code" that set standards to reduce sexuality and violence on the screen. However, in the face of pressure to attract crowds in the early days of the Depression, it was ineffective. A spate of gangster and sexually charged romances and musicals followed. These movies infuriated moralists, especially for their seeming danger to youth, who made up a large proportion of the audience. Henry James Forman's widely read *Our Movie Made Children* (1933) claimed that children imitated the sexuality of the films of Jean Harlow, Barbara Stanwyck, and Mae West, and of the gangster movies of Edward Robinson and James Cagney. Outrage led to the enforcement of the Production Code in 1934. Just as moralists marginalized the freak show, they drove the carnivalesque cinema to the skid-road "grindhouse" movie house. Hollywood confirmed its role as a producer of "family" middlebrow entertainment. Similarly, bowing to conservatives, British authorities barred the viewing of films on Sundays until 1933, and their censorship board was even more strict than the American, banning, for example, many Hollywood horror films until the late 1950s.[12]

Continued Efforts to Uplift the Carnival Crowd

These efforts to outlaw, marginalize, or censor the commercialized carnival were not the only strategy of genteel and middle-class tastemakers. As in the nineteenth century, there were numerous efforts to offer uplifting alternatives to the intoxication of the bar, the freakish spectacle, and the "immoral" film. As we shall see, however, most of these initiatives reached only the middle class and those aspiring to that status. As noted in chapter 5, the American park and playground movements of the late nineteenth century won renewed enthusiasm after World War I. Public golf courses, tennis courts, and especially swimming pools sprouted across the country during the 1920s. The number of public park and recreation departments in the US rose from 146 in 1921 to 428 by 1931. The same uplifting endeavor was seen in the opening of museums, whose number climbed from 94 in 1910 to 149 in 1930. Even more impressive were New Deal public works projects that built a wide array of recreational and cultural facilities. In the 1930s, 867 public recreation areas and over 9,000 libraries, museums, and other cultural sites were built or improved. Many were committed to physical exercise and nonviolent competition in sports and games. Other organized programs were devoted to preserving or restoring traditional crafts and folkways. Still more offered modern arts activities and individual hobbies, often explicitly to contest the excitement and novelty of commercial amusements. These sites challenged consumer entertainment while affirming genteel values.[13]

Radio was another potential venue of uplift. As early as 1923, just three years after the first commercial broadcast, there were already seventy-two educational radio stations that featured classical music, children's educational programs, and even book reviews. In the 1930s, even the commercial radio networks occasionally presented opera from the New York Metropolitan Opera and classical music appreciation programs without advertising. These were efforts to popularize high culture to an audience that otherwise heard only a steady stream of sitcoms, cop shows, soap operas, and chat programs, along with the songs on the "hit parade," shot through with increasingly intrusive advertisements. All this was perhaps a presumptuous and ultimately futile attempt to reach a middle-class and even mass audience, but it reflects the confidence and commitment of the highbrow community to proselytize their values to the general public. Apparently, network executives shared this view (or at least accommodated it), broadcasting these highbrow programs rather than consigning them to college radio and urban FM stations, as is the case today.[14]

Other efforts at cultural uplift included the curious endeavor by Charles Eliot, the former president of Harvard University, to offer to those who missed a formal liberal arts education an opportunity to catch up as adults. From 1909, Eliot promoted his selection of the basic texts of classical education in his Five-Foot Shelf of Books. Presumably, junior executives read these books on the bus or subway to and from work. The Book-of-the-Month Club, created in 1926, was intended to keep the busy middle-class reader up to date in the latest literature. Despite charges of watering down high culture, the club's board of judges upheld genteel standards rather than picking popular books of fantasy, adventure, or sentiment.[15]

In 1930s Britain, in addition to the classical music programs on BBC radio, volunteer associations and local government promoted hobbies (craft classes and folk dancing, for example), as well as adult education. According to their supporters, such activities were alternatives to the "deadening compulsion always to be in a crowd," a not-too-subtle put-down of commercial leisure. In the 1930s, the BBC even promoted discussion groups for educational radio programs in the BBC's magazine, *The Listener*.[16]

While many of these improving activities were surely marginal or reached primarily the young and already "cultured," there were more direct efforts to challenge and transform commercialized carnival. A good example is the efforts of New York officials not merely to suppress the sideshow at the boisterous summer-long carnival of Coney Island but to turn it into a site of promenades and family togetherness. Since the building of three amusement parks on Coney Island around 1900 and the extension of the subway to the site by 1920, politicians had tried to make Coney a Central Park by the Sea. They hoped to induce crowds to abandon amusement park novelties for green space, sandy beaches, and even enlightened entertainment (like the aquarium that was finally erected in 1957 at Coney Island). The seaside boardwalk, opened in 1923, was supposed to be a counter to the catchpenny attractions on the shore and the thrill rides of the amusement parks. In the 1920s, the boardwalk attracted a genteel crowd of men in dark suits and women with fancy flowered hats promenading with babies in perambulators. Meanwhile, beginning in 1924, the Long Island Park Commission built fourteen parks accessible by car via new state highways. These parks offered relatively uncommercialized settings of seaside nature for family picnics, but also an escape from the Coney Island plebs. In fact, these parks were accessible only by car (not subway or bus). These efforts met with mixed success. They probably contributed to the long-run decline of Coney as it was abandoned by the more affluent offspring of the working class and immigrant visitors of the early twentieth century. But the new parks did foster a family-oriented and nature-loving ethos in the middle class.[17]

Once again, the intrusiveness of American reformers was more muted elsewhere. Coney Island's English counterpart, Blackpool, was more diverse and reached a more multiclass audience than did Coney. Throughout most of the twentieth century, Blackpool was essentially a regional entertainment center with a wide range of stage shows and pier entertainment, as well as a site for freak shows and amusement park rides. It did not drift down-market, as did Coney. Blackpool had more political support for public improvements that preserved a middle-class clientele long after Coney had been abandoned by the more affluent fun seekers. Most important, at Blackpool there was not the same impulse to crush the carnival sections of the seaside resort or to "reform" the tastes of its working-class holidaymakers. Highbrow missionaries, of course, prevailed in England and elsewhere (as with the uplifting programming on the BBC and the gentry home and castle preservations of the National Trust). However, in the arena of popular amusements, American elites were more prone to try to impose gentility than were their British counterparts. The larger issue, as it pertains to the US, is not the success or failure of these uplifting efforts but that they existed at all, trying to challenge commercialized carnival of the early twentieth century.[18]

Behind these attacks on carnivalesque street culture was a persistent affirmation of domesticity and the time and goods of the family. Part of the legacy of genteel culture was an effort to expand home ownership. The frequent argument made by reformers was that property-owning workers became stable and industrious, willing to accept long hours and work discipline to provide for the welfare of their families and communities. Home ownership was supposed to make the working class join the middle class. Already in 1900, 46.7 percent of American homes were owner occupied, rising to 47.8 percent in 1930. The issue became central in the Depression when, in 1933, half of American mortgages were in default (reflected in the fact that homeownership dropped to 43.6 percent in the 1940 census).[19]

The belief that homeownership meant "good citizenship" was embraced both by Republican Herbert Hoover in his 1928 presidential campaign and by his Democratic successor, Franklin Roosevelt. In 1934, Roosevelt's Federal Housing Administration guaranteed private loans and established the standard thirty-year mortgage with a ten percent down payment. His New Deal also began a program of highway construction that helped to create a new wave of suburban housing. In 1939, tax deductions on mortgage interest further encouraged home ownership. New home construction increased from 93,000 in 1932 to nearly 600,000 in 1941. The impact of this pro-homeownership policy would be fully realized only after World War II. In 1960, home ownership reached 61.9 percent. By 1973, almost 40 percent of African American families and 70 percent of White wage earners owned their own homes. Serious economic and social inequality remained, but Americans across the political spectrum embraced the idea that unending growth had finally arrived. And at its core was the mortgaged (owned) home and its demand for time and money. Famous suburban housing developer William Levitt made the point plain: "No man who owns his own house and lot can be a Communist. He has too much to do."[20]

Despite all the celebration of economic individualism, the government did not simply stay out of the marketplace but helped citizens get into it. In the G.I. Bill of Rights of 1944, Congress provided low-interest loans for war veterans, promising a future of family and privacy for the sacrifice of service. The government-backed loans to veterans constituted nearly half of new mortgages between 1947 and 1957. Added to this was the 1956 Interstate Highway Act, which created a great network of freeways that led to modern suburbia and its malls. All this was part of a great shift from the urban crowd culture that had so worried the early twentieth-century gentility and its intellectuals. It was probably the most successfully realized goal of the reformers of free time, likely because it met the desires of many working people for domestic space and life.[21]

The Irrepressible Carnival

Despite these notable efforts to repress and provide alternatives to the carnival and its crowd, the modern saturnalian festival and its patrons could not be denied or replaced. Why would anyone ever have thought otherwise? Yet, reformers from Mill onward expected that the gradual improvement in the wages and social stability of working people would lead to a "civilizing" of their leisure, replacing the carnival appeals of sensuality, violence, and psychotropics with "uplifting" family and refined pleasures. They did not expect commercialized carnival.

In part, this "civilizing" process actually came to pass. With greater and more certain wages, discretionary working-class income increased and shifted from casual drinking to excursions or movie tickets and even to home-improvement purchases. New technologies and higher incomes opened vistas for free time beyond the neighborhood bar and seasonal festival. The revolution in transportation and communications that accelerated after 1850 resulted in both new leisure opportunities and a measure of social convergence, as middle-class free-time culture trickled down to working-class people. The railroad began to make distant travel possible, gradually opening up travel to time-starved workers. By the end of the century, the tram freed wage earners from exclusive reliance on the neighborhood pub or ethnic fraternal society for leisure. The streetcar gave them access to the football or baseball game, amusement park, dance hall, and theatre district. At least in the US, by the 1920s the car widened further those vistas to include family camping and vacation travel. All this resulted in a shift from a narrow and unchanging range of carnival pleasures, sometimes even moves in the direction advocated by the genteel.[22]

The dynamics of commercialization itself also tended to soften or modify carnivalesque leisure. Capitalist goals of profit maximization often led to the melding of class cultures, mixing carnival and genteel elements to reach a wider market. This is obvious in popular amusements like the circus that offered both the sideshow with its three-legged man and bearded lady but also the top-hatted ringmaster and the elegant trapeze walker. By contrast, an originally uplifting leisure like the railroad excursion was gradually shorn of its moralizing lectures and austerity to appeal to wider and more popular markets. By the 1920s, American movie makers had become masters at combining plebeian thrills and more middle-class romance and moralism. The result was a softening of the carnival-genteel conflict. Moreover, competition encouraged innovations that took popular entertainment far from its traditional carnival roots. The entertainment industry was often the first to adopt new technology (such as electricity for amusement park rides and night lighting). The commercialized entertainment industry was increasingly wed to novelty, quickly adapting to both changing tastes and innovations. By 1900, leisure was torn from its traditional roots in community and history.[23]

But commercialization hardly created a classless free-time culture. Providers still often appealed to age, class, and cultural differences in efforts to define, segment, or even monopolize markets. Higher-class pleasure-seekers have long resisted the invasion of the rowdy crowd on a limited budget to "their" resorts, hotels, and concert halls. And often to win or keep respectable customers, entrepreneurs did their utmost to ensure exclusivity. But it worked the other way too: carnival survived the commercialization of free time precisely because these differences in class and age survived. And commercial providers recognized this. The entertainment business sometimes served the submerged class or rebellious age group with the aesthetic of thrills, disruption, mockery of conventional or authoritative values, and celebration of sensuality so amply displayed in the traditional carnival. These values were often revved up and recontextualized in a new commercial setting. The thrills of bullbaiting or cudgeling contests survived in professional wrestling and horror films. Naturally, this commercialized carnival still challenged genteel sensibilities and standards and prompted a reaction. Let us return to the three pleasure settings that reformers sought to control or ban—bars and drinking, amusement parks, and movies—to consider briefly how commercialization kept the carnival going.

Obviously, drinking and other consciousness-alternating practices have prevailed, despite prohibition and other codes of constraint. But it is important to remember that the bar was always much more than a site of intoxication. In many ways, the frequent gaiety and sometimes elegance of the Victorian saloon offered a contrast with the dreary homelives of working people. This was extended in the array and fashions of twentieth-century "night spots."[24] Moreover, as Madelon Powers notes, early twentieth-century American bars often catered to a "regular crowd" of mostly working-class males seeking comradery far from the interference of the "do-gooders" who wanted them to go to museums and parks. Bars were an escape from the confines of the family home as well. They were always commercial, often closely supplied and regulated by breweries, and proprietors expected regular purchases of drinks from customers. The saloon was also the site of a culture with distinct customs: "treating" one another along the bar, small-stakes gambling, group singing, and conversation, but seldom drunkenness.[25] Sometimes bars were settings for social, job, and political networks, live entertainment, and even sexual contacts. All this has declined in the past two generations with the rise of home-based media and even a general withdrawal from social interaction. The psychotropic impulse has become increasingly privatized in the home. Ultimately this is the culmination of the transference of the communal ecstasy of the festival to the commercial exchange between the individual drinker and the market provider. As imbibing has become less communal (and seasonal), it has remained a central form of mood self-regulation and escape, often on a daily basis.

A more obvious survivor of the popular carnival is the amusement park. It appeared at the end of the nineteenth century, just as a mass consumer culture was emerging. Often located on cheap suburban land, amusement parks attracted urban wage earners via streetcar and subway. Though they had origins in genteel pleasure gardens and often attempted to draw crowds across class lines, they also preserved the core of the carnival culture. Again, Coney Island is the best example. With origins as a seaside venue as early as the 1820s, this oval-shaped peninsula at the southern end of Brooklyn, New York, underwent many transformations in the nineteenth century. It served both as an exclusive resort area on its eastern shore and a haven for gamblers and swindlers on the west end. By 1900, much of central Coney Island became the home of three amusement parks: Steeplechase Park (1897), followed by Luna Park (1903), and Dreamworld (1904). These parks offered mechanized play that reassured the respectable, but they also offered excitement at five or ten cents a ride. Still Coney primarily served as an industrial-era carnival.[26] As the historian John Kasson notes, "Coney Island located its festivity not in time as a special moment on the calendar but in space as a special place on the map. . . . Coney Island signaled the rise of a new mass culture no longer deferential to genteel tastes and values."[27]

As a perfect expression of modern saturnalia, Coney's amusement parks introduced roller coasters that offered the rush of seeming danger. The parks broke Victorian moral codes in rides like the "barrel of fun," which threw young men and women together. But they offered more than thrill rides. Luna Park and Dreamworld especially gave consumers the immersive experience of a walk-through fantasy, romantically reminiscent of European city squares or the Orient, especially when illuminated at night by the recent innovation of electric lighting. In contrast to the daily life of factory work and dark, often gloomy tenements, Coney provided an electric extravaganza that harked back to the colorful decorations of the traditional festival. Within the parks were an amazing array of spectacles: compressed scenic tours of distant or imaginary places, reenacted disasters like the recent flood in Johnstown, Pennsylvania, simulations of recent battles and tenement fires (viewed from grandstands), and even pseudo-trips to the moon and hell, all feasts for the senses and imagination. Blackpool's Pleasure Beach, along with Copenhagen's Tivoli Gardens and Vienna's Prater, was a bit more sedate (no rides to hell or mock blazes), but it shared the carnivalesque spirit, brought into the industrial urban era.[28]

These twentieth-century amusement parks amplified the traditional festival with new technology and entrepreneurial innovation. The boisterous crowds, the unrelenting intensity, and the thrills of bodily motion followed the traditions of the older festival, but the new carnival was not contained in a few days a year; it was accessible with a subway or train ticket all summer long and sometimes throughout the year as at Walt Disney World in Florida. Moreover, the saturnalian opportunity for emotional release and even social inversion remained in the mocking of convention. Coney and Blackpool were not sites for quiet strolls through manicured city parks as their patrons' genteel superiors desired. Instead, descendants of peasant carnival revelers flocked to Blackpool and Coney Island for the thrill of rides, perhaps a chance romantic or sexual encounter, and simulated confrontations with danger or others' misfortune.

Still, things had changed: these modern playful crowds abandoned "blood sports" like cockfighting and physical contests like intergroup brawling. In their place, Coney's crowds jousted playfully with thrill-ride machines and engaged in an exciting, continuously changing encounter with sights, sounds, smells, and strangers. The new carnival was not only less seasonal but more innovative. However, it still was a carnival—no longer an escape from the annual drudgery of the agricultural or craftwork cycle, but an escape nevertheless from the lifelong monotony of wage earning, the expectations of elders, and the dreariness of tenement life.

Moreover, since the 1970s, modern amusement parks have dramatically accelerated the visceral thrill in rides. New parks such as Magic Mountain and Six Flags replaced the wood and rail coasters of the past with faster, higher, more elaborate, and suggestively more dangerous rides, based on tubular steel. These innovations roughly coincide with the rise of the thrill-seeking video game culture that has appealed especially to teens and young adults. Even Knott's Berry Farm of Southern California, dating from mid-1920s as a fruit stand and in the 1930s and early 1940s a folksy restaurant with a "ghost town," became a state-of-the-art amusement park, catering to thrill seekers as the new coasters invaded the once placid park. In 1975, it introduced a steel tubular coaster, the Corkscrew. At the same time, Disney's parks in Orlando and Anaheim introduced thrill rides appealing to teens, as did Universal and others.[29] In modern commercial form, the carnival survives. In fact, it thrives.

The Modern Carnival and Youth Rebellion

Over the twentieth century, however, the carnival has become less identified with workers and more with rebellious youth, especially from the middle class. Notably, we see this in the 1960s counterculture in the defiant rejection of the genteel values of the older generation when a group of young people identified themselves as "freaks." Unlike the "conventional freak," who was mostly an involuntary social outcaste because of physical abnormality, countercultural freaks chose that status as a mark of estrangement from conventionality in an intentional break from the norms of constraint and compromise.[30] This freakery took cultural form in camp and unhinged horror (or the creepy).

Among other things, camp was a put-on. An example of this was a new type of freak show that peaked in the 1990s in the bizarre and vulgar acts of middle-class performers who appeared at rock clubs pretending to be "freaks" while audiences pretended to be dismayed and treated the whole thing as a joke. Jim Rose's Sideshow Circus featured, for example, a man covered in tattoos that looked like a jigsaw puzzle and who swallowed live bugs. Camp appeared also in shock-talk TV (like *Jerry Springer*), where psychological freaks engaged in over-the-top outrage while studio audiences cheered. Similar, too, were the cosplay performances of crowds at showings of *Rocky Horror Picture Show* and other midnight movies from the 1970s. Camp performers and audiences celebrated the outrageous, sometimes pretending to be the freak or the rube, but always in a rejection of middle-class expectations and taste. Since the 1960s, subsequent cohorts of youth have returned to the carnivalesque, which the middle class had rejected, both in admiration of that tradition's "earthiness" and in energized defiance of genteel values of constraint and refinement. Obvious examples are punk rock and later hip hop concerts.[31]

A second form of middle-class youth rebellion through the carnivalesque was expressed in the mainstreaming of shock and horror. As noted above, movies always have exhibited elements of the carnival, though this impulse was repeatedly checked by the vigilance of censors. This changed in the 1960s. The collapse of the family audience for movies (due to TV), the need to draw the young to theaters with what was taboo on "family" TV, and a general decline of genteel constraint ended old controls. The old Production Code of the 1930s was replaced by an age-graded rating system in 1968 that separated G films open to children from R-rated movies for adults. Ostensibly freeing movies from constraints on realism (often sexual), the new rating system also opened the door to the return of the carnival's "earthiness" in the form of unhinged horror.[32]

Arguably, the turning point came with *Night of the Living Dead* (1968), a radical transformation of the comparatively tame Hollywood monster and horror movie. It features the onslaught of flesh-eating zombies on a defenseless and divided group of ordinary people holed up in an American farmhouse. Without the comfort of a happy ending or a safely distant fantasy setting in a European village, the movie exhausts the audience with unrelenting graphic violence. All this broke the rules of the traditional horror film. Produced by an unknow independent filmmaker, George Romero, *Living Dead* became the model of much horror that followed. The fear and disgust evoked by the traditional carnival freak show were accelerated.[33]

These horror films were part of a broader trend toward sensual intensity (seen in everything from action-adventure movies and violent video games to modern tubular roller coasters).[34] The commercialized carnival intensified the saturnalian rebellion and thrill seeking of the traditional festival. This modern revving up of the violence, sensuality, and bizarreness of the carnival was very much a manifestation of what I call fast capitalism and its irrepressible popular appeal (chapter 7). Genteel tastemakers had no chance of containing it.

As Daniel Bell suggests in his famous *Cultural Contradictions of Capitalism* (1976), the rational efficiency of bourgeois industrialism has produced not just a genteel culture of free time but its opposite. This was a hedonistic impulse that rejected capitalist rationality and efficiency. This inclination came not only from the descendants of the carnival-going peasants and traditional aristocracy but, surprisingly, from within the bourgeoisie itself. Though historians might date this challenge to capitalist efficiency from the Romantic movement of the nineteenth century, it reached its fullness only in the middle of the twentieth century, led by middle-class youth. Despite elements of antimaterialism in that youth rebellion, the "counter" in the counterculture was not anticonsumerism but the affirmation of consumerism in a new carnival culture. Though the counterculture seemed to threaten the bourgeois work ethic, this essentially hedonistic movement was vital to expanding consumer markets upon which capitalism depended for growth. As a result, hedonism has become irrepressible and insidious.[35]

We can question Bell's pessimistic interpretation of capitalist hedonism today as reflecting a middle-aged intellectual's displeasure with what he saw as the excesses of the counterculture of the 1960s and early 1970s. Still, it is hard to discount his broad analysis: the mid-twentieth century witnessed the culmination of a long trend—the cultural division between middle-class culture (both genteel and middlebrow) and a new youth-shaped carnival culture. The result has been a decades-long despair, especially within the middlebrow middle class, regarding the pleasure choices of the young, leading to repeated "moral panics" over everything from video games to horror movies. This division remains and makes problematic any consensus over the future of free time.

Middlebrow Kitsch but Also "Fun"

The frustration of genteel culture makers went further. While much of their fire was directed toward the modern carnival (in all its forms), they also lamented the emergence of a middlebrow culture. This is seen in their endless mockery of kitsch, the often garish, sentimental, and "easy" culture of a presumed unrefined section of the middle class.[36] But of greater interest here is the fact that the middlebrow crowd rejected that highbrow elite. An emerging portion of the middle class, usually without the education or "pedigree" of the genteel, disdained the plebeian and countercultural carnival but also recoiled from the "refinement" and austerity of highbrow culture. Middlebrow culture denied elite claims of cultural authority and without embarrassment embraced the conventional and accessible. The middlebrow crowd, however, could not be reduced to boorish consumers of kitsch, as often claimed by highbrow elites. They also wanted something that the genteel elite would not provide—fun. This is a point often missed in the literature. Of course, fun for the middlebrow could not come in carnivalesque form. Instead, it was a new expression of delight best evoked, I believe, through the cult of the indulged child.[37]

After 1900, genteel standards were under attack, not only by commercial popular culture but also from within the aspiring middle classes themselves. Ultimately, this was because high culture (whose gatekeepers were academic and self-appointed elites) could not stop the intrusion of commercial culture providers who encouraged personal choice and streamlined access to culture as a surefire way of expanding sales. And this applied both to low and middlebrow consumers. This is simplistic, but genteel elites were very much aware of this trend when they attacked middlebrow consumerism as a threat to highbrow values. As Joan Rubin notes, by the 1920s middlebrow magazines in the US rejected the authority of highbrow tastemakers in favor of the "ready-made capacity for independent judgment" of ordinary middle-class people. And the "Babbitts," a name introduced by Sinclair Lewis in his famous novel of 1922, abandoned their Five-Foot Shelf of Books for a comfortable and familiar culture of *Reader's Digest* and later Oprah Winfrey and Dr. Oz. By the 1920s, the view that a specific path to cultured status was necessary for the successful and superior person gave way to the idea that business success was a sufficient measure of accomplishment. There was no need to attend grand opera or read "serious" books. Culture became a matter of personal choice, an idea echoed forty years later by prominent economists like Gary Becker. No longer did the genteel elite have the right to impose standards of taste and refinement. Highbrow standards were replaced by a personally chosen goal of self-realization and comfortable conformity. Consumer culture offered the rising middle class an opportunity for self-gratification and, perhaps with the aid of self-help books like those written by Dale Carnegie, a chance to "win friends and influence people."[38]

But the middlebrow abandonment of the tastemakers of the genteel elite went beyond rejecting difficult-to-achieve aesthetic standards and the expectation of refinement. The middlebrow also objected to the austerity and didacticism of the genteel. This group wanted fun without any higher purpose other than shared enjoyment with the family. Fun had become a "right," noted the anthropologist Martha Wolfenstein in the 1950s. And providing it to children became a parental duty, partially replacing the old obligation of character formation and self-control.[39]

The fun ideal meant an exciting and emotionally fulfilling experience, neither "uplifting," as required by highbrow tastemakers, nor ecstatic, as expected in the carnival. It often was simply whatever "ordinary" folk, just entering the middle class, found amusing and entertaining. And commercial pleasure makers understood this far better than genteel reformers. Still, even the elite were forced to make compromises with the middlebrow "fun morality." In the early years of the cinema, British cultural gatekeepers had prohibited Sunday exhibition of movies and regulated the showing of American films; but by the 1930s, they had to give in to popular taste by abandoning this Sabbatarian prohibition. At the same time, the BBC had to supplement its highbrow programming with more popular musical and educational formats (in large part to counter pressure from commercial radio stations across the channel).[40] Similarly, American museum designers were obliged to compromise with their goals of presenting exhibits of nature with scientific accuracy and realism by including more engaging displays of dinosaur fossils and dioramas of birds and jungle animals.[41]

The fun morality, however, was most clearly revealed in the focus on the delightful and delighted child. It is here that modern middlebrow pleasures diverged most sharply from modern gentility and the carnival. The early twentieth century that fully commercialized middlebrow culture also produced a new understanding of the child, especially in the US. Increasingly, small children especially were understood, not as innocents in need of sheltered training and still less as willful sinners (as in the past), but as fonts of "wondrous innocence." Children were no longer understood primarily as heirs or future workers that had to be trained but instead as bringers of delight and wonder. As such, young people became much more central to the fun aspirations of adults. In the child's wonder was an alternative to genteel refinement and constraint. The delightful and delighted child was also an answer to the pleasures of the traditional carnival crowd. The middlebrow view of fun was radically different from the fun of Coney Island circa 1900, which offered mostly young adults thrills, novelty, and rebellion against genteel standards. Instead, this new form of fun fixated on the delighted gaze of the child rather than the stare of the freak or saturnalian disruption.[42]

Disney best illustrates this. With its ordered space and restrained frivolity, Disneyland attracted suburban families when it opened in 1955. Disney's park was radically different from the seedy amusement parks of the era (as Blackpool and Coney had become by midcentury). Disney eliminated elements of the plebeian pleasure crowd that the middlebrow population found objectionable—the physical crush and disorder of the throng, the cacophony of sideshow barkers, and those "disgusting" freaks. The swarm of strangers at Coney that unsettled the rising middle class, accustomed to their personal space in their cars and detached suburban houses, was replaced by a small cluster of family and friends that could ignore the encircling crowd. And at the center of that circle was often the delighted and delightful child. The sideshow freak had turned into the "wonderful" Mickey Mouse.[43]

Disney represented an important shift in the composition of amusement park crowds in the twentieth century. In 1900, grown-ups may have acted like children, but they seldom burdened themselves with kids when they went to amusement parks. Most important, the thrills and adventures that excited them—the dance halls, the freak shows, and even early amusement park spectacles—had little to evoke innocent childlike wonder. It was only with Disney in 1955 that a whole amusement park was organized on the principle of adults sharing fun with kids.[44]

The Disneyland that opened in 1955 in Anaheim, California, and the Walt Disney World that opened in 1971 outside Orlando, Florida, adopted much from the commercialized carnival of Coney (its fantasy walk-through environment especially), but in most ways Disney defined itself against Coney. It offered not industrial saturnalia or commercial carnival but middlebrow "fun." From 1955, Disney's fantasy world reflected the nostalgia of middle-class visitors for their own childhoods in small towns (Main Street, USA) and, even more, for movie characters that they had seen as children (Disney's Peter Pan and Dumbo, for example). Disney offered a distinct escape from daily life for middlebrow Americans of the mid-twentieth century. They sought relief not from work discipline and the stultifying world of late Victorian society through the childlike play of young adults (as at Coney in 1900), but from the freeways and fragmentation of midcentury suburban life through the child-centered play of families. The resulting experience at Disney was not merely sentimentalized or sanitized, as often claimed, but a playful episode of cross-generational togetherness that attracted a middlebrow audience.[45]

What made it playful was the presence of children. The young were not expected to "learn" at Disneyland (at least not seriously). They were supposed to respond with wonder and to remind their elders of their own childhood wonder as they traversed the fantasy "lands." Remembering watching Disney movie cartoons as children, adults hopped on the delightful, but seldom thrilling, Disney-themed rides. Remember taking the "It's a Small World" ride? Disney's attractions included storybook simulations of Tom Sawyer's Island, the Jungle Cruise, and the Rocket to the Moon—attractions very different from the offerings at museums of natural history or heritage sites like Colonial Williamsburg in the US and the Beamish Open-Air Museum in the UK. While adults enjoyed their delighted offspring and relished their own childhood memories, children thrilled to the novelty of walking through three-dimensional cartoon sets. "Fun" had become childish delight and nostalgia for childhood.[46]

Many academics and other descendants of Victorian gentility find Disney fun to be phony. Still, in the celebration of wondrous innocence or the "cute" child, middlebrow fun was a challenge to the austerity of the genteel and the saturnalia of the carnival. And the cute was more than kitsch or simple sentimentality. It was a celebration of the delightful and delighted innocent. Moreover, the cute has its "edginess," with its sometimes celebration of the "naughty" child, for example, as many (including myself) have noted. It is true that this middlebrow aesthetic, built around family nostalgia and contained "fun," does not work as well today as it did a generation ago (a fact distressing to the middlebrow). The "cool" of the camp and the creepy has invaded its terrain on TV, at the movies, and in amusement parks (even Disney's). Yet this invasion is a big part of the modern popular cultural landscape and our story.[47]

The cute in Disney form once again shows a measure of American exceptionalism. By contrast, in Britain this role of the child was slower to develop. Many Britons have long enjoyed Disneyland, Disney World, and Disneyland Paris, but they did not build one of their own. Despite imitations of Disney-like characters and themes in amusement parks in Britain, such figures never became successful competitors to Disney. And heritage sites like Beamish, which cultural studies commentators often accuse of Disneyfication for its prettified portrayal of a traditional mining village, always intended to "uplift" visitors by imparting learning about the past.[48] In the US, the flight from gentility was more extreme, taking both carnivalesque and distinctly middlebrow forms. Middlebrow Americans rejected the late Victorian plebeian crowd at Coney, but not their fun in the rides, bright lights, and fantasy of the amusement park. The middlebrow found this pleasure and perhaps other forms of the carnival acceptable when expressed as the playfully childlike.

Three Cultures in Perpetual Conflict and the Dilemma of Free Time

These brief stories of the fates of genteel and carnival culture and the rise of middlebrow culture in the twentieth century help us understand a modern dilemma: the confusing and ultimately debilitating conflict over what we should do with our free time. In the last chapter, I considered how the failure of genteel reformers to win Americans to alternatives to consumerism frustrated hopes for a progressive reduction of work time. Here I want to expand on that theme by considering an equally important disappointment: frustration over the free-time culture that we have. In one sense, the frustrated are the inheritors of genteel culture who have failed to win over or even find compromises with carnival or middlebrow culture. This is where a good deal of the criticism of modern consumer culture originates. According to genteel expectations, the traditional culture of carnival and aristocratic display was supposed to disappear, and the values of refined self-development and enlightened conviviality prevail. However, not only did elements of the carnival (and aristocratic leisure) survive, perpetuated by commercialization and people still wed to its values, but a new aesthetic emerged from a middlebrow section of the middle class. It accepted only part of the genteel project, embracing kitsch and the cute. Moreover, a group of the middle class, especially the young, adopted the new carnival in rebellion from their respectable roots. The result was three modern free-time cultures in perpetual conflict with each other about what the "good life" is or should be. The misunderstanding between these groups continues to cloud a vision of time freer from the market.

Genteel free-time culture has survived (often with modernist modifications) in mostly urban and college-educated centers. Readers of this book are likely to be members of that culture. Yet we should not forget that genteel values were rooted in the ancient world in the philosophy of Aristotle, with his celebration of cultivated leisure but disdain for physical labor. The decadence of ancient Rome provoked ascetic Christian revulsions, though it allowed for the perpetuation of festival and aristocratic cultures in the Middle Ages. Religious and cultural reform along with the development of capitalism challenged those cultures and laid the foundations for the genteel values of the nineteenth century. Of course, few today wholeheartedly embrace this Victorian vision. But it remains, sometimes hidden from view.

The modernist successors of the Victorians, of course, claimed to go beyond that culture and its religious and capitalist origins. No doubt, the Victorian vision of free-time culture was compromised by exclusivity, familism, and aristocratic holdovers, especially status-seeking spending and patriarchal presumption. Yet, many modern would-be tastemakers shared with their predecessors a belief that free time should be devoted to personal development and constrained engagement with others and nature. Such essentially genteel values lay behind the reformers and intellectuals who called for playgrounds, the cultivation of hobbies, and adult education in the early twentieth century. Though clearly direct descendants of Victorian "rational recreation," these more recent reformers were rather less paternalistic. The name "democratic leisure" was a reasonably accurate description of their goals. And they sought alternatives to consumerism. As noted in the previous chapter, they insisted that free time should be more than compensation for or relief from toil. It had a purpose beyond spending to keep the economy growing. Echoing Keynes in 1930, these reformers believed that consumer needs were limited, and when they were met, that time free from the economy could bring personal transformation and form interactive communities outside of work. This was to be the real purpose of life. Frankly, there is a lot about these ideas that warrant our attention, even emulation.

Yet, as we have seen, these ideas failed to win popular support. Again, that failure was largely the inability of the modern genteel to acknowledge and adapt to the needs and dreams of people beyond their own circle. Moreover, frustration with the failure of this vision (especially with the growth of the commercial carnival) further weakened and often destroyed any hope of an alliance between the "cultured minority" and the popular classes. That partnership was always at best tenuous, even as, during the 1930s, a portion of the intelligentsia and policy makers attempted to create such an alliance.

By the 1950s, however, most intellectuals abdicated any role in promoting this alternative vision for a common culture (or even mutual respect in diversity). Instead, amid the emerging politics of growth and the Cold War, many thinkers linked mass culture to commercial manipulation and totalitarianism. Building on Ortega's fears of a "revolt of the masses" in a commercialized carnival culture of the 1930s was the American Dwight Macdonald's attack on "midcult" kitsch in the 1950s. While Ortega had lamented the rise of a mass of peasant-workers in early twentieth-century European cities, Macdonald anguished over the expanding suburban middle class and its embrace of commercialized kitsch in 1950s America. Macdonald's views were typical of intellectuals of the period: the problem was not traditional popular culture but commercially imposed mass culture. While "folk art grew from below. . . . mass culture is imposed from above . . . fabricated by technicians hired by businessmen; its audiences are passive consumers." Macdonald claimed to honor folk culture, but he was comfortable that the old division between high and low culture had been "watertight." And any seepage of highbrow into midcult was particularly damning. McDonald was dismayed that kitsch (or the midcult) of the middle-class crowd fed off high culture because only that culture's "more easily understood and enjoyed" elements were adopted. Presumably, sophistication and refinement were lost on the middlebrow. Decorative and sentimental painting, easy-listening light classical music, "uplifting" stories in mass-produced magazines, and Hollywood musicals all qualified as kitsch. Clement Greenberg echoed this view: "Kitsch pretends to demand nothing of its customers except their money—not even their time." This disdain contributed to a growing cultural (and political) conservativism evidenced by these intellectuals who had abandoned the Marxist and liberal views of their youth.[49]

The famous author of *The Lonely Crowd*, David Riesman, joined the attack on the modern cultural barbarian in a 1958 essay. He found that especially "southerners coming North, white or Negro, [had become] fodder, not for the machines of production so much as for those of consumption; for coming from a pre-industrial culture, they lack sales resistance." They were inevitably victimized by merchandisers. "This injection at the bottom is, I believe, responsible for much of the American economy of leisure." In Riesman's view, this infusion of unrefined consumers "more than makes up for the withdrawal of those people in the educated strata . . . who no longer find in the purchase of possessions a sufficient agenda for living." No longer expecting a refined leisure culture from the masses, Riesman believed that work had become a necessary and valued "psychological stabilizer." Riesman noted that few workers wanted (in the mid-1950s) a four-day workweek (though the better educated labor leaders did). Reeducation for more discerning leisure was unlikely, he argued. Though a liberal, Riesman shared much of the cultural pessimism (or elitism) of Ortega and MacDonald.[50]

A common belief, with deep historical roots and echoes today, was that affluence threatened to pamper the masses, reducing their willingness to work. In 1961, sociologist Harold Wilensky insisted that only the managerial and professional classes, like worker bees, still put in long hours of work; the masses, like drones, fed off the productivity of capitalism. Their primary role was to be consumer markets for the ingenious entrepreneurial elite. This presumption that affluence (and the propensity of the inferior to breed more than the intelligent) led to social degradation is echoed in the satirical movie *Idiocracy* (2006). For other intellectuals of this period, the free time of the masses was little more than compensation for boring or stressful labor.[51] While these intellectuals might concede that a shortage of free time may explain the commercialized inferiority of mass leisure, none had any confidence that the masses (both middlebrow and lowbrow) would make "good" use of their free time. For these influential thinkers, free time was used for little more than culturally debilitating consumption. They saw no hope for a more liberatory culture. These views reflected an ongoing and ultimately unresolvable clash between genteel and popular leisure values.

Of course, there is much evidence that these elitist attitudes have softened in the last fifty years. Research shows that consumption patterns have become less defined by class and income than by age, gender, sexuality, and other cultural factors.[52] Moreover, sections of the bourgeoisie and its intellectuals have turned themselves into "outsiders," no longer following the cloistered highbrow elite in the academy or in New York. In fact, many of these intellectuals have embraced the popular, even the kitsch, so long condemned by an older generation of thinkers. Beginning in the 1950s, some estranged middle-class Whites (mostly men) abandoned the mass culture of the White suburb for that of the exotic outsider (beatniks and later hippies, for example). According to Grace Hale, they sought to find identity and community in the alien cultures of African Americans and even White evangelicals (groups that presumably still possessed individuality and sociability), even if only symbolically via literature, music, or even language. As Hale notes, this response was largely escapist, contributing little to the lives of the outsiders. It also ignored (and often simply disdained) the everyday people struggling with work and the allure of commercial culture. All this often lacked any clear political or social goal.[53] Again, the intelligentsia did little to support a free-time culture that could transcend either middlebrow or the commercialized carnival.

Although perhaps more subtle than in the past, these middle-class rebels continued to display attitudes of cultural superiority. Most obviously, such attitudes survive today in the disdain of coastal elites for the Americans in the "fly over" territory in the middle of the country. Cultural critics continue to make both commercial carnival and the kitsch/cute the opposite of the "real leisure" that could be experienced only by the Aristotelian few. The cultural elitism of late twentieth-century intellectuals like Sebastian de Grazia and Tibor Scitovsky is still with us. The dominance of this perspective in proposals for "better" free time has long reduced leisure advocates to marginal status, easily dismissed. We see them today as sometimes thoughtful, maybe even thought-provoking, but essentially unrealistic or even just cranks. Recall my discussion of the minimalists in the introduction.

Meanwhile, stepping into the breach have been the legions of commercial populists who regularly condemn or mock the elitist critics of consumerism. Rejecting or ignoring the possibility of manipulated or dysfunctional consumption, these populists disdain the entire culture of constraint. They insist that the only discipline required is that of a market governed (presumably) by the rational (or even just personal) calculation of consumer desires and costs. Rather than seeking new and more satisfactory ways of addressing the problem of free time, consumer populists celebrate consumer choice and identity. They insist that consumer goods have produced not passivity and conformity but individuality and unique, often liberatory, communities.[54]

In any case, neither genteel cultural critics nor commercial populists (sometimes corporate shills) have looked much beyond consumerism (of either the carnival or middlebrow kind) in the free time of working people. Neither group often acknowledges, for example, that activities like gardening, sewing, car customizing, or angling can meet the standard of refined self-development and conviviality. Again, this disinterest in the variety of working people's culture is not a good starting point for proposing personal fulfillment and engagement with others or nature outside the work-and-spend culture.

Even more important is the fact that the conflict and misunderstanding between the free-time cultures has not been just one way. Reciprocal disdain, mistrust, and misunderstanding prevails between the three cultures. This has made very difficult any serious political discussion of the work-and-spend economy or of ways to create a more satisfactory free-time culture. Sections of those participating in the modern carnival culture have become militant opponents of the modern inheritors of the genteel tradition—the college educated, often urban, "elite." This has led to an aesthetic of aggressive masculinity and tribal, even race-bonding, cultures (often with clear carnival roots) built, as some say, around guns, trucks, and bars. This group, indiscreetly dubbed "deplorables" by Hillary Clinton during her 2016 campaign for the presidency, is partially composed of overworked wage earners. Yet these people have defined themselves against any challenge to their carnival/kitsch cultures. To that crowd has been added large sections of the White evangelical community, anxiously adhering to patriarchal familism and often linked culturally to the middlebrow.[55] Though traditionally hostile to the carnival, the middlebrow, with their even greater alienation from modern genteel cultural values—secularity, individualism, internationalism, and embrace of racial and sexual diversity—have sometimes become the allies of the "deplorables." This is seen clearly in the populism of the right since 2016. The American cultural wars of the early twenty-first century can be understood as still another example of the division of the modern genteel from carnival and kitsch.

In any case, it is hard to find any sign of the alliance between progressive reformers and the working class that we saw at the end of World War I—an alliance that won the eight-hour day. The contemporary diversion of the culture wars reinforces the hegemony of the ideology of work, growth, and consumption, and this distraction continues to hinder any productive discussion of free-time culture. Neither expectations of a progressive liberation from work and the market nor a widely embraced personally and socially uplifting leisure culture emerged out of the economic miracles of the twentieth century.

Those failed expectations, however, went beyond the political and cultural eclipse of earlier hopes for free time and culture. The defeat of those ideas was not just the victory of consumerism over free time, but of a particular kind of consumerism that has come to dominate our free time. Consumer culture has changed since 1900 in ways that have further consolidated our work-and-spend regime. Key here are two broad technological and economic changes that I will explore in the next two culminating chapters: the acceleration of consumption in what I call "fast capitalism," and the impact of new forms of mobility and media that have transformed free-time culture in what I label "funneled capitalism." These broad trends further impact how we think about free time and our potential for more satisfying uses of it.

7

Fast Consumer Capitalism

AN EMERGING BIAS AGAINST SLOW CULTURE

The failure of Keynes's expectations of fifteen-hour workweeks and of cultured leisure tells us a lot about our modern world and the prospects for any alternative. So far, I have emphasized the political and cultural reasons for this disappointment. But perhaps even more intractable are a series of technological and marketing changes in the twentieth century that transformed consumption and thus influenced free time and its prospects. In the following two chapters, I want to focus broadly on two ways this was so.

First, there was a great speedup of our encounter with consumed objects and experiences, radically transforming how consumption shaped free time. Second, the range of consumption greatly expanded but was experienced in increasingly personalized ways (in effect, "funneling" consumption as with the phonograph or cell phone). In effect, this funneling transformed personal and social life in free time. These were changes that Keynes and our genteel forebearers had not anticipated, producing a distinctly modern kind of "materialism" that reinforces our bias toward consumption. This modern materialism goes way beyond the traditional "deadly sins" of avarice, gluttony, and envy. The acceleration of consumption shapes the modern experience of time, and funneled consumption offers alternatives to traditional personal and social meanings of free time. Fast and funneled consumption was particularly driven in the twentieth century by mass production and electronic media. I will show how these two trends radically altered liberated time and our attitude toward it.

These changes began early in the twentieth century, just as free time was becoming more available with the eight-hour day and the weekend.

Thus, I will focus on these formative years. In this chapter, I will concentrate on the impact of the mass production of goods and consumed experiences in speeding up consumption in what can be called "fast capitalism." In the following chapter, I will consider more explicitly how mass media and other innovations like the car changed the personal and social meaning of free time, creating "funneled capitalism," in which a global culture is channeled to the often-isolated individual.

Fast and funneled capitalism led to amazing satisfactions, but also disappointments. We must remember regular time free from work was rare and episodic for most people before the twentieth century; and consumer goods, especially new and rapidly changing goods of pleasure, played a minor role up to that point in how free time was used. The rise of the mass and fast consumer economy after 1900 radically changed what free time meant just as free time was becoming available. Much of this was liberating, but ultimately it was also frustrating.

The mass production that took off about 1900 made possible more free time (as in the eight-hour day), but it also filled free time with new goods and activities. This new consumer culture went well beyond simply the growing quantity and variation of consumer goods or the increasing sophistication of advertising. Modern consumer capitalism also led to the turnover of commodities at a much faster rate than before. This acceleration was built into modern capitalism: an increasingly rapid pace of production and purchase created profit through the fast turnaround of investment. This produced a new intensity of economic activity that radically changed consumers' relationship with commodities. With fast capitalism, durable goods came more rapidly than the durations of their usability, which had once governed their production and consumption. Stuff was discarded for new stuff before the old stuff was worn out. Objects of pleasure particularly began to mark time and even increased the pace of time. All this changed the meaning of time.

Fast capitalism had three basic dimensions that impacted time: First, goods and commodity experiences sped up time as they came and went at a faster pace. Second, commodities became easier and more convenient to use. Finally, these goods were both packaged and sensually "packed," producing an intensified consumer experience, a third form of "fastness." New foods, drinks, novelties, phonograph records, movies, and other consumer goods that emerged around 1900 created a new era of "packaged pleasures." The trend toward faster-changing, more accessible, and more intense consumer goods was rooted in the historic drive for profit, accelerated with new manufacturing, transport, and communication technology. More goods, produced at a faster rate, with easier access, and often increased sensual intensity also created scarcities of free time as additional commodities (and their care) occupied additional minutes of free time.

The turnover and convenience of fast goods and consumed experiences had three broad effects: 1) fast capitalism required more time than otherwise necessary at wage work to obtain the money needed to purchase more stuff; 2) fast capitalism also led modern consumers to adopt a bias toward fast over slow goods because fast goods made more efficient use of scarce free time when more goods "saturated" that time; and 3) fast goods and experiences did not require the effort or the long and continuous periods of free time demanded by slow goods and experiences, which required self-cultivation and real-world engagement, making the desire for more free time less pressing. In fact, for some, work became a respite from fast-paced and often stressful "leisure."[1]

This may be familiar, but this was not all that fast capitalism did. The packed and packaged pleasures of many new consumer goods offered new forms of sensual intensity that became part of everyday life. Think of the power and speed of cars and aircraft or even the experience of riding roller coasters at the amusement park, all of which emerged around 1900. Thereafter, product engineers developed goods that tapped into human psychological and biological proclivities (eventually with the aid of science). Often exciting and alluring, fast goods and experiences displaced slow-paced and more diffuse forms of leisure. Fast consumption often required little preparation and offered a rapid and easily accessible succession of sensations (like phonographs and packaged foods and later TV streaming and video games).

Such pleasures were not simply manufactured. They emerge from our biological inheritance and natural needs and thus become immediately appealing. In our ancestors' world of scarce and defuse pleasure, a biological attraction to sugary fruit, for example, had evolutionary benefits, aiding survival. However, from about 1900, sensual pleasures became packed and prevalent, no longer scarce or difficult to obtain (that is, "fast"). As a result, these pleasures impacted our lives in ways very different from our ancestors. The most obvious are obesity and addiction. I can purchase and eat a three-hundred-calorie candy bar or a supersized hamburger in seconds; my distant ancestors might take hours to do the same with scarce seeds and berries, which provided many fewer calories.

If we have a biological (and problematic) preference for fast consumption, our longings for "slow" alternatives to modern fast goods (like hobbies, country walks, conversation, spiritual encounters, and even leisurely dining) are cultural legacies, learned and cultivated. Often, however, the biological trumps the cultural, especially when the biological urge comes in the form of modern packaged pleasures. As often noted, with the coming of twentieth-century consumer culture, insufficient training in "consumer skills" (despite efforts of the consumer movement from the 1920s) further led to consumption of fast goods. Especially since the advent of mass education, schools have largely prepared the young for jobs (sometimes) rather than for cultivating free-time "life"—much less for being knowledgeable consumers.[2]

Slow goods became comparatively less appealing (especially with the expansion of advertising by fast competitors in the mass media). The combination of time scarcity when working hours remained unchanged and the advantages of fast goods frustrated further expectations of cultural refinement. People chose fast consumption in everyday life decisions, even though many people in moments of reflection preferred the slow, especially because the slow seemed to offer more self-realization and worldly engagement. Who has not lamented time surfing the net instead of cultivating hobbies, faith, or friendships? Yet, for many, these experiences of constant novelty as well as immediate and intense pleasure served as substitutes for the old hope of a spiritual life in an increasingly secular age. The point has become to fill time with novelty and intensity. This displaced other meanings of free time (both personal and communal).

The result has been Linder's "harried leisure class," where free time seemed to have become as psychologically pressing as work time, even when no boss or other external authority was imposing a "speedup." Free time became fast time because of fast goods. That intensification of time changed economic calculations: a slow activity like reading a book became more costly in terms of foregone income than many fast goods. As wages increased, the opportunity costs of foregoing an extra hour of work went up, reducing interest in another hour free from work, especially if it was a "slow" hour. This speedup altered and frustrated cultural expectations (especially as defined by critics of consumer culture). In sum, with unfettered economic growth, even with more time liberated from work, free-time culture became more burdened and often surprisingly unsatisfying for many—even as it became sometimes also alluring and pleasurable. This contradiction lays at the heart of our modern dilemma.[3]

But to understand this dilemma, we need to go beyond these abstractions and look a little more closely at the history of fast consumer capitalism and its impact on our experience of free time. Work and conditions of employment (usually set by employers and a global competitive economy) certainly have impacted access to free time and even the cultural content of free time. But I argue here that also important is the nature and character of modern consumption. Fast consumer culture has shaped the broader question of free-time culture and indirectly encouraged more work than was once expected. Let me situate fast consumer capitalism in American history and give some examples of how it has worked over the past century to shape time and culture.

Fast Capitalism: Early Twentieth-Century Origins

Why is our economy so fast? In part, it is because the fast turnover of capital and inventory is key to profit and modern capital accumulation. Turnover, rather than pillage or even monopoly of scarce goods and resources, is at the heart of much modern wealth. Capitalists try to speed up production and consumption when possible. But fast capitalism also needed consumers amenable to such rapid turnover. Both were insufficient before 1900. Let us briefly consider both sides of the coin of fast capitalism.

The term, fast capitalism, was introduced by Ben Agger in the late 1980s, making a now familiar argument. From the end of World War II until the 1970s, a relatively stable era of America society had prevailed. American corporate hegemony globally, paired with unions in heavy industry and the welfare state, had produced an era of mass production and mass consumption based on relatively efficient American factories and well-paid suburbanized working families. Often called "Fordism," that era ended in the 1970s with a series of economic changes. One significant change was the introduction of "just-in-time" batch production, designed for increasingly focused and changing global markets based on new, especially digital, technologies and business processes. This led to other changes: globalized production, the decline of American economic dominance, and the reduction of American union jobs and secure working-class consumers. The result, too, was a decrease of the time between product development and consumer purchase—that is, fast capitalism. Drawing on the theories of postmodernism, Hartmut Rosa finds that "social acceleration" took off in the 1970s, with fast capitalism, globalization, and especially digitalization.[4]

I find a lot to value in this analysis. But here I argue that fast capitalism has much earlier origins—around 1900. It was rooted in a cluster of technological and business innovations that accelerated dynamics inherent in capitalism. While production for profit has always required the turnover of investment, technology and marketing practices limited this turnover until the end of the nineteenth century. About then, faster transportation and communications as well as factory innovations like the assembly line and consumer packaging moved goods more quickly from product design and manufacture to consumer purchase. These technologies increased the rate that bankers could finance production, manufacturers could turn out and sell goods to stores, and retailers could change, display, and sell goods to consumers.

Around 1900, a diverse range of innovative producers of new consumer goods introduced frequent, sometimes annual model changes. These products ranged from automobiles and snapshot cameras to phonographs and electric household appliances. A vast array of novelty and fashion manufacturers of toys, knickknacks, and apparel did the same. Some even prospered by creating commercial fads in games like tiddlywinks (1886) or toys like teddy bears (1906). Technologically innovative products like phonographs and movie cameras and projectors, along with records and films, accelerated and democratized the flow of products and novelty, taking the turnover economy of books and periodicals to new, faster, and more sensual heights. Moreover, there were new methods of persuasion, inducing consumers to adapt more rapidly to change: enticingly decorated shop windows and displays in department stores, carefully designed product labeling, magazine advertising to promote the latest models of stoves and cars, and innovations in toiletries, snack foods, bottled soft drinks, cigarettes, and canned goods. Fast capitalism also meant planned obsolescence, a term popularized by Vance Packard in 1960 in his *Waste Makers*. But, as historian Philip Scranton observes, 1920s merchandisers who had traditionally sold goods like furniture for their heritage and durability (often passed down as heirlooms) adopted the strategy of garment and novelty makers, transforming their durables into objects of fashion. Must-have furnishings soon became out-of-date, requiring fresh purchases. In the business of continually convincing Americans of the need to buy new, better, and more were legions of salespeople, whipped to a frenzy through emotionally charged sales conventions and cutthroat competition. This first era of fast capitalism extended until the Great Depression.[5]

The Fastness of Phonographs

Let us focus on two consumer innovations of the first three decades of the twentieth century—the phonograph and the automobile—to understand this process better. The phonograph, invented in 1877 by Thomas Edison using a cylinder and improved with Emile Berliner's disc record of 1887, led to a radical speedup of music production and consumption. What emerged on a mass scale were musical "hits" that briefly gained public excitement and regard. Thousands of mass-produced and constantly changing phonograph records exactly reproduced centrally manufactured tunes and voices in their spiral of grooves. Early phonographs were very simple devices. They reproduced recorded sounds when a vibrating needle (attached to a mechanical amplification system involving a "horn") was inserted into a spiral groove while the record revolved. This offered listeners the latest tunes that could be replayed and heard anytime and almost anywhere. The phonograph became a household appliance by 1900, offering a revolutionary replacement for the slowly changing aural experience of concerts and amateur music on parlor pianos.

Around 1900, an oligopoly of three major producers—Victor, Edison, and Columbia—transformed Edison's original novelty for capturing the voice (first used as a business machine) into an industry of fast goods: constantly improving phonograph players and an ever-fresh output of recordings for a home entertainment market. Aggressive advertising and retail-store promotion familiarized consumers with the phonograph, made more appealing as the Big Three introduced technological advances in their players and recordings.[6]

All of this encouraged rising expectations and a presumption of the inevitable obsolescence of the recently new. Fast change became the norm. The phonograph also introduced a cardinal principle of modern merchandising, linking product improvement with personal advancement over time. Everything was supposed to be better now than when we were younger, and we should expect more with age. In the late 1890s, the big phonograph companies developed a technique copied a generation later with immense success by General Motors and other car companies: they introduced a full line of products, graduated by features and price. The object was not just to segment the market by consumer income. It was to invite the consumer to climb up the product ladder over time. In 1899, Edison offered the entry level "Gem" phonograph for children, expecting them as adults to move on to pricier models; about 1900, Victor sold cheap phonographs like the "Toy" for three dollars, but also the elegant "Monarch" for 150 dollars for the genteel rich "who have hitherto scorned the talking machine." In 1906, Victor upped the prestige factor and fully addressed the concern of the refined bourgeoisie by introducing the "Victrola," which hid the machine-like horn in fancy cabinetry. This made the phonograph suitable for the bourgeois parlor. The Victrola came with a wide choice of regal models (the William and Mary, Queen Ann, and Louis XIV). The full line of phonographs represented a status hierarchy, but it also suggested that life was not to be static. Many could rise in time; next year perhaps, one could get the new, improved, and better model.[7]

This anticipation of turnover was radically accelerated with mass-duplicated recordings. This was an early example of "razor and razor blade" marketing based on the initial purchase of hardware (razors or phonographs) that required the seemingly endless purchase of razor blades or records. Victor sold high end "Red Seal" records that featured European opera celebrities (like Enrico Caruso) singing classics that appealed to a middle-class listener seeking genteel status. However, the object of much commercial recording was to create musical hits—meaning popular, but usually ephemeral, songs that were catchy and emotionally accessible, even to those with untrained ears. The result was a new type of sensory experience: two-to-three-minute-long bursts of musical sensation, much like eating a candy bar or smoking a cigarette (other fast products). This was the age of the "hit" in both meanings of the word—a popular and quick experience of sensual intensity.[8]

The phonograph record's success roughly paralleled the rise of Tin Pan Alley—the commercialized song industry, which created the modern "hit" tune, first for sheet music, then for records. Tin Pan Alley dominated commercial popular music from the late 1880s (even though, after 1920, songs were no longer published at the "alley" along West Twenty-Eighth Street between Fifth and Sixth Avenue in New York City). Only about 1955 did this system of popular tune-smithing succumb to an industry dominated by rock music. From the beginning, success for song writers required producing tunes that attracted mass sales but were essentially ephemeral. The tunes were elemental, often written by young amateurs like Irving Berlin, who famously could not read music or play the piano with any sophistication. The key was being timely (referring to contemporary events like the Spanish American War) and using just the right combination of novelty and familiarity to fit in a widely recognized category (story, comic, sentimental, march, and even racist "coon" songs, for example). All depended on the tune catching the wave of popularity.[9]

Before radio and, today, the internet, new songs were "plugged" in New York by Vaudeville singers, who were paid by sheet music producers to perform new tunes on the stage. Sometimes, small-time pluggers sang a new tune on the streetcar to create popular interest. Because hits were impossible to predict and were quickly replaced, the industry had to offer a continual parade of songs, most of which failed to reach an audience. A few hits between 1902 and 1907 sold over 250,000 sheet music copies. About a hundred songs sold as many as 100,000 copies by 1910. This rarity made the hit almost universally recognized. Insofar as consumers tended to crowd around a few hits at any point in time (seeking to share a common aural experience), repeated listening in a few weeks to these hits produced a rapid turnover when the audience grew tired of them (as compared to traditional folk songs heard over a lifetime on special occasions). Record makers understood that they had to produce endless novelty and consumers came to expect this.[10] On all three levels (turnover, access, and intensity), the phonograph and its records were the quintessential fast goods of the early twentieth century, creating the path to radio, TV, and the smartphone.

Automobility and the Speedup of America

Again around 1900, other fast commodities emerged on the market. Easily the most important was the automobile. Carl Benz's first automobile of 1886 was scarcely more than a tricycle powered by a one-cylinder internal-combustion engine. In the decade after 1900, however, the auto rapidly changed, producing the expectation of fast-moving innovation as well as faster transportation. The common horseless carriage of 1900, basically a wagon with a chain-driven under-the-seat engine and a tiller for steering, was transformed into a far more powerful and intimidating vehicle with a protruding front engine, steering wheel, pneumatic tires, drive shaft, and multicylinder engine. Internal combustion vehicles prevailed by 1910 over electric and steam cars because of their ease of startup (as compared to the twenty minutes to get up the "head of steam" on the steam car and the electric with its hours of charging the battery). Internal combustion also offered power and range (over the electric car, especially). The electric starter (after 1912), which eliminated the annoying crank start-up procedure and improved transmissions, sealed the deal for internal combustion. It offered not just speed and power but convenience.[11]

Most of these innovations were offered first on high-priced prestige cars, but the Ford Model T (1908–1927) provided a modern car for the masses. The Model T offered the instant power of twenty horses, speeds of 45 mph, and about a hundred miles of driving per tank of gas, a dramatic change from the carriage or wagon pulled by horses. Moreover, the Model T gave ordinary Americans personal and on-demand mobility in a large country with a dispersed population. It was also an attractive alternative to the communal and station-based transportation of trains. Horses, too, had offered personal transportation, to which Americans were accustomed, possessing over twice the number per capita as did Britons in 1900. The auto was just faster and did not need to rest. The car gave ease of use and speed. But even more, the automobile presented the seeming prospect of endless innovation (much as would the personal computer in the 1980s and 1990s). It was fast in multiple ways.[12]

In the 1910s, the Model T was king, but it hardly changed from 1908 to 1927. Moreover, though innovations like the introduction of the enclosed car with roof and side windows became standard by the 1920s, innovation throughout the car industry declined, leading to a manufacturer's nightmare—market saturation. A new form of fast capitalism—less dependent on technological change—was required to turn over car inventory. This came with the rapid style changes in what would later be called planned obsolescence, and this required a new innovator. In 1924, instead of offering a basic car at rock bottom prices as did Ford, General Motors (GM) chose to emphasize style over technological innovation when it presented a sleek, colorful, and stylish Chevrolet to compete with the black and boxy, if utilitarian, Ford Model T. GM's Alfred P. Sloan soon introduced regular stylistic innovations in the body and interior of his vehicles to persuade car buyers to dispose of their old "out-of-date" cars for the new model, even if the old car was still serviceable. Eventually, this became the "annual model change" under the guidance of GM's Harley Earl, who favored long and low cars with curves. Sloan recognized, as did the phonograph companies, that American consumers were positioned along a long and rising slope of incomes. Elsewhere, social classes were more sharply differentiated. In hopes of attracting customers all along that slope, Sloan created a full line of cars with distinct price ranges and features. The line began with the entry-level Chevrolet, rising to the Pontiac, then to the Oldsmobile, Buick, and, at the top, the Cadillac. This vehicular slope, in theory, offered Americans a path upward to mark their personal progress. Buyers presumably moved up from the Chevrolet to the Cadillac over time, marking economic success and increasing status. This too revved up sales and more frequent purchases.[13]

Not only did all this rescue GM—in the early 1920s a weak company loaded up with unprofitable midpriced cars—but it created a new form of fast capitalism. In all, this strategy made GM the dominant carmaker in the US from the mid-1920s until the end of the century, when Asian and European carmakers finally supplanted it. Ford and other makers followed GM's lead by the end of the 1920s. The car culture became the lodestar of American fast capitalism. While there were only about 1,000 cars on the road in the US in 1900, by 1930 there were over 23 million. In fact, Americans owned about 80 percent of the global output of vehicles in January 1927. The automobile not only revolutionized American mobility but also transformed the American consumer. Cars and phonograph records turned over fast, creating a whole new way of experiencing free time.[14]

Producers had an incentive not only to turn over goods faster and to make their use easier but also to increase the sensual load of many commodities, transforming time by making it more intense. Entrepreneurs, with the aid of product engineers and other innovators, learned how to increase the sensuality of products. I have already noted early examples: in the early modern period, capitalists vastly expanded the market for mood- and mind-altering consumables like tobacco and distilled liquors, and even tea, coffee, and sugar increased dietary intensity. However, in the late nineteenth century new technologies created a wide range of new sensually intense products. Some examples will suffice. James Bonsack's cigarette rolling machine of 1881 and new methods of curing tobacco reduced the cost and ease of access to tobacco. The new cigarette also offered a milder smoke that could be drawn deep into the lungs (unlike earlier forms of tobacco use such as the pipe and cigar). This made the chemical rush quicker and more intense and the health side effects more dire. With slot machines (from 1891), gambling became even faster and more absorbing, as well as less social.[15]

Product intensification also took more benign forms. By 1900, soda fountain drinks with their sugar, fizz, and often caffeine were mass distributed in bottles; and bitter chocolate was blended with milk and sugar in the Hershey's Bar, for example. New technologies sped up the consumption of new visual delights. As early as 1839, the daguerreotype photograph did the work of a painting in minutes. This magic was gradually accelerated and made reproducible, culminating in 1888 with George Eastman's Kodak amateur snapshot camera. The Eastman-

Kodak company eliminated the skill required for picture development with rolled film and commercial picture development and printing. Three years later came the motion picture camera, which dramatically sped up the flow of images and created the illusion of a moving picture. The modern roller coaster offered another form of sensual intensity. In 1884, La Marcus Thompson's coaster gave consumers the simulated thrill of danger, packed into a two-or-three-minute gravity-powered rail journey on a twisting and undulating slope. By the 1890s, this thrill had become the familiar roller coaster with its steam-engine, chain-driven trip up a wooden incline and its speedy downward journey through vertigo-inducing dips and curves. In 1886, another version of intensity was Thompson's scenic railroad. With its painted images of exotic nature and fantasy scenes, this amusement compressed into a short period sights that would have required days of "regular travel." These rides, along with other multisensory spectacles that simulated disasters or battles, were concentrated into a few minutes in amusement parks (mostly notable at New York's Coney Island).[16]

Competition between purveyors of these engineered pleasure systems led to ever more rapid and intense hits of audio-visual-tactile sensuality after 1900. It meant ever quicker mass production of recordings of ephemeral popular tunes, and even faster and more shocking amusement park rides. Fast capitalism in all these ways created successful businesses for investors. Yet, we still need to ask, Why did consumers embrace this speedup of life and experience?

Fast American Consumers in the Early Twentieth Century

Obviously fast goods appealed to people lashed to dull, repetitive work, offering an escape from boredom with episodic rushes of delight that broke up the unceasing and unchanging beat of work time. These goods also filled the "emptiness" of time free from work with stimulation that offered hits of dopamine. This is perhaps inevitable and certainly common to industrializing societies. But, as often asked, why have Americans been more attuned to speed than others? The explanation usually begins with the rather unique character of American society, especially as it emerged after 1900. David Riesman's *Lonely Crowd* (1950) famously claimed that the US became in the twentieth century a society of mobile, insecure, and relatively detached people—the "other directed," in his words. The values and behavior of these Americans were no longer dictated by the individualistic and fixed standards of the "inner-directed" Victorian bourgeois of the nineteenth century, nor by the tradition-determined expectations of the immobile villager of the more distant past, but by the shifting standards of twentieth-century peer groups. While often challenged in its details, this analysis has frequently been echoed in understandings of modern and postmodern society.[17]

But what does this analysis have to do with my understanding of fast capitalism? The most direct answer is that the other-directed American was attracted not only to transient peer groups but also to ephemeral goods. Americans, as quintessentially "modern" (or even "postmodern") people, notable for mass mobility and for relatively weak bonds of family and ethnicity, were a perfect match for a fast-capitalist transformation. The rapid flow of goods was an effective and relatively stress-free way for Americas in a nation of immigrants, where the self and community were historically unfixed and unstable, to express both their individuality and their social identity. These fast-changing goods were the language of quickly shifting peer-group interaction. Key here was the possibility of changing that self, and its social relations, swiftly in response to fast capitalism. In fact, Americans pioneered many of the features of fast capitalism precisely because Americans, compared to Europeans and others, were so free of tradition. There has always been an American bias toward novelty and youth. Some Americans, especially the recently urbanized, over time abandoned one identity for another—often through the display of fashion. Though hardly a tendency restricted to Americans, as the German sociologist Georg Simmel noted in 1904, fashion became a way that insecure people (especially) could find identification in a group (of the fashionable) while distinguishing themselves from others (deemed unfashionable).[18]

Consumer goods allowed Americans to free themselves from their old communities and to express their individuality in a dynamic mass society where novelty was its essential feature. For example, children of immigrants in 1900 wore "American" clothes and attended amusement parks and dance halls that featured the "latest thing" in order to distance themselves from their parents' control, values, and culture. Innovative commodities gave immigrants and other Americans a sense of freedom and sometimes served as a substitute for the often traditional identities provided by fast-disappearing skilled crafts or farming. Individuality no longer meant a fixed, integral personality, so valued in genteel culture, but a series of identities, presumably self-chosen, and often attached to a series of consumer goods (cars, clothes, and other rapidly changing commodities).[19] There is even an argument that the succession of fast experiences and goods became, with secularization in the twentieth century, a substitute for the expectation of an eternal afterlife. Doubtless, Americans (as well as others) pursued novelty in fear of missing out on an opportunity for "fulfillment."[20]

Along with a search for identity came a longing for community. Consumer goods, especially the branded and pleasure commodities that emerged at the end of the nineteenth century, offered tickets into consumption communities, as Daniel Boorstin noted long ago. No longer was there a need for birth right, cultural training, or even social skills. A Jewish immigrant to New York or a recent Black youth arriving in Chicago from Alabama could find instant security in a community of consumption with the purchase of the "right" clothing and music. The fact that these "communities" were not based on tradition or institutions designed for longevity was not necessarily a problem. As shown by historian Andrew Heinz, that ephemerality and superficiality eased entry into a new group and exit from an old one. Fast goods both appealed to and perpetuated a society of the "other directed," and that "direction" often came from goods.[21]

Since the early twentieth century, social ephemerality has often provided a personal and social flexibility missing in non-consumer-based social groups (religious, ethnic, and neighborhood, for example). As already noted, when social clubs or service organizations were run by their members, they often unintentionally excluded others or became factionalized. Today, staff on cruises easily get people to join in. There is less personal risk in disclosing oneself as a "member" of a community of cruisers than in actually chancing humiliation by joining a book group that demands long-term personal interaction. Unattached people begat fast goods, and vice versa.

Fast goods often facilitated both rebellion from and submission to the group—as did fashion in general, offering both separation from and membership in groups, a dynamic that sometimes accelerated the pace of change. Elsewhere I argue that these social functions of modern consumerism provided a substitute for political values of individual freedom and democratic participation (perhaps as evidenced by the decline in voting in the early twentieth century). Freedom no longer meant primarily civil rights but opportunity for personal pleasure, experienced in and through chosen goods. And that free choice was expressed through continually changing goods. Democracy as a right to equality in political participation became personally sharing with others a standard bundle of goods that continually "improved."

The "American way of life" was and is a moving target, promising ongoing progress through choice and a shared standard of consumption. Fast consumer culture did this with *relatively* little self-destructive behavior and personal humiliation. Consumerism did not often produce crazed antisocial loners or intolerant and aggressive fascists (even though it probably undermined personal commitments and social solidarities that made civil societies work in the past). This interlocking relationship between fast goods and "other-directed" people has made it hard for defenders of the simple or cultivated life to have much impact on modern free-time culture. Fast changing goods, rather than the "slow" objects and culture of the past, seemed to fit the needs of modern people. Fast consumers interlocked with fast producers.[22]

The Consumer Appeal of Intensity

The fast consumer was also attracted to sensually intense goods. These ranged from the phonograph and film to the readily available candy bar and bottle of soda, and to the mass-produced car and the popular amusement park. However, these needs for sensual intensity did not appear ex nihilo around 1900 but were rooted in human evolution and deep history. Let me summarize.

As often noted, people have inherited from their prehistoric ancestors a craving for intensity—first in a pursuit of energy-packed foods like sugar and fat (as in honey or meat rather than low-energy vegetables). Our biological forebears craved these foods because they were rare and thus winning access to them improved their chances of survival. Through evolution, these cravings were passed on to modern people. Human ancestors were naturally attracted to certain sights and sounds, even smells and motions that helped them survive and pass these longings to offspring. For example, bright colors, certain odors, and skills of bodily movement helped our forebears identify food and potential mates, and to escape or prevail over threats. Since the Neolithic revolution, humans have tried to make rare or fast-decaying foods more readily accessible by containing and preserving them with the invention of pots and later bottles. Even natural or easily fabricated substances were concentrated with distillation (turning wine to brandy or flowers into perfume, for example). And early civilizations strove to contain and intensify sensations beyond taste and smell. Long before the phonograph and movie camera, innovators tried to capture and extend sound and fix or create visual scenes. Singing songs that could be easily memorized and repeated is an obvious example of preserving sound.[23]

Our human ancestors spent scarce resources on gathering pigments of red, orange, and even the naturally rare blue for colorful decorations on walls and bodies that defied the drab everyday of greens, browns, and greys. Long after humans needed to hop over rocks or swing from tree branches to chase animals for food (or escape predators), civilizations cultivated and accentuated such movements in sport: the first Olympic Games in Greece in the eighth century BCE or the medieval joust are obvious examples of this quest for bodily exhilaration. And dancing has obvious mating and social values. The thrill simply of running, so essential for our highly vulnerable prehistoric ancestors, was multiplied with the horse, which also gave its riders power over unmounted humans. All these efforts were part of a civilized humanity's effort to magnify and preserve sensation and the advantages that this gave.[24]

This inherited quest for intensity was dramatically accelerated at the end of the nineteenth century. Entrepreneurs exploited this quest when they offered foods that featured sugar and fat, taking advantage of consumers' biological (and cultural) proclivity, rooted in ancient conditions of great scarcity. The fact that this scarcity no longer exists is ultimately problematic, but people still crave intensity. In turn, these desires have been stimulated by advertising, packaging, and manufacturing. Entrepreneurs have also tapped other desires for intensity in sensations that formerly were scarce. Note the fast-paced and visually intense movies that are conveniently at hand and constantly changing, and the thrill rides that offer the simulated stimulation of the primeval hunt and chase.[25] A variety of new goods illustrate this point—from roller coasters to movies. But let me focus again on the phonograph and automobile. They tell the story of the mass appeal of intensity in fast consumer capitalism.

The phonograph offered an avalanche of sound that put to shame the occasional hearing of songs and musical instruments at festivals and concerts. The home phonograph may have made music like wallpaper—a background sound hardly noticed (a phenomenon greatly expanded with radio and today's digital smart speakers). But it also increased the expectation of emotionally stimulating sound and reduced toleration of the "boring bits," resulting in the need to move on to another recording. Recorded sound was purely aural, disassociated from other sensations (crowds and musicians, for example). Less was there to distract or diffuse the recording's impact. More subtly, because consumers associated songs with a particular time in their lives (having heard them repeatedly in a short period), they recalled the past through these tunes as "oldies." This pattern of musical memory results from the intense ephemerality of the recorded hit that then is associated with a particular time of life. These hits, heard later in life, evoked nostalgic memories of first loves and carefree youth. In this way, these popular tunes were, like other ephemeral consumer goods (e.g., toys, dolls, and cars), gateways to nostalgic memory. Phonographs set modern people on a new path in the way that time was experienced. Recordings encouraged consumers to rush to the future, impatiently seeking the next novelty, but also to long for the past in the sensuality of sounds associated with cherished times and relations in life, and to expect daily (sometimes almost constant) encounters with "hits" of sound. This intensity of aural experience shaped the future, past, and present.[26]

The car provides an even more obvious example of the appeal of intensity. From first entering the vehicle, it offered personal power at the touch of the foot on the accelerator. In early years, the rich, especially their youth, dashed down country roads in their automobiles, terrorizing locals still stuck in the old world of foot or hoof. And those still relegated to the newer, but annoyingly crowded and fixed, routes of the railroad were often jealous of the automobility of the wealthy. But the car was quickly democratized, reaching into rural America and, by the 1930s, available even to some working-class high-school boys. The driver at the wheel had much more "horsepower" than did a person at the reins of a horse-drawn wagon. A ride on a galloping horse could not match the speed, acceleration, and power offered by the car. Men especially understood the car this way. The power of automobility compensated for the loss of independence and of craft, agricultural, and business skills in an age of wage work in routinized jobs. Working-class men especially preserved a measure of dignity behind the wheel and working under the hood. The car was a machine that they mastered, unlike the machines at the factory or office. Some men claimed a position of superiority by making fun of women drivers, despite often significant female proficiency in driving early automobiles and knowledge of their operation. Cruising down the "open road" offered freedom from the burdens of family, work, and even one's own cares. Cars, like other fast goods, offered intensity and were often empowering. They met not only biological needs but conformed to particular characteristics of American life.[27]

Fast Capitalism: 1930 to 1960

The dynamics of fast capitalism were put in place in the three decades after 1900, but they took a more familiar form in the decades after 1930. Innovation did not slow down during the economic slump of the 1930s as one might have expected. Rather, the very fact that consumer sales shrunk so dramatically after 1929 obliged manufacturers and advertisers to attract anxious buyers with "consumer engineering," designing new products and new appeals to reverse "underconsumption." The product designer, noted advertising executive Ernest Calkins, had to "anticipate wants and desires not yet realized, but foreshadowed by trends and implicit in the habits and folkways" of the nation. What this meant practically was accelerating the turnover of goods by finding new ways of increasing consumer spending. Consumer engineers assumed that there were plenty of cautious consumers with money in their bank accounts who could be enticed into spending by offering new and exciting products. Beyond making goods disposable to counter the "slow" mood of the decade, many innovations stressed speed—streamlined cars, trains, and mobile trailers, and a faster pace of the pop music hit parade. Streamlining—a sleek, forward-looking design—replaced the utilitarian appearance of many products like home appliances, which often had mechanical parts showing. Not only trains and cars were streamlined but so was the Sears Coldspot refrigerator, which dispensed with the older boxy look of models with condensers open on top. All this was to suggest forward-looking modernity despite the glum of the Depression. Added to the list of innovations were the high-pressure "hard sell" and saturated radio advertising, often with cheerful jingles.[28]

Another common strategy was to speed up sales by reducing prices (like cigarettes, toys, and phonograph records). Department stores and other retailers, hoping to increase the turnover of their inventory, offered frequent bargains and convenient shopping Saturday or Thursday evenings. Major League baseball even largely abandoned the old bourgeois preference for leisurely afternoon games by installing lights for evening exhibitions, when more people could attend. Most important was the coming of the discount retailers. Among the first was Michael Cullen's self-service supermarket opened in 1930 on New York's Long Island. Many followed with discount clothing and furniture sales set up in bankrupt factories. Shopping at discounters was not only cheaper but faster. None of this was discarded when the economy recovered. In fact, discount retail was the beginning of the abandonment of the relatively slow-paced shopping at department stores. These "palaces of consumption," as William Leach describes them in the late nineteenth century, had intrusive sales staff, arty displays, fitting rooms, and leisurely restaurants that distracted from the rapid exchange of money and commodities. The discount store, however, eliminated most sales staff and counters as well as enclosed merchandise cabinets that kept customers from inspecting goods. The encounter between buyer and product became direct and immediate with goods on open display. All this set the stage for suburban discount retailers like Kmart, Target, and Walmart in the mid-1960s and later for big-box specialty electronics, hardware, and even pet stores. Discounters offered consumers low prices for quick volume sales and unencumbered purchases. Mostly gone was the grocer offering advice and meeting neighbors for gossip. It is no surprise that the latest step in this process is one-click online buying with Amazon. Faster shopping made bargain hunting an end in itself and shopping much less of a time-consuming social experience.[29]

Another fast capitalist trend from the 1930s was the aggressive merchandising of novelties to young people and their parents. While the first decade of the 1900s saw the birth of child-oriented commercial fads (notably the teddy bear craze of 1906), the Depression marked the full flowering of character licensing, especially with Disney-branded products. Such licensing led to massive sales of Mickey Mouse merchandise (toys, dolls, apparel, comics, even watches). During the Depression, Disney capitalized on the publicity from blockbuster movies to license products featuring movie characters and themes (especially *Snow White and the Seven Dwarfs*). This marketing ploy became common after World War II, when Mattel pushed its latest toy guns and Barbie dolls directly to children in TV ads on the *Mickey Mouse Club*. By the end of the 1970s, the commercial fad was mastered by George Lucas, whose Star Wars movie trilogy sold licensed toy figures and space vehicles to millions of kids. With licensed marketing of toys and the creation of a "full line" of toys related to a movie (especially with the action figures of Lucas and many others), toy purchases no longer were a sometime thing (done for birthdays and Christmas, for example) but happened far more frequently when new products came out. The marketing of minitoys offered with McDonald's Happy Meals (since 1979) and other fast-food specials for kids advanced this almost weekly expectation of new toys. The pace of consumption increased with these commercial fads.[30]

In the meantime, fast-changing and ever more accessible goods became more intense. The best example again is cars. Henry Ford abandoned his four-cylinder Model A in 1932 for a far more powerful car with double the cylinders in its V-8 engine. Cheaper cars were no longer sold "stripped down" and later possibly accessorized with aftermarket add-ons. They increasingly included new features (radios, automatic transmissions, effective heaters, and greater comfort) and, most notably, more power. The Depression era also offered consumers a flood of sound with network radio and cheap tabletop receivers. By the 1930s, network radio was filling American homes with sound all day, without more effort than a turn of a knob. This is nothing special today, but it was a radical transformation in the 1930s, as commercial sound became easy and constant (in contrast to the effort required to play a stack of phonograph records). But, like the phonograph, radio programs came and went quickly. Even the smash sitcom hit of 1929, *Amos 'n' Andy* (famous for its comic routines featuring caricatures of Black characters played by White men), lost its top billing by 1931.[31]

Though weekly movie attendance dropped from ninety million in 1929 to sixty million in 1932, the studios responded with more thrilling features (gangsters with blazing guns, horror, and musicals), all aided by the new technology of the soundtrack. Cinemas also offered double features, twice the excitement for the same price. Very quickly, sensual appliances became common in American homes. It took merely a decade for half of these homes to contain radios and for three quarters of them to include TVs. What made these products attractive was that they offered sensual arousal, changing people's expectations. As the economic historian Avner Offer notes, "sensual inactivity is a psychic burden." Again, intensity went with fast capitalism.[32]

Following the war, Americans returned to accelerating waves of spending for new suburban housing, with furniture and appliances to fill them, along with cars to get to new shopping centers. After 1945, the appeal of new cars (unavailable for four years due to the war) and then the possible purchase of television sets (similarly delayed by the war) led the postwar consumerist onslaught. The "conformist 1950s" were, in fact, extraordinarily innovative for consumers, as rising household income, increasingly shared (at least by Whites) across the classes, provided spending opportunities for symbolic and pleasure goods.[33]

Postwar fast capitalism carried on the interwar shift from technological to stylistic innovation insofar as many goods were sold for rapidly changing style and fashion rather than durability and utility. Much of the spending was for temporary purchases of furniture and appliances. Modernistic home furnishings, often popularizations of experimental and elite designs from the 1920s and 1930s, became fashionable even to the "stodgy" middle class (which had formerly preferred Victorian styles of wood and upholstered furniture). Plastic, once considered cheap, became the rage in clocks and radios, replacing traditional wood casings with bright color, modernistic shapes, and sometimes even whimsy. Many bought chairs and lamps of modern materials like plywood, aluminum, and fiberglass, for their modernity. After 1945, the quest of many Americans for long-deferred household goods sometimes took a flashy turn that later generations found distasteful and excessive. Remember those bright green bathroom fixtures? Everything moved faster. In fact, by the late 1950s, 20 percent of American families were moving every year. They did so for jobs, of course, but also to "step up" in housing, just as they moved up with car trade-ins. TV shows came and went faster than radio. Even the wildly popular Milton Berle (a comic with a variety show) lasted merely eight years and only after several changes of format, dropping from number one in 1948 to five in 1952.[34]

Again, the phonograph record and the car can serve to illustrate these trends. No phase of fast capitalism after 1945 was faster than the popular music industry, especially when it focused on a new generation of restless young consumers. While the phonographic recording industry declined with the advent of radio in the late 1920s and later the Depression, phonograph records got a boost with the LP (long-playing) record introduced to consumers by Columbia in 1948. LPs had a playing time of twenty minutes on each side. This allowed the hearing of longer pieces (like movements of symphonies and multiple numbers from musicals) on a single disk, reducing the chore of record changing as compared to the old four-minute-long, 78 RPM (revolutions per minute) records. This innovation at first appealed primarily to older listeners with longer attention spans than required for pop music, especially starting in 1957 with the coming of high fidelity and stereophonic records and phonograph equipment.[35]

But for youth, the introduction of the 45 RPM record by RCA in 1949 had a greater impact. The 45 record included a single song on either side like the old 78 RPM, but the 45 was smaller, more rugged, and more convenient to play and exchange (especially with multi-record changers). The LP/45 division replicated the old partition between the highbrow (and relatively "slow") music of Victor's Red Seal records and the Tin-Pan-Alley recordings of would-be hits. With the 45 RPM record and player, speed and convenience again were paramount. More important, delivery to consumers was fast and concentrated on the most novel-seeking sector of the population—teenagers.[36]

Youth were attuned to the "latest thing" via peer groups in high school (attended by most teens by the 1950s). From that time, radio stations, too, were increasingly geared toward youth as adults shifted to TVs. The teen especially sought an escape from the living room with its TV console, usually controlled by the father in the evening. Cheap 45s, conveniently available at neighborhood drug and variety stores, were bought weekly by millions of American youths. Teen-oriented radio repeatedly played a short list of "hits," leading often to an even faster turnover of tunes as the popular music of Tin Pan Alley gave way by the mid-1950s to rock. Having abandoned the sentimental ballads and relatively complex arrangements of the big bands of the past, rock performers offered quick repetitive tunes, often adopting the rhythmic, raw, rhythm-and-blues and hillbilly musical styles of African American and rural working-class White artists. Performers and styles came and went, ironically creating later an ongoing demand for "oldie" songs, reminding older Americans of their past youth.[37]

As for cars, the speedup took different forms. First, from 1949, mass-produced vehicles were increasingly equipped with high-compression engines that could go up to 120 mph (and speedometers made that point by including that number). But fastness also came in the form of the rapid turnover of the family car and the quick change of the car's look. While in 1956 American car companies changed the "shell" of their vehicle bodies every two to three years, in 1958 GM replaced its car bodies after one year. This was part of a consumer trend to trade in new cars after only 2.5 years. Most new car buyers relished novelty, not only high-compression engines, powered windows, steering and brakes, and automatic transmissions, but the famous tailfin holding the back lights and a long and low look. This stylistic speedup was an example of planned obsolescence that made the 1953 sedan look very dated by 1955. Car companies had long wanted to increase the turnover of cars to increase sales. Their dreams were fulfilled in the 1950s: car registrations more than doubled between 1945 and 1960 (rising from 25.8 to 61.7 million). Consumers embraced the fast-changing car, just as they accepted novelty in other products like music.[38]

But this enthusiasm for speed came not only from youth (or the working class) but from the supposedly stodgy middle class. In 1958, a car marketing expert told the *US News and World Report* that new cars were sold primarily to "middle and upper-income families." New cars were a special marker of status. Because the new vehicle often looked so different from used cars, even a two-year-old car looked obsolete, magnifying the owner's humiliation at being left behind. Even only slightly used cars showed poorer Americans their financial inability to keep up. Such used cars were for the losers. Moreover, relatively cheap, fuel-efficient, or utilitarian cars (like the Nash, Crosley, and Henry J) failed in the market. More expensive cars, loaded with accessories and the latest styling, dominated sales to the status-conscious affluent. In the 1950s, the small and practical Volkswagen Beetle remained the car of the eccentric (my father had one).[39]

But why did the middle class seem to abandon their presumed traditional self-restraint? One obvious answer was that their status-seeking desire to be at the cutting edge of consumerism trumped old-fashioned ideals of practicality and simplicity. The excesses of planned obsolescence by the end of the 1950s and competition with the utilitarian Beetle led to the smaller American "compacts" (like the Ford Pinto or Chevrolet Corvair) and a more restrained styling. However, the embrace of continuous change hardly disappeared. In 1960, the popular sociologist Vance Packard condemned this status-seeking quest for novelty as a threat to traditional American pragmatism and individualism (as well as a waste of resources). But nothing could slow down this acceleration of the product life cycle.[40]

Fast Capitalism from the 1960s

By the 1960s, fast capitalism took new forms. First, planned obsolescence was partially superseded by purchases of cars, TVs, and other formerly "family" goods for individual use. This led to families with multiple cars and TVs. This may have slowed the acceleration of product turnover, but fewer people shared these goods and more individualized vehicles and media often made for more intense interaction with them.

Second, the 1970s brought not only more individualized consumption but also technological and marketing innovations that further increased the pace of spending. Many Americans and other affluent people experienced a new wave of invention, especially in analog entertainment technologies (e.g., CDs and VCRs). From the 1980s, digital devices, especially the rapidly changing personal computer and its accessories, accelerated consumer experience. And these devices entered the home rapidly. By one estimate, it took fifty years for household ownership of wired phones to rise from 10 percent to 65 percent; but it took only seven years from 2010 for ownership of computer tablets to increase from 3 percent to 65 percent.[41] But let us leave more of that story for the next chapter.

Since the 1970s, not only has the churning of consumer goods increased but so has the pace and intensity of media. One obvious indicator of this trend is the shortening of TV ads: reduced from commonly a minute in the 1950s to thirty seconds by the 1970s and to today's length of fifteen seconds at times. The result is exposure to as many as sixty ads per hour. Digital ads on the internet are even shorter, sometimes one second. Not only have ads gotten shorter and increased in number, but the length of a single image has shortened. In 1978, the average shot length in American television ads lasted 3.8 seconds; by the early 1990s, it had dropped to 2.3 seconds. A study from 2009 claims that the average shot length for an ad aired on a soap opera was scarcely one second compared to the program's shot length of 4.84 seconds. With the advent of the TV remote and multiple cable channels, the commercial message had to be delivered before the remote-control operator could change the channel. But the expectation, especially among the young, of a rapid succession of shots has made not only advertising on the Superbowl a blizzard of images but also the half-time show.[42]

The pace of movies and TV shows has also dramatically increased. The average shot length in movies has declined in English language films from 12 seconds in 1930 to 2.5 in 2010. This is obvious to us all. Just consider Stanley Kubrick's 1968 blockbuster *2001: A Space Odyssey*, with its then modern special effects of spaceships and planets, but also with its luxuriously slow scenes. Compare it to a contemporary sci-fi movie with its quick cuts and short shots. James Cutting estimates that the duration of camera shots in movies has dropped from an average of 12–15 seconds in the 1950s to just 3–5 seconds seventy years later. Barry Salt finds twenty-first-century action films to be even shorter (with shots lasting from 1.63 to 1.95 seconds). Or just watch a few minutes of a 1950s sitcom like *The Adventures of Ozzie and Harriet*, with its hardly adventurous, slow-moving, and simple story line. Contrast it with contemporary sitcoms that feature multiple plots with different dilemmas and fast-talking exchanges between characters, alternating in short montages. Today, a slow scene is boring; the fast, pleasurable.[43]

Of course, this visual acceleration is more evident in some media than others. A particularly graphic form is the development of the action-adventure movie where dialog, character development, and plot have been sacrificed for frequent "hits" of action. Note the shift in westerns and crime movies that began in the late 1960s. Relatively slow moving and plot dependent for decades, westerns became not only less moralistic and more violent (Sam Peckinpah's *The Wild Bunch* from 1969, for example) but action moved faster. This was even more true of action films, notable especially with Clint Eastwood's *Dirty Harry* series (from 1971) and Sylvester Stallone's *Rambo* series (from 1982). Arnold Schwarzenegger's *Terminator* (1984) turns sadistic in its fast-paced mayhem. Similarly, movies of Chuck Norris, Steven Seagal, and Jean-Claude Van Damme display mostly the body in violent motion. In the past, such exhibitions of the muscled male in fast-paced violence attracted the insecure teenage boy. But from the 1970s this show of virility was offered as a blockbuster attraction. As Eric Lichtenfeld notes, "Action pulls free of any narrative context: it is fighting for the sake of fighting." The violence becomes almost tedious in what Rikke Schubart called "aggravated redundancy."[44]

The speedup of action in movies is closely related to the advent of violent video games. While the video game was invented by computer scientists for personal amusement (*Tennis for Two* in 1958 and *Spacewars* in 1961), by 1972, Nolan Bushnell's Atari had packaged such games for arcade machines and home consoles for children and youth. From the late 1980s, Nintendo and Sega offered more powerful devices and more intense games. The player at the controls had to act quickly to get Mario past barrels thrown at him by a gorilla or to move Sonic the Hedgehog through an endless series of digital obstacles. I have to admit, when I first saw a six-year-old play *Sonic* in the early 1990s I found it dizzying, a pace that was like nothing I had experienced watching *Cisco Kid* on TV in the 1950s.[45]

But that habit of fastness extends far beyond action movies and video games. It has become so embedded in the culture that it seems natural. Respectable middle-class Americans embraced fast capitalism in the annual model change of tailfin-bedecked cars in the 1950s while their children bought this week's 150-second hit record. And even the childish thrills of action movies and video games of the 1970s and 1980s became a lifelong habit as adult men held onto their teen thrills.[46] Fast capitalism is practically everywhere and with everyone. It is part and parcel of the cyber experience, beginning with personal computers that have made sensual (especially visual) pleasure immediate and virtually unlimited. I do not write this as a scold, arguing for a return to a contemplative life and to the virtues of simplicity and living closer to nature. We are all part of fast capitalism and often benefit from it. But we still need to think about how fast capitalism has made us who we are and how that has shaped our free time.

Fast Goods and Slow Goods

Having considered the origins of our modern fixation on fast goods and experiences, we can now step back and reflect on how fast goods explain our free-time settlement and why so many of us do not want more of their opposite—slow goods and more free time. Basically, the answer lies in the logic of fast capitalism that explains why we do not optimize the allocation of goods and free time as once expected. As we have seen, a speedup of consumption only accentuated the bias toward goods. Higher wages raised the cost of taking more free time but also provided access to more consumer goods (especially "fast" durables like cars and entertainment devices) that required more hours of work to pay for them. Fast goods created an unexpected link with work that contradicted old expectations. They did not produce "enervated" people, devastated psychologically by the rush of stuff, as once feared (at least by genteel intellectuals). Instead, the welter of stimuli in the form of cars, movies, fashion, candy, and novelties has actually reinforced the work ethic, leading people to work longer and probably harder than formerly expected.

But this bias toward consumption is about more than materialism. Increased access to consumer goods by itself has not displaced "leisure" (as I may have argued in earlier work). Much leisure involves goods gained by work-derived income. But the advent of fast consumer goods and experiences has often displaced "slow" free-time activities and consumer goods. To participate in fast consumer capitalism, one must work more than one might otherwise, but also the bias toward the fast makes more free time less important: fast goods and experiences take less time than the slow; and free time that is not saturated by fast goods becomes "empty." All this at least partially explains the bias toward money rather than time in fast capitalism.

Still, there may be more to the question of why so few of us have resisted the pied piper of fastness and not demanded more time for the slow. After all, the slow often requires less money and thus less work time. Some have made a choice for the slow as I noted in the introduction. But it is not really that obvious why most have not. Many might simply say that the majority are making a personal choice (which intellectuals have no right to challenge). Efficiency demands priority of the fast over the slow and we live in a time-saving culture.

But the choice for the fast is not all that rational. Fast goods have certainly become a habit, an expectation, and time efficient. But these commodities are seldom fully "consumed," be they cars, fashionable shoes, or, especially today, electronic devices. According to one recent estimate, 82 percent of smartphones collected for recycling work fine. Consumers bought new ones every eighteen months simply because they wanted the new model, often with very minor improvements. They embraced rapid turnover irrationally.[47] As Stephen Rosenberg argues, such goods represent "stored potential free activity," but their "utility" is seldom cashed in fully. This may be because accumulating these goods has become a fetish. Some work to purchase the Ford F-150 pickup but do not have much time to use it (and may have no idea just how much work time it was worth in sacrificed free-time activity). But this waste of utility in goods is also because stuff goes too fast down the consumption conveyor belt to ever be used up. The obvious question is why do we put up with this? Why do we not pick what we really want off the line and use our free time in cultivating it—perhaps even slowly. Some do, of course, but the fast-moving belt is a large part of the pleasure of consumption, essential to the success of fast capitalism. The expectation that the next commodity and consumer experience is faster, more convenient, and more intense is part of the appeal, despite our thoughtful claims of wanting things slower and more time to enjoy them. Still, the question comes up: Why do we continue to expect that the next shiny thing will be faster and thus better, especially when we have experienced disappointment?[48]

To some readers these questions may raise a red flag—oh, here is another jeremiad against modern pleasure and choice. But my intent is to explore the puzzle of why we seem to prefer goods (predominantly fast ones) over time (even time to use these goods). So let me pull together ideas from this book to add a bit more to the discussion of why fast beats slow, even if ultimately the fast often does not satisfy and even provokes countermovements.

First, obviously fast is easier than slow. As noted above, fast goods require less training and preparation than slow goods (computer games versus learning to play a violin). When so many things are so convenient and so easy to use, and the payoff of refinement is so uncertain and often frustrating, the bias toward the quick shot of dopamine is obvious. The slow path may require the discipline of the persistent parent (monitoring piano practice, for example) or isolation from the fast (as attempted by rural utopians and religious conservatives like the Amish). But the former often leads to rebellion and the latter to costly withdraw from the advantages of modernity or even reactionary bitterness. Self-discipline in adulthood is hard to pull off because fast has become a habit; and imposed or self-imposed isolation from it is riddled with inconsistencies. Also, adults do not have to practice the piano like they might have been forced to do by parents when they were children. How many parents today still insist on the effort? Much more can and has been said on this subject.[49]

Second, fast goods make the slow seem boring, unappealing, and even tiring. These goods and experiences have come to be experienced as mere tedium. Many fast goods are "packed" with sensuality, often missing in nature or book groups. The fast-cut, rich and striking pallet of color, and the throbbing sounds of modern animation, win out over the restfulness of strolls along nature trails, with their mere greens, browns, and grays. Biologically, this means that fast goods/media provide frequent hits of dopamine and the expectation of such hits. Slower, less frequent infusions produce boredom and anxiety. Compared to the fast good—from which the "boring bits" have been taken out—even the beauty of nature can appear dull and unattractive, especially if accessing nature requires lengthy preparation, such as a long car ride over the desert to get to the Grand Canyon.[50]

At the same time, the speed and ease of access to fast flows of goods and sensation may decrease people's attention spans, reducing their willingness to read long books or ponder complex writing and images. Fewer may be willing to dig deeply into a topic—or even to use information sources that are not digitized, and which require turning off the computer or smartphone and walking over to the library (a problem that teachers and librarians today constantly complain about in students). To "surf the net" means to slide quickly from one web site to another. This leads to "extensity," notes Byung-Chung Han; surfing "does not permit the development of any duration or allow for any completion." At the same time, the computer's capacity for multitasking encourages users to expect to do more than one thing at a time. The computer's speed creates pressures to accelerate the pace of life, leading to a "density of time." Email and text messaging, for example, have produced the expectation that messages are answered in hours or even minutes, and correspondence has become sloppy. Texting has become a substitute for verbal exchange and computers have led us to the "tyranny of the moment" (as Thomas Eriksen pessimistically claims), replacing the pleasures of cultivating a skill or planning an activity.[51] Many of us may despair over these trends, but few will abandon their fast devices. There is no turning back to an idealized world of Victorian gentility, much less the carnival culture of traditional society. But we still miss aspects of these slow worlds and experience surprising degrees of psychological and social stress with our fast culture.

Third, these slow goods and activities require a complex response that many lack skill or time to activate. There is pleasure in the "tension and arousal" in anticipating and planning an encounter with leisure activity, as Tibor Scitovsky notes; and then there is further pleasure in the "resolution of tension and diminishing arousal" as the activity is engaged and completed (as in cultivating a garden). But this is a difficult process for most of us. In fast capitalism, arousal is maintained at near the optimum level from start to finish (as consumers seek to minimize discomfort or boredom). This is most obvious in the continual pursuit of pleasurable hits (what Scitovsky calls "comfort"). Scitovsky's contempt for what he sees as Americans' "disdain for culture" may reflect his European genteel background. Still, he may be right that American higher education (especially since it ceased being largely training of the elite for a lifetime of refined leisure) has emphasized job training rather than preparation for skilled and cultivated consumption and leisure. As a result, only a small minority in adulthood have the training and background necessary to appreciate and participate in slow culture. Scitovsky attributes this bias to American puritanism, but it could equally, or even better, be explained by the emergence of the conventional modern expectation of working for and spending on fast goods, a goal that coincided with the emergence of mass education.[52] Education for cultivated leisure is not even an argument that professors in the liberal arts are willing to make. In any case, as the economist Avner Offer notes, "the flow of novelty and innovation undermines conventions, habits, and institutions of commitment" such as service clubs, political organizations, and churches, creating "a bias toward the short term."[53]

As Hartmut Rosa observes, "The compression of experience fosters adaptation to instruments of fastness that require no formal training and only short periods of engagement—like TV." Thus, without the time for slow hobbies, contemplation, and conversation that consumers have repeatedly claimed they favor, TV becomes a filler requiring "neither buildup nor follow-up." James Robinson and Geoffrey Godbey note in their survey of American time use in the 1980s that 38 percent of the 37.6 hours of weekly free time was devoted to TV. Instead of an actual reduction in the quantity of free time in recent years, they found a perception of time loss with the speedup of nonworking hours. This acceleration has resulted in insufficient durations of free time for the cultivation of that elusive pursuit of "flow," "deep relaxation," and "losing oneself in an activity." Instead, time-pressed Americans have used their leisure hours in "tiny packets" and "in a superficial series" of activities—as in watching TV.[54] This is as true today as it was when Robinson and Godbey wrote their book in the 1990s. The time-consuming hobby, the challenging book, or joining the bowling league require more continuous periods of time. All this may appear to be an affirmation of the basic principles of Victorian culture against modern trends. And it is to a degree, but a call for the slow does not have to mean a return to Victorian values in toto. Nor should it.

Fourth, fast goods dominate our attention simply because over decades they have been marketed in ads and other promotions. They have burrowed into our desires and responses. Nature trails are not usually advertised, but fast cars and action movies are, and incessantly. Ads compound the attraction of the wrapper of the candy bar or cigarette package with attractive associations to romance, adventure, or simply memories of fun times. As often noted, the point of advertising is not just to sell a product but to train consumers to shop incessantly. And shopping itself, of course, has become fast with the internet: it is quicker, more convenient, and often more intense on the screen than at the mall. This leads to satiation and disappointment. Instead of getting off the consumption treadmill, however, consumers often respond with a desire for more intensity, more fastness in new stuff. As Colin Campbell notes, modern consumers have a romantic tendency to believe the next car, pair of shoes, or cell phone will satisfy. In this way, the drive to consume is less materialistic (or even a quest for social status) than it is rooted in a mental expectation of satisfaction. One imagines a red sports car will bring happiness, and when it does not, it is followed by a new fantasy.[55]

Fifth, over time fast goods (and their promotion) have been adapted to our cultural, psychological, and even biological needs and wants. As noted earlier in this book, this may not mean just intensification but optimization. Manufacturers long ago realized that there were limits to accelerating intensity and have adopted various strategies of modulation—for example, by reducing the sugar rush in candy with salty nuts or semisweet chocolate as in the Snickers bar or limiting vertigo in coaster rides with calibrated drops and twists. Food scientists created "flavor profiles" that offered consumers a mix or even succession of taste sensations—sweet, bitter, and salty—or a pleasant feeling in the mouth with fat in ice cream. Both surpass the simple rush of sugar. The layering of sensation has often been an alternative to its simple intensification. Pleasure engineers have also created products that sustain everyday living rather than provide that occasional rush of the saturnalian experience. They have offered consumers regular punctuations of the day with candy bars and cigarettes that lift us out of the boredom and tension of everyday life. Even popular songs and TV serials have provided daily upbeats (rather than disruptions), delivering relief from the forgettable blur of life's routine. And these often small marks of intensity have almost never threatened the work ethic; indeed, they often make the workaday life bearable. Nor have they hampered physical or mental health, at least in the short run. They have become habitual.

Sixth and finally, some fast goods are simply addictive. Cigarettes and alcohol are the obvious examples, but others are still habit-forming, if not necessarily life-threatening. Many fast goods doubtlessly displace other uses of time. Think of video games. While researchers are divided as to whether such goods are addictive (especially if the cigarette is the standard), there is little doubt that some (such as video games) have replaced pleasures that require training, are sensually diffuse, and take time—slow time.[56] The marketing of intensity tapped into biological needs born of scarcity, but it also created satiation because that intensity became so plentiful. New goods evoked feelings of delight, even "awe," which, as we all know, quickly disappear as they become habitual. Satiation produces demand for more intensity. A growing intolerance of boredom, caused in part by modern plentitude and convenience, seems to require more novelty, convenience, and intensity—in other words, fast goods. This describes the process of addiction, driven by the biology of dopamine.[57]

Traditional religion had another name for this—concupiscence—and demanded restraint or "spirituality" as an alternative to the "sin" of giving in to "temptation." But religion has less power in our secular age, and modern people often find traditional moral codes obsessive and neurotic. In any case, these codes were born in an age of scarcity when community survival and social peace required a measure of constraint. In our age of plenty, these moral demands have largely lost their power.

While the ubiquity of accessible desires has led to frequent calls for the restoration of traditional morality, for many, traditional self-control no longer seems necessary. The "addiction" to fast stuff has become far more subtle than the pains of heroine withdraw. But giving up or reducing the desire for fast stuff is still difficult. Simply stated, fast goods and fastness have become habits, learned in childhood, and perpetuated in ever advancing waves of the new, convenient, and intense. We click past TV shows and scroll quickly through song lists on streaming services the second we feel bored. We move quickly past the latest novelty or "must-have" purchase on to the next, filling our garages and basements with hardly used stuff. Our obsessions with the quickly changing and the immediate make us forget the past (both last week's news and our deeper heritage).[58] Fast capitalism makes us less interested in the possibilities of the slow in free time.

Inevitably all this produced a reaction. This can be seen in the individual pursuit of the unchanging, be it the medieval Latin Mass by traditionalist Catholics who do not even know Latin, or those attempting to resurrect seasonal rituals like Celtic Samhain, or those who even devote themselves to bygone eras (from the Confederate South to "Merry England"). Some, but surely not all, of these infatuations are positive or harmless. But the point of these activities and beliefs is to soften and retard the bewildering pace of change and to restore the past.[59]

Nostalgia is one such effort. The longing for a simpler past has produced a curious phenomenon. Until recently, nostalgia has often been for past regimes or cultures (such as for the ancien régime in Europe after the French Revolution, for the Russian Empire in post-Soviet Russia, or for the 1950s among some White Americans). Today this has been supplemented, if not surpassed, by a new form of nostalgia characterized by a personal attachment to ephemeral consumer goods from childhood (toys and dolls) or one's coming-of-age (oldie songs and vintage cars). This form of nostalgia is a manifestation of fast capitalism. Such "consumed nostalgia" is an attempt to reverse the psychological stress of consumer acceleration, not through a restoration of deep cultures and societies of the past but by making the personal experience of the ephemeral and commercial "eternal," at least to the collector of the consumer goods of their youth.[60] Another common form of contemporary nostalgia is the modern festival, ranging from county fairs to weekend celebrations of local "heritage." They are usually geared toward perpetuating memory of lost or diminished cultures (e.g., farming and crafts) or of the "glory days" of communities in decline.[61]

Of course, there are many perfectly good and harmless reasons to be attracted to fast goods. Many democratize pleasure, offering sensations that in the past only the rich had. As Robert Proctor wrote in our book, *Packaged Pleasures*, "Of course, people were overjoyed to be able to play Caruso records whenever they wished in 1910, just as they were eager to download and hear the latest techno song on their MP3 players a century later."[62] The convenience of digital shopping is obvious to all. But we cannot forget how fast capitalism has changed us.

This brings me back to how fast goods have transformed our understanding of time and the possibility of alternatives. The central fact is that slow goods offer individual expression and social or worldly engagement in ways that many fast goods do not. And these forms of expression and engagement have long been primary objectives of free time. However, individuality requires lengthy self-cultivation and real community demands extensive interaction—and both of these take time. But fast goods do not require this as much and they often do not result in self-development or community. Fast goods seem to economize on free time, but in their plentitude and habituality they absorb free time, leaving little time for time-consuming opportunities like hobbies, nature walks, or conversation. They short circuit free time and its satisfaction.

At least since the advent of modernity, self-fulfillment and social exchange have defined the quest for free time. Though often denied to the masses and used to create exclusivity, the paucity of these two experiences in free time remains key to what modern people find disappointing about fast capitalism. The "choice" of time efficiency over self-expression and social interaction is not the result of mere personal thoughtlessness or a simple succumbing to materialism and immediate gratification. As we shall see in the next chapter, that "choice" is shaped by modern alternatives to the slow form of self-expression and social interaction. These alternatives were built into fast capitalism. Automobility and the mass media especially created a particular nexus of self and the world that funneled and short-circuited goals of self-expression and social interaction. The next chapter will try to explain this.

8

Funneled Capitalism

THE CHANGING MEANINGS OF SELF AND SOCIETY IN FREE TIME

A century of fast capitalism has transformed what free time means and how we value it. But there is still another factor that explains the pleasures and frustrations of free time. Increasingly, we experience much consumption in a funnel—as relatively isolated individuals encountering a wider, though distant, world. Fast consumer culture displaced slow time, but this funneling process also created substitutes for slow forms of self-expression and social interaction. In this process, two areas of consumer culture were particularly important: automobility and new media, the second of which emerged in the phonograph and movies, radio and TV, and eventually, in digital media. Both transformed the meanings of the personal and social in free time that had been so central to earlier (often genteel) ideals of leisure.

Twentieth-century mass consumption has often offered personal identity and social participation. Commonly this is seen in the form of emulation, especially as consumption has been democratized. With rising incomes, new goods and commercialized experiences expanded a traditional pattern of elite competitive consumption (status seeking) to include a much larger population than the "leisure class" of the Gilded Age of the late nineteenth century.[1] But this process went beyond "keeping up with the Joneses." New goods, be they fashionable clothes or furniture, offered more nuanced ways of both defining the self and joining consuming communities. As suggested in the last chapter, these products provided ways of displaying self and participating in communities without necessarily possessing the skill, ancestry, or resources formerly required to express individuality and join communities. For some, the emotional costs and difficulties of disclosing oneself to others (or even oneself) were overcome through these symbol-laden goods. Consumer goods, be they cosmetics or cars, did the work of creating and displaying the self and shared values. This, of course, explains the insecure teen who is obsessed by consumer trends and fads. But the same principle applies to immigrants, minorities, and, if we are honest, many of the rest of us who do not fit those categories. For many Americans, the car on the road or in the driveway, for example, has long stood for the self while providing membership in a consumers' community of car owners. The Cadillac or the Chevrolet told people something about who you were and who you associated with. Arguably consumerism can also be a substitute for political engagement (both in unjoining and joining groups) and for many other "isms," be they religious or cultural.[2]

In this chapter, I want to take this thinking a step further. In the cases of automobility and mass media, the consumer culture not only provided a means of forming personal and social identity through symbolic consumer goods but also supplied alternative ways of expressing the self and participating in communities. These alternatives were attractive because they were often "fast" (accessible and intense as we have seen), even as they frequently short-circuited slower pathways to happiness.

Efficiency in providing individuality and sociability is perhaps most evident in cars. Automobility liberated the individual from the neighborhood and the street throng. At the same time, automobility offered access to the wider social world without the constraint of timetables or fixed routes of public travel. In addition to "fastness," the car brought the radical possibility of personal choice and an unimpeded range of experience and contacts. The car freed the individual for a wider, often self-selected, world, but in doing so, it sometimes took from Americans some of the individuality and community that they could have in a closer, more intimate world before the car. However, for many, this loss was worth the gain. The substitute form of the personal and social worked for many.

This pattern is even more obvious with new media. Beginning with the phonograph, new media partially replaced time-consuming self-cultivation (like hobbies or book reading) with more immediate personal gratifications (like listening to a three-minute record). The movie substituted many socially interactive activities (local theater) with an abstracted sharing of pleasures (as in a mass, but passive, engagement with movie stars). The new media combined the quest for the personal and social in new ways. Key was the way that people experienced the new media as a process rather than an object. Again, beginning with the phonograph recording, media devices funneled pleasure into private (even isolated) and ephemeral experiences (as in listening to today's hit record) when those pleasures came from the centralized dispersal of a wide range of sensations (as in mass-produced and distributed recordings).

To a degree, this meant the eclipse of older, but also modern, paths to personal fulfillment and social or worldly engagement that required cultivated individuality and real social contact. Modern media offered a substitute with an immediate isolated personal access to the wider (though only virtual) world. This nexus of the individual and the social grew tighter as we moved from the phonograph to the radio and television. The extreme form of this today, of course, is the smartphone. Over time, the private reception of shared goods and experiences became faster (less deliberative and less personally cultivated) and more global (less communal or familial). In the process, both the ideal of the contemplative/refined personal experience (for instance through daydreaming, gardening, and book reading) and the once-commonplace crowd or intimate social experience (the high-school football game or the local book club) passed to the fringes of modern life. Instead, through media, many people learned to experience a succession of identities and virtual communities via the screen or speaker. The result has been much choice and excitement that came with access to a global and diverse culture, but it also meant ephemerality and sometimes real (if not virtual) social isolation. For the American teenager, this was especially notable. As the

American Time Use Survey found, fifteen-to-nineteen-year-olds spent eleven hours less per week in real contact with friends in 2021 than in 2010–2013.[3]

Self-mobility and mass media both affirmed and transformed American culture. The car fulfilled old American dreams of freedom from crowds and access to "great open spaces." Media technology vastly expanded personal choice, long a hallmark of American culture, to nearly everyone. At the same time, these technologies produced a global (although often self-selected) culture built around the isolated individual in the car and in the media-equipped home. Increasingly people traveled alone but encountered worlds beyond their family and neighbors. They were first entertained in crowds at the movies but later listened and watched in the seclusion of home while sharing this experience with millions. A mass, but privatized, culture was the result.

Perhaps surprisingly, this phenomenon was hardly expected by the educated and well informed at the beginning of this process in the early twentieth century. As noted in chapter 5, intellectuals worried about popular exposure to the pleasures and excitement of the street or the wider world, anxious that this access would make people succumb to consumerist temptation or would undermine the remains of genteel culture. Elites hoped that the home would provide an antidote to the consuming crowd. They dreamed that family life in the home but also in the car would protect the masses from the consumerist allure of the street and perhaps even create a universal culture of uplift. The home, family life, and especially the "innocent" child would preserve tradition, constrain excess, and promote cultivation against the ephemerality, ecstasy, and immediacy of the consuming crowd. As it turned out, these elites had nothing to worry about, but neither were their hopes realized. Instead of succumbing to the hysteria of the crowd, Americans got privacy (even if in traffic in the car) and individuality (even if "choice" was provided by corporate media). And they still got the "street" (if at the mall and, increasingly, in the confines of their home through media). The private turned out not to be an escape from the world. The personal and global came together, but not as self-cultivation and social or worldly engagement but something entirely different—as a commercialized private-public nexus. And this linkage offered a problematic alternative to other forms of self-realization and social meaning.

These automotive and media cultures cannot be reduced to the image of the passive consumer controlled by the manipulative merchandiser, as presented by many culture critics, be they conservative or progressive. Neither did automobility and media-saturated consumption produce primarily self-creating consumers, who transformed their daily lives and commercial popular culture into self-chosen identities and communities, as claimed by some cultural studies scholars and corporate apologists. This new culture offered choice and participation, but in ways that often short-circuited goals of self-fulfillment and engagement with others and with the physical world.

This private-public nexus is an ultimate achievement of fast capitalism. This linkage has largely eliminated the slowness of past culture. It has replaced the time-consuming cultivation of the self with serial selves, constructed or reflected in the flickering stream of global media. That private-public nexus has also substituted often difficult interactions with others with the sociality of virtual communities of consumption. Little time and motivation remain for self-fulfillment or face-to-face community. The car and the new mass media brought new forms of individual and social expression that shaped modern free time while biasing Americans toward fast goods and fast consumption over slow free time. Let us expand on these generalities.

Automobility: The Vehicular Self in Search of Open Spaces

Henry Ford famously summed up the revolutionary implications of the car for the twentieth century with a pledge: "I will build a car for the great multitude. It will be large enough for the family, but small enough for the individual to run and care for. . . . It [should be] so low in price that no man making a good salary [would] be unable to own one—and enjoy with his family the blessings of hours of pleasure in God's great open spaces."[4] For Ford, the car should be just large enough to contain a single family (neither sufficient for the crowd, like a train, nor adequate only for the individual, like the horse) and yet small enough for the male owner to maintain. It was an ideal personal machine in an age of impersonal machines and bureaucratic work, maximizing the self while the factory machine or office work minimized it. This individualism was no longer just for the rich in their motorized carriages but for the "great multitude." Yet, the car was not for the poor making a poor wage; rather, the car was for the man "making a good salary," entitled to escape the throng with his family. In fact, "success" could have been defined by the ability to break from the crowd, a gift of the male provider. Ford expected few women to buy his car. It was for the vast but individualistic middle class. At the same time, the car was a private access to the wider world, a flight from the confines of neighborhood, crowd, and city to the "great open spaces." It was a call to go out to the world, but to a place where there was no throng (and no limits like those imposed by train schedules and cramped seating with strangers). The car was a welcome emancipation from bodily contact with strangers on the street. This combination of individualism and qualified worldliness was also an abandonment of intermediaries like the people met at neighborhood get-togethers and the owner of the local shop with personal service. The car freed the individual from the oppressiveness of propinquity (the constant observance, judgment, and interaction with neighbors and nearby family, for example). It also enabled the individual to create a wide network of friends and associates. Automobility magnified both American individualism and a quest for expanded horizons, at least from the anonymous vantage of the vehicular shell.[5] Despite the dangers of driving and frustrations of traffic, early twentieth-century Americans quickly sacrificed time (at work) and money to possess the car. It became a quintessential funneling device that took the isolated individual to the wider world. In the Depression, Americans held on to their cars even when they could not afford other things.[6]

Individualism was the most obvious appeal insofar as the automobile meant self-sufficiency. A peculiar form of that self-reliance was the pride the multitude took in customizing and upgrading their vehicles, adding luggage carriers, lights, and other accessories, when factories had not yet installed these features. Cars became "personal technologies," as were other appliances introduced early in the twentieth century (phonographs and radios, especially) that were improved through consumers' tinkering. Early car owners often expected to learn the workings of their vehicles and took pride in repairing them (as they frequently required). Gradually, as accessories like trunk storage and heaters became standard, middle-class car owners abandoned tinkering. This practice was passed on to the young from the late 1920s; however, tinkering turned to modifying old basic cars like the Model T for speed rather than convenience or beauty. Because of the relative simplicity and low cost of the Model T, young men and teens could replace iron engine pistons with lightweight aluminum ones on used Model Ts. When "unnecessary weight" like the roof and even seats were removed, a Model T could reach 70 mph or more instead of the 40–45 mph of the original. These hot rods in their various forms were the perfect expression of the radical individualism of working-class (mostly White) male youth from the 1930s through the 1980s. Hot rods gave them independence from their families and dignity in a world where they often were humiliated, such as in high schools designed for the upwardly mobile middle class or at work where they were subordinated and paid little.[7]

More broadly, as historian Cotten Seiler observes, the car seemed to promise the twentieth-century male a chance to regain the "authoritative, robust, creative, and mobile traits" that presumably he had before industrialization. The early car offered a particularly male form of individualism. In driving and customizing, men gained power and competence over the automotive machine that contrasted with the machines of the factory and office owned and controlled by the boss. The young viewed such power and competence as the supreme marker of adulthood, even citizenship. The driver's license indicated that its holder had the independence and skill to drive. But that person presumably also had knowledge of the rules of the road, the perfect combination of liberty and constraint signifying membership in a "republic." As Susan Seo notes, "The automobile came to represent individual solitude and freedom." In fact, "more than any other technology, the automobile had enlarged perceptions of the self." However, auto driving rapidly on narrow corridors with frequent cross-traffic exchanges required many laws and often strict policing that ordinary law-abiding citizens had not previously encountered. The right to a driver's license implied full awareness of these contradictory dynamics of individual freedom and social responsibility. This status naturally was sought by women who had just been granted the franchise in 1920 and by youth who eagerly applied for driver's licenses at the earliest possible age (often sixteen, which, until 1971, was five years before they could vote). Automobility became a marker of personal participation in civil society.[8]

By its very name, the automobile denoted the mobile self, but its ability to move in any direction at any time and at speeds far greater than by foot or horse fostered even more individualism: it encouraged the diffusion of an already dispersed American population (noted for its isolated farmhouses rather than nucleated villages) simply because car travel did not require bus stops or train stations that necessitated "close-in" housing on small lots. Cars did not cause suburbs. Railroad suburbanization long predated the auto. But autos further dispersed housing, as suburbanites were linked to cities and each other with a web of arterial streets and, from the 1950s, with ribbons of freeways to downtown and other worksites and shopping centers.[9]

This residential dispersal led to new ideals of domestic space by 1920. The car culture caused the disappearance (at least for a time) of the Victorian-era home with its large and deep front porch, from which people could greet neighbors on sidewalks out on evening strolls. The porch was gradually replaced by the attached garage. Space-wasting, one-story ranch houses, made possible by cheaper housing lots in the suburbs, replaced two-story homes through the 1960s. Despite reports of a new neighborliness in popular sociology of the 1950s (by writers like William Whyte especially), the suburbs compounded the individualism fostered by automobility. Residential neighborhoods became a "mass of small, private islands," notes historian Kenneth Jackson, as encounters with neighbors declined.[10] And suburbanites related to their neighbors through displays of landscaping and home improvements, thus "keeping up with the Joneses" with exhibits of individual skill and ingenuity. The retreat to car and home often reduced neighborly social contacts as propinquity was replaced by more extensive social networks requiring automobility.

Also because of the spatial inefficiency of cars (taking up more space per traveler than required with trains and buses), parking costs due to high-priced land in downtown business districts forced major retailers like department stores to construct large outlets in suburban roadside tracts with free and easy-access parking lots. Kansas City's Country Club Plaza, built in 1923, was probably the first shopping center of the auto age. After 1960, the shopping mall finally began to replace downtown shopping districts, further liberating Americans from the concentrated crowd of downtowns and public transportation hubs. The crowd that had so worried early twentieth-century intellectuals largely disappeared with the car and the mall. The drive-in restaurant (from 1921) and drive-in movie (from 1933) as well as drive-through banking (first in 1949, though common only from the 1970s) added to this transformation. All were part of a new culture of personal mobility and convenience that reduced physical contact with others (while often speeding up consumer transactions). Is it any surprise that today we have embraced a totally desocialized form of shopping in the internet purchase?[11]

A final example of this phenomenon needs to be mentioned: the shift from the family car (that Henry Ford touted) to vehicles for individual drivers in multiple-car households. Until 1960, only about 22 percent of American households possessed more than one car; most had to make do with a family vehicle that had to be shared by the whole household. The family car was a point of pride for many breadwinners who showed their importance by keeping the family up to date with a frequent car change, purchased every three years or less. Cars throughout the early post–World War II years were mostly sold as vehicles of family togetherness and status.

Beginning in the mid-1960s, however, as boomers were reaching driving age and women increasingly worked outside the home, a new way of selling novelty emerged. Car companies offered personalized alternatives to the family sedan and station wagon. Leading the way in 1964 was the Mustang, designed for young singles with its many individualized features and models. Other vehicles were advertised to appeal to women (like the Corvair). Added to this in the 1970s were small personal luxury cars like the BMW for young professionals who rejected the traditional expectation of waiting for luxury (as in GM's oversized Cadillac) until they had "arrived," usually with a family. All this contributed to multicar households, which rose to 28 percent by 1970, climbed to 52 percent by 1980, and stabilized at 58 percent in 2017. Cars became objects of individual, rather than primarily family, use and expression. This included cars for work, for family activities (e.g., the minivan), and for male play and fantasy (such as in the curious sight of pickup trucks, originally designed for farm use, in the driveways of suburban houses). There were 816 cars for every 1,000 Americans in 2019. In Britain the number was 472 (2018), and in China, it was 207 (2021). Other formerly shared goods also became individualized (radios, TVs, and later computers and phones). Everyone seemed to get their own toy box.[12]

This quick summary is sufficient to make the point that the car was not only the quintessential commodity of "fastness" but of social fragmentation and individualism. Yet it also promised open spaces. It is not surprising that millions of Americans embraced this idea soon after the Model T became available. Although mass tourism certainly came with the train (as early as the 1840s in England), the car eliminated the crowded tubes of railcars and throngs congregating at terminal hotels that railroad touring required. Instead, the car allowed for far more individualized travel, but still across a wide range of destinations and routes.

Inevitably, by the 1920s, the auto gave rise to the motel, with its private entrance a short distance from the parked car. The car brought open spaces to city dwellers in autumn day trips to picturesque New England towns, summer vacations to Western National Parks, and winter treks to the Florida seashore.

The auto delivered the world in ways that people never had known—combining the personal and the global. That these expanded vistas were experienced privately was part of the appeal of the car. Such tourism was a prelude to the ultimate enhancement of the self—the freedom of the "open road"—and to liberation from the constraints of family, neighborhood, and, of course, the crowds so often romantically remembered and portrayed in writing and on the screen.[13] The appeal of the open road brought together the quest for longed-for individuality and social engagement in a new way. The question that arises here is whether all this widened, but highly personalized, experience was an enhancement of or even a substitute for other forms of self-expression and social involvement.

Transforming the Self and the Social: The Phonograph, 1900–1940

While the auto took the isolated individual out into the wider world, modern media ultimately offered the self the entire world without even having to move. Even more than the car, modern media was a "funneled" experience. Again, it begins with the phonograph in the home. This simple device quickly and efficiently brought not just the fast audio recording to the masses but a global speed culture to the privacy of the home. In one sense, the phonograph was merely one of many new domestic appliances offered to households after 1850. These included the cast iron stove, the piano, and the sewing machine, or, with home access to electricity at the end of the nineteenth century, devices like electric fans, vacuum cleaners, and, of course, lighting, all of which impacted domestic life.[14]

However, unlike most of these appliances, the phonograph offered more than easing housework or domestic comfort: it privatized much entertainment, shifting it from public places. The phonograph also created access to a larger geographic (and eventually global) culture of reproduced voice and music. Added to the bargain, it introduced continuous innovation in sharp contrast to the relative constancy of these other consumer durables. In effect, the commercial recording of sound fused the public and private, offering fast-changing celebrity entertainment in the private parlor or living room, which families often filled with "timeless" furnishings. This intrusion of global fast capitalism on the personal space of the home was revolutionary for Victorians, who had linked the home with cultural stability—a shelter from the bustle of work, the market, and the wider world. The slow culture of reading about the world or playing (or singing) from commercial sheet music was one thing, but the instantaneous sensation of a bundle of global musical "hits" was another.[15]

Nothing like this was expected when Edison invented the phonograph. Edison thought that the phonograph would serve as a business machine for dictating letters, for example. For him, recording sound was as important as playback, presumably allowing individuals to capture the voice of the famous or even just a family member. The phonograph, however, became an entertainment device in 1889 when coin-operated record players, equipped with individual hearing tubes, were placed in commercial public settings for a quick private listen. Modeled after mechanical coin-operated music machines, these coin-operated phonographs soon became a rage in saloons and arcades, often placed adjacent to train stations for a working-class audience eager to hear the latest popular tune in transit to work or home. This novelty gradually declined and disappeared by 1908, partially due to lack of amplification (solved by the 1930s with the revival of the jukebox in cafés and bars). Far more successful was the phonograph for home use. By the mid-1890s, it was becoming a domestic appliance for the middle class. The personal hearing tube was replaced with a horn projecting recorded sound to a family living room—a new form of privatization.[16]

This was an example of a shift to an emerging market for domestic durables and the private ownership of machines that formerly had been placed in commercial businesses for public consumption. Other examples at this time were Gillette's safety razor, which supplanted barbershop shaves, Kodak's snapshot camera, which opened up amateur photography as an alternative to photograph studios, and eventually home-based washing machines, which replaced many commercial laundries. The middle person was eliminated (professional barber, photographer, and launderer), and the individual consumer was newly linked to a small number of corporate manufacturers and distributors (to Kodak's film developing service, for example). The phonograph became one of many commodities linking corporate production and privatized consumption, a connection that challenged and ultimately eliminated much of the commercial and social life of small shops. Amazon shopping is a culmination of this trend. This dyad of the corporate and the personal hollowed out much of the social and customary life in between.

The domestic phonograph not only privatized the arcade talking machine, making it respectable to a property-obsessed, home-owning middle class, but, like the car, it eliminated social interaction, freeing the listener from the crowd at the live performance. While a small number of companies (principally Edison, Victor, and Columbia in the early twentieth century) provided these recordings, these centralized sources offered much more choice than did the local music venue. These recordings also offered celebrity voices and musical ensembles that now could be heard anywhere without going to the New York Metropolitan Opera or Milan's La Scala. Though heard privately, recorded celebrities became even more famous when their voices were consumed across the nation and even ocean. The intimacy of the listening experience encouraged the audience to identify with celebrity personalities like Enrico Caruso (as they would with mass-culture movie stars a few years later).[17] The commercial recording of sound created a new kind of fusion of individuality (privacy, choice, identity) with the global.

Consumers were satisfied with a phonograph that no longer offered personal recording (it was of poor quality anyway) but only passive music playback. By 1900, instead of recording the voice of a beloved family member, the phonograph reproduced the voice or music of an admired celebrity with whom one had a virtual rather than real relationship. The apparent preference for the global luminary over the local and personal was defining. It was a significant change on the path to impersonal Facebook "friends." Phonograph records became less a way to preserve memory of one's personal relationships than a means to personally keep up with a community of novelty makers. Records offered an alternative to the slow culture of self and society. In the familiar and private setting of the home, the phonograph was about participating in shared "hits" of sound with a consumption community, free of contact with a physical group nearby.[18] The phonograph maximized the personal and the social, offering both choice and the virtual world, but often minimizing self-expression and social engagement.

Of course, the radical implications of the phonograph were hidden to late Victorian consumers. They wanted the home to remain a refuge from the world, not the narrow end of a funnel to a global culture and business. But, as noted in chapter 7, Victor made the talking machine acceptable in the 1906 bourgeois parlor in the form of the Victrola. This phonograph was a machine but looked decidedly nonindustrial, blending in with family heirlooms, when the company hid its mechanical workings under finely finished wooden cabinetry (as did many models of sewing machine of the era). The bourgeois consumer could have the world of the new and famous in the privacy of the timeless home (presumably full of heirlooms), even when that recorded world was radically novel. The contradiction bothered few.

The phonograph was also sold as the very fulfillment of domestic stability and privacy in that it was an alternative to the "dangerous" street "out there." No need to go to the nightclub or crowded bar or even risk venturing out to a vaudeville theater if one had a Victrola. Edison's ads for its phonographs repeatedly made this appeal: "Make home [with the Edison phonograph] a competitor of downtown, the club, the café, the theatre and the concert hall" (about 1900). The record player was supposed to provide an escape from the crowd as well as bring the family together to listen to recordings that would appeal to all its members. Yet the logic of the phonograph was not to build family togetherness but to foster radical individualism. By 1913, Victor began to understand this when it offered portable phonographs, often at low prices, to young people to accompany them while vacationing away from family. The phonograph encouraged individual listening and personal choice across a universe of recordings. It inevitably broke up family listening and fostered generational differences as the young found their own listening pleasure. This, of course, culminated in the 1950s with teen rock music, which parents hated.[19]

With the phonograph, the home became more than an escape from the job, market, and public strife. It became the narrow point of a funnel drawing in a global celebrity culture for personal consumption. This V-shaped linkage of the global to the personal became far more evident as this nexus was extended to radio, television, cable entertainment, and the internet. First, however, a visual element had to be added to the aural, and, of course, this came with the movies.

The Personal-Global Nexus Expands with Movies and Radio

Motion pictures paralleled phonographs, both appearing around the same time, but with far different trajectories. Both began in the form of an individualized but public machine. Edison's kinetoscope of 1893, a short peep show, could be used by customers for a coin in arcades like those that featured the coin-operated phonograph. But the kinetoscope's success was even shorter than Edison's arcade phonograph. By 1896, in contrast to the phonograph, the motion picture became a crowd rather than private experience when film was projected on a screen (following the model of the magic lantern of projected slides). Though movies were first silent on the screen, the audience sometimes was not. Still, crowd interaction was limited. Though viewers were not alone, for the individual in the crowd the experience was often solitary. The movies became even more isolating with the introduction of sound movies in 1927. This naturally silenced the audience when the screen began to speak. But again, as with the phonograph, from the beginning what was experienced at the movies was "global," with the moving pictures portraying life far beyond the individual viewer's community.[20]

Still, the global reach of the movies was limited: at first, audiences were socially homogeneous, mostly working class and young. Movie content naturally reflected the interests of this crowd. Until about 1908, movies were short shows of news, acrobatics and other vaudeville acts, and visual thrills (chases, teasing sexuality, special effects, even horror with little or no story line). Moreover, after 1905, movies were mostly shown at nickelodeons located in the back of cigar stores or abandoned shops, sites of working-class entertainment (certainly in the public imagination).[21] Neither the audience nor the programs reached beyond a narrow "world."

When Edison attempted in 1909 to create a patent pool monopoly, the Motion Picture Patent Company (MPPC), he presumed that this situation would continue indefinitely.[22] However, by 1916, a group of independent moviemakers and distributors had successfully challenged the MPPC. They did so, in part, by creating new viewing spaces and new content that extended the audience and programming. Important to their success was expanding the movie audience beyond the working class to include the middle class, creating a mass audience. These independent show business entrepreneurs did this by building "movie palaces" that offered comfort and middle-class respectability, challenging the down-market nickelodeons. They also expanded movie content to include feature-length narratives, appealing to a wider audience. This set the stage for a multiclass or mass audience for a wide-ranging movie experience. In time, a handful of major film studios located in Hollywood dominated the film industry, including Fox (1912) and Adolph Zukor's Paramount (1913) and later Warner Brothers (1923), MGM (1924), and RKO (1928), along with several smaller studios (Columbia, Universal, Republic, and United Artists). Benefitting from economies of scale as well as targeting a wide-ranging audience, these studios outcompeted the European film industry with its fragmented markets. By 1918, the US produced 85 percent of the films shown worldwide and the US film industry earned a third of its income abroad. The present-day global dominance of American popular culture began with the early motion pictures.[23]

Thus, over the course of all these changes, the movie industry connected the individual viewer with a global culture, creating a media funnel of images (and eventually audio) that extended beyond that of the phonograph's sound. The movies did this not simply by expanding the "world" of the viewer but by linking the viewer with the world-famous star. From 1910, leading players in movies were identified in publicity and the opening credits. This led audiences to identify with their favorites. The "star system" of course had precedents—for example, on the stage and in the variety show. Movie stars, however, were seen simultaneously across the country by countless viewers, and stars were projected on a screen literally bigger than life. This created a curious viewer response: the movie star appeared to be both intimate and approachable in close-ups, but also, like celestial stars, above the ordinary and earthy. Moviegoers swooned over and idolized the personalities of actors, following their glamorous lives off the screen in fan magazines, such as *Photoplay*, appearing as early as 1911. Yet, movie fans often believed stars were their personal friends. This was a powerful combination in linking the individual viewer to a global corporate entertainment business.[24]

The movies created new communities of consumption. Unlike traditional pleasure crowds (gathered at village festivals, for example), these communities were widely dispersed with limited or no social interaction. Viewing "communities" at local cinemas were linked by national entertainment companies that distributed regularly changing features to national chains of movie theaters. Within weeks, audiences, especially in cities, saw *Gone with the Wind* in 1939. This pattern was anticipated in 1890 by the French sociologist Jean-Gabriel Tarde, who observed that the spectacle was being transformed from the seasonal, local, and unchanging event (as in the festival or fair) to a nearly daily, perpetually changing entertainment, experienced and shared by viewers across the nation and even the globe.[25] The key to this shared experience was that it was seldom interactive but instead was a mass experience, individually encountered.

The radio was still another vehicle for introducing twentieth-century people to the individual-universal nexus. It was the beginning of an emerging electronic funnel. Like the phonograph, the radio offered a shared experience, consumed domestically and in private. And like the record player, the radio, too, did not begin as an entertainment receiver. Rather, it was invented in 1897 as an interpersonal communication device, a wireless telegraph. Though in the next few years inventions made possible the transmission and reception of voice, the expectation remained that the radio was to be a point-to-point communication device (in this case a wireless telephone). However, the logic of "funneled capitalism" soon prevailed. By 1916, David Sarnoff, future chief of NBC, understood that the radio receiver could also be an alternative to the home phonograph, replacing the record with sound that was electromagnetically radiated into homes from a chain of transmitters at radio stations. This system was centralized nationally in 1926 with the National Broadcasting Network (NBC), which linked local transmitters across the country through long-distance telephone lines. Soon there was an oligopoly of three broadcast networks, dependent on advertising revenue from merchandisers of mostly national name-brand goods. For listeners, the funnel of diverse entertainment from the network to the home was a dramatic advance over the phonograph and record. It required no more effort than a turn of the radio dial.[26] The radio was a perfect vehicle for promoting fast capitalism and the individual-universal nexus. All that was missing was the visual.

The central transmission of sound to private listeners of network radio created a national popular culture, dispersing not only music but narrative. As early as 1928, the first situation comedy was heard on radio. Other genres (adventure, variety talk, and children's shows) quickly followed. Programming was familiar in format, even with ever new content, much of it coming from stage, screen, or even magazines. As Douglas Gomery notes, "A problem starts the narrative, closure ends it. Opposing forces clash and are resolved in a unified ending. The skill came with integrating the advertising." Radio offered listeners the "world," but one that promised not to challenge the middle-class audience desired by advertisers. By 1938, 40 percent of American households on a typical winter evening were listening to the radio. Since evening schedules mixed programs designed for different ages and sexes, they encouraged families to listen together. The radio was the new family hearth and often looked like one with its lit vacuum tubes.[27]

Even so, like the phonograph, the radio also promoted individual listening with time-specific programming for stay-at-home women during the day and children after school. With the Depression of the 1930s, the still often social trip to the movie theater, with its admission price, was already taking a backseat to the domestic and "free" radio programming (if incessant advertising was ignored). The radio was not only cheaper and more convenient than the movies; it did not require leaving the home to travel to a sometimes dangerous or crowded part of town or sitting next to strangers. Again, like the appeal of the auto, radio offered crowd-adverse Americans a private way of participating in the wider world. Moreover, radio listeners could turn the radio on or off and change the volume or station at will. They could even listen while working, in bed, or in their underwear. After the war and with improvements in FM broadcasting, radio became more diverse and audiences even more segmented across stations devoted to talk, rock, religion, and even high culture (with public broadcasting).[28] The major reason for the change in the role of radio was a new competitor, television, which "videoized" the radio of the 1930s and 1940s, beginning a new era of media funneling.

Television and Other Electronic Funnels

Television was a visual extension of radio, further consolidating the link between the domestic and the global. TV was developed largely by the same companies as radio (NBC especially, of which ABC was a spinoff, but also CBS and AT&T). Commercial broadcasting from New York began in 1941 even though World War II delayed mass purchase of the "box" until after 1945. But then its mass adoption was phenomenally fast: In 1949, only 2 percent of American homes had TVs; five years later, the figure was 59.4 percent. By 1967, it was 95 percent. As early as 1955, households consumed an average of 3 ½ hours of TV per day, stabilizing at 6 ½ hours in 1976. Like the radio, commercial TV, dominated by NBC, CBS, and ABC, delivered families to national advertisers. Since the advent of the phonograph and radio, Americans had become acclimatized to being linked via personal media to the centralized media provider, making TV a welcomed addition to the electronic hearth. By 1957, Americans saw 420 advertisements per week, totaling five hours and eight minutes. From 1960, TV shows were mostly on film (rather than live from New York as they were at first), often produced in the old movie studios. The networks offered a predictable menu of sitcoms, variety, crime, and westerns. With the shift from live dramas and comedies to film came a surge in action scenes, especially in westerns (reaching twenty-eight serials per week in prime-time evening watching by 1959). Many of these early shows started on radio. But in the early 1950s, adults who had been brought up on radio abandoned it at home as a family entertainment center.[29] As a result, radio gradually dropped its serials, becoming a personal media device, even an electronic jukebox, repeatedly playing a small set of popular songs, heard while working and driving and especially by the young seeking an escape from "family TV."[30]

Television was supposed to be for all members of the family to share. To be sure, early television recognized age and gender difference. Like radio before it, early TV programming was segmented by time of day:

housewife TV in the mornings and early afternoons; kids' shows after school and on Saturday morning, and male-dominated programming during prime-time evenings and weekend afternoons. But in the 1950s households still had only one TV, which had to be shared (even if dad often controlled the channel knob and later the remote). Family togetherness was promised with network self-censorship and programming. Variety shows like Ed Sullivan on Sunday night offered something for everybody. To be sure, teen and adult nonfamily entertainment could be found at the movies—especially from 1968 with the introduction of the rating system that opened up movies to the "adult" entertainment of sex, graphic violence, and horror. But TV remained a refuge of the family and its programing remained global only in the sense of a wide range of family-friendly fare.[31]

As Joshua Meyrowitz notes in his *No Sense of Place* (1985), radio and television had the effect of merging social groups once separated by "information boundaries," such as in face-to-face or book communication that preserved status barriers. The new media, however, blurred sex, age, and other roles as well as undercut behavioral expectations, explaining in part the decline of distinctions between highbrow and lowbrow, adult and child programming. By bringing a diverse world into the home, TV created—in Marshall McLuhan's words in his famous *Understanding Media* of 1964—an electronic "global village."[32] This, of course, presumed a shared TV-viewing experience (as in broadcast TV in a family living room).

But by the mid-1960s, the privatizing logic of the personal-general nexus was already beginning to challenge television, both as a family "hearth" and a "global village," with the introduction of multiple TVs per household. Small-screen portable Sony TVs were designed and sold for use by homemakers in the kitchen. The family no longer had to share. "Togetherness" and the tensions that it often engendered could be replaced with personal choice.[33]

The proliferation of television channels from the 1980s, combined with the growth of the multiple-set household, radically extended the possibilities of personalized viewing of "global" programming. The global village became many global villages, radically changing the meaning of the global in media. Not only was the small end of the electronic funnel increasingly narrowed to the individual, but the wide end was becoming a self-chosen "world."

This occurred, of course, with nationally distributed cable TV, growing from 5 percent of households in 1980 to 61 percent by 1991, reaching 95 percent of households by 2000. Beginning with Home Box Office's national service in 1972, cable challenged broadcast TV, not just with an improved signal but with many channels. Between 1976 and 1994 many of the now familiar cable networks appeared. The launching of the Fox network in 1986 added to the cable landscape. Early advocates of cable suggested that a variety of channels would create opportunities for refined and specialized shows for audiences neglected by the broad middle-class programming of broadcast TV. These expectations faded in the 1990s as cable channels like The Learning Channel and Arts and Entertainment fell under pressure to sell ad time that would reach beyond a "refined" niche audience. Cable consolidated into control by a handful of companies (of course, dominated by old media conglomerates). By 2022, there was Disney-ABC; Comcast, owner of NBC-Universal; Fox; AT&T, owner of WarnerMedia; and Paramount Global, owner of Viacom-CBS, further limiting real diversity.[34] But channels, segmented by age, gender, and media preference, certainly prevailed, adding still more individualization to media without challenging the centralized source.

Another avenue for individualized media was personal video devices and software. The video cassette recorder (VCR) first appeared in 1975 with Sony's Betamax, followed by the VHS player in 1977. These machines allowed for tape-recording TV shows, freeing the consumer from the fixed schedule of cable or network programs. Even more, they led to commercial home videotape recordings. By 1990, rental and sales of VCR cassettes were undercutting network broadcasting, further fragmenting viewership (not to mention weakening the old social ritual of "going to the movies"). These technologies seemed to threaten the personal consumer–global corporate nexus, so firmly established by network and cable TV. They even suggested a revival of private accumulations of media, as in the old habit of individualized collections of phonograph recordings.

But these technologies were short-lived. VCRs declined in the 1990s after the arrival of the DVD in 1997. More important, physical recordings were replaced by another form of technology—the internet. This technology offered (as did the radio in comparison to the phonograph) much greater ease of personal access to an even wider range of globalized "information." The corporate connection (at least for a time) became more subtle: internet browsers mediated between producers and consumers of information, offering corporations access to buyers but also new opportunities for interpersonal communication—social media and email, especially. In any case, the internet radically extended the individual-global nexus, even revolutionizing TV broadcasting and cable with online streaming from 2005.[35] In fact, the internet was the end product of a rapidly changing series of media innovations that shaped consumer expectations of the electronic funnel.

This process began with two interrelated technologies: solid-state electronics and digital technology. The transistor, the solid-state replacement for the fragile and relatively large electronic vacuum tube, made possible smaller, potentially portable electronics. Unlike tubes, transistors required very little power, generated little heat, rarely burned out, and, most importantly, often could be run on batteries for mobile devices. In 1947–1948, Bell Lab engineers invented the transistor, and in 1954 Sony and later other manufacturers purchased licenses to develop new consumer products based on the transistor. This led to a wide range of small and often portable devices that culminated thirty-six years later in the smartphone. In 1957, the transistor radio appeared, key to the independence of youth from their parent's home-bound TVs and radios receivers. In 1963, Phillips introduced the audio cassette player/recorder. This analog device did what no record player could do—provide music on demand in the car or in the pocket. Personal access was extended with mobility. In contrast to the phonograph with its cumbersome vinyl record, stylus, tone arm, and turntable, the self-contained cassette tape could be easily slipped into its player and operated with the push of a button. This made the cassette player easily adaptable to cars in the 1970s, supplementing or even replacing the car radio. Sony's battery-operated Walkman cassette player (introduced in 1979) allowed both private listening via earphones and complete portability. Its portability and easy-to-choose audio cassette tapes made the "world" more accessible and the experience more personal and private than was offered by the fixed programs on the radio or the phonograph, which could not be carried while operating.[36]

Like the old phonograph record, the cassette was still an analog device. The compact disc (CD) of 1983 introduced the digital format, replaying sound off an easily stored plastic disc. By 1988, CDs were outselling cassettes. In 1991, stores abandoned the sale of both vinyl records and cassettes. With the CD, the sound wave was no longer copied analogically but recorded in "samples" of that wave in digital signals, recorded thousands of times per second. Even more, the CD extended once again the duration of play, allowing eighty minutes of music, the equivalent of both sides of the LP without the bother of having to turn it over. Convenience again triumphed. In a world of accelerated fast capitalism, however, the digital CD victory was also short-lived, as sales stalled as early as 1996. The new competition, of course, was the internet and the personal digital computer, together the consummation of the electronic funnel.[37] It is to this technology that we must now turn.

The Culmination: From PCs to Smartphones

Step by step and in fact quite rapidly, digital innovations changed our lives, often by refining the electronic funnel. The first digital computers of 1946 were large, bulky, and powered by vacuum tubes, requiring miles of wire and suitable only for government (military) and corporate business use. The key to the computer's development and adaptation for consumers was its simultaneous miniaturization and enhanced power (memory, storage, speed of processing, etc.). Here solid-state and digital technologies came together as groups of components were miniaturized in the integrated circuit board in 1958 and still more in the microprocessor chip in 1971. This led to the personal computers (PCs) of Apple in 1977 and of IBM in 1981. The PC went through amazing changes in the 1980s. Storage and data access were vastly improved with hard drives in 1980, data disks in 1983, and CD-ROMs in 1984. Ease of use was revolutionized with graphic interface software like Windows in 1983, along with great improvements in microprocessor and RAM chips. By the end of the 1980s, computer games, encyclopedias, and music were easily accessible and storable, doing what records and cassettes could never do. Until then, however, PCs still depended on what could be stored on hard drives or on digital discs.[38]

Once again, as with the record and cassette that preceded it, the critical storage function of the recording (in this case the hard drive, CD, or DVD) gave way to another "wireless" transmission system—the internet. While the internet began as a system for linking data across computers via telephone lines and modems for the military, by 1983 it was used by universities. The breakthrough for personal use on the World Wide Web came in 1992 with a text-based web browser, but it was quickly supplanted by the graphic web browser in 1994. Thereafter it took only a point and click of the mouse to gain access to the World Wide Web. Again, at first this required a telephone line, but, in 1997, Wi-Fi was introduced.[39] Change in the 1990s was as dizzying as it was in the 1980s.

In the mid- to late 1990s, personal access to the "world" had radically changed. Information and entertainment that once had required physical recordings (be they vinyl phonograph records, cassette tapes, VCRs, CDs, CD-ROMS, DVDs, or hard drives) or wired connections (via phones and modems or even just wired electricity) were available with a wireless router and internet connection. The battery-powered laptop (1988) and tablet (1993) even eliminated the constant need for a power cord and made the tabletop PC seem like a needless inconvenience. This set the stage for personal and immediate access to a world of sensation—from centrally produced movies and music to social media linkages to virtual "friends."

Only one technology was missing in the final (so far) phase of this integration of self and world via modern electronic media: the smartphone. With it, the digital world became available on the go without even the need for a stationary Wi-Fi router. This handheld personal device was the culmination of it all: speakers, screen, and touch access to the "world." We just need a few lines more to complete this story.

While the idea of a wireless phone dates to the earliest days of the radio, it became practical only in the early 1980s, when solid-state electronics reduced the size and power needs of portable phones and cell towers emerged for linking phones over distances. Moreover, from the late 1990s a wide range of single-purpose personal devices came to the market (e.g., MP3 players, digital cameras, personal digital assistants or PDAs, and GPS navigators). Most notable was the iPod of Apple, which quickly dominated the market for downloaded music. After the digitalization of the cell phone, beginning in 1992, all these functions, including the internet, were combined with a mobile phone into the smartphone. That breakthrough came in 2007 with Apple's iPhone. Within a year, Apple faced a competitor in the Android system of Google.[40]

This blizzard of digital innovation since 1981 radically transformed the electronic funnel, making the innovations of the first eighty years of the twentieth century pale in comparison. Most importantly, the incessant waves of innovation, one after the other, acclimatized us to the further refinement of the electronic funnel. Free time had changed fundamentally.

With the smartphone, the full potential of the electronic funnel seems to have been realized: miniaturizing and mobilizing constant personal access to global information on an apparently unlimited scale and with little limit on access and storage. Gone are the constraints of recordings, wired linkages, and cumbersome fixed points of access. The smart watch is only a variation. There may well be more changes ahead, including other forms of individualized and mobile access to global media as well as devices to extend funneled experience beyond sight and sound. These innovations may or may not gain favor. Still, this technology, as it exists in the third decade of the twenty-first century, has revolutionized daily life, taking the electronic funnel to its near logical conclusion. What is the most curious to me is just how readily and quickly people have adapted to it.

I suspect a cause of this often unquestioned embrace of the smartphone is the gradual introduction of its characteristics across time, not just since the first PCs in 1981 but dating back to the introduction of TV, radio, and ultimately the phonograph. The smartphone is the logical culmination of the principle first introduced with the phonograph: the unmediated linkage of the individual to the global. And impediments to that linkage have been eliminated in a long series of innovations from the radio to the smartphone. What has been constant is that this modern phenomenon has met a contradictory need for personal liberation from the actual world while experiencing that world "virtually."

Ultimately, this process has created a substitute for a longing that long predates the twentieth century—a need to cultivate self and to interact socially in free time. With the electronic funnel, that longing, however, has become free of the "slowness" of traditional (and sometimes modern) aspirations. This began with the globalized sound of the phonograph but was radically extended with its successors by adding video (movie and TV); enhancing access to the global wirelessly (radio, TV, and the internet); increasing the personal and mobile (cassettes, CD devices, and computer tablets); overcoming the limits of the capsulized experience of the recording with continuous flows of sensuality (radio, TV, and the internet); and, ultimately, by bringing together the private and the global in all of their convenience with the smartphone.

We have largely embraced electronic funneling in our work and even more significantly in our play or free time without much reflection or resistance. Maybe we need to think a little more about it (without moral panic or undue nostalgia for what has been lost). A brief review may inform us about our regular disappointment with our free time and help us consider whether this funneled capitalism has contributed to why we do not have more of it.

Funneled Free Time: The Fast and Slow in Perspective

The story of the internet is about far more than personal isolation in a flickering world, alien to physical life. The computer has delivered a vast range of experience and knowledge to nearly everyone. It truly annihilates space and time. It and the smartphone vastly extend access to almost everything, often without reference tools. The internet and digital "clouds" (from about 2005) have allowed for immediate links to unfathomably large deposits of data and entertainment that formerly came only in often difficult-to-access physical recordings, books, and periodicals. From simple email and texting to social media and video teleconferencing, the digital connection helps maintain ties to family, friends, customers, and suppliers, often across great distances. This has become vital in a society as dispersed and mobile as modern America. It is far superior to the old long-distance calls that often cost a dollar a minute. During the ongoing COVID-19 pandemic, internet calls have been life or sanity savers, an essential replacement for face-to-face contact that the virus made impossible. The contact between parents and children especially has increased in recent years, even if that sometimes means the helicopter mom or dad, phoning or texting offspring daily or more.[41]

The internet lifts social and cultural constraints on individual choice, often despite the desire of closed societies and politicians to control their populations. A decade before the internet, "futurologists" like John Naisbitt anticipated a world networked through the computer that would challenge the hierarchies of traditional power structures. Of all the forms of the funneled experience discussed above, the various forms of the internet offer the greatest challenge to any critique of the electronic funnel because of the possibility of person-to-person linkage. It has not created yet the dystopia of Orwell's *1984*.[42]

More specifically, the digital funnel has transformed old forms of individuality and sociability. The smartphone has led to new ways for young people to define themselves and socialize. Take, for example, a perhaps surprising change: recently there has been a declining interest in sixteen-year-olds obtaining a driver's license and using the car to display themselves and socialize with others. These uses of the car by teens had occurred in many American communities from the early 1950s to about 1990. But the culture of teens cruising down Main Street in personalized vehicles (customized and "souped up") to show off and meet others has been challenged by the internet. The physical cruise is largely superseded by an electronic one. The personal and social needs that the cruise provided were not about to disappear, but, in ways, the internet was an improvement. Getting noticed or meeting someone is more efficient at the touch screen than at the windshield. We can all think of many other examples of this type of change resulting from the internet.[43]

Taking a wider view, the internet can be seen as a culmination of a long transformation of free time and meanings of the individual and the social. The smartphone completes a drive that dates from early modern times, as discussed in chapter 3. It offers a new way to realize an old urge to escape from the other in a private space, but also to experience the wider world. In the past, that escape was from the crowded one-room cottage full of people or from the public scrutiny of the ritualized festival at the village square or in the hall of the castle. Relief came perhaps in the privacy of a room of one's own and in the exposure to the beyond through reading a book. Today the smartphone offers far more privacy and worldly adventure. The isolation is liberating just as the virtual world at the other end of the electronic funnel is fulfilling. The funneled pleasure is an extraordinarily alluring sensory experience: fast and packed, but also private and extensive. This funnel has become part of a modern quest for freedom from the social world near us (in a physical sense) without giving up access to the social in the wider culture—a quest undertaken through the phonograph and ultimately through the internet.

Still, despite the benefits of the electronic funnel and the long roots of its appeal, there were considerable costs. First, and most obviously, the early expectations that the internet would allow for free exchange and self-realization without centralized or corporate control have been compromised. Throughout the whole history of the funnel, corporate control of what is delivered and how it is received has been paramount. This began with Kodak and Victor, extended through network radio and TV and cable, and culminates now with the oligopoly of internet browsers and social media providers. British journalist Samuel Earle may not be exaggerating much when he noted in 2021: "The internet now stands as a vast web designed to capture our tastes, attention, and patterns of thought, and to push them along profit-making lines. The goal is not a world where anything is possible—but a world where everything is predictable and purchasable."[44]

There are many downsides to the internet (cybercrime and vulnerability to online predators, identity thieves, and misinformation, for example). But I want to emphasize how the electronic transformation of individuality and the social have impacted free time. Inevitably, this leads to an implicit comparison with the past—as shown in how those still wed to the older culture disparage funneled culture. Note how the older generation often mocks kids with their tiny earphones so engrossed in the latest rap star that they ignore the scenery on the family road trip or, worse, their grandparents at Thanksgiving. Sherry Turkle has often noted the contradiction of being "alone together" on the internet. This criticism may be more than nostalgia or hostility to change. Today's internet-driven devices seem to encourage new forms of narcissism: Facebook and other social media have fostered self-promotion, the angling for "likes," and obsessing in posted messages about daily feelings or experiences, assuming internet "friends" really care. Especially for the teen, social media can produce anxiety over the competition to gain notice and the fear of humiliation. The openness of the virtual world sometimes lacks the protection of a chosen group of real friends.[45]

It is inarguable that the hours that children spend playing computer games are taken away from physical play, reading, and self-enhancing hobbies. Video games may offer the visceral rush of real sports, but they do so without the burning of calories and the building of muscle, contributing to growing childhood obesity rates. Face-to-face social skills, so complex and difficult to learn, are not developed at the screen either. Playing video games with others across the internet really does not count as conversation. As the cultural critic Byung-Chul Han notes, "communication without community prevails" today, with its ephemerality and lack of group-building purpose. With perhaps some exaggeration, he claims that "digital communication is extensive communication; it does not establish relationships, only connections."[46]

In a recent Facebook posting I received, a fourth-grade teacher reported how he was met with groans from his classroom when he insisted that his students spend a few minutes talking with each other. Many went to their smartphones when given a chance. Of course, in chat rooms, emails, and especially text messages (requiring less time and effort than phone calls), youth do communicate, but is this really conversation? And social media has become progressively "fast" (as in Twitter, Instagram, or Snapchat). Does anyone learn how to cope, compromise, or share thoughts through these "fast" interactions? Is it any surprise that by 2015 American teenagers were spending about nine hours a day consuming electronic media? But adults also have abandoned conversation and interaction for internet-accessed cultural silos.[47] This may be obvious, but it should also be of concern.

An apparently ironic effect of the internet is that it seems to make some people lonely as people interact less physically with others, and yet the internet attracts lonely people without meeting their need for others. Luke Fernandez and Susan Matt note how the obsession with internet "likes" and "friends" leads to the belief that being alone or lonely is negative, even a health hazard, rather than a "human condition," as people once believed. Likewise, the electronic funnel with its increasing ease of access offers an immediate "cure" to any sign of "micro-boredom," those dull moments where nothing particular commands our attention. But banishing boredom with an internet fix may eliminate opportunities for creative thought or that old virtue, introspection.[48] These concerns and complaints all seem to point to a sense that there has been a loss of slow culture for a fast culture of funneled time. In one way or another, the electronic funnel short-circuits self-realization and social interaction.

The internet and its predecessors foster variety and choice but seldom enhance the integral person with cultivated preferences and skills, rootedness in past cultures and a clear direction for the future. The internet offers an easy substitute for encounters with others and the physical world. The modern goal of creating an integrated identity has been undermined by fast media and goods that fragment the self. Compounding this is the electronic funnel, which provides encounters with a rapid series of decontextualized and unrelated experiences. Such digital flashes encourage short-term and superficial attention, frustrating the development of integral identities that require time and focus to develop. Concentration on any topic or even amusement is constantly challenged by the "link" to the next site that beckons the finger to the mouse or touch screen. Fast capitalism, especially in the form of the electronic funnel, creates an intense focus on the present instead of deepening one's ties to the past or future. Decontextualized digital encounters deprive the individual of a sense of "belonging in the world."[49] Of course, we may reject the value of the steady and developed self as outdated and insist that the "flexible" self is well adapted to a fast world.[50] The rigidity of the inner-directed person of a century ago certainly is problematic. But is not also the digital-surfing self?

The other end of the funnel is also compromised. The virtual world delivered to the individual may be wider than one's physical world, but it is often an abstract and fantasy version of the real world. This is the culmination of a far longer trend that dates at least from the emergence of the media star on stage, on screen, and in recordings. The personal and familiar disappeared in a winner-take-all celebrity economy when a small number of stars began to monopolize the marquee, radio playlist, broadcast prime-time slot, and record or video store shelf. The internet with its promotions of "sponsored" links exacerbates this trend. A radical asymmetry often emerges as fewer people produce culture for a larger number of consumers. Of course, this concentration is reversed somewhat with the emergence of digital "influencers" on Twitter and podcasts, each vying for internet audiences who are drawn by a seemingly endless array of interests, enthusiasms, or even casual curiosity. But such "celebrities" are often short-lived and their audiences only superficially engaged.

The virtual world is sometimes a distortion and illusory. It is also often a world of confusion. As we all know, the internet is a portal to education and business, but also to shopping and entertainment. It has blurred the boundary between information and commercialism (devaluing the former) and between work and play (sometimes threatening productivity and sabotaging fun times). Moreover, the plethora of "information" and the ease of shifting from one internet site to another clutters people's lives, creating what David Shenk calls "data smog," with no clear way of sorting it all out. Recognition of this state of confusion, in fact, long predated the computer—decades earlier Erich Fromm found "negative freedom" without purpose or direction led to an "escape from freedom" in the embrace of authoritarianism. The very idea of making sense of the world almost seems naive or passé. Also, the internet, with its nearly unlimited websites, has taken to ridiculous proportions what occurred when broadcast media was supplanted by the narrowcasting of cable. Some sites gain millions of (usually temporary) hits, but mostly the Web has reduced the sharing of information that was common when large portions of the population watched the same "nightly news." While having multiple options can be advantageous, the result has been people hunkering down in their digital silos, freeing them from having to reassess their prejudices, habits, or ideologies.[51] The virtual society has created not a common culture or even tolerance for diversity but siloed cultures, sometimes defined against each other (as in the culture wars).

This media combination of the self and society has produced two additional contemporary anomalies worth mentioning here. First, the personal stockpiling of the "world" in the cloud or on hard drives. Coming along with media access to the world was the hope of accessing it anytime. The appeal of the phonograph was more than the diversity of the recordings; it was also the fact that these records that captured the ephemeral voice or sound could be stored and replayed at any time. People not merely accessed an ephemeral world but possessed it. This, of course, led to stockpiling and repeated efforts to ease the storing process: substituting the bulky cylinder recording for the disc, replacing the large and fragile record with a cassette tape and CD disc, storing recordings on hard drives, and ultimately accessing the digital cloud. This accumulation magnified personal choice and made the world more immediately accessible (even owned). But stockpiling also became a fetish and compounded the phenomenon of "overchoice" or "data smog." It has led to large collections of videos in streaming libraries (as I admit, I have). What to choose? It is easier sometimes just to accumulate more. The digital collection, precisely because of the removal of limits to electronic storage, magnifies the hoarding impulse and often contributes to our isolation from other people (and their collections).[52] In sum, stockpiling becomes a substitute for self-development and reaching out to the social and physical world.

Second, the electronic funnel has exacerbated a fundamental tension in American society between the individual and society. As Grace Hale notes, the modern American's search for a balance of self and community has often failed. Fernandez and Matt find that this balance has been often lost in a hyperindividualism that presumes unlimited opportunities for self-expression and expansion. While rooted in a deep cultural rejection of the "crowd" and a quest for autonomy, the electronic funnel from the phonograph to the smartphone has aggravated this imbalance. It promises a cure for loneliness in the electronic gift of the right to infinite sociability even while making people more sensitive to their isolation. Yet, the quest for community is largely lost, in part because the funnel at base promises primarily freedom from the crowd and the opportunity for unrestrained self-expression. All this often leads to an obsessive individualism, even to narcissism. The digital world seldom checks that obsession. It does not demand that the individual listen to or exchange with the other. The funnel is both the cause and effect of this preoccupation. What is sometimes lost, of course, is the often difficult cultural work of self-discovery and development in and through social commitment and engagement. Thus, free time has sometimes become frustrated time.[53]

In the end, automobility and modern media offer both a substitute for and a displacement of these goals. They do so by accentuating personal access to the universal in ways that "ordinary" life cannot match. Before the funnel, the quest for individuality in free time was constrained by limited personal space. Automobility has largely eliminated this, freeing the individual from propinquity and providing the "great open spaces." Before modern media, people had neither the will nor the way to get much beyond their personal expectations and biases. But in its replacement of old forms of individuality, modern media has substituted the slow with the fast, which got progressively faster. This acceleration meant that the private reception of shared goods and experiences became less deliberative, less personally cultivated. Fastness prevailed over contemplated choice in free time.

The result was the substitution of the integral self as a goal with serial selves, corresponding to fast, and thus superficial, media encounters. In the process, the individual became more isolated (requiring less shared or interactive contact with others in the funneled experience of the "world"). This sometimes produced the strange combination of the solipsistic self, immersed in the wide world. This nexus has seldom produced a cultivated, integrated self or a coherent, much less interactive, encounter with the world. At the same time, that global reach, while obviously freeing the individual from the parochial, seldom created an active social exchange, communal feeling, or community support. The electronic funnel has transformed liberated time in ways that ultimately are a substitute for or displacement of what people say they want.

Despite its distortions, the electronic funnel offers a reasonable (or accustomed) substitute for older and slower forms of individuality and sociability. As a result, both the intimate and restrained experience favored by the genteel and the mass and ecstatic experience of the traditional carnival crowd have drifted to the fringes of modern life. The slow activity of personal refinement as well as the communal experience of the unchanging and infrequent festival have become psychologically inaccessible, often empty of meaning and unvalued. In particular, free time with the slow became wasted time. And the funnel offers substitutes.

9

Making Time for Culture

For millennia, making time for culture has been the goal of elites living off the time of others. With industrialization, this goal seemed to be a possibility for the broad masses, freed from some of the labor required to support themselves and those elite. That potential has yet to be realized. The twentieth century proved capitalism was about more than lashing time to work for production and profit: it was also about time fixed *to a kind* of consumption that both perpetuated devotion to work and economic growth and reduced the value of freeing time for culture. I have argued that the end of economics should not be just more economics but the opportunity to make time for self-development and social and worldly engagement, that is, for culture. This formulation is certainly incomplete, and much more could be said about the quality of our relationships in free time with the world.[1] But in my argument, I have tried to avoid the presumptions of genteel "superiority" and tribal bias. While these cultural goals may be part of a bourgeois strategy of separation from the "carnival culture" of the popular classes and the self-indulgent rich (as noted in chapter 3), they need not be.

For many, and not just the academic few, the quantity of free time has been disappointing, as has the free time available for personal realization and community enrichment. In part, the evolution of Western society and capitalism has frustrated both objectives. I have stressed four ways in which this occurred.

1. The modern work-life settlement of "full-time" employment in the forty-hour workweek has prioritized market work and economic growth over free time, creating a relatively unchanged work year. This was a resolution to the crises of the early twentieth century. It has produced a work-time settlement that has become largely fixed

for more than eighty years in the US in large part because of the simple dominance of capital and the supposed impossibility of accepting a steady-state economy where human needs would be met with a real decline in work. Capitalism obscures and frustrates any desire for time over money in its incessant drive for growth and profit. The common assumption among social scientists that we personally choose between time and money ignores the historical evidence that worker-consumers never have had much of a choice. Benefits are often tied to "full-time employment," and employers generally set working hours. In fact, over the course of industrialization, work time has decreased far less often than wages have increased. Despite often true claims that reduced work can mean increased productivity, business has consistently and continually rejected reduced hours because of fears that it would limit or even reduce the circulation of capital and profit.

A fifteen-hour workweek, as anticipated by Keynes, even with general affluence, would mean the end or reduction of growth and the accumulation of capital. Without remediation, such a reduction might destroy the dream of "rags to riches," not to mention frustrate a work ethic built into a value system extending over centuries. The choice between time and money usually has been the option of the relatively well-compensated professional. Moreover, the beneficiaries of the Fordist trade-off of time for money at mid-century (in unionized sectors, especially) generally accepted (even if they did not choose) the trade-off of the unchanging forty-hour week for progressively higher wages.

This acceptance may have always been inevitable, but the failure of elites to provide realistic free-time alternatives to Fordist work-and-spend solutions reinforced this trend. And, coming out of the Depression's family crisis, the forty-hour standard for the mostly male breadwinner seemed reasonable for many. That might have changed had Fordism continued. However, since the 1970s, insufficient wages to support modern expectations (health care, education, and a socially tolerable standard of living) have meant many workers had to maximize money over time. One change was the double-income family, with socially beneficial, but also for some costly, results in terms of lost family time. There is considerable variation in this settlement of the forty-hour norm, but it remains normative (even with two-income households). And to change it will require political will and possibly international agreement (given the global impact of any reduction).

2 There are many reasons why there has not been that political will. Among them is the unbridgeable and often hostile division between the cultures of high/genteel modernism, middlebrow, and the commercial carnival—a division that has impeded any common free-time culture or even mutually tolerant cultural diversity. The genteel and their modernist successors, with their sometimes laudable ideals but also elitist assumptions, have little in common with the middlebrow and their traditional culture of family and religion but also consumer delight; meanwhile, a complex popular culture of youth, the poor, and the marginal challenges the other groups with their commercialized carnival. While elements within the genteel group joined workers by promoting more free time (especially early in the twentieth century), divisions between the genteel and popular and working classes have prevented a long-lasting alliance between the two groups. Instead, modern gentility remains largely fixed on highbrow notions of free-time culture, repeatedly raising the question whether the "masses" would ever want or wisely use additional free time. Elite disdain for both middlebrow and popular culture has been answered with the rejection of the snobbish and often secular values of the modern genteel by the other two groups. And added to this, especially in the US, is racism that reduces further the hope of any alliance for time and culture by dividing the working classes and justifying widespread prejudice against African American cultures.[2] A basic toleration of diverse paths to happiness is essential. This requires an ideal of individuality and community that is not based on the denial of the personhood and society of others. We are far from realizing this in our divided and increasingly confrontational cultures. Unfortunately, modern media and consumer capitalism thrive on the inequality that drives much of the misunderstanding and hostility between free-time cultures.

3 The transformation of consumer culture has also limited the possibilities of more free time and its culture. Commodities and the market have progressively crowded out personal and community culture with the ever-encompassing dynamic of fast capitalism and its ephemerality, convenience, and intensity. Ultimately fast capitalism eliminates the slowness of culture—replacing the cultivation of self with serial selves realized in the flicker of global media and reducing social interaction to virtual communities of consumption. Fast goods generally did not save time or stimulate demand for more free time. If anything, they called for more work (and income) to obtain the parade of fast goods, and they easily accommodated the scarcity of free time (noted in exhausted consumers' preference for watching TV, made far more evident in internet surfing).

Self-cultivation and social interaction take time, and as these goals are displaced by fast capitalism, free time that is not saturated with fast goods seems "boring." At the same time, we work for income to purchase stores of potential free time in goods that we actually do not have the free time to enjoy. Often these goods remain in "storage," collecting dust in garages or sheds. More often, perhaps, income from work time is cashed in for semi-addictive fast goods that form our serial identities and the ever-changing "communities of consumption." All this is a poor, though often alluring, substitute for developing an integral self and for engaging with others and the wider world.

4 Added to these effects of fast capitalism is the electronic funnel. Growing in scope and impact from the phonograph to the smartphone, the funneling of the mediated "world" to the linked individual has offered an appealing alternative to integral individuality and interaction with the "slow" (and often frustrating) world of the immediate and physical. The challenges of personal realization and the "dangers" of the real crowd are replaced by individual choice of access to an unlimited virtual world. All this gives the fast funnel priority over the slow culture of free time.

The dynamics of market growth and capital accumulation are at the heart of the problem. They make nearly impossible any alternative to the full-time settlement and subvert making time for culture. Still, fast capitalism and the funnel have brought so much—novelty, convenience, and intensity, as well as a broadening of exposure to ideas and experiences, liberation from the confines of the close by, a massive reduction in the costs and accessibility of sensation and information, and so much more. All this has made any alternative more difficult to achieve or even to image. The problem is that there needs to be more—more free time and more slow culture.

This comfort with consumer capitalism is central. A major part of the dilemma is the simple fact that the settlement, the three cultures, as well as fast and funneled consumption, all have become accustomed fixtures in our lives. Over the years, we have "naturalized" them with our failure to demand a change in the definition of "full-time work," our prejudices against other cultures' free time, and our embrace of fastness and funneled free-time culture. Simultaneously, we have failed to develop the tools and skills necessary for more free time, greater toleration for others, slow goods, or a different way of making our own cultures personally and socially. Many of us cannot even conceive of an alternative to growth capitalism and the work-and-spend life. And what would be a satisfactory resolution to our culture wars? Any realistic alternative to continual product innovation, convenience, and intensity seems empty and boring to most of us most of the time. Personal fulfillment in hobbies often turns into an obsession or becomes tedious; social engagements in conversation become gossip fests and whining about others.

Encounters with nature often seem boring in comparison with mediated sensations. The thought of going out and away from our personal globalizing devices to find common ground or exchange ideas and experiences is frightening or just too much trouble. Even more difficult is getting beyond the obvious fact that the settlement has contributed much to the prosperity since World War II. In the end, there are real and perhaps unresolvable cultural conflicts—the fast may be really what we want, and our electronic funnels may be what we desire with their amazing choices that spare us of the crush of crowds. Frustrations may not outweigh satisfactions, at least in the short term.

In all honesty, I need to note that there are other plausible explanations of our behavior of working more than we need to and pursuing free time to unsatisfying ends. Doubtless, our modern quest for health, safety, comfort, and economic and professional advancement for our children creates costs in medical care, insurance, housing, and education that make us work longer and harder and cause us to neglect making time for culture. Capitalism is not alone to blame for our free-time culture wars: negative drives in our quest for identity and community limit our toleration and understanding of others who are joined in the same pursuit. Tribalism and aggressive behavior may be in our DNA. Still, I think such tendencies can be combatted. That is the whole point of civilization and most religious teachings.

Nevertheless, the problem goes beyond the issue of free time; it must also include our attitudes toward work. As many have noted, work is at the moral and psychological center of many people's existence, especially when positive understandings and models of free time are neglected. More than that, work gives us the right to free time in the eyes of others—and of ourselves. Income without work for some will always be questioned and often resented by those who work for pay. Work is also a setting for personal achievement and social contribution. Many of us feel guilty when not working; if we are not wasting "God's time," as believed by Puritans centuries ago, we still feel we are wasting "valuable" time.

Yet for most people, most of the time, work is primarily the means to obtain the income to cover everyday bills and to make and enjoy culture in free time. The joy of crafts and the dignity and sacred mission of the "calling," much trumpeted in the past (and in modern nostalgia), mean little to most in routinized and "managed" jobs today. The goal of a free-time culture can be and mostly will be realized in the market, where choices (for those with money) abound and where productivity and innovation have freed time from toil. Work is the necessary trade-off for free-time culture. And in the modern world that work, even if dull and repetitive, provides the income to enjoy free time, even if it is mostly fast and funneled. Still, it is hard to know when enough work is enough.

All this suggests that our work-and-spend culture cannot be explained or condemned easily. Books like this seem always to be long on critical analysis and short on solutions. And books that offer solutions tend to advocate personal remedies, applicable, if at all, to the privileged, or they are narrowly "practical" but hardly touch the surface of the problem. This may suggest less the lack of imagination of their authors than the intractable character of the problem of making time for culture.

This remains so despite the obvious disappointment with over two centuries of industrial and capitalist progress. We must admit that we have a work-driven and productivity-obsessed society, which is crisis-prone and ultimately unsustainable. Our work-and-spend society is susceptible to breakdown when investor confidence and the flow of consumption are interrupted (as in recessions or natural disasters like the COVID-19 pandemic). Despite economic growth and gains in productivity, many people still lack free time. And during free time, many find themselves with a limited capacity to engage socially or to realize themselves personally. What Barbara Ehrenreich wrote about the 1980s American middle class may still be true: "When more is not enough but only serves as a springboard to further excess, we have entered a state analogous to physical addiction."[3] The seemingly inevitable is unstable and often dissatisfying.

As a society, we are largely bereft of utopias and visions of the future that would provide alternatives to our impoverished free-time culture. With globalization and the speedup of the flow of goods and information with digital technology, many of us see current trends as irreversible and inevitable. In our age of profound skepticism regarding the possibilities of revolutionary change, there appears to be no alternative to capitalism, with its imperative of endless growth and capital accumulation, even though that necessity is ultimately self-destructive environmentally and, I believe, socially and psychologically.[4]

Even personally, the choices seem like nonstarters: withdrawal, cults, self-help regimens. There are no easy or obvious solutions. Moreover, there is the constant and convenient temptation to claim that this is all an exaggeration or a nostalgic rejection of the virtues of the late-modern world out of an elitist defense of a dying world of gentility. The political and social possibilities evident in the early 2020s are not encouraging, as we are mired in cultural distractions and short-term thinking.

But that does not mean that the issues raised in this book should not be broadcast. Despite all this, many of us claim to others and ourselves that we want something different. Markets may create wealth, but many of us still expect to have time liberated from the economy, even as for many of us our job is to colonize the free time of others with markets. Most of us know that commodities alone do not create culture and can impede its creation.

Offering a detailed blueprint for the personal realization of free time for culture is beyond the scope of this book, as is a "what is to be done?" outline of a political and social path that would ease such personal realization. I leave to others specific recommendations for work time and its use. I am not very encouraged by the fact that a hundred years of advancement in productivity and innovation has not produced a better outcome than the cultural politics that seem to dominate discussions in halls of government and in homes today. But it is worth a few pages to summarize the terms of what may be necessary—with a clear eye.

The Settlement Reconsidered

I have argued that the persistence of long working hours is rooted in many factors, but a neglected issue is politics and especially the difficulty in changing a foundational settlement like the forty-hour law of 1938. It not only set the standard of "full-time work" but the assumption that the payoff of further improvements in productivity and affluence would primarily come to workers in the form of higher wages and consumption. Of course, affluence has made possible longer periods of schooltime and retirement and, to a small extent, increased vacations (but not as a statutory right in the US). Still, the forty-hour standard remains, especially impacting workers with children at home. Politically, it is difficult to imagine today a statutory reduction, but, if the past is consequential, a political revision of the settlement may be necessary. Such changes have taken place in the context of a political opening, as in the postwar crisis of 1919 with the coming of the eight-hour standard. That breakthrough came only with the support of a temporary combination of elite reformers and popular insurgency, and then only at an international level. Given the progress of economic globalization, such a revision today may also require an international agreement. As seen by the difficulties in getting international tariff and climate change agreements signed and adhered to, this will be no easy task. Throughout the history of modern work time, it has been difficult for a single nation to break from the working hours of competitors. The US may have done so for a time in 1938, as did France in 1998 with the thirty-five-hour week (though often evaded).[5] But an international agreement may no longer be possible with the recent rise of populist nationalism.

The time question appears regularly in the press as a social issue (as we have seen, often couched in the language of the "work-life balance") but seldom in political discourse. This may be in part due to its "utopian" character and the dominance of growth politics, even on the left. Moreover, the time issue is overwhelmed by the weight of class divisions that are manifested in culture, especially differences in the use of free time that are expressed in clashes of identity that dominate electoral politics. Seldom have there been cross-class cultural alliances; today, they are even more difficult to create. The educated and genteel modernists, today often associated with the left, sometimes mock the "kitsch" of the middlebrow and "carnival" culture of the working class. At the same time, elements of the middlebrow and working class despise the modernist-genteel elite with their "San Francisco values" and their disdain for "flyover" America. Conservative politicians take advantage of this division by pitting these people against the "arrogance" and "liberalism" of the cultured elite. As a result, the culture wars submerge the politics of time (as well as other pressing issues).

Still, though my themes of time and culture are not front and center, these topics are embedded in other issues, suggesting the possibility of coalitions for change. Let me suggest three: 1) a growing threat of technological unemployment with robotics and artificial intelligence, 2) a crisis in family care (and gender equality), and 3) a pending ecological disaster with unchecked growth. As part of addressing these issues, we may have to reconsider the work-time settlement of the early twentieth century. A revision of that settlement will require a broad international and cross-cultural alliance over these three concerns. It will certainly necessitate cooperation from all interested parties, including labor, family advocates, and environmentalists. Let us briefly consider these three issues.

First, without getting too theoretical, a major tendency of capitalism is to displace workers. In part this is due to the way that capitalism tends to turn labor into capital, substituting workers with machines and other technologies, including, more recently, software. But, as often noted, this has been deferred by the so-called occupational migration of workers from primary to tertiary employment over the past nearly three hundred years of industrialization, as farm and factory workers have shifted to employment in the health, education, finance, and leisure industries. There is, however, no reason to expect this to continue indefinitely. Today, the technological unemployment of semiskilled factory workers caused by robotics and digital technology is also impacting white-collar and professional staff. Some threatened by the new automation may embrace the mostly forgotten call of Paul Lafargue in his *Right to be Lazy* (1883) to abandon the goal of more work and embrace the possibilities of technology to free people from excessive market labor.

In any case, the prospect of technological displacement raises once again the argument for reduced working hours to create more jobs. In 2021, experiments with the four-day workweek were being conducted in Spain, Sweden, and Japan, among other countries. Recent studies have returned to the early twentieth-century concern that long hours have actually reduced productivity. However, the argument for shorter work time has always been about more than job creation and efficiency; it is also about life beyond the market. As Erika Page wrote in 2021, "gradually reducing the workweek could contribute to an economy where growth and productivity take a subordinate role to values like balance and sustainability."[6] We could go further and claim a right to free time to make culture. Still, we must recognize that this perspective did not win the day during the Depression of the 1930s, and it is a long way from doing so today.

Second, the trend toward multiple employment in families, especially since the 1970s, makes the problem of full-time work more problematic. It undermines the "logic" of the forty-hour standard that originally presupposed the full-time (mostly male) provider and the housewife. Forty hours of market work per family with a home-based worker long seemed sensible to most. Of course, there is little chance that the Victorian solution of the mostly male wage earner and the mostly female domestic caregiver will or should return. A reduction of weekly work, however, can be a path to what feminists and allies have long favored: the symmetrical family with men and women sharing income work, family labor, and personal life. The COVID-19 pandemic highlighted an ongoing problem of the time-scarcity of working families in which single parents and couples work "full-time." The result was often a greater burden of income work and family being placed on women, especially mothers, when schools and other child-support institutions were closed.[7] This issue was part of an aborted legislative agenda of the Biden Administration in 2021 with modest goals of parental paid leave and support for child daycare. But the pressing issue of time as well as financial stress on working families hardly broke through in the media. Still work time is a family issue, and it will long remain so.

Third, added to the issue of technological unemployment and family stress is the urgent environmental crisis, especially the link between the growth economy and the predicament of global warming. Concern over this issue could lead (and has sometimes already led) to still another alliance. For years, economists and policy makers, even those supporting environmentalism, claimed that the global economy could both grow and avoid global warming (with controls on greenhouse gases). But some environmentalists are beginning to argue that phasing out fossil fuels that cause those gases may not be enough. In 2019, in excess of eleven thousand scientists advocated a "shift from G.D.P. growth" toward "sustaining ecosystems and improving human well-being." Jason Hickel, author of *Less is More: How Degrowth Will Save the World*, insists that a planned reduction in energy and resource use is essential to reduce global inequality and foster happiness. Indefinite growth on a finite planet is impossible and greenhouse gas emissions cannot decrease fast enough to avoid catastrophe, even with renewable energy. This group insists that the global north is responsible and must degrow. Kerryn Higgs argues that it is unrealistic to expect technological fixes and raising prices on polluting resources (leading to substitutions) to provide a smooth transition from fossil fuels to a green economy. Though controversial and politically unrealistic today, renewed discussion of the steady-state economy may need to accompany any revival of calls for a four-day week or similar goals. In light of increasing evidence of global warming and climate change, Higgs's warning may gain wider appeal. For her, there is no alternative to "socialism or the taming of the capitalist economy." She argues that "structural change is indispensable," with the goal "to meet needs rather than create them." Reduced work time is obviously an essential part of this goal.[8]

Without doubt, degrowth is a hard sell politically when the shift to renewables is itself so tough. This again has become part of the culture wars as "anti-elitists" cling not only to their God and guns but to their SUVs and oversized Ford F-250 pickup trucks. Eric Levitz argues that "nothing short of an absolute dictatorship would affect such a transformation at the necessary speed. And the specter of eco-Bolshevism does not haunt the Global North. Humanity is going to find a way to get rich sustainably or die trying." Perhaps there can be a middle ground: abandoning growth for its own sake and finding a "sweet spot" between meeting universal needs and the "environmental ceiling," as the economist Kate Raworth argues.[9]

These looming threats to work and family return us to the ideas of the free-time movements of the nineteenth and early twentieth centuries, while the environmental crisis makes us think of the looming future. We hear calls for reducing work time and for sharing jobs (though not as much as for guaranteed income as a partial substitute for lost work income). The ongoing burden of combining full-time work with bearing and raising children has brought forth serious proposals for family leave and other profamily legislation. And, if these proposals may mean slower rates of growth, so much the better for the environment. In time, a new settlement of our political economy that seriously addresses these problems will be necessary. As unimaginable as it may seem, that may well require new international free-time and work standards to replace those of nearly a hundred years ago.

Of course, a beginning requirement is to recognize the obvious fact that Americans work significantly more than almost all European and other affluent countries. Obvious immediate solutions involve updating the Fair Labor Standards Act regarding overtime pay, especially because American workers since the 1970s have been increasingly excluded from overtime pay benefits for working more than forty hours per week. Increasing holiday time (via statute or other means) and instituting a paid family leave law would also get Americans closer to the European standard.[10]

Making Time for Culture

The problem is not only freeing time from work but making time for culture. Perhaps ironically, it seems as if the challenge of free time has increased since more of it has become available after the coming of the eight-hour day. The conservative intellectuals who fretted about "Sunday neuroses" of people liberated from work and control by their genteel "betters" were wrong. The problem has not been the uneducated submitting to the temptations of free time so much as how that time was colonized by fast and funneled consumer capitalism. The simple appeal of fastness—novelty, convenience, and intensity—has been irrepressible to almost everyone, while the slow, cultivated, and defuse has become fundamentally unattractive. Opponents of the fast have few practical alternatives. Ultimately, most critiques of modern sensuality and materialism are rooted in philosophical and religious ideas that long predate the coming of modern consumer goods. The traditional mix of solutions—regulating access to pleasures, ascetism for the elite, or cycles of abstention and indulgence for the masses—really evades the complexity of the modern problem. None are realistic options in the modern world, where pleasure has become ever more accessible and intense—and comforting.

It is perhaps possible that the fast and funneled consumer society can be slowed and expanded as people ascend to a more positive and less self-destructive stage. That was the dream of early twentieth-century optimists like Simon Patten (and later psychologists like Alfred Maslow) who looked for a less hedonistic and more social society in a more advanced form of capitalism. Today, a few look to a market solution to the problem of fast and funneled capitalism: entrepreneurs, armed with the findings of positive psychology, will offer programs of "experience" and self-creation as alternatives to commodities and passive consumption.[11]

While this may well be a worthwhile effort, I am skeptical about the possibilities of an "experience economy" based on the market. The point of many enterprises is to create repeat customers, not create self-developers. And business success seems always to lead to corporate buyouts of the "good" businesses and the imposition of the logic of fast capitalism. But I can understand why one might despair of the public and nonprofit sectors. Senior and local recreation centers as well as public gardens, museums, arts programs, charities, and recreational sports are critical additions to modern society and even in a small way challenge the commercial. Yet, as we have seen, these institutions of the slow and intimate have hardly displaced or even offered a clear alternative to the fast and funneled. They lack the resources to compete. Volunteer groups that support these institutions and create free-time communities beyond the market are often plagued by internal division and exclusion. Merchandisers are often more "welcoming" to participants and are far better at recognizing (and exploiting) evident and latent human needs than are noncommercial book clubs and recreational organizations. The leisure market often meets those needs by making appeals precisely to the fast and funneled.

But we should not just fall into despair and skepticism. In the introduction, I noted some efforts to practice slow culture. As Rosa notes, there are "islands of deceleration" (examples might be rooms in houses furnished with heirlooms or slow-food banquets) that promise an escape from fast and funneled capitalism, even if they often are places of "re-creation" that help people get back on the treadmill. For many, like the social psychologist Tim Kasser, an answer may simply be "mindfulness" of our choices. The economist Avner Offer offers "commitment," combining making a thoughtful decision to reject the allure of consumerism with skills ("a personal and social repertoire of working traditions and routines") to find alternatives. This, of course, often requires character traits valued by the genteel (and which, as Offer and others note, are more present in the educated and affluent): self-control, cultivated refinement, and openness to others and new experiences.[12]

Perhaps the challenge is to combine promotion of these "working traditions and routines," which many might associate with the cultivation of the arts and bourgeois restraint, with support for diversity and openness. There is no reason that hunting and needlepoint should be excluded from these "traditions and routines." Along these lines, Jennifer Rauch proposes as an alternative to a "Neo-Luddite" abandonment of modern consumer society an "enlightened consumerism that accommodates environmental concerns, social politics and individual creativity." This "post-Luddite" solution may be a middle ground between the rejection and embrace of technology, a solution which "promote[s] human well-being, community health, economic justice, political freedom, individual dignity and the public interest."[13]

But mindfulness, commitment, and a "post-Luddite" balance are mere attitudes and perspectives—and awfully vague at that. How are they realized? They may require training (at a young age) or later a retraining of the senses. This may mean pursuing skills, hobbies, experiences, contemplation, and relationships that are not immediately gratifying but rather increase in satisfaction with time. Any successful challenge to the fast and funneled life of modern consumer culture may involve stretching and diffusing enjoyment as an alternative to the endless string of "hits." Despite its flaws, the old genteel culture with its presumed goal of focused refinement may still have something to teach us. But that retraining is no easy task, and the temptation to become self-righteous ascetics always remains.

Such a challenge to our modern free-time culture may lead to an appreciation of what Rosa calls "resonant relationships with the world." Drawing on the Romantic tradition and Critical Theory, Rosa insists that resonance experiences require personal receptiveness, engagement, and change, as well as a recognition of the elusiveness of those experiences. All this challenges the "idea of the intellectual, technological, moral and economic *mastery of the world*." Resonance may take place between people and with things and activities like work and sports, as well as with history, nature, and religion. Modernity, in fact, has made resonance increasingly available with the increase in personal freedom and greater material resources.[14] But modernity also brought an unlimited quest for "growth, acceleration, and innovation," along with an environmental crisis, political unresponsiveness to change, and psychological overload, stress, and exhaustion. And all of this frustrates the promise of resonance. Rosa insists that structural change is needed: we must limit growth and provide a guaranteed personal income and new taxes on wealth. But he insists this is not sufficient. Also required is a change in the "existential sensibilities" of us all. And that, in turn, demands time as well as greater psychological openness and security.[15]

The Romantic and rather vague tone of this call for resonance may trouble the practical (or "modernist") reader. For me, this critique of contemporary culture also seems to discount the abiding problem of the allocation of time between obligation and freedom, work and leisure. Neither the historical quest for free time nor new choices between time and money seem to be an important issue in resonance theory and allied thought. In part, this may be because free time has so often been spent on "islands of deceleration," where we merely recover from the stresses of work rather than experience "resonance." But it may also suggest an unwillingness to address the persistent need to reallocate time between necessary work and life-affirming leisure. It is important to recognize the workaday lives of those with fixed time schedules and their limited opportunity for cultured leisure.[16]

I admit that these proposals to counter fast and funneled society may not satisfy the reader, but the question remains: Is that society sustainable, not just environmentally but psychologically? The slow is boring, but then so is the fast in the long run. The obvious fact is that fast and funneled capitalism has not brought happiness (or at least the measure of happiness that we had expected).[17] Perhaps, as Peter Stearns argues, that expectation has been a fundamental mistake of modernity since the eighteenth century. Toning down that expectation of happiness through capitalism might help resolve our frustration (and reduce the constant appeal of consumerism, built on that anticipation).[18]

Clearly, the consumerist culmination of capitalism is deeply problematic and no certain bringer of happiness. As noted again and again by Peter Whybrow and others, the consumer imperative exploits an "instinctual striving of more" that "puts the dopamine system on high alert," and leads to exhaustion and addiction. In his well-documented economic history, Avner Offer claims that affluence in the US and elsewhere, especially since the mid-1970s, "has been producing a reduction in aggregate welfare" as rampant individualism has been promoted through "easy" access to hedonistic stimuli. "The proliferation of cheap rewards makes the rewards that need an investment of patience and time that much more difficult and expensive to achieve." Echoing decades of admonition from religion and philosophy, he insists that the elite show restraint and that all must learn that societal well-being requires a "balance of meeting our needs and the needs of others on whose good will and approbation our own well-being depends." However, the pervasive individualism that the fast and funneled encourage has made this appeal even less often heard than in the days of Victorian gentility.[19]

Moreover, the individualism that fast and funneled capitalism promotes has hardly created a culture of personal security, as Kasser notes. Instead, for many, it leads to the fragmentation of the self. The continuous pressure of emulation has produced in many a "fragile self-worth." Echoing Offer, even the evenhanded Stearns finds that the recent phase of consumerism "risks eliminating too many life options and creating too many stresses in the daily routine."[20]

The modern work-and-spend trade-off may still prevail with the widespread assumption that the stuff and services of consumer capitalism are worth the life lost in work time. But it may not continue. That trade-off was a product of the consumerist explosion of the early and mid-twentieth century. However, more recently, that exchange may have lost its luster. Since the 1970s, the stagnation and often decline in real wages have made work for many a grim necessity rather than a trade-off of sacrificed time for wages. And, for some of the more affluent, the trade-off has led to a garage full of those "exchanges" of time for goods (RVs and other toys, for example) that are seldom or never used.[21] Even as the immediate gratification of the fast and funneled has freed us from the wait for the next festival, it also often has led to satiation and boredom, so often seen in the techno-indulged teen.

So where does all this end? Of course, I do not know, nor does anyone else. Rosa's magisterial *Social Acceleration* ends with a pessimistic conclusion. He finds no "bearers" of a "politics of deceleration" and laments the thought that perhaps only "the breakdown of the economic system will stop the rush." But then he admits that this might mean the "unbridled rush into an abyss." His subsequent call for a renewed quest for "resonance" in daily life may appeal to some, but it seems unlikely to reverse trends for the great many. Kerryn Higgs argues that, in the long run, there is no alternative to some form of the steady-state economy. But she also admits that all governments today "exist at the pleasure of market forces."[22] Is this irreversible? It may have to be.

On the personal and cultural front, at least some of us are beginning to look for self-realization and community beyond the work-and-spend status quo. There is a need to get past the dead-end quests for personal meaning and community in addictive consumption and media. There are alternatives, however limited, both in but also outside the market (in public services, voluntary organizations, and religious movements devoted to substitute paths to happiness). By recognizing where we are and how we got there, and by admitting our frustration with our short-circuited quests for liberation, some people and even nations may come to a better work-life balance and find more satisfying free time.

Notes

Chapter 1. The Trouble with Time Today

1 Alec MacGillis, *Fulfillment: Winning and Losing in One-Click America* (New York: Farrar, Straus and Giroux, 2021), chap. 4.

2 See Lauren Weber, "Navigating the Coronavirus," *Wall Street Journal*, April 3, 2020; and J. F. Reyes, "A Recipe for Burnout," *Philadelphia Inquirer*, May 31, 2020, for examples of a large journalistic response to the onset of COVID-19 in the spring of 2020.

3 Erin Kelly and Phyllis Moen, *Overload: How Good Jobs Went Bad and What We Can Do About It* (Princeton, NJ: Princeton University Press, 2020), 4. Among the many critiques of the modern work obsession are Rahaf Harfoush, *Hustle and Float: Reclaim your Creativity and Thrive in a World Obsessed with Work* (New York: Diversion Books, 2019); Brianna Abbott, "Physicians Burnout Is Widespread," *Wall Street Journal*, January 15, 2020; Brigid Schulte, "Millennials Want a Work-Life Balance, But Their Bosses Don't Understand," *Washington Post*, May 7, 2015; and Cindy Krischer, "Wrong Work-Life Balance Could Be Costly," *Chicago Tribune*, August 2, 2013.

4 Joyce Russell, "Work-Life: Career Coach," *Los Angeles Times*, September 6, 2015; Arlie Hochschild, *Outsourced Self* (New York: Picador, 2012); Michael Birnbaum, "While Covid-19 Continues to Force Remote Work, Europe Looks to Enforce a Right to Disconnect," *Washington Post*, September 4, 2020; Antonia Farzan, "Spain Will Experiment with Four-Day Workweek, a First for Europe," *Washington Post*, March 15, 2021; Christine Hauser, "In Britain, a New Test of an Old Dream: The 4-Day Workweek," *New York Times*, June 6, 2022; K. Rushton, "New Yorkers Unfazed by Work-Life Balance," *Daily Telegraph*, July 26, 2013.

5 Jamie K. McCallum, *Worked Over: How Round-the-Clock Work is Killing the American Dream* (New York: Basic, 2020), 10, 28, 30–31, 45; "Average Annual Working Hours per Worker in OECD-Countries in 2021," *Statista*, August 5, 2022, https://www.statista.com/; Lydia Saad, "The '40-Hour' Workweek Is Actually Longer—by Seven Hours," *Gallup*, August 29, 2014, https://news.gallup.com. In *Empire of Things: How We Became a World of Consumers, from the Fifteenth Century to the Twenty-First* (New York: Harper, 2017), 443–51, Frank Trentmann challenges the difference between American and European work time and the claim by Juliet Schor and others that work time has increased since World War II, though his evidence shows little increase in leisure time.

6 Valerie Ramsey and Neville Francis, "A Century of Work and Leisure," *American Economic Journal: Macroeconomics* 1, *no.* 2 (2009): 189–222, quotation at 210; Trentmann, *Empire of Things*, 445; David Surdam, *Century of the Leisured Masses: Entertainment and the Transformation of Twentieth-Century America* (New York: Oxford University Press, 2015), chap. 5. A good review of the actual reduction of vacation time taken by Americans in recent years is in Andrew Van Dam, "The Mystery of the Disappearing Vacation Day," *Washington Post*, February 10, 2023.

7 Bruce Ward, "Americans Are Choosing to Be Alone. Here's Why We Should Reverse That," *Washington Post*, November 23, 2022.

8 Among the best known and most influential and thoughtful of those advocates of spending less to make possible more time is Juliet Schor, *The Overspent American: Why We Want What We Don't Need* (New York: Harper, 1999).

9 A useful survey of the literature is Clare Kelliher, Julia Richardson, and Galina Boiarintseva, "All of Work? All of Life: Reconceptualizing Work-Life Balance in the 21st Century," *Human Resource Management Journal* 29, no. 2 (April 2019): 97–112.

10 Harvard Business Review, Stewart D. Friedman, Elizabeth Grace Saunders, Peter Bregman, and Daisy Dowling, *Harvard Business Review Guide to Work-Life Balance* (Boston: Harvard Business Review Press, 2019).

11 Stewart D. Friedman of Harvard Business School finds success in those who take charge of their lives, make the most of their constraints, and who practice the thirty-six exercises he offers to, for example, "embody your values" and "manage boundaries" as well as "focus on results" and "create cultures of innovation." Stewart D. Friedman, *Leading the Life You Want: Skills for Integrating Work and Life* (Boston: Harvard Business Review Press, 2014), 153–56. A similar approach is Mason Donovan, *The Golden Apple: Redefining Work-Life Balance for a Diverse Culture* (Brookline, MA: Bibliomotion, 2016).

12 Matthew Kelly, *Off Balance: Getting Beyond the Work-Life Balance Myth to Personal and Professional Satisfaction* (New York: Hudson Street Press, 2011), xi. Similar views are taken by Henry Cloud, *One-Life Solution* (New York: Collins Business, 2008); Ben Peterson, "Don't Call it Work-Life Balance: People Don't Have 2 Identities, So Focus on Office Culture Instead," *Chicago Tribune*, January 19, 2017; and Kelly and Moen, *Overload*, 11.

13 Ben Shapiro, "How a Silicon Valley CEO Masters Work-Life Balance," *New York Times*, August 16, 2018; Tony Schwartz, *The Power of Full Engagement: Managing Energy, Not Time* (New York: Free Press, 2003). Schwartz (ghost writer of Donald Trump's *Art of the Deal*) advises executives to adopt the techniques of athletes to maximize and renew personal energy.

14 Laura Vanderkam and others insist that professional women not throw away their gains but instead find the skills to maximize success in both spheres. Laura Vanderkam, "The Problem with Work-Life Balance," *USA Today*, March 19, 2013; Laura Vanderkam, "The Other Princeton Mom," *Wall Street Journal*, September

29, 2015. Sharing Vanderkam's perspective are Alison Bowen, "5 Things High-Powered Women Need to Know about Work-Life Balance," *Chicago Tribune*, July 11, 2017; and Alan Belasen, *Women in Management* (New York: Routledge, 2017).

15 Roxanne Gay, "My Colleagues Have Great Work-Life Balance," *New York Times*, August 21, 2020; Paul Sullivan, "Work-Life Balance is Tricky All the Way Up the Income Ladder," *New York Times*, October 10, 2015; McCallum, *Worked Over*, 12–14, 178.

16 Weekly working hours rose 3.5% for the bottom 20% of wage earners between 1979 and 2016, while they rose only 1.8% for the top 20%. Longer hours perhaps were necessary for the bottom group whose income rose only 24% compared to 95% for the top. Valerie Wilson and Janelle Jones, "Working Harder or Finding It Harder to Work: Demographic Trends in Annual Work Hours Show an Increasingly Fractured Workforce," *EPI*, February 22, 2018, www.epi.org; Kelliher, Richardson, and Boiarintseva, "All of Work," 97–112; Kelly, *Off Balance*, 13; T. Warren, "Work-Life Balance/Imbalance: The Domination of the Middle Class and the Neglect of the Working-Class," *British Journal of Sociology* 66, no. 2 (2015): 691–717.

17 Joshua Fields Millburn and Ryan Nicodemus, *Minimalism: Live a Meaningful Life* (Missoula, MT: Asymmetrical Press, 2011); Patrick Rhone, *Enough* (self-pub., 2016). Some websites focusing on "decluttering" are www.decluttr.com, www.happinesscouncil.org, and www.awhillans.com. This may remind readers of President Jimmy Carter's famous (and frequently mocked) "Crisis of Confidence" speech of July 15, 1979, where he claims that "owning things and consuming things does not satisfy our longing for meaning." Carter's speech is found on the American Rhetoric website, updated July 10, 2021, www.americanrhetoric.com/.

18 Schor, *Overspent American*, esp. chaps. 5 and 6.

19 The Project 333 website is https://bemorewithless.com. See also Courtney Carver, *Project 333: The Minimalist Fashion Challenge that Proves Less Really Is So Much More* (New York: TarcherPerigee, 2020); Christine Koh and Asha Dornfest, *Minimalist Parenting: Enjoy Modern Family Life More by Doing Less* (New York: Routledge, 2013); Joshua Becker, *Clutterfree with Kids: Change Your Thinking. Discover New Habits. Free Your Home* (Loveland, CO: Becoming Minimalist, 2014); and Katrina Onstad, *The Weekend Effect: The Life-Changing Benefits of Taking Time Off and Challenging the Cult of Overwork* (New York: HarperCollins, 2017), chap. 5.

20 This critique is rooted in the anthropology of Dan Miller, author of many books on the social meaning of consumption, for example, *The Comfort of Things* (Cambridge, UK: Polity, 2008). Classic texts are Mary Douglas and Baron Isherwood, *The World of Goods: Towards an Anthropology of Consumption*, rev, ed. (New York: Routledge, 1996); Grant McCracken, *Culture and Consumption* (Bloomington: University of Indiana Press, 1990); and Ben Fine, *The World of Consumption: The Material and Cultural Revisited* (New York: Routledge, 1996).

21 See Daniel Siegel, *The Developing Mind: Toward a Neurobiology of Interpersonal Experience*, 2nd ed. (New York: Guilford Press, 2012), 9, for a popular and positive treatment, arguing for a common and complex human need both for differentiating and integrating experiences. Martin Seligman, *Flourish: A Visionary New Understanding of Happiness and Well-Being* (New York: Free Press, 2011), spells out a psychology based not on dysfunctional behavior and consciousness but on psychological traits that positively foster happiness. Joseph Pine and James Gilmore in *The Experience Economy* (Boston: Harvard Business Review Press, 2011) draw on positive psychology to make a case for improving consumer experiences.

22 Benjamin Hunnicutt, *The Age of Experiences: Harnessing Happiness to Build a New Economy* (Philadelphia: Temple University Press, 2020), 1–18, 30–33, 90, 104–5, 122.

23 Mihaly Csikszentmihalyi, *Flow: The Psychology of Optimal Experience* (New York: Harper, 2008) and *Beyond Boredom and Anxiety* (New York: Jossey-Bass, 1975). See also Stuart Brown, *Play: How It Shapes the Brain and Invigorates the Soul* (New York: Penguin, 2009), 17, 32–37. Popular treatment of positive psychology is in Martin Seligman, *Authentic Happiness: Using the New Positive Psychology to Realize Your Potential for Lasting Fulfillment* (New York: Free Press, 2002).

24 Hunnicutt, *Age of Experiences*, xix, chaps. 5 and 6, esp. 49–58, 80, 95, 150–54, 170–73.

25 Simon Patten, *The New Basis of Civilization* (1907; repr., Cambridge, MA: Harvard University Press, 1968).

26 The defining text, of course, is Mikhail M. Bakhtin, *Rabelais and his World* (Bloomington: Indiana University Press, 1984).

27 A far more elaborate and nuanced argument for the need for such a disinterested exchange of self and the world is found in Hartmut Rosa's *Resonance: A Sociology of Our Relationship to the World* (Cambridge, UK: Polity, 2019). To keep my text manageable and clear, I focus on the social dimension of the "world," while Rosa explores issues like nature, history, political institutions, and even religion. More about this will be discussed in the conclusion.

28 The best known text promoting this classical Greek ideal is Sabastian de Grazia's *Of Time, Work and Leisure* (New York: Doubleday, 1964).

29 John S. Mill, *Principles of Political Economy (1848; repr.,* Toronto: University of Toronto Press, 1965), 753–96. See Herman Daly, *Steady-State Economics* (San Francisco: Freeman, 1977), for a modern update.

30 McCallum, *Worked Over*, 26–27, quotation at 27. See also Hugh Cunningham, *Time, Work, and Leisure: Life Changes in England since 1700* (Manchester: Manchester University Press, 2015), for a similar argument about England.

31 McCallum, *Worked Over*, chaps. 6 and 7. See also Diane Fassel, *Working Ourselves to Death* (Lincoln, NE: iUniverse, 2000); and Bryan Robinson, *Chained to the Desk* (New York: New York University Press, 2014).

32 Tibor Scitovsky, *The Joyless Economy: An Inquiry into Human Satisfaction and Consumer Dissatisfaction* (New York: Oxford University Press, 1976); Peter Whybrow, *American Mania: When More Is Not Enough* (New York: Norton, 2005).

33 Scitovsky, *Joyless Economy*, 6, 23, 27, 34, 71, 206–7, 225. An interesting update of Scitovsky appeared in a special issue on "The Joyless Economy" in *Critical Review* 10, *no.* 4 (Fall 1996). A thorough analysis is also Avner Offer, *The Challenge of Affluence: Self-Control and Well-Being in the United States and Britain since 1950* (New York: Oxford University Press, 2006), esp. chaps. 2–4.

34 Whybrow, *American Mania*, esp. chaps. 1, 4, and 5.

35 Also consider Tim Kasser, *The High Price of Materialism* (Cambridge, MA: MIT Press, 2002).

36 Gary Cross, *Time and Money: The Making of Consumer Culture* (New York: Routledge, 1993). See also Cunningham, *Time, Work, and Leisure*, 202.

Chapter 2. Two Traditional Cultures and the Capitalist Revolution

1 Challenging a simple narrative of agricultural determinism is David Graeber and David Wengrow, *The Dawn of Everything: A New History of Humanity* (New York: Farrar, Straus and Giroux, 2021).

2 Peter Farb and George Armelagos, *Consuming Passions: The Anthropology of Eating* (Boston: Houghton Mifflin, 1980), 52; Gary Cross and Robert Proctor, *Packaged Pleasures: How Technology and Marketing Revolutionized Desire* (Chicago: University of Chicago Press, 2014), chap. 2.

3 David Smail, *On Deep History and the Brain* (Berkeley: University of California Press, 2008), 166–67.

4 Marshall Stahlins, *Stone Age Economics* (1974; repr., London: Routledge, 2012), 1–39.

5 Angus Maddison, *The World Economy*, vol. 1 (Paris: OECD, 2007), 46–52.

6 Carlo Cipolla, *Before the Industrial Revolution*, 3rd ed. (New York: Norton, 1993), 137–38; Stephen Broadberry et al., *British Economic Growth, 1300–1850: Some Preliminary Estimates*, Economic Historic Society, working paper, September 8, 2009, 31, http://cgeh.nl.

7 A summary is in James Davis, "The Economy of Work," in *A Cultural History of Work in the Medieval Age*, ed. Valerie Garver (New York: Bloomsbury, 2019), 15–29; and Josef Ehmer, "Work and Workplaces," in *A Cultural History of Work in the Early Modern Age*, eds. Bert De Munck and Thomas Safley (New York: Bloomsbury, 2019), 20, 31. Classic studies include Steven Epstein, *Wage Labor and Guilds in Medieval Europe* (Chapel Hill: University of North Carolina Press, 1991), chap. 3; Steven Epstein, *An Economic and Social History of Later Medieval Europe, 1000–1500* (New York: Cambridge University Press, 2009), chap. 4; and James Farr, *Artisans in Europe, 1300–1914* (New York: Cambridge University Press, 2000), 114, 122.

8 Seth Bernard, "The Economy of Work," in *A Cultural History of Work in Antiquity*, ed. Ephraim Lytle (New York: Bloomsbury, 2019), 19–32; Keith Bradley, *Slaves and Masters in the Roman Empire* (New York: Oxford University Press, 1987); Cameron Hawkins, *Roman Artisans and the Urban Economy* (Cambridge: Cambridge University Press, 2016).

9 Lynn White, *Medieval Technology and Social Change* (New York: Oxford University Press, 1962), chaps. 2 and 3; Steven Epstein, *An Economic and Social History of Later Medieval Europe, 1000–1500* (New York: Cambridge University Press, 2009) 197–205; Jean Gimpel, *The Medieval Machine* (New York: Penguin, 1977), chaps. 1, 7; David Landes, *Revolutions in Time: Clocks and the Making of the Modern World*, rev. ed. (Cambridge, MA: Belknap Press of Harvard University Press, 2000), chap. 7.

10 J. P. Griffin, "Changing Life Expectancy Throughout History," *Journal of the Royal Society of Medicine* 101, no. 12 (December 1, 2008): 577; Farr, *Artisans in Europe*, 128–41.

11 A famous analysis is Keith Thomas, "Work and Leisure in Preindustrial Society," *Past and Present* 29 (December 1964), 50–66. See also Christopher Dyer, *Making a Living in the Middle Ages: The People of Britain, 850–1520* (New Haven, CT: Yale University Press, 2002), 281; and Davis, "The Economy of Work," 15–22.

12 Cipolla, *Before the Industrial Revolution*, 76; Keith Thomas, "Work and Leisure," 51–53; Davis, "The Economy of Work," 17–18.

13 Josef Ehmer, "Work and Workplaces," 84–85.

14 Catherina Lis and Hugo Soly argue that preindustrial elites often justified their daily activities (hunting, preparing for war, etc.) as socially essential and that they became more openly devoted to a leisure life only in the nineteenth century. *Worthy Efforts: Attitudes to Work and Workers in Pre-Industrial Europe* (Leiden: Brill, 2012), 552–53. See also Alessandro Arcangeli, "Work and Leisure," in *Work in the Early Modern Age*, ed. Munck and Safley, 166–67.

15 Ronald Hutton, *The Rise and Fall of Merry England: The Ritual Year, 1400–1700* (New York: Oxford University Press, 2000), 37–44; Peter Laslett, *The World We Have Lost* (New York: Scribner, 1973), chap. 2; Christina Hole, *British Folk Customs* (London: Hutchinson, 1976), 63, 137.

16 Michael Judge, *The Dance of Time: The Origins of the Calendar* (New York: Arcade Publishing, 2004) 6, 56, 143, 199–202, 145–59, 203; Hole, *British Folk Customs*, 137.

17 Roger Caillois, *L'Homme et le sacré* (Paris: Leroux 1939), 125, cited in Peter Burke, *Popular Culture in Early Modern Europe* (New York: Harper, 1978), 178–204; Hutton, *Merry England*, 8–27; Emmanuel Le Roy Ladurie, *Carnival in Romans* (New York: G. Braziller, 1979), 305–24.

18 Barbara Ehrenreich, *Dancing in the Streets: A History of Collective Joy* (New York: Metropolitan Books, 2007), chaps. 4 and 5; Gary Cross, *The Cute and the Cool: Wondrous Innocence and Modern American Children's Culture* (New York: Oxford

University Press, 2003), chap. 4; Edward Shorter, *The Making of the Modern Family* (New York: Basic, 1975), 129–38.

19 Compton Reeves, *Pleasures and Pastimes in Medieval England* (London: Alan Sutton, 1993), 151–61; Burke, *Popular Culture*, 183–84.

20 Mark Judd, "Popular Culture and the London Fairs, 1800–1860," in *Leisure in Britain*, eds. John Walton and James Walvin (Manchester: Manchester University Press, 1983), 24–25; Jack Santino, *All Around the Year: Holidays and Celebrations in American Life* (Urbana: University of Illinois Press, 1994), 90, 145–64.

21 Joseph Strutt, *The Sports and Pastimes of the People of England* (1830; repr., Bath, UK: Firecrest Pub., 1969), 339–41.

22 Burke, *Popular Culture*, 178–204; Bakhtin, *Rabelais and His World*, chap. 1. For American variations on carnival, see Santino, *All Around the Year*, 88–96.

23 Bakhtin, *Rabelais*, 301–436.

24 Richard Altick, *Shows of London: A Panoramic History of Exhibitions, 1600–1862* (Cambridge, MA: Harvard University Press, 1978), 37; Richardson Wright, *Hawkers and Walkers in Early America* (New York: Frederick Ungar, 1927), 179–80, 189–91; Gary Cross, *Freak Show Legacies: How the Cute, Camp, and Creepy Shaped Modern Popular Culture* (New York: Bloomsbury, 2021), chap. 2.

25 Robert W. Malcolmson, *Popular Recreations in English Society, 1700–1850* (Cambridge: Cambridge University Press, 1973), 36–37; Reeves, *Pleasures and Pastimes*. 91–92. For other examples of violent festival games, see Robert Davis, *The War of the Fists: Popular Culture and Public Violence in Late Renaissance Venice* (New York: Oxford University Press, 1994), and Farr, *Artisans in Europe*, 265–68.

26 Malcolmson, *Popular Recreations*, 43–44; Strutt, *Sports and Pastimes*, 80–84; Henri Misson, *Memoirs and Observations in his Travels over England* (1719; repr., London: Creative Media Partners, 2018), 24–27.

27 Jane Carson, *Colonial Virginians at Play* (Williamsburg: University Press of Virginia, 1965), 151–52; J. B. Ancelet, "Falling Apart to Stay Together: Deep Play in the Grand Marais Mardi Gras," *The Journal of American Folklore* 114, no. 452 (2001): 144–53; Cross, *Freak Show Legacy*, chaps. 5–7.

28 Robert Levine, *A Geography of Time* (New York: Basic, 1997), 12; M. A. Bienefeld, *Working Hours in British Industry: An Economic History* (London: Weidenfeld and Nicolson, 1972), 19.

29 D. A. Reid, "The Decline of St. Monday, 1776–1876," *Past and Present* 71 (1976): 76–101; Eric Hopkins, "Working Hours and Conditions During the Industrial Revolution, A Re-appraisal," *Economic History Review* 35 (February 1982): 52–57.

30 Jeremy Goldberg and Emma Martin, "Work and Leisure," in *Work in the Medieval Age*, ed. Garver, 170–71; Maxine Berg, Pat Hudson, and Michael Sonenscher, eds., *Manufacture in Town and Country Before the Factory* (Cambridge: Cambridge University Press, 1983), chap. 1; Arthur Young, *The Farmer's Tour through the East of England*, vol. 4 (London: W. Strahan, 1771), 361.

31 Following E. P. Thompson and others, Hugh Cunningham makes this point in *Leisure in the Industrial Revolution*, 1780–1880 (New York: St. Martin's Press, 1980), chap. 2.

32 Norbert Elias, *Power and Civility* (1939; repr., New York: Pantheon, 1980), 236–37; Reeves, *Pleasures and Pastimes*, 103–22; J. R. Barker, *The Tournament in England* (Woodbridge, UK: Boydell, 1986); Peter Borsay, *A History of Leisure: The British Experience since 1500* (New York: Palgrave, 2006), 82–83; Roger Manning, *Hunters and Poachers: A Social and Cultural History of Unlawful Hunting* (New York: Oxford University Press, 1993), 35–36.

33 Thorstein Veblen, *The Theory of the Leisure Class* (1899; repr., New York: Oxford University Press, 2009).

34 Katherine Dunbabin, *The Roman Banquet: Images of Conviviality* (New York: Cambridge University Press, 2003); Francis Joannès, "The Social Function of Banquets in the Earliest Civilizations," in *Food: A Culinary History from Antiquity to the Present*, eds. Jean-Louis Flandrin and Massimo Montanari (New York: Columbia University Press, 1999), 32–37.

35 Garrett Fagan, *Bathing in Public in the Roman World* (Ann Arbor: University of Michigan Press, 2002); Katherine Welch, *The Roman Amphitheater: From its Origins to the Colosseum* (New York: Cambridge University Press, 2007).

36 Massimo Montanari, *Food Is Culture* (New York: Columbia University Press, 2006), 11, 38, 49–50, 63; Strutt, *Sports and Pastimes*, 24–47, 111–49, 305–38; Reeves, *Pleasures and Pastimes*, 74–80, 111–12.

37 Julia Berral, *The Garden: An Illustrated History from Ancient Egypt to the Present Day* (London: Thames & Hudson, 1966); Robert Berger, *In the Garden of the Sun King* (Washington, DC: Dumbarton Oaks, 1985); Karen Jones and John Wills, *The Invention of the Park* (Cambridge, UK: Polity, 2005), 9–25.

38 Burke, *Popular Culture*, 25–26; Farr, *Artisans in Europe*, 268; Frederick Douglass, *The Life of Frederick Douglass* (New York: New American Library, 1968), 84–85.

39 Carolyn Korsmeyer, *Making Sense of Taste* (Ithaca, NY: Cornell University Press, 1999), 16–33; Anthony Synnott, "Puzzling over the Senses: From Plato to Marx," in *The Varieties of Sensory Experience*, ed. David Howes (Toronto: University of Toronto Press, 1991), 61–71.

40 This is tersely noted in Sabastian de Grazia, *Of Time, Work, and Leisure* (Garden City, NY: Anchor, 1964), 24.

41 De Grazia, 14–16.

42 David Landes, *Unbound Prometheus: Technological Change and Industrial Development in Western Europe from 1750 to the Present*, 2nd ed. (New York: Cambridge University Press, 2003), 56–59; David Landes, *Revolution in Time: Clocks and the Making of the Modern World* (Cambridge, MA: Belknap Press of Harvard University Press, 2000), 228–29; E. P. Thompson, "Time, Work-Discipline, and Industrial Capitalism," *Past and Present* 38 (1967): 56–97.

43 Karl Marx, *Capital*, vol. 1 (1867; repr., New York: International Publishers, 1967), 233.

44 For example, see Landes, *Unbound Prometheus*, chap. 2; E. P. Thompson, *The Making of the English Working Class* (New York: Vintage, 1966), 333–40.

45 Lewis Mumford, *Techniques and Civilization* (1934; repr., Chicago: University of Chicago Press, 2010), 14–17; Frederick Engels, *The Condition of the English Working Class* (1844; repr., Stanford, CA: Stanford University Press, 1958), 202. Jonathan Martineau, *Time, Capitalism and Alienation: A Socio-Historical Inquiry into the Making of Modern Time* (Leiden: Brill, 2015), chaps. 2–3.

46 Emma Griffin, *Liberty's Dawn: A People's History of the Industrial Revolution* (New Haven, CT: Yale University Press, 2013), 37–39, 70; Thomas Dublin, *Women at Work: The Transformation of Work and Community in Lowell, Massachusetts, 1826–1860*, 2nd ed. (New York: Columbia University Press, 1981), 25–26; Clive Behagg, "Controlling the Product: Work, Time, and the Early Industrial Workforce in Britain, 1800–1850," in *Worktime and Industrialization*, ed. Gary Cross (Philadelphia: Temple University Press, 1988), 42–3; Karl Ittmann, *Work, Gender, and Family in Victorian England* (New York: New York University Press, 1995), 45.

47 Lois Carr and Lorena Walsh, "Economic Diversity and Labor Organization in the Chesapeake, 1650–1820," in *Work and Labor in Early America*, ed. Stephen Innes (Chapel Hill: University of North Carolina Press, 1988), 145–54; Ludovic Frobert and François Jarrige, "The Economy of Work," in *A Cultural History of Work in the Age of Empire*, ed. Victoria Thompson (New York: Bloomsbury, 2021), 22–26. Others stressing rural work intensification include Peter Kriedte et al., *Industrialization Before Industrialization: Rural Industry in the Genesis of Capitalism* (New York: Cambridge University Press, 1981).

48 Jan de Vries, *The Industrious Revolution: Consumer Behavior and the Household Economy, 1650 to the Present* (New York: Cambridge University Press, 2008), 43–47, 62–71, 114, quotation at 115.

49 Critics include Carmen Sarasúa, "The Economy of Work," in *A Cultural History of Work during the Age of Enlightenment*, eds. Deborah Simonton and Anne Montenach (New York: Bloomsbury, 2019), 22–28; Hugh Cunningham, *Time, Work, and Leisure: Life Changes in England since 1700* (Manchester: Manchester University Press, 2015), 45; and Frank Trentmann, *Empire of Things: How We Became a World of Consumers, from the Fifteenth Century to the Twenty-First* (New York: Harper Collins, 2017), 74–75.

50 Voth argues that this rise in work time resulted largely from increased demand for consumer goods, as does Jan de Vries, but admits that employers recognized that longer work time was advantageous to them. In any case, "Stalinist growth" in the period 1769–1831 was based on increased work rather than technological innovation or savings. Hans-Joachim Voth, *Time and Work in England, 1500–1830* (Oxford: Clarendon Press, 2000), 130, 175, 192–98, 202–9, 244–45, 271–74, 226, quotation at 233.

51 Classic studies of English artisans in the Industrial Revolution are Thompson, *English Working Class*, chap. 8; Eric Hobsbawm, *Labouring Men* (1964; repr.,

London: Wiedenfeld & Nicholson, 2015), chaps. 2, 4, 15, 17. American artisan history can be found in Howard Rock, *Artisans of the New Republic* (New York: New York University Press, 1979); and Sean Wilentz, *Chants Democratic: New York City and the Rise of the American Working Class, 1788–1850* (1984; repr., New York: Oxford University Press, 2004), 36–53.

52 Howard Rock and Paul A. Gilje, introduction to *American Artisans: Crafting Social Identity*, eds. Howard Rock, Paul A. Gilje, and Robert Asher (Baltimore: Johns Hopkins University Press, 1995), xi–xx; Howard Rock, "Independent Hours: Time and Artisans in the New Republic," in Cross, *Worktime and Industrialization*, 22; Rock, *Artisans of the New Republic*, 264–73.

53 Duncan Bythell, *The Sweated Trades: Outwork in Nineteenth Century Britain* (London: Batsford Academic, 1978); Nancy Green, *Ready-to-Wear and Ready-to-Work: A Century of Industry and Immigrants in Paris and New York* (Durham: Duke University Press, 1997).

54 Cunningham, *Leisure in the Industrial Revolution*, 60–61; Reid, "The Decline of St. Monday," 76–101; Behagg, "Controlling the Product," 47–50.

55 Voth, *Time and Work in England*, 130; Behagg, "Controlling the Product," 47, 55; Reid, "St. Monday," 76–101.

56 Burke, *Popular Culture*, 296; Hutton, *Merry England*, 261.

57 Puritan quotation from Perry Miller, *The New England Mind: The Seventeenth Century* (1954; repr., Cambridge, MA: Harvard University Press, 1983), 44. The classic text is Max Weber, *The Protestant Ethic and the Spirit of Capitalism* (1905; repr., New York: Dover, 2003).

58 Dennis Brailsford, *Sport and Society: Elizabeth to Anne* (London: Routledge, 2007), 54, 128–32; Bruce Daniels, *Puritans at Play: Leisure and Recreation in Early New England* (New York: Palgrave, 1995); Hutton, *Merry England*, 143–46, 203–5.

59 Matti Peltonen, "The Weber Thesis and Economic Historians," *Max Weber Studies* 8, no. 1 (January 2008): 79–98; Burke, *Popular Culture*, 207–43; Robert Muchembled, *Popular Culture and Elite Culture in France, 1400–1750* (Baton Rouge: Louisiana State University Press, 1985), 49–61.

60 Malcolmson, *Popular Recreations*, 98–110, 152–60; Hutton, *Merry England*, 246: Borsay, *History of Leisure*, 102; William Waits, *The Modern Christmas in America: A Cultural History of Gift Giving* (New York: New York University Press, 1993), chap. 2; Stephen Nissenbaum, *The Battle for Christmas* (New York: Knopf, 1996), 14–45.

61 Peter Bailey, *Leisure and Class in Victorian England: Rational Recreation and the Contest for Control, 1830–1885* (London: Routledge, 1978), 20–23. Accounts of the withdrawal of leisure space in England are Malcolmson, *Popular Recreation*, 116–18; Thompson, *English Working Class*, 402–3; Borsay, *History of Leisure*, 102–3.

62 Hutton, *Merry England*, 241–50; Cunningham, *Time, Work*, 42–46; Cunningham, *Leisure*, 42–46, 78–79.

63 Benjamin Franklin, *The Autobiography and Selections from His Other Writing* (New York: Liberal Arts Press, 1952), 85–89, 93, and 231.

64 Benjamin Franklin, *Poor Richard Improved: Being an Almanack and Ephemeris . . . for the Year of our Lord 1751*, Founders Online, National Archives website, accessed February 9, 2023, https://founders.archives.gov/.

65 Thompson, *English Working Class*, 350–400; David Hempton, *Methodism and Politics in British Society, 1750–1850* (Stanford, CA: Stanford University Press, 1984), 27; Reid, "St. Monday," 86–98; Griffin, *Liberty's Dawn*, chap. 8; Malcolmson, *Popular Recreations*, 100–7; Jan Butler, *Awash in a Sea of Faith: Christianizing the American People* (Cambridge, MA: Harvard University Press, 1990). An update is in Merrill Miller, *The Making of Working-Class Religion* (Urbana: University of Illinois Press, 2016).

66 Landes, *Unbound Prometheus*, 56–59; Thompson, "Time, Work-Discipline," 56–97.

67 Christopher Lasch, *Haven in a Heartless World* (New York: Norton, 1977), chap. 1. For a critique of the romantic image of the domestic economy, see Amanda Vickery, "Golden Age to Separate Spheres: A Review of the Categories and Chronology on English Women's History," *Historical Journal* 36, no. 2 (1993): 383–414.

68 Basic sources include Nancy Cott, *The Bonds of Womanhood: "Woman's Sphere" in New England, 1780–1835* (1977; repr., New Haven, CT: Yale University Press, 2021), 57–64; and Thompson, "Time, Work-Discipline," 56–59. For an update, see Vanessa Ogle, "Time, Temporality and the History of Capitalism," *Past & Present* 243, no. 1 (May 2019): 312–27.

Chapter 3. Modernizing Free Time

1 Peter Borsay, *A History of Leisure: The British Experience since 1500* (New York: Palgrave, 2006), 137; Peter Clark, *British Clubs and Societies, 1580–1800* (Oxford: Clarendon Press 2000).

2 Norbert Elias, *Power and Civility* (1939; repr., New York: Pantheon, 1982), 11, 86, 229, 232, 236; Norbert Elias, *The Civilizing Process*, vol. 1, *History of Manners and State Formation and Civilization* (1939; repr., Oxford: Blackwell, 1994), 48–95.

3 Baldassare Castiglione, *The Book of the Courtier* (1526; repr., New York: Penguin, 1976), 11, 29, 34, 38, 39, 43, 58–59, 67, 117; Ehrenreich, *Dancing in the Streets*, chap. 5.

4 William Baker, *Sports in the Western World* (Urbana: University of Illinois Press, 2021), 42–57; Francis Henry Cripps-Day, *The History of the Tournament in England and France* (London: B. Quaritch, 1918).

5 F. M. L. Thompson, *Rise of Respectable Society* (Cambridge, MA: Harvard University Press, 1988), 153; Margaret Hunt, *The Middling Sort: Commerce, Gender, and the Family in England, 1680–1780* (Berkeley: University of California Press, 1996), 207–15.

6 Peter Burke, *Popular Culture in Early Modern Europe* (New York: Harper, 1978). See also Robert W. Malcolmson, *Popular Recreations in English Society, 1700–1850* (Cambridge, UK: Cambridge University Press, 1973).

7 John Crowley, *Invention of Comfort: Sensibility and Design in Early Modern Britain and Early America* (Baltimore: Johns Hopkins University Press, 2001), 2–5, 8–17, 45–55, 90–93; Michael McKeon, *Origins of the English Novel* (Baltimore: Johns Hopkins University Press, 1987), 217–28, 241, 260–61, 324–25; Raffaella Sarti, *Europe at Home: Family and Material Culture, 1500–1800* (New Haven, CT: Yale University Press, 2001), 91–106, 129–47.

8 Michael McKeon, *Secret History of Domesticity: Private, Public, and the Division of Knowledge* (Baltimore: Johns Hopkins University Press, 2007), chap. 2; Simon Schama, *Embarrassment of Riches: An Interpretation of Dutch Culture in the Golden Age* (New York: Knopf, 1987), 375–78, 391; Keith Thomas, *Man and the Natural World: Changing Attitudes in England, 1500–1800* (New York: Oxford University Press, 1983), 119.

9 Jon Stobart and Mark Rothery, *Consumption and the Country House* (Oxford: Oxford University Press, 2016); chap. 2; Nicholas Cooper, *Houses of the Gentry, 1480–1680* (New Haven, CT: Yale University Press, 1999), 273–77, 288–92; John Brewer, *The Pleasures of the Imagination: English Culture in the Eighteenth Century* (New York: Farrar, Straus and Giroux, 1997).

10 Burke, *Popular Culture*, 25; William Warner, *Licensing Entertainment: The Elevation of Novel Reading in Britain, 1684–1750* (Berkeley: University of California Press, 1998), chap. 1; Richard Altick and Jonathan Rose, *The English Common Reader: A Social History of the Mass Reading Public, 1800–1900*, 2nd ed. (Columbus: Ohio State University Press, 1998).

11 Crowley, *Comfort*, chap. 7; Thomas, *Natural World*, 253, 301; Cooper, *Houses of the Gentry*, 293–94.

12 Crowley, *Comfort*, 22–26, 114–17, 129, 139, 151; Peter Hoffner, *The Sensory World in Early America* (Baltimore: Johns Hopkins University Press, 2003), 20; Sarti, *Europe at Home*, 91–97.

13 Maxine Berg, *Luxury and Pleasure in Eighteenth Century Britain* (New York: Oxford University Press, 2005), 1–16, 22–26, 220, 295, quotation at 39; Frank Trentmann, *Empire of Things: How We Became a World of Consumers, from the Fifteenth Century to the Twenty-First* (New York: Harper Collins, 2017), 32–77, 95–118; Neil McKendrick, John Brewer, and J. H. Plumb, *The Birth of Consumer Society: The Commercialization of Eighteenth-Century England* (Bloomington: Indiana University Press, 1982), 9–33; Stobart and Rothery, *Country House*, 9, 12, 14, 16; David Hume, *Essays, Moral, Political and Literary* (Indianapolis: Liberty Classics, 1987), 268, cited in Crowley, *Comfort*, 157. Also see Linda Peck, *Consuming Splendor: Society and Culture in Seventeenth-Century England* (New York: Cambridge University Press, 2005).

14 Trentmann, *Empire of Things*, 107.

15 Berg, *Luxury*, 26, 29, 37, chap. 6, quotation at 19; Stobart, and Rothery, *Country House*, 9, chap. 2, quotation at 11; Woodruff Smith, *Consumption and the Making*

of Respectability (London: Routledge, 2002); Laurence Klein, "Politeness and the Interpretation of the British Eighteenth Century," *History Journal* 43 (2002): 869–98; Elias, *Power and Civility*, 315.

16 Thomas, *Natural World*, 37, 92–99, 107, 144–45, 147–48.

17 Heiner Gillmeister, *Tennis: A Cultural History* (New York: New York University Press, 1998); Norbert Elias and Eric Dunning, *The Quest for Excitement: Sport and Leisure in the Civilizing Process* (London: Blackwell, 1986), chap. 3; Ehrenreich, *Dancing in the Streets*, 87, 122, 138, 149, 179.

18 John A. R. Pimlott, *The Englishman's Holiday: A Social History* (1947; repr., Brighton, UK: Harvester: 1976), 1–36; Christopher Hibbert, *The Grand Tour* (New York: Putnam, 1969), 10–25; Andrew Wilton and Ilaria Bignamini, eds., *The Grand Tour: The Lure of Italy in the Eighteenth Century* (London: Tate Gallery Pub., 1996); Edward Chaney, *The Evolution of the Grand Tour*, 2nd ed. (London: Taylor & Francis, 2000).

19 Malcolm Andrews, *The Search for the Picturesque: Landscape Aesthetics and Tourism in Britain, 1760–1800* (London: Scolar Press, 1989), 36, 39, 51; T. A, Hose, ed., *Appreciating Physical Landscapes: Three Hundred Years of Geotourism* (London: The Geological Society of London, 2016). 1–21, 41–57; Hartmut Berghoff, ed. *The Making of Modern Tourism: The Cultural History of the British Experience, 1600–2000* (New York: Palgrave, 2002).

20 Some sources on spas and seaside resorts are Melanie King, *The Secret History of English Spas* (Oxford: Bodleian Library, 2021); Phyllis Hembry, *The English Spa* (London: Athlone Press, 1990); Peter Borsay, *The Image of Georgian Bath* (Oxford: Oxford University Press, 2000); John K. Walton, *The English Seaside Resort: A Social History, 1750–1914* (Leicester: Leicester University Press, 1983); John Sears, *Sacred Places: American Tourist Attractions in the Nineteenth Century* (New York: Oxford University Press, 1989); Jon Sterngass, *First Resorts: Pursuing Pleasure at Saratoga Springs, Newport, and Coney Island* (Baltimore: Johns Hopkins University Press, 2001); and Alain Corbin, *The Lure of the Sea* (Cambridge, UK: Polity, 1994).

21 Karen Jones and John Wills, *The Invention of the Park* (Cambridge, UK: Polity, 2005), 9–39; Marie Luise Gothein, *History of Garden Art: From the Earliest Times to the Present Day*, vol. 1 (London: J. W. Dent, 1928), 25–30; Julia Berral, *The Garden: An Illustrated History from Ancient Egypt to the Present Day* (London: Thames & Hudson, 1966), 35–39.

22 James Granville Southworth, *Vauxhall Gardens* (New York: Columbia University Press, 1941), 36–71; Roy Porter, *English Society in the Eighteenth Century* (New York: Penguin, 1982), 242–50; David Coke, *Vauxhall Gardens* (New Haven, CT: Yale University Press, 2011), chap. 2.

23 Heath Schenker, "Pleasure Gardens, Theme Parks, and the Picturesque," in *Theme Park Landscapes: Antecedents and Variations*, eds. Terence Young and Robert Riley (Washington, DC: Dumbarton Oaks, 2002), 69–89; Roy Rosenzweig and

Elizabeth Blackmar, *The Park and the People: A History of Central Park*, rev. ed. (Ithaca, NY: Cornell University Press, 1998).

24 Sears, *Sacred Places*, 28, 185–88; Sterngass, *First Resorts*, 7–74, 117–45, 204–20, 227.

25 Gary Cross and Robert Proctor, *Packaged Pleasures: How Technology and Marketing Revolutionized Desire* (Chicago: University of Chicago Press, 2014), chap. 2. Good surveys are David Courtwright, *Forces of Habit: Drugs and the Making of the Modern World* (Cambridge, MA: Harvard University Press, 2001), 14–18, 30, 72–75; David Courtwright, *The Age of Addiction: How Bad Habits Became Big Business* (Cambridge, MA: Belknap Press of Harvard University Press, 2019), 33–34; Wolfgang Schivelbusch, *Tastes of Paradise* (New York: Vintage, 1992), 159; Michael Coe, William Clarence-Smith, and Steven Topik, eds, *The Global Coffee Economy in Africa, Asia, and Latin America, 1500–1989* (Cambridge: Cambridge University Press, 2003); Michael Pollan, *Botany of Desire* (New York: Random House, 2001), chap. 1; Robert Proctor, *The Golden Holocaust* (Berkeley: University of California Press, 2012).

26 Courtwright, *Age of Addiction*, 17, 27–34, 91–93; Schivelbusch, *Tastes*, 110.

27 Daniel Lord Smail, *On Deep History and the Brain* (Berkeley: University of California Press, 2008), 164–83, 186; Roy Porter and Dorothy Porter, *In Sickness and in Health: The British Experience, 1650–1850* (London: Fourth Estate, 1988), 217, 220. The classic on alcohol use in the early nineteenth-century US is William J. Rorabaugh, *The Alcoholic Republic: An American Tradition* (New York: Oxford University Press, 1979).

28 Jessica Warner, *Craze: Gin and Debauchery in the Age of Reason* (London: Random House, 2002). Among many sources on regulation is John Burnham, *Bad Habits: Drink, Smoking, Drugs, Gambling, Sexual Misbehavior, and Swearing in American History* (New York: New York University Press, 1993).

29 Schivelbusch, *Tastes*, 131–32; Courtwright, *Forces of Habit*, 57.

30 John Kasson, *Rudeness & Civility: Manners in Nineteenth-Century Urban America* (New York: Hill and Wang, 1990), 11–13, 131, 161, 173–81; Hoffner, *Sensory World*, 247–9; Linda Young, *Middle-Class Culture in Nineteenth Century America, Australia, and Britain* (London: Palgrave, 2003), 68–73.

31 Much of the best work on this issue dates from the 1980s: Bonnie Smith, *Ladies of the Leisure Class: The Bourgeoises of Northern France in the Nineteenth Century* (Princeton, NJ: Princeton University Press, 1981); Leonore Davidoff and Catherine Hall, *Family Fortunes*, rev. ed. (New York: Routledge, 2002), chap. 5; Carroll Smith-Rosenberg, *Disorderly Conduct: Visions of Gender in Victorian America* (New York: Oxford University Press, 1986).

32 John Tosh, *A Man's Place: Masculinity and the Middle-Class Home in Victorian England* (New Haven, CT: Yale University Press, 2007), 6, 31–33, 49, quotation at 1; Peter Borsay, *History of Leisure*, 121–27, 187–89; Steven Gelber, *Hobbies: Leisure and the Culture of Work in America* (New York: Columbia University Press, 1999);

Margaret Marsh, *Suburban Lives* (New Brunswick, NJ: Rutgers University Press, 1990), chap. 3.

33 The classic histories of early suburbs are Kenneth Jackson, *Crabgrass Frontier: The Suburbanization of the United States* (New York: Oxford University Press, 1985), chap. 4; Robert Fishman, *Bourgeois Utopia: The Rise and Fall of Suburbia* (New York: Basic, 1989), chaps. 1 and 5. A good compendium is Becky Nicolaides and Andrew Wiese, eds., *The Suburb Reader*, 2nd ed. (New York: Routledge, 2016).

34 Classics on this topic are Colleen McDannell, *The Christian Home in Victorian America, 1840–1900* (Bloomington: Indiana University Press, 1994), 48–49; and Katherine Grier, *Culture and Comfort: People, Parlors, and Upholstery, 1850–1930*, rev. ed. (Washington, DC: Smithsonian Books, 2010).

35 John Gillis, "Gathering Together: Remembering Memory Through Ritual," in *We Are What We Celebrate: Understanding Holidays and Rituals*, ed. Amitai Etzioni (New York: New York University Press, 2004), 89–103.

36 Penne Restad, *Christmas in America: A History* (New York: Oxford University Press, 1996), 43, 44, 58–68, 96; John Gillis, *A World of their Own Making: Myth, Ritual, and the Quest for Family Values* (Cambridge, MA: Harvard University Press, 1996), 163–86; Stephen Nissenbaum, *Battle for Christmas* (New York: Vintage, 1997), 49–65; Karal Ann Marling, *Merry Christmas: Celebrating America's Greatest Holiday* (Cambridge, MA: Harvard University Press, 2000), 122–30; John Pimlott, *The Englishman's Christmas* (London: Branch Line, 1974), 94, 110; Timothy Larsen, *Oxford Handbook of Christmas* (New York: Oxford University Press, 2020).

37 I develop this in my book *The Cute and the Cool: Wondrous Innocence and Modern American Children's Culture* (New York: Oxford University Press, 2004), chap. 4.

38 Jean-Jacques Rousseau, *Emile*, quoted in *Education in the United States: A Documentary History*, ed. Sol Cohen, (New York: Random House 1997), 207.

39 Stephen Mintz, *Huck's Raft: A History of American Childhood* (Cambridge, MA: Harvard University Press. 2004), chaps. 7 and 8.

40 Joseph Kett, *Rites of Passage: Adolescence in America, 1790 to the Present* (New York: Basic, 1977), chap. 5; F. J. Harvey Darton, *Children's Books in England: Five Centuries of Social Life*, 3rd ed. (London: British Library and Oak Knoll, 1999); Seth Lerer, *Children's Literature: A Reader's History, from Aesop to Harry Potter* (Chicago: University of Chicago Press, 2008); Jacqui Reid-Walsh, *Interactive Books: Playful Media Before Pop-ups* (New York: Routledge, 2019).

41 I develop this theme in my book *Kids' Stuff: Toys and the Changing World of American Childhood* (Cambridge, MA: Harvard University Press, 1997), chap. 2.

42 Cross, *Cute and Cool*, chap. 2; C. John Sommerville, *The Rise and Fall of Childhood* (New York: Vintage, 1990), chap. 13.

43 Marina Moskowitz, *The Standard of Living: The Measure of the Middle-Class in Modern America* (Baltimore: Johns Hopkins University Press, 2004), 3–7, 18; Leigh

Schmidt, *Consumer Rites: The Buying and Selling of American Holidays* (Princeton, NJ: Princeton University Press, 1997); Crowley, *Comfort*, 145–46; Young, *Middle-Class Culture*, 88; Paul Mullins, *The Archaeology of Consumer Culture* (Gainesville: University Press of Florida, 2011), chaps. 1 and 3; Richard Bushman, *The Refinement of America: People, Houses, Cities* (New York: Knopf, 1992), chap. 8.

44 Alexis McCrossen, *Holy Day, Holiday: The American Sunday* (Ithaca, NY: Cornell University Press, 2000); Paul Boyer, *Urban Masses and Moral Order in America, 1820–1920* (Cambridge, MA: Harvard University Press, 1978), chap. 3; Thomas W. Laqueur, *Religion and Respectability: Sunday Schools and Working-Class Culture, 1780–1850* (New Haven, CT: Yale University Press, 1976).

45 Quotation from *New York Crystal Fount* (September 14, 1842), cited in Ian R. Tyrrell, *Sobering Up: From Temperance to Prohibition in Antebellum America, 1800–1860* (Westport, CT: Praeger, 1979), 181; Brian Harrison, *Drink and the Victorians: The Temperance Question in England, 1815–1872* (Pittsburgh: University of Pittsburgh Press, 1971), chap. 15; Kenneth Meier, *The Politics of Sin: Drugs, Alcohol, and Public Policy* (Amonk, NY: M. E. Sharpe, 1994), 48, 65. A recent survey is Daniel Okrent, *Last Call: The Rise and Fall of Prohibition* (New York: Scribner, 2010).

46 Hugh Cunningham, *Leisure in the Industrial Revolution* (London: Croom Helm, 1980), 66–73; Borsay, *History of Leisure*, 42–43; Peter Bailey, *Leisure and Class in Victorian England* (London: Routledge, 1978), 39–40.

47 Cunningham, *Leisure*, 78–89.

48 J. A. Mangan, *Athleticism in the Victorian and Edwardian Public School* (Cambridge: Cambridge University Press, 1981), 69–70, 113, 187–201. Tony Collins, *Sport in Capitalist Society: A Short History* (New York: Routledge, 2013) is an accessible introduction.

49 Bailey, *Leisure and Class*, 41; Cunningham, *Leisure*, 85–88.

50 Frederick Olmsted, "Public Parks and the Enlargement of Towns" (1870), cited in *Civilizing American Cities: A Selection of Frederick Law Olmsted's Writings of City Landscapes*, ed. S. B. Sutton (Cambridge, MA: Harvard University Press, 1971), 80–81; David Schuyler, *The New Urban Landscape* (Baltimore: Johns Hopkins University Press, 1986), chaps. 6 and 7.

51 Clarence Rainwater, *The Play Movement in the United States* (1922; repr., New York: Forgotten Books, 2017), 100–5; Henry Curtis, *The Play Movement and Its Significance* (1917; repr., New York: Kessinger Pub., 2007), 60–65, 108–9.

52 H. Cunningham, *Time, Work and Leisure: Life Changes in England since 1700* (Manchester: Manchester University Press, 2014), 83–86; Steven Conn, *Museums and American Intellectual Life, 1876–1926* (Chicago: University of Chicago Press, 1998); Karen Rader and Victoria Cain, *Life on Display: Revolutionizing U.S. Museums of Science in the Twentieth Century* (Chicago: University of Chicago Press, 2014), chap. 1.

53 Quotation in Rader and Cain, *Life on Display*, 23.

54 Robert Rydell, *All the World's a Fair: Visions of Empire at American International Expositions, 1876–1916* (Chicago: University of Chicago Press, 1987); John Kasson, *Amusing the Million: Coney Island at the Turn of the Century* (New York: Hill and Wang, 1978); Gary Cross and John Walton, *The Playful Crowd: Pleasure Places in the Twentieth Century* (New York: Columbia University Press, 2005), chaps. 2 and 3; Dennis Downey, *A Season of Renewal: The Columbian Exposition and Victorian America* (Westport, CT: Praeger, 2002); Rebecca Graff, *Disposing of Modernity: The Archaeology of Garbage and Consumerism During Chicago's 1893 World's Fair* (Gainesville: University Press of Florida, 2020), chap. 2.

55 Roger Manning, *Hunters and Poachers* (Oxford: Clarendon Press, 1993), 35–67; Roger Longrigg, *The English Squire and His Sport* (New York: St. Martin's Press, 1979), 99–178; Borsay, *History of Leisure*, 82–3.

56 In the American colonies, hunting was as much for food and eliminating livestock predators such as wolves as it was for sport. Hunting there was done with far less concern for conservation than in Europe. Early on deer, wild turkey, and pigeons were plentiful, though the carrier pigeon was hunted to extinction by 1914. Hunting became increasingly recreational through the nineteenth and into the twentieth century, becoming a rite of male bonding. This background influenced the modern idea that Americans have an unassailable right to bear arms. See Jan Dizard, Robert Muth, and Stephen Andrews, *Guns in America* (New York: New York University Press, 1999).

57 Wray Vamplew, *The Turf* (London: Allen Lane, 1976), 25–30; Charles Cotton, *The Compleat Gamester* (London, 1674), reprinted in Cyril H. Hartmann, ed., *Games and Gamesters of the Restoration* (1930; repr., London: Kennikat Press, 1971), 1–115.

58 Richard Moss, *Golf and the American Country Club* (Urbana: University of Illinois Press, 2001), 20–21, 49, 51, quotation at 47.

59 Borsay, *History of Leisure*, 85.

60 Clifford Clark, *The American Family Home, 1800–1960* (Chapel Hill: University of North Carolina Press, 1986), chap. 5; Robert Roberts, *The Classic Slum: Salford Life in the First Quarter of the Century* (Manchester: Manchester University Press, 1971), 35; Thompson, *Respectable Society*, 176, 193.

61 Friedrich Engels, *The Condition of the English Working Class* (Stanford, CA: Stanford University Press, 1968. Original: 1844), 162–63.

62 Richard Price, "The Working Men's Club Movement and Victorian Social Reform Ideology," *Victorian Studies* 16 (1971): 117–47; John Taylor, *From Self-Help to Glamour: The Working Man's Club, 1860–1972* (Oxford: Oxford University Press, 1972); W. Scott Haine, *The World of the Paris Café: Sociability Among the French Working Class, 1789–1914* (Baltimore: Johns Hopkins University Press, 1996), 3–4. A survey is Mack Holt, ed., *Alcohol: A Social and Cultural History* (Oxford, UK: Berg, 2006).

63 Richard Hoggart, *Uses of Literacy* (London: Penguin, 1957), 72, quoted in Borsay, *History of Leisure*, 86.

Chapter 4. Time Struggles and the Settlements of the Twentieth Century

1 A handy survey of working hours research is provided by the Economic History Association in "Hours of Work in U.S. History," https://eh.net/. Also see the US Bureau of Labor Statistics, "Labor Force Statistics from the Current Population Survey," last modified January 20, 2022, https://www.bls.gov.

2 The topic of the history of work time and the labor movement in general has long been neglected by historians, a situation reflected in many of the sources in this as well as other chapters. David Brody, *In Labor's Cause: Main Themes of the History of the American Worker* (New York: Oxford University Press, 1993), 3–26.

3 Quotation from "On the Reduction of the Hours of Labour," *New England Artisan*, June 21, 1834, quoted in Brody, *Labor's Cause*, 34. Classic American treatments of this theme are in Alan Dawley, *Class and Community: The Industrial Revolution in Lynn* (New York: Cambridge University Press, 1976), 20–32; Jonathan Prude, *Coming of the Industrial Order: Town and Factory Life in Rural Massachusetts, 1810–1860* (New York: Cambridge University Press, 1983), 3–63; Thomas Dublin, *Women at Work: The Transformation of Work and Community in Lowell, Massachusetts, 1826–1860*, 2nd ed. (New York: Columbia University Press, 1993), 58–86.

4 Brody, *Labor's Cause*, 86 (quotation); David Roediger and Phillip Foner, *Our Own Time: A History of American Labor and the Working Day* (New York: Verso, 1989), 19–31. The "republican" theme is classically developed in Sean Wilentz, *Chants Democratic: New York City and the Rise of the American Working Class, 1788–1850* (1984; repr., New York: Oxford University Press, 2004).

5 David Thompson, *The Chartists: Popular Politics in the Industrial Revolution* (New York: Pantheon, 1984), 333.

6 Roediger and Foner, *Our Own Time*, chaps. 3 and 4. Richard Price, *Masters, Unions, and Men* (New York: Cambridge University Press, 1980), 53.

7 Ivy Pinchbeck and Margaret Hewitt, *Children in English Society*, vol. 2, *From the Eighteenth Century to the Children Act 1948* (London: Routledge, 1973), 350–406; Peter Bailey, *Leisure and Class in Victorian England: Rational Recreation and the Contest for Control, 1830–1885* (London: Routledge, 1978), 42–45. An update is in Jane Humphries, *Childhood and Child Labour in the British Industrial Revolution* (New York: Cambridge University Press, 2011).

8 For details, see Gary Cross, *A Quest for Time: The Reduction of Work in Britain and France, 1840–1940* (Berkeley: University of California Press, 1989), chap. 2.

9 Teresa Murphy, "Work, Leisure, and Moral Reform: The Ten-Hour Movement in New England, 1830–1850," in *Worktime and Industrialization*, Gary Cross, ed. (Philadelphia: Temple University Press, 1988), 59–76; Norman Ware, *The Industrial Worker, 1840–1860: The Reaction of American Industrial Society to the Advance of the Industrial Revolution* (New York: Ivan Dee, 1990), chaps. 8 and 10.

10 E. L. Hutchins and A. Harrison, *A History of Factory Legislation, 3rd ed.* (1926; repr., London: Routledge, 2013), chaps. 7 and 8; David Montgomery, *Beyond*

Equality: Labor and the Radical Republicans, 1862–1872 (Urbana: University of Illinois Press, 1981), 243–90; Roediger and Foner, *Our Own Time*, 101–9.

11 Eric Hobsbawm, *Labouring Men: Studies in the History of Labour* (New York: Basic, 1965), 371–86; Brody, *Labor's Cause*, 103–4; Roediger and Foner, *Our Own Time*, 124; Sharon Smith, *Subterranean Fire: A History of Working-Class Radicalism in the United States* (Chicago: Haymarket, 2006), 27–28; Elizabeth Faue, *Rethinking the American Labor Movement* (New York: Routledge, 2017), 42; David Roediger, *Wages of Whiteness: Race and the Making of the American Working Class* (London: Verso, 1991); For issues of divisions over race and immigration on a wider scale, see Neville Kirk, *Comrades and Cousins: Globalization, Workers, and Labour Movements in Britain, the USA, and Australia from the 1880s to 1914* (London: Merlin Press, 2003).

12 Sidney Webb and Harold Cox, *The Eight Hours Day* (London: Walter Scott, 1891), 110–13, 118–20; Ira Steward, "A Reduction of Hours: An Increase of Wages" (1865), in *A Documentary History of American Industrial Society*, ed. John Commons et al., vol. 9 (New York: Russell & Russell, 1958), 283–301; Roediger and Foner, *Our Own Time*, chap. 5.

13 George Gunton, *Wealth and Progress* (New York: D. Appleton, 1887), 4–5, 11, 21–32, 84, 88, 212, 232–48. More discussion is in Roediger and Foner, *Our Own Time*, 99–101, 124.

14 Classical analyses are in Neil Smelser, *Social Change in the Industrial Revolution* (Chicago: University of Chicago Press, 1959) 180–212, 235–66; and Maxine Berg, *The Machinery Question and the Making of Political Economy, 1815–1848* (New York: Cambridge University Press, 1982), 23–27.

15 Robert Giffen's views are stated in Royal Commission on Labour, *Minutes of Evidence with the Fourth Report*, vol. XXXIX (1893), 486–88.

16 Roediger and Foner, *Our Own Time*, 149; Gerald Friedman, *State-Making and Labor Movements: France and the United States, 1876–1914* (Ithaca, NY: Cornell University Press, 1998), 57, 62.

17 The "Eight Hours" song was published in 1878 and widely sung up to the Haymarket Affair of 1886. See Philip S. Foner, *American Labor Songs of the Nineteenth Century* (Urbana: University of Illinois Press, 1975), 81–2; and Roediger and Foner, *Our Own Time*, 127. The text of the song is available as "Eight Hours" at www.marxists.org, updated April 2002.

18 Paul Lafargue, *The Right to Be Lazy* (1883; repr., Ardmore, PA: Fifth Season Press, 1999).

19 Gompers quoted in Mike Konczal, *Freedom from the Market* (New York: New Press, 2021), 45.

20 Sidney Webb, "The Limitation of the Hours of Labour," *Contemporary Review* 56 (December 1889): 859. See also Cross, *Quest for Time*, chap. 3; and Roediger and Foner, *Our Own Time*, for a full bibliography.

21 William E. Murphy, *History of the Eight Hours Movement*, vol. 1 (Melbourne: Spectator, 1896), 75–81.

22 The cautious British did not join the international protest on May Day but waited until Sunday, May 4, when a large crowd could be assured for an eight-hour demonstration, avoiding the risk of a one-day general strike. William Murphy, *History of the Eight Hours Movement*, vol. 2 (Melbourne: Spectator, 1906), 54–56, 81–86. Note also Michelle Perrot, "The First of May 1890 in France: The Birth of a Working-Class Ritual," in *The Power of the Past: Essays for Eric Hobsbawm*, eds. Pat Thane, Geoffrey Crossick, and Roderick Floud (Cambridge: Cambridge University Press, 1984), 143–72; Friedman, *State-Making*, 161.

23 For a classic analysis, see Henry Mussey, "Eight-Hour Theory in the American Federation of Labor," in *Economic Essays: Contributed in Honor of John Bates Clark*, ed. Jacob Hollander (1927; repr., New York: American Economic Association, Books for Libraries Press, 1967), 220–24. See also, Lawrence Glickman, "Workers of the World, Consume: Ira Steward and the Origins of Labor Consumerism," *International Labor and Working-Class History* 52 (Fall 1997): 72–86; Roediger and Foner, *Our Own Time*, chap. 8; Julie Greene, *Pure and Simple Politics: The American Federation of Labor and Political Activism, 1881–1917* (New York: Cambridge University Press, 1998), 97–110.

24 Cross, *Quest for Time*, chap. 5; Peter Stearns, *Revolutionary Syndicalism and French Labor* (New Brunswick, NJ: Rutgers University Press, 1971), 43–45.

25 Classic studies include Samuel Haber, *Efficiency and Uplift: Scientific Management in the Progressive Era, 1890–1920* (Chicago: University of Chicago Press, 1964); Sudhir Kakar, *Frederick Taylor: A Study in Personality and Innovation* (Cambridge, MA: Harvard University Press, 1970); and Daniel Nelson, *Frederick W. Taylor and the Rise of Scientific Management* (Madison: University of Wisconsin Press, 1980).

26 Still the best source is Anson Rabinbach, *The Human Motor: Energy, Fatigue, and the Origins of Modernity* (Berkeley: University of California Press, 1992); Arthur Shadwell, *Industrial Efficiency: A Comparative Study of Industrial Life in England, Germany, and America* (London: Longmans, 1906); Cross, *A Quest for Time*, 116–20.

27 John S. Mill, *Principles of Political Economy* (1848; repr., Toronto: University of Toronto Press, 1965), 753–96; Adam Smith, *Wealth of Nations* (1776; repr., New York: Modern Library, 1937), 78–83; Alfred Marshall, *Principles of Economics*, (1890; repr., London: Macmillan, 1920), 694.

28 Rodney Lowe, *Adjusting to Democracy: The Role of the Ministry of Labour in British Politics, 1916–1939* (New York: Oxford University Press, 1986), chap. 3; Josephine Goldmark, *Fatigue and Efficiency: A Study in Industry* (New York: Russell Sage, 1912), chaps. 2 and 3. Good surveys are Maureen Flanagan, *America Reformed: Progressives and Progressivisms, 1890s–1920s* (New York: Oxford University Press, 2007); Daniel Rodgers, *Atlantic Crossings: Social Politics in a*

Progressive Age (Cambridge, MA: Harvard University Press, 1998); and David Roediger, "The Limits of Corporate Reform: Fordism, Taylorism, and the Working Week in the United States, 1886–1929," in Cross, *Worktime and Industrialization*, 135–54.

29 George Barnes, *History of the International Labour Office* (London: Williams and Norgate, 1926), 28–29; Jasmien van Aele, "The International Labour Organization (ILO) in Past and Present Research," *International Review of Social History* 53, no. 3 (December 2008): 485–511.

30 Cross, *Quest for Time*, 6; Greene, *Pure and Simple*, 267–68.

31 Cross, *Quest for Time*, chap. 6.

32 Barnes, *International Labour Office*, xi–xii, 36–37, quotations at 39 and 59.

33 David Lloyd-George quoted in Keith Middlemas, *Politics in Industrial Society* (London: André Deutsch, 1979), 142–43; Olga Hidalgo-Weber, "Social and Political Networks and the Creation of the ILO," in *Globalizing Social Rights: The International Labour Organization and Beyond*, eds., Sandrine Kott and Joëlle Droux, (London: Palgrave, 2013), 17–31, esp. 24–5.

34 Formally known as the "Hours of Work (Industry) Convention, 1919 (No. 1)," General Conference of the International Labour Organisation, adopted November 28, 1919, International Labour Organization (website), www.ilo.org; International Labor Conference of the ILO, *First Annual Meeting* (Washington, DC: ILO, 1920), 222–27; David Montgomery, *Workers' Control in America* (New York: Cambridge University Press, 1979), 97.

Chapter 5. Why Free Time Stopped Growing

1 See Lorenzo Pecchi and Gustavo Piga, eds., *Revisiting Keynes: Economic Possibilities for Our Grandchildren* (Cambridge, MA: MIT Press, 2008). Of the fifteen invited essays, the most germane were by Joseph Stiglitz, 41–86; Richard Freeman, 135–42; Robert Solow, 87–93; Gary Becker and Luis Rayo, 179–84; and Leonardo Becchetti, 185–87. See also John Owen, *The Price of Leisure: An Economic Analysis of the Demand for Leisure Time* (Montreal: McGill-Queens University Press, 1969), chaps 1 and 2; and Clem Tisdell, ed., *The Economics of Leisure*, 2 vols. (Northampton, MA: Egar, 2006).

2 Owen, *Price of Leisure*, chap. 1; Stephen Rosenberg, *Time for Things: Labor, Leisure, and the Rise of Mass Consumption* (Cambridge, MA: Harvard University Press, 2021), 50; US Bureau of Labor Statistics, "Labor Force Statistics from the Current Population Survey," https://www.bls.gov.

3 Gary Becker, "A Theory of the Allocation of Time," *Economic Journal* 75 (September 1965): 493–517; Robert Levine, *A Geography of Time: The Temporal Misadventures of a Social Psychologist* (New York: Basic, 1997), 13–14; Hartmut Rosa, *Social Acceleration: A New Theory of Modernity* (New York: Columbia University Press, 2015), 68–69; Staffan Linder, *The Harried Leisure Class* (New York: Columbia University Press, 1970), 40–46, 55, 78–80, 125–30; Tibor Scitovsky,

The Joyless Economy: An Inquiry into Human Satisfaction and Consumer Dissatisfaction (New York: Oxford University Press, 1976) , 162–64.

4 A classic critique of the orthodox economist position is in Juliet Schor, *The Overworked American: The Unexpected Decline of Leisure in America* (New York: Basic, 1991), 60–78, 128–32.

5 Hunnicutt, *Age of Experiences*, chap. 1.

6 Benjamin Hunnicutt stresses the persistence and even growth of the work ethic in twentieth-century America to explain the failure of shorter work time and the success of the growth economy. I agree that the work ethic was a powerful attitude and idea, but, with Hunnicutt, I also argue that the necessity of capital accumulation fosters the persistence of the work ethic and the growth of the market. Hunnicutt, *Age of Experiences*, xvi; Benjamin Hunnicutt, *Work Without End: The Abandonment of Shorter Hours for the Right to Work* (Philadelphia: Temple University Press, 1988); Benjamin Hunnicutt, *Free Time: The Forgotten American Dream* (Philadelphia: Temple University Press, 2013).

7 Charles Mills, *Vacations for Industrial Workers* (New York: Ronald Press, 1927), 24–25, 70, 76; US Department of Labor, Bureau of Labor Statistics, *Vacations with Pay in Industry, 1937* (Washington, DC: United State Printing Office, 1939), 7–8.

8 Irving Bernstein, *The Lean Years: A History of the American Worker, 1920–33* (1969; repr., New York: Haymarket Books, 2010), 476; US Bureau of the Census, *Historical Statistics of the United States*, vol. 1 (Washington: USPO, 1965), 135; Sean Glynn and John Oxborrow, *Interwar Britain* (London: Allen & Unwin, 1976), 154.

9 Lionel Robbins, *Economic Planning and International Order* (1937; repr., London: Hassell Street Press, 2010), 178–82.

10 Hunnicutt, *Work Without End*, 148–52. His chapter 5 has an excellent bibliography dealing with this theme. Also note Jan Logemann, "Beyond the Mad Men: Consumer Engineering and the Rise of Marketing Management, 1920–1970s: An Introduction," in *Consumer Engineering, 1920s–1970s: Marketing between Expert Planning and Consumer Responsiveness*, ed., Jan Logemann, Gary Cross, Ingo Koehler (New York: Palgrave, 2019) 1–17.

11 Greene's views are from the *New York Times* (February 17, 1932), cited in David Roediger and Eric Foner, *Our Own Time: A History of American Labor and the Working Day* (New York: Verso, 1989), 245. See also Louis Walker, *Distributed Leisure: An Approach to the Problem of Overproduction and Underemployment* (New York: The Century Co., 1932), 34.

12 International Labor Office, *Hours of Work and Unemployment Report of the Preparatory Conference, January 20 to 25, 1933* (Geneva: ILO, 1933), 8–13, 22–23.

13 Gary Cross, *Time and Money: The Making of Consumer Culture* (New York: Routledge, 1993), chap. 4.

14 Hunnicutt, *Work Without End*, chaps. 3 and 5; Irving Bernstein, *Turbulent Years: A History of the American Worker, 1933–1941* (New York: Houghton Mifflin, 1970), 22–31. See Michael Denning, *The Cultural Front: The Laboring of American*

Culture in the Twentieth Century (New York: Verso, 1997) for the broader implications of a cultural alliance of labor and the left in the Depression.

15 Hunnicutt, *Work Without End*, chaps. 6–8; Irving Bernstein, *The Caring Society: The New Deal, the Worker, and the Great Depression* (Boston: Houghton Mifflin, 1985), 116–19. During the 1930s, income tax rates rose from 0.4% to 4.4% for households earning 10,000–15,000 dollars and from 14.5% to 71% for incomes over one million. During World War II rates increased to 18.6% for the 10,000–15,000 dollars income range and to 85% for income over one million dollars, though with deductions real rates were lower. US Bureau of the Census, *Historical Statistics of the United States* (Sanford, CT: Fairfield, 1965), 717.

16 M. S. Eccles, "Government Spending is Sound," speech of January 23, 1939, quoted in Hunnicutt, *Work Without End*, 205. Paul Douglas and James Hackman, "The Fair Labor Standards Act of 1938," *Political Science Quarterly* 53 (December 1938): 502–31.

17 Basic sources on the 1938 Act include Douglas and Hackman, "The Fair Labor Standards Act," 502–31; George Paulsen, "The Legislative History of the Fair Labor Standards Act" (PhD diss., Ohio State University, 1959); and Bernstein, *The Caring Society*, 126–31, 142.

18 Roediger and Foner, *Our Own Time*, 259–62.

19 Maurice Leven, Harold Moulton, and Clark Warburton, *America's Capacity to Consume* (Washington, DC: Brookings Institution, 1934), 127–32; Harold Moulton and Maurice Leven, *The Thirty Hour Week* (Washington, DC: Brookings Institution, 1935), 7, 13, 20. Note also Mordecai Ezekiel, *Jobs for All Through Industrial Expansion* (New York: Knopf, 1939), 219–24.

20 Harold Ickes, *Back to Work. The Story of PWA* (New York; Macmillan, 1935), 195; Rexford Tugwell, *The Industrial Discipline and the Governmental Arts* (New York: Columbia University Press, 1933), 222–23; Hunnicutt, *Work Without End*, chap. 9.

21 Alvin Hansen, *Fiscal Policy and Business Cycles* (New York: Norton, 1941), chaps. 4, 12, and 14; Kathleen Donohue, *Freedom from Want: American Liberalism and the Idea of the Consumer* (Baltimore, MD: Johns Hopkins University Press, 2003), 247, 278–83; Liz Cohen, *A Consumer's Republic: The Politics of Consumption in Postwar America* (New York: Vintage, 2003), chap. 3; Nelson Lichtenstein, *The Most Dangerous Man in Detroit: Walter Reuther and the Fate of American Labor* (New York: Basic, 1995), 175–90.

22 Robert Collins, *More: The Politics of Economic Growth in Postwar America* (New York: Oxford University Press, 2000), chaps. 2 and 5, quotations at 39, 186, and 196. Note also Barbara Ehrenreich, *Fear of Falling: The Inner Life of the Middle Class* (New York: HarperPerennial, 1985), chap. 1; Alan Wolfe, *America's Impasse: The Rise and Fall of the Politics of Growth* (New York: Pantheon, 1981), 13–49; Kerryn Higgs *Collision Course: Endless Growth on a Finite Planet* (Cambridge, MA: MIT Press, 2014), chaps. 1 and 2; Lawrence Glickman, *Free Enterprise: An American History* (New Haven, CT: Yale University Press, 2019), chap. 5.

23 Wikipedia, s.v. "List of Countries by Average Annual Labor Hours," last modified January 15, 2023, https://en.wikipedia .org/; Jan Logemann, *Trams or Tailfins? Public and Private Prosperity in Postwar West Germany and the United States* (Chicago: University of Chicago Press, 2012), chaps. 3–6; "Average Annual Hours Actually Worked per Worker," OECD.Stat, 2021, https://stats.oecd.org.

24 National Bureau of Economic Research, *Recent Economic Changes in the United States*, vol. 2 (New York: McGraw-Hill, 1929), 625–26; Lance Davis, *American Economic Growth* (New York: Harper and Row, 1974), 213.

25 Rosenberg, *Time for Things*, 14, 57, 79, 83, quotation at 139.

26 *Facts and Figures of the Automobile Industry, 1928 Edition* (New York: National Automobile Chamber of Commerce, 1928), 53; Reynold Wik, *Ford and Grassroots America* (Ann Arbor: University of Michigan Press, 1972), 223; James Flink, *The Automobile Age* (Cambridge, MA: MIT Press, 1993), 131–33.

27 Lendol Calder, *Financing the American Dream: A Cultural History of Consumer Credit* (Princeton, NJ: Princeton University Press, 2001). Mass advertising played a role too. See Paul Rutherford, *The Adman's Dilemma: From Barnum to Trump* (Toronto: University of Toronto Press, 2018), chap. 2.

28 John Blum, *V Was for Victory* (New York: Harcourt Brace Jovanovich, 1976), 101; Inger Stole, *Advertising at War: Business, Consumers, and Government in the 1940s* (Urbana: University of Illinois Press, 2012), chaps. 1 and 2.

29 Thomas Hine, *Populuxe* (1987; repr., New York: Fine Communications, 1999), 4, 15–58.

30 Charles McGovern, *Sold American: Consumption and Citizenship, 1890–1945* (Chapel Hill: University of North Carolina Press, 2006), chaps. 5 and 6. Sources on prewar consumer protection include Stuart Chase, *The Tragedy of Waste* (New York: Macmillan, 1925); Arthur Kallet and Frederick Schlink, *100,000,000 Guinea Pigs: Dangers in Everyday Foods, Drugs, and Cosmetics* (New York: Vanguard Press, 1933); and Ruth Lamb, *American Chamber of Horrors* (New York: Farrar & Rinehart, 1935).

31 Roediger and Foner, *Our Own Time*, 262–72; Rosenberg, *Time for Things*, 56, 83, 89, 122, 139–48.

32 Robert Lynd and Helen Lynd, *Middletown in Transition* (New York: Harcourt, 1937), 11, 26, 245.

33 T. J. Jackson Lears, *Fables of Abundance: A Cultural History of Advertising in America* (New York: Basic, 1994), 222, 253; George Katona, *The Mass Consumption Society* (New York: McGraw Hill, 1964), 51; Rosenberg, *Time for Things*, 21, 58–59.

34 Émile Durkheim, *Suicide: A Study in Sociology* (1897; repr., Glencoe, IL: Free Press, 1951), 246–58; Émile Durkheim, *The Division of Labor in Society* (1893; repr., Glencoe, IL: Free Press, 1964), 17, 353–73; Ferdinand Tönnies, *Community and Society* (1887; repr., New York: Harper, 1957).

35 Gustave Le Bon, *The Crowd: A Study of the Popular Mind* (1895; repr., New York: Loki's Publishing, 2016); Sigmund Freud, *Group Psychology*, (1922; repr., New

York: Liveright Publishing, 1967), 5–22; Sigmund Freud, *Civilization and its Discontents* (1929), 97, 103, and *Future of an Illusion* (1927), 2, 7–8, 10, both in *The Standard Edition of the Complete Psychological Works of Sigmund Freud*, ed., James Strachey, vol. 21 (London: Hogarth Press, 1961).

36 José Ortega y Gasset, *The Revolt of the Masses* (1929; repr., New York: Norton, 1957), 88, chap. 3. Similar views are in Oswald Spengler, *The Decline of the West*, 2 vols. (New York: Knopf, 1926–28); and Leonard Woolf, *Barbarianism Within and Without* (New York: Harcourt, Brace & Co., 1939). The classic history is Patrick Brantlinger, *Bread and Circuses: Theories of Mass Culture as Social Decay* (Ithaca, NY: Cornell University Press, 1983), 186–99, chaps. 1 and 3.

37 Michael O'Malley, "That Busyness That is Not Business: Nervousness and Character at the Turn of the Last Century," *Busyness: Social Research* 72, no. 4 (Summer 2005): 371–406; George Beard, *American Nervousness: The Causes and Consequences* (New York: Putnam, 1881), 96–122; Trentmann, *Empire of Things*, 149–51. Examples of Progressivist disdain for immigrant spending are in Louise More, *Wage-Earners' Budgets: A Study of Standards and Cost of Living in New York City* (New York: Henry Holt, 1907), 170–80; and A. Clark and Edith Wyatt, *Making Both Ends Meet: The Income and Outlay of New York City Working Girls* (New York: Macmillan, 1911).

38 William Orton, *America in Search of Culture* (Boston: Little, Brown and Company, 1933), 246–60; Wendell S. Dysinger and Christian Ruckmick, *The Emotional Responses of Children to the Motion Picture Situation* (New York: Macmillan, 1933); Bruce Lenthall, *Radio's America: The Great Depression and the Rise of Modern Mass Culture* (Chicago: University of Chicago Press, 2007), 21–29; Brenton Malin, *Feeling Mediated: A History of Media Technology and Emotion in America* (New York: New York University Press, 2014), 14, 21, 155–56, 158–59, 166; Susan Currell, *The March of Spare Time: The Problem and Promise of Leisure in the Great Depression* (Philadelphia: University of Pennsylvania Press, 2005), chap. 6.

39 Stuart Chase, *Men and Machines* (New York: Macmillan, 1935), 264, quoted in Currell, *Spare Time*, 20, 21–30.

40 Victoria de Grazia, *Politics of Consent* (Cambridge: Cambridge University Press, 1982), chap. 1; Cross, *Time and Money*, chap. 5.

41 De Grazia, *Politics of Consent*, chap. 2; Shelley Baranowski: *Strength through Joy: Consumerism and Mass Tourism in the Third Reich* (New York: Cambridge University Press, 2004).

42 Cross, *Time and Money*, chap. 5. Examples of British "democratic leisure" are in E. B. Castle, *The Coming of Leisure* (London: New Education Fellowships, 1935), 18–19, 35; and Lancelot Hogben, *Education for an Age of Plenty* (London: British Institute for Adult Education, 1937), 10–14.

43 Clarence Rainwater, *The Play Movement in the United States* (Chicago: University of Chicago, 1922), 100–5; Henry Curtis, *The Play Movement and Its Significance*

(New York: Macmillan, 1917), 60–65; Dom Cavallo, *Muscles and Morals: Organized Playgrounds and Urban Reform, 1880–1920* (Philadelphia: University of Pennsylvania Press, 1981), 46–48.

44 Eleanor Ells, *History of Organized Camping: The First 100 Years* (Martinsville, IN: American Camping Association, 1986); Leslie Paris, *Children's Nature: The Rise of the American Summer Camp* (New York: New York University Press, 2008).

45 Jesse Steiner, *Americans at Play* (New York: Harper Brothers, 1933), chap. 3; Currell, *Spare Time*, chaps. 3 and 4.

46 The classic on this subject is David Shi, *The Simple Life: Plain Living and High Thinking in American Culture* (New York: Oxford University Press, 1985), 50–214.

47 Currell, *Spare Time*, 77–88, 103–4.

48 The best books on consumerism and ethnicity in the period are Andrew Heinze, *Adapting to Abundance: Jewish Immigrants, Mass Consumption, and The Search for American Identity* (New York: Columbia University Press, 1990); and Liz Cohen, *Making a New Deal: Industrial Workers in Chicago, 1919–1939* (New York: Cambridge University Press, 1990).

49 Currell, *Spare Time*, 188.

50 Jeff Bishop and Paul Hoggett, *Organizing Around Enthusiasms: Mutual Aid in Leisure* (London: Comedia, 1986), 55, 122, chap. 3; Gary Cross, *Machines of Youth: America's Car Obsession* (Chicago: University of Chicago Press, 2018), 153–64.

51 Gary Cross, *An All-Consuming Century: Why Commercialism Won in America* (New York: Columbia University Press, 2000), chap. 1.

52 George Orwell, *The Road to Wigan Pier* (London: V. Gollancz 1937), 77.

53 Robert and Helen Lynd, *Middletown in Transition* (New York: Harcourt, Brace, 1937), 246; Glenn Elder, *Children of the Great Depression* (Chicago: University of Chicago Press, 1974), 183–87, 192.

54 E. Wight Bakke, *Citizens Without Work: A Study of the Effects of Unemployment upon the Workers' Social Relations and Practices* (New Haven, CT: Yale University Press, 1940), 191.

55 E. Wight Bakke, *The Unemployed Man: A Social Study* (London: Nisbet, 1933), chap. 6; Eli Ginzberg, *The Unemployed* (New York: Harper, 1943), 65, 71, 75.

56 Elder, *Children of the Great Depression*, 26, 53, and 61.

57 Lynd and Lynd, *Middletown in Transition*, 265; Bakke, *Unemployed Man*, chap. 6; Cross, *All-Consuming Century*, chap. 3; Trentmann, *Empire of Things*, 280–82.

58 Mirra Komarovsky, *The Unemployed Man and his Family* (1940; repr., New York: AltaMira Press, 2004), 42; Winifred Wandersee, *Women's Work and Family Values, 1920–1940* (Cambridge, MA: Harvard University Press, 1981), chaps. 1–6.

Chapter 6. Why Free-Time Culture Frustrates

1 John M. Keynes, "Economic Possibilities for Our Grandchildren," in *Essays in Persuasion* (New York: Harcourt, 1932), 365–73. An interesting recent take on this "permanent problem" in the modern age of presumed "post-scarcity," from a center-right point of view, is Brink Lindsey, "What is the Permanent Problem?" *Niskanen Center*, October 6, 2022, www.niskanencenter.org.

2 Jose Ortega y Gasset, *The Revolt of the Masses* (New York: Norton, 1957. Original: 1929), chap. 3.

3 Lawrence Levine, *Highbrow/Lowbrow: The Emergence of Cultural Hierarchy in America* (Cambridge, MA: Harvard University Press, 1990).

4 Madelon Powers, *Faces Along the Bar: Lore and Order in the Workingman's Saloon, 1870–1920* (Chicago: University of Chicago Press, 1998), 82; F. Scott Haine, "Work and Leisure," in *A Cultural History of Work in the Age of Empire*, ed. Victoria Thompson (New York: Bloomsbury, 2019), 149–53; Purley Baker, *ASL Yearbook* (1914), 16, cited in Paul Boyer, *Urban Masses and Moral Order in America, 1820–1920* (Cambridge, MA.: Harvard University Press, 1978), 208.

5 W. J. Rorabaugh, *The Alcoholic Republic: An American Tradition* (New York: Oxford University Press, 1979); W. J. Rorabaugh, *Prohibition: A Concise History* (New York: Oxford University Press, 2018); David Courtwright, *The Age of Addiction: How Bad Habits Became Big Business* (Cambridge, MA: Belknap Press of Harvard University Press, 2019), 95–123; John Burnham, *Bad Habits: Drinking, Smoking, Taking Drugs, Gambling, Sexual Misbehavior and Swearing in American History* (New York: New York University Press, 1993), 26–49; Peter Stearns, *The Battleground of Desire: The Struggle for Self-Control in Modern America* (New York: New York University Press, 1999), chap. 9.

6 John Burnett, *Liquid Pleasures: A Social History of Drinks in Modern Britain* (London: Routledge, 1999), 172–73.

7 James Cook, ed., *The Colossal P. T. Barnum Reader* (Urbana: University of Illinois Press, 2005), 1–9; Neil Harris, *Humbug: The Art of P. T. Barnum* (Chicago: University of Chicago Press, 1973), chaps. 2 and 3; Benjamin Reiss, *The Showman and the Slave: Race, Death, and Memory in Barnum's America* (Cambridge, MA: Harvard University Press, 2001); James W. Cook, *The Arts of Deception: Playing with Fraud in the Age of Barnum* (Cambridge, MA: Harvard University Press, 2001); Gary Cross, *Freak Show Legacies: How the Cute, Camp, and Creepy Shaped Modern Popular Culture* (New York: Bloomsbury, 2021), 28–32; Lauren Rabinovitz, *Electric Dreamland: Amusement Parks, Movies, and American Modernity* (New York: Columbia University Press, 2012), 25–59.

8 Cross, *Freak Show Legacies*, chap. 3.

9 Edo McCullough, *Good Old Coney Island* (New York: Scribner's, 1957), 250–83; Oliver Pilat and Jo Ranson, *Sodom by the Sea: An Affectionate History of Coney Island* (Garden City, NY: Doubleday, 1941), 333–34; Gary Cross and John Walton, *The Playful Crowd: Pleasure Places in the Twentieth Century* (New York: Columbia University Press, 2005), 132–40.

10 N. Morgan and A. Pritchard, *Power and Politics at the Seaside* (Exeter: University of Exeter Press, 1999), chaps. 6 and 7. John Walton, *Blackpool* (Edinburgh: Edinburgh University Press, 1998), chap. 6.

11 Charles Musser, *The Emergence of Cinema* (Berkeley: University of California Press, 1990); Richard Abel, *Americanizing the Movies and "Movie-Mad" Audiences, 1910–1914* (Berkeley: University of California Press, 2002); Wanda Strauven, ed., *Cinema of Attractions Reloaded* (Amsterdam: Amsterdam University Press, 2006); Douglas Gomery, *Shared Pleasures: A History of Movie Presentation in the United States* (Madison: University of Wisconsin Press, 1992); David Robinson, *From Peep Show to Palace: The Birth of American Film* (New York: Columbia University Press, 1996).

12 Hugo Munsterberg, *The Photoplay: A Psychological Study* (New York: Appleton, 1916), 95; Jane Addams, *The Spirit of Youth and City Streets* (New York: Macmillan, 1909), 75–76, 86; Henry Forman, *Our Movie Made Children* (New York: Macmillan, 1933); Sheri Biesen, *Film Censorship Regulating America's Screen* (London: Wallflower, 2018), 17–23; Garth Jowett, Ian Javie, and Kathryn Fuller, *Children and the Movies: Media Influence and the Payne Fund Controversy* (New York: Cambridge University Press, 2006); Jennifer Fronc, *Monitoring the Movies: The Fight over Film Censorship in Early Twentieth-Century Urban America* (Austin: University of Texas Press, 2017).

13 Jesse Steiner, *Americans at Play* (New York: Harper Brothers, 1933), chap. 3; Susan Currell, *The March of Spare Time: The Problem and Promise of Leisure in the Great Depression* (Philadelphia: University of Pennsylvania, 2010), chaps. 3–4; The President's Committee on Recent Social Trends, *Recent Social Trends in the United States*, vol. 2 (New York: McGraw-Hill, 1933), 995; Victoria Grieve, *The Federal Art Project and the Creation of Middlebrow Culture* (Urbana: University of Illinois Press, 2009); Jeff Wiltse, *Contested Waters: A Social History of Swimming Pools in America* (Chapel Hill: University of North Carolina Press, 2007).

14 Susan Smulyan, *Selling Radio: The Commercialization of American Broadcasting, 1920–1934* (Washington, DC: Smithsonian Institution Press, 1994), 65–66; Cynthia Meyers, *A Word from Our Sponsor: Admen, Advertising, and the Golden Age of Radio* (New York: Fordham University Press, 2014), chaps. 4 and 5.

15 Joan Rubin, *The Making of Middlebrow Culture* (Chapel Hill: University of North Carolina Press, 1992), chaps. 1, 3–5; Lawrence Levine, *Highbrow/Lowbrow: The Emergence of a Cultural Hierarchy in America* (Cambridge: Harvard University Press, 1988), 23–30.

16 E. B. Castle et al., *The Coming of Leisure* (London: Educational Fellowship, 1935), 18–19, quotation at 35; Lancelot Hogben, *Education for an Age of Plenty* (London: British Institute for Adult Education, 1937), 10–14; W. E. Williams and A. E. Heath, *Learn and Live: The Consumers' View of Adult Education* (London: Meuthen, 1936), 11, 31–44.

17 Robert Caro, *The Power Broker: Robert Moses and the Fall of New York* (New York: Vintage Books, 1975), 318–19; Cross and Walton, *Playful Crowd*, 132–40; Charles Denson, *Coney Island: Lost and Found* (Berkeley, CA: Ten Speed Press, 2002),

26–29, 40–44; Michael Immerso, *Coney Island: The People's Playground* (New Brunswick, NJ: Rutgers University Press, 2002), 159–60.

18 Cross and Walton, *Playful Crowd*, 140–45, 152–65.

19 "Historical Homeownership Rate in the United States, 1890–Present," DQYDJ (finance website), accessed February 13, 2023, https://dqydj.com.

20 Jackson, *Crabgrass Frontier*, 172–87, 204–18; Mark Foster, *From Streetcar to Superhighway* (Philadelphia: University of Pennsylvania Press, 1981), 65–70; Paul J. P. Sandul and Katherine Solomonson, eds., *Making Suburbia: New Histories of Everyday America*, (Minneapolis: University of Minnesota Press, 2015). The familiar Levitt quotation is cited in David Kushner, *Levittown: Two Families, One Tycoon, and the Fight for Civil Rights in America's Legendary Suburb* (New York: Walker, 2009), xiv.

21 David Nye, *Consuming Power* (Cambridge, MA: MIT Press, 1998), 194; Jackson, *Crabgrass Frontier*, 204; Tom Lewis, *Divided Highways: Building the Interstate Highways, Transforming American Life* (Ithaca, NY: Cornell University Press, 2013).

22 P. S. Bagwell, *The Transport Revolution since 1770* (London: Routledge, 1988); Albro Martin, *Railroads Triumphant: The Growth, Rejection, and Rebirth of a Vital American Force* (New York: Oxford University Press, 1992).

23 Though focused on Britain, Hugh Cunningham's *Time, Work, and Leisure* (Manchester: Manchester University Press, 2014) and Peter Borsay's *A History of Leisure* (London: Palgrave, 2006) discuss with much subtly these technological and commercial transformations of the carnival/festival, which apply broadly.

24 For early twentieth-century urban pleasure sites, see David Freeland, *Automats, Taxi Dances, and Vaudeville: Excavating Manhattan's Lost Places of Leisure* (New York: New York University Press, 2009).

25 Powers, *Faces Along the Bar*, chaps. 5, 7, 9; Perry R. Duis, *The Saloon: Public Drinking in Chicago and Boston, 1880–1920* (Urbana: University of Illinois Press, 1999), chap. 1. An update is Christine Sismondo, *America Walks into a Bar* (New York: Oxford University Press, 2014).

26 John Kasson, *Amusing the Million: Coney Island at the Turn of the Century* (New York: Hill and Wang, 1978), 29–87; Cross and Walton, *Playful Crowd*, chaps. 2 and 3; Rabinovitz, *Electric Dreamland*, 25–59.

27 Kasson, *Amusing the Million*, 50.

28 Cross and Walton, *Playful Crowd*, chap. 3.

29 Scott Rutherford, *American Roller Coasters* (Osceola, WI: MBI Pub. Co., 2000), 102–3; "Knott's Berry Farm Upgrades with New Thrills and Themes," *Architectural Record* 187, no. 11 (November 1999): 50.

30 Leslie Fiedler, *Freaks: Myths and Images of the Secret Self* (New York: Simon and Schuster: 1978), 13–14; Robert Bogdan, *Freak Show: Presenting Human Oddities for Amusement and Profit* (Chicago: University of Chicago Press, 1988), 2; Michael

Chemers, *Staging Stigma: A Critical Examination of the American Freak Show* (London: Palgrave, 2008), chap. 1.

31 Cross, *Freak Show*, chap. 5.

32 Kevin Heffernan, *Ghouls, Gimmicks, and Gold: Horror Films and the American Movie Business* (Durham, NC: Duke University Press, 2004), 67, 185; Rich Worland, *Horror Film* (London: Blackwell, 2007), 75–92, 116; William Paul, *Laughing, Screaming: Modern Hollywood Horror and Comedy* (New York: Columbia University Press, 1994), 30–33; Jon Lewis, *Hollywood v. Hard Core: How the Struggle over Censorships Saved the Modern Film Industry* (New York: New York University Press, 2000), chap. 4.

33 R. H. W. Dillard, "Night of the Living Dead: It's Not Just like a Wind Passing Through," in *American Horror*, ed. Gregory A Waller (Urbana: University of Illinois Press, 1988): 14–29; Kendall Phillips, *Projected Fears: Horror Film and American Culture* (Westport, CT: Praeger, 2005), 82.

34 Todd Trogmorton, *Roller Coasters* (Jefferson, NC: McFarland, 1993), 8–11, 32–33, 35; Eric Lichtenfeld, *Action Speaks Louder: Violence, Spectacle, and the American Action Movie* (Westport, CT: Praeger 2004), 22–25, 186–87.

35 Daniel Bell, *The Cultural Contradictions of Capitalism* (New York: Basic, 1976).

36 The classic sources are in Bernard Rosenberg and David M. White, eds., *Mass Culture: The Popular Arts in America* (Glencoe, IL: Free Press, 1957); and Gillo Dorfles, *Kitsch: The World of Bad Taste* (New York: Universe Books, 1969). Of course, modernists eventually found mass culture and embraced elements of it. See James Naremore and Patrick Brantlinger, *Modernity and Mass Culture* (Bloomington: Indiana University Press, 1991); and Robert Boyers, ed., "On Kitsch: A Symposium," *Salmagundi* (Winter–Spring 1990), 197–312.

37 Rubin, *Middlelbrow Culture*; Martha Wolfenstein, "The Emergence of Fun Morality," *Journal of Social Issues* 7, no. 4 (Fall 1951): 15–25.

38 Stanley Coben, *Rebellion Against Victorianism: The Impetus for Cultural Change in 1920s America* (New York: Oxford University Press, 1991), chap. 3; Rubin, *Middlebrow Culture*, 25, 31–32; Dale Carnegie, *How to Win Friends and Influence People* (New York: Simon and Schuster, 1936).

39 Wolfenstein, "Fun Morality"; Peter Stearns, *Satisfaction Not Guaranteed: Dilemmas of Progress in Modern Society* (New York: New York University Press, 2012), chap. 1.

40 D. L. LeMahieu, *Culture for Democracy: Mass Communications and the Cultivated Mind in Britain between the Wars* (New York: Oxford University Press, 1988), 66–99; Paddy Scannell and David Cardiff, *A Social History of British Broadcasting* (Oxford: Blackwell, 1991), chap. 2.

41 Steven Conn, *Museums and American Intellectual Life, 1876–1926* (Chicago: University of Chicago Press, 1998), 245; Karen Rader and Victoria Cain, *Life on Display: Revolutionizing US Museums of Science in the Twentieth Century* (Chicago: University of Chicago Press, 2014), 19, 22, 27.

42 Cross, *Freak Show Legacies*, chap. 5; Gary Cross, *The Cute and the Cool: Wondrous Innocence and Modern American Children's Culture* (New York: Oxford University Press, 2003), chap. 3.

43 Cross and Walton, *Playful Crowd*, chap. 5.

44 Woody Register, *The Kid of Coney Island* (New York: Oxford University Press, 2001), 300–303. William Mangels, *The Outdoor Amusement Industry from Earliest Times to the Present* (New York: Vantage, 1952), 27–28; Cross and Walton, *Playful Crowd*, chap. 3.

45 Cross and Walton, *Playful Crowd*, chap. 5.

46 Neil Harris, "Expository Expositions: Preparing for the Theme Parks," in *Designing Disney's Theme Parks*, ed. Karal Ann Marling (New York: Flammarion, 1997), 27. In addition to the cartoon and storybook fantasies of Fantasyland, Disney promoted values and interests that one would find in 1910, when Walt Disney was nine, in boy's magazines like *Youth's Companion*. This included fascination with the colonized world beyond Europe and the "White man's burden" to "civilize" it (Adventureland), the "Manifest Destiny" of European pioneers to prevail in the West (Frontierland), and the glories of new technology and progress (Tomorrowland). Still, the overriding theme was not knowledge or chauvinism, but childlike fun. Disney's vision came not from the museum but the imagination of a middle-class boy who grew up in the first decade of the twentieth century.

47 Daniel Harris, *Cute, Quaint, Hungry and Romantic* (New York: Basic, 2000), 5–10; Sianne Ngai, *Our Aesthetic Categories: Zany, Cute, Interesting* (Cambridge, MA: Harvard University Press, 2012), 3, 64, chap. 2; Simon May, *The Power of Cute* (Princeton, NJ: Princeton University Press, 2019), 2, 127, chap. 14; Joshua Dale, "The Appeal of the Cute," in *The Aesthetics and Affects of Cuteness*, ed. Joshua Dale et al. (New York: Routledge, 2017), 25–53; Cross, *Cute and Cool*, chap. 3; *Freak Show Legacies*, 124–30.

48 Cross and Walton, *Playful Crowd*, chap. 6.

49 José Ortega y Gasset, *The Revolt of the Masses* (New York: Norton, 1957. Original: 1929), chap. 3; Dwight Macdonald, "A Theory of Mass Culture," *Diogenes* 3 (Summer 1953): 1–17, reprinted in Rosenberg and White, *Mass Culture*, 59–73, quotation at 69; Clement Greenberg, "Avant-Garde and Kitsch," *Partisan Review* (1946), 278–89, reprinted in Rosenberg and White, *Mass Culture*, 98–110, quotation at 107. Similar was the view of Leslie Fiedler, "The Middle Against Both Ends," *Encounter* 5 (1955): 16–23; and of T. S. Eliot, *Christianity and Culture* (New York: Harcourt, Brace & Co., 1949). For a good analysis of the political and social limits of this perspective, see Grace Hall, *A Nation of Outsiders: How the White Middle Class Fell in Love with Rebellion in Postwar America* (New York: Oxford University Press, 2014), 35–43.

50 David Riesman, "Leisure and Work in Post-Industrial Society," in *Mass Leisure*, eds. Eric Larrabee and Rolf Meyersohn (Glencoe, IL: Free Press, 1958), 363–85 (quotations at 364–65). Most of the articles in this volume were less critical than those in *Mass Culture*, but still they were concerned about the "quality" of free time of immigrants and workers in a commercial society. See also Daniel Horowitz, *Consuming Pleasure: Intellectuals and Popular Culture in the Postwar World* (Philadelphia: University of Pennsylvania Press, 2012), chap. 2.

51 Harold Wilensky, "The Uneven Distribution of Leisure: The Impact of Economic Growth on Free Time," *Social Problems* 9, no. 1 (Summer 1961): 32–56.

52 Alan Warde, "Consumption and Critique," in *Handbook of Cultural Sociology*, eds. John Hall, Laura Grindstaff, and Ming-Cheng Lo (New York: Routledge, 2010), 408–416; Pierre Bourdieu, *Distinction: A Social Critique of the Judgment of Taste* (New York: Routledge, 1984).

53 Hall, *Nation of Outsiders*, 5–7, 34–35.

54 Classics here are Dick Hebdige, *Subculture: The Meaning of Style* (London: Methuen, 1979); John Fiske, *Understanding Popular Culture* (Boston: Unwin Hyman, 1989); James Twitchell, *Lead Us into Temptation: The Triumph of American Materialism* (New York: Columbia University Press, 1999); Stanley Lebergott, *Pursuing Happiness: American Consumers in the Twentieth Century* (Princeton, NJ: Princeton University Press, 1993).

55 An early observer of this is Thomas Frank, *What's the Matter with Kansas? How Conservatives Won the Heart of America* (New York: Henry Holt, 2004). Among the many more recent observations is Valerie Scatamburlo-D'Annibale, "The 'Culture Wars' Reloaded: Trump, Anti-Political Correctness and the Right's 'Free Speech' Hypocrisy," *Journal for Critical Education Policy Studies* 17, no. 1 (2019): 69–119.

Chapter 7. Fast Consumer Capitalism

1 Arlie Hochschild, *The Time Bind: When Work Becomes Home and Home Becomes Work* (New York: Holt, 2001).

2 Charles McGovern, *Sold American: Consumption and Citizenship, 1890–1945* (Chapel Hill: University of North Carolina Press, 2006), chaps. 5 and 6; Tibor Scitovsky, *The Joyless Economy* (New York: Oxford University Press, 1976), 230–31.

3 Staffan Linder, *The Harried Leisure Class* (New York: Columbia University Press, 1970); Gary Becker, "A Theory of the Allocation of Time," *Economics Journal*, 75 (September 1965):493–517.

4 Ben Agger, *Fast Capitalism: A Critical Theory of Significance* (Urbana: University of Illinois Press, 1988). According to Hartmut Rosa, this social speedup led to a loss of stable personal identities, creating narrow cohorts with limited capacity for relationships across age (in contrast to the generational identities of the modern era and intergeneration relations of traditional societies). As a result, "societal synchronization" and "social integration" were no longer possible. This acceleration, Rosa finds, fundamentally disrupted the "modernist agenda": pursuit of progress, individualism, and even domesticity. Hartmut Rosa, *Social Acceleration:*

A New Theory of Modernity (New York: Columbia University Press, 2015), 19, 20, 110–11, 212, 285, 290.

5 Philip Scranton, *Endless Novelty: Specialty Production and American Industrialization, 1865–1925* (Princeton, NJ: Princeton University Press, 1997); Gary Cross, *Kids' Stuff: Toys and the Changing World of American Childhood* (Cambridge, MA: Harvard University Press, 1997), chap. 3; Walter Friedman, *Birth of a Salesman: The Transformation of Selling in America* (Cambridge, MA: Harvard University Press, 2005).

6 James Weber, *Talking Machine Advertising: A History of the Berliner Gramophone and Victor Talking Machine* (Midland, ON: Adio, 1997), 94–95, 112; Victor Talking Machine Company, Phonograph advertisement, *Colliers*, November 19, 1902, 73.

7 Weber, *Talking Machine Advertising*, 94–95, 99; Roland Gelatt, *The Fabulous Phonograph, 1877–1977* (New York: Macmillan, 1977), 71. Victor Talking Machine Company, Phonograph advertisement, *Voice of the Victor*, 1919, 42.

8 David Suisman, *Selling Sound: The Commercial Revolution in American Music* (Cambridge, MA: Harvard University Press, 2012). For the integration of music clips in advertising, see Timothy Taylor, *The Sounds of Capitalism: Advertising, Music, and the Conquest of Culture* (Chicago: The University of Chicago Press, 2012).

9 Suisman, *Selling Sound*, chap. 1; David Jansen, *Tin Pan Alley: The Composers, The Songs, the Performers, and their Times* (New York: Donald Fine, 1988), xv, xvi, xx

10 Jansen, *Tin Pan Alley*, 3, 71, chap. 7; Isaac Goldberg, *Tin Pan Alley: A Chronicle of American Popular Music* (New York: Ungar, 1930), chaps. 5 and 8. Note also David Freeland, *Automats, Taxi Dances, and Vaudeville: Excavating Manhattan's Lost Places of Leisure* (New York: New York University Press, 2009), 85–105; and David Monod, *Vaudeville, and the Making of Modern Entertainment* (Chapel Hill: University of North Carolina, 2020), chap. 2.

11 James Flink, *The Automobile Age* (Cambridge, MA: MIT Press, 1993), 47–51; James Rubenstein, *Making and Selling Cars: Innovation and Change in the US Automotive Industry* (Baltimore: Johns Hopkins University Press, 2001), 18–31.

12 Robert Casey, *The Model T: A Centennial History* (Baltimore: The Johns Hopkins University Press, 2008), 60, 84.

13 Especially revealing is Alfred P. Sloan, *My Years with General Motors* (New York: Doubleday, 1963), 152–53; Casey, *Model T*, 87, 93; James Flink, *Car Culture* (Cambridge, MA: MIT Press, 1975), 141, 151; Flink, *Automobile Age*, 293; David Gartman, *Auto Opium: A Social History of the American Automobile* (New York: Routledge, 1994), chap. 3.

14 United States Bureau of the Census, *The Statistical History of the United States* (New York: Basic, 1976), 8, 716; National Automobile Chamber of Commerce, *Facts and Figures of the Automobile Industry* (New York: National Automobile Chamber of Commerce, 1928), 53; 1920-1930.com, "World Car Market as It was in 1927," http://

www.1920-30.com; Reynold Wik, *Ford and Grassroots America* (Ann Arbor: University of Michigan Press, 1972), 223; Flink, *Automobile Age*, 131–33.

15 Wolfgang Schivelbusch, *Tastes of Paradise: A Social History of Spices, Stimulants, and Intoxicants* (New York: Vintage, 1993), 152–59; David Courtwright, *Forces of Habit: Drugs and the Making of the Modern World* (Cambridge, MA: Harvard University Press, 2001), 114–22; David Courtwright, *The Age of Addiction: How Bad Habits Became Big Business* (Cambridge, MA: Belknap Press of Harvard University Press, 2019), 51–56.

16 Robert Proctor and I develop this theme in *Packaged Pleasures: How Technology and Marketing Revolutionized Desire* (Chicago: University of Chicago Press, 2014), chaps. 4, 6, 7.

17 Luke Fernandez and Susan Matt, *Bored, Lonely, Angry, Stupid: Changing Feelings about Technology, from the Telegraph to Twitter* (Cambridge, MA: Harvard University Press, 2019), 155–68; David Riesman, Nathan Glazer, and Reuel Denney, *The Lonely Crowd: A Study of the Changing American Character* (New Haven, CT: Yale University Press, 1950).

18 Georg Simmel, "Fashion," *International Quarterly* 10 (1904): 130–55; Jukka Gronow, "Fads, Fashions and 'Real' Innovations," in *Time, Consumption, and Everyday Life*, eds. Elizabeth Shove, Frank Trentmann, and Richard Wilk (London: Berg, 2009), 129–42.

19 This analysis is suggested in the classic theoretical works by Frederic Jameson, *Postmodernism, or, The Cultural Logic of Late Capitalism* (Durham, NC: Duke University Press, 1997); and David Harvey, *The Condition of Postmodernity* (Cambridge: Blackwell, 1990). But its ideas are implied by historians like Karen Halttunen regarding nineteenth-century urbanization and self-created identity in *Confidence Men and Painted Women: A Study of Middle-Class Culture in America, 1830–1880* (New Haven, CT: Yale University Press, 1982); Kathy Peiss in her study of the relationship between cosmetics and women's self-image in the 1920s in *Hope in a Jar: The Making of American Beauty Culture* (Philadelphia: University of Pennsylvania Press, 2011); Andrew Heinze in his study of Jewish urban immigration in the beginning of the twentieth century in *Adapting to Abundance: Jewish Immigrants, Mass Consumption, and The Search for American Identity* (New York: Columbia University Press, 1990); and Susan Matt in her analysis of social alienation, American mobility, and the quest for objects of stability in *Homesickness: An American History* (New York: Oxford University Press, 2014).

20 T. J. Jackson Lears, *No Place for Grace: Antimodernism and the Transformation of American Culture, 1880–1920* (Chicago: University of Chicago Press, 1994), especially chap. 5; Rosa, *Social Acceleration*, 134, 180.

21 Daniel J. Boorstin, *The Americans: The Democratic Experience* (New York: Random House, 1973), 69–164; Heinz, *Adapting to Abundance*, chap. 1.

22 Gary Cross, *All-Consuming Century: Why Commercialism Won in Modern America* (New York: Columbia University Press, 2000), chap. 1.

23 Lionel Tiger, *Pursuit of Pleasure* (Boston: Little, Brown, 1992), 21; Diane Ackerman, *Natural History of the Senses* (New York: Vintage, 1990), 6, 27, 82–83, 202–6, 213–14; Steven Mithen, *The Singing Neanderthals: The Origins of Music, Language, Mind, and Body* (Cambridge, MA: Harvard University Press, 2007), 234.

24 Yanko Tsvetkov "A Brief History of the Color Blue," Alphadesigner (website), June 13, 2001, https://alphadesigner.com; Ehrenreich, *Dancing in the Streets*, 22, 23, 184, 210–215; William McNeill, *Keeping Together in Time: Dance and Drill in Human History* (Cambridge, MA: Harvard University Press, 1995), 4.

25 Cross and Proctor, *Packaged Pleasures*, chaps. 2, 3, 5.

26 Evan Eisenberg, *The Recording Angel: Music, Records, and Culture from Aristotle to Zappa*, 2nd ed. (New Haven, CT: Yale University Press, 2005), 23, 38, 43; Mark Katz, *Captured Sound: How Technology has Changed Music* (Berkeley: University of California Press, 2010), 29, 66–70.

27 Kathleen Franz, *Tinkering: Consumers Reinvent the Early Automobile* (Philadelphia: University of Pennsylvania Press, 2005), chap. 3; Robert Lucsko, *The Business of Speed: The Hot Rod Industry in America, 1915–1990* (Baltimore: Johns Hopkins University Press, 2008), 16–18, 41–45, 64–68; Katie Mills, *The Road Story and the Rebel: Moving Through Film, Fiction, and Television* (Carbondale: University of Southern Illinois Press, 2006).

28 Ernest Calkins, "What Consumer Engineering Really Is," in *Consumer Engineering*, eds. Roy Sheldon and Egmont Arens (New York: Harper, 1932), 1; Jeffrey Meikle, *Twentieth-Century Limited: Industrial Design in America, 1925–1939* (Philadelphia: Temple University Press, 2001), 4, 52–54, 59, 101–10; Adrian Forty, *Objects of Desire* (New York: Patheon, 1986), 156–60; Taylor, *The Sounds of Capitalism*, chap. 3.

29 William Leach, *Land of Desire: Merchants, Power, and the Rise of a New American Culture* (New York: Vintage, 1993), 114–15; Jan Logemann, *Trams or Tailfins? Public and Private Prosperity in Postwar West Germany and the United States* (Chicago: University of Chicago Press, 2012), 94, 188–91; Ellen Shell, *Cheap: The High Cost of Discount Culture* (New York: Penguin, 2009), chap. 3.

30 Cross, *Kids' Stuff*, chaps. 4 and 7.

31 Gartman, *Auto Opium*, chap. 5; Cross, *All-Consuming Century*, chap. 3; Bruce Lenthall, *Radio's America: The Great Depression and the Rise of Modern Mass Culture* (Chicago: University of Chicago Press, 2007), chap. 2; Susan Smulyan, *Selling Radio: The Commercialization of American Broadcasting, 1920–1934* (Washington: Smithsonian Institution Press, 1994), 126–32.

32 Ben Wattenberg, ed., *Statistical History of the United States* (New York: Basic, 1976), 400; Iwan Morgan and Philip Davies, eds. *Hollywood and the Great Depression: American Film, Politics and Society in the 1930s* (Edinburgh: Edinburgh University Press, 2016); Avner Offer, *The Challenge of Affluence: Self-Control and Well-Being in the United States and Britain since 1950* (New York: Oxford University Press, 2006), 175–80.

33 Thomas Hine, *Populuxe* (New York: Knopf, 1986).

34 Hine, *Populuxe*, chap. 1; Stephen Fenichell, *Plastic: The Making of a Synthetic Century* (New York: HarperCollins, 1996), chap. 5; Gary Edgerton, *The Columbia History of American Television* (New York: Columbia University Press, 2007), 114.

35 Mark Coleman, *Playback: From the Victrola to MP3, 100 Years of Music, Machines, and Money* (New York: Da Capo, 2003), 39, 59–68; Greg Milner, *Perfecting Sound Forever: An Aural History of Recorded Music* (London: Faber and Faber, 2009), 109–12.

36 Coleman, *Playback: From the Victrola to MP3, 100 Years of Music, Machines, and Money* (New York: Da Capo, 2003) 76–85.

37 Marc Fisher, *Something in the Air: Radio, Rock, and the Revolution that Shaped a Generation* (New York: Random House, 2007), 5–15. Other sources on rock music include Bill Bentley, *Smithsonian Rock and Roll: Live and Unseen* (Washington, DC: Smithsonian Books, 2017); Mitchell Hall, *The Emergence of Rock and Roll: Music and the Rise of American Youth Culture* (New York: Routledge, 2014); Paul Friedlander, *Rock and Roll: A Social History*, 2nd ed. (New York: Routledge, 2018); Jim Miller, *Flowers in the Dustbin: The Rise of Rock and Roll, 1947–1977* (New York: Touchstone, 2000); Richard Aquila, *That Old-Time Rock & Roll: A Chronicle of an Era, 1954–63* (Urbana: University of Illinois Press, 2000).

38 James Flink, *The Automobile Age* (Cambridge, MA: MIT Press, 1993), 287; Vance Packard, *The Waste Makers* (New York: David McKay, 1960), 93; "Biggest Year in Auto History," *US News and World Report*, May 13, 1955, 26–28.

39 "New Cars: Who Buys Them?" *US News and World Report*, March 14, 1958, 84–86; Offer, *Challenge of Affluence*, 198, 279.

40 Packard, *Waste Makers*, chaps. 8 and 9.

41 "Share of US Households Using Specific Technologies, 1860 to 2019," Our World in Data (website), Oxford Martin School, University of Oxford, accessed January 26, 2023, *https://ourworldindata.org*; David Edgerton, *The Shock of the Old: Technology and Global History Since 1900* (New York: Oxford University Press, 2007), chap. 2. As noted by Richard John, *Network Nation: Inventing American Telecommunications* (Cambridge, MA: Belknap Press of Harvard University, 2010), business interests and political influence long impeded the emergence of "universal service" of the telephone.

42 "Average Ad Time Per Hour of Primetime National TV on Cable Network Groups in the United States in 1st Quarter 2019," Statista (website), 2023, www.statista.com; J. MacLachlan and M. Logan, "Camera Shot Length in TV Commercials and their Memorability and Persuasiveness," *Journal of Advertising Research* 33, no. 2 (1993): 57–63; Jeremy Butler, *Television Style* (New York: Routledge, 2009), 124; James Cutting, *Movies on Our Minds: The Evolution of Cinematic Engagement* (New York: Oxford University Press, 2021), chap. 7.

43 "Data from a Century of Cinema Reveals How Movies Have Evolved," *Wired*, September 8, 2014, www.wired.com; Cutting, *Movies on Our Minds*, 142; Barry

Salt, *Film Style and Technology: History and Analysis*, 3rd ed. (London: Starword, 2009), 377–78; James Gleick, *Faster: The Acceleration of Just about Everything* (New York: Pantheon, 1999), 173–202; Simon Gottschalk, "Speed Culture: Fast Strategies in Televised Commercial Ads," *Qualitative Sociology* 22, no. 4 (1999), 312; Wendy Parkins and Geoffrey Craig, *Slow Living* (Oxford: Berg, 2006), 38.

44 Eric Lichtenfeld, *Action Speaks Louder: Violence, Spectacle, and the American Action Movie* (Middletown, CT: Wesleyan University Press, 2007), 114–15, 186–87; Rikke Schubart, "Passion and Acceleration: Generic Change in the Action Film," in *Violence and the American Cinema*, ed. J. David Slocum (New York: Routledge, 2001), 192–208; Amy Rust, *Passionate Detachments: Technologies of Vision and Violence in American Cinema, 1967–1974* (Albany: State University of New York Press, 2017), chap. 3.

45 Stephen Kline, Nick Dyer-Witheford, and Greig de Peuter, *Digital Play: The Interaction of Technology, Culture, and Marketing* (Montreal: McGill-Queen's University Press, 2003); 84–108, 128–50.

46 Kline, Dyer-Witheford, and de Peuter, *Digital Play*, 128–150; Gary Cross, *Men to Boys: The Making of Modern Immaturity* (New York: Columbia University Press, 2008), 212–25.

47 Jennifer Rauch, *Slow Media: Why 'Slow' is Satisfying, Sustainable, and Smart* (New York: Oxford University Press, 2018), 72.

48 Stephen Rosenberg, *Time for Things: Labor, Leisure, and the Rise of Mass Consumption* (Cambridge, MA: Harvard University Press, 2021), 139, 266–68.

49 Scitovsky, *Joyless Economy*, 206–12.

50 Jonathan Gershuny, "Busyness as the Badge of Honor for the New Superordinate Working Class," *Social Research* 72, no. 2 (Summer 2005): 287–314; Peter Toohey, *Boredom: A Lively History* (New Haven, CT: Yale University Press, 2011), chap. 6; Robert Levine, *A Geography of Time: The Temporal Misadventures of a Social Psychologist* (New York: Basic, 1997), 36–38.

51 Byung-Chul Han, *The Disappearance of Ritual* (Medford, MA: Polity, 2020), 7. See also Byung-Chul Han, *The Scent of Time: A Philosophical Essay on the Art of Lingering* (New York: Polity, 2020); and Thomas Eriksen, *Tyranny of the Moment: Fast and Slow Time in the Information Age* (London: Pluto Press, 2001), 19–20.

52 Scitovsky, *Joyless Economy*, 68–71.

53 Offer, *Challenge of Affluence*, 358.

54 John Robinson and Geoffrey Godbey, *Time for Life: The Surprising Ways American Use their Time* (University Park, PA: Penn State University Press, 1999), xviii, 55, 125–26, 292; Rosa, *Social Acceleration*, 137–39.

55 Colin Campbell, *The Romantic Ethic and the Spirit of Modern Consumerism* (London: Blackwell, 1989).

56 Daniel Lord Smail, *On Deep History and the Brain* (Berkeley: University of California Press, 2008), 118, 127–28, 131, 147.

57 A popular treatment of this is Anna Lembke, *Dopamine Nation: Finding Balance in the Age of Indulgence* (New York: Dutton, 2021).

58 Fernandez and Matt, *Bored, Lonely*, 282–83, chap. 3; Peter Stearns, *Satisfaction Not Guaranteed: Dilemmas of Progress in Modern Society* (New York: New York University Press, 2012); Cross and Proctor, *Packaged Pleasures*, chaps. 1 and 8.

59 Parkins and Craig, *Slow Living*, 52; Carl Honoré, *In Praise of Slow* (London: Orion, 2004), 4; Geoff Andrews, *The Slow Food Story: Politics and Pleasures* (Montreal: McGill-Queen's University Press, 2008); Carlo Petrini, *Slow Food Revolution: A New Culture for Dining & Living* (New York: Rizzoli, 2006); Alice Waters, *We Are What We Eat: A Slow Food Manifesto* (New York: Penguin, 2021).

60 I develop this in my book *Consumed Nostalgia: Memory in the Age of Fast Capitalism* (New York: Columbia University Press, 2015), chap. 6. For a treatment of modern forms of nostalgia and their critics, see Tobias Becker, *Yesterday: A New History of Nostalgia* (Cambridge, MA: Harvard University Press, 2023). See also Rauch, *Slow Media*, 73; and Daniel Rodgers, *Age of Fracture* (Cambridge, MA: Belknap Press of Harvard University, 2011), 225–37, 247–49.

61 A good bibliography and summary of nostalgic folk festivals is in Lisa Gabbert, "American Festival and Folk Drama," in *The Oxford Handbook of American Folklore and Folklife Studies*, ed. Simon Bronner (New York: Oxford University Press, 2018), 277–97; Robert H. Lavenda, *Corn Fests and Water Carnivals: Celebrating Community in Minnesota* (Washington, DC: Smithsonian Institution Press, 1997); Lisa Gabbert, *Winter Carnival in a Western Town: Identity, Change, and the Good of the Community* (Logan: Utah State University Press, 2011); and Simon J. Bronner, *Killing Tradition: Inside Hunting and Animal Rights Controversies* (Lexington: University Press of Kentucky, 2008).

62 Cross and Proctor, *Packaged Pleasures*, 232.

Chapter 8. Funneled Capitalism

1 Some classics are T. Veblen, *The Theory of the Leisure Class* (New York: Oxford University Press, 2007. Original: 1899); Juliet Schor, *The Overspent American: Why We Want What We Don't Need* (New York: Harper Collins, 1999); Fred Hirsch, *The Limits to Growth* (Cambridge, MA: Harvard University Press, 1976); Susan Matt, *Keeping Up with the Joneses: Envy in American Consumer Society, 1890–1930* (Philadelphia: University of Pennsylvania Press, 2002).

2 Gary Cross, *All-Consuming Century: How Commercialism Won in Modern America* (New York: Columbia University Press, 2000), esp. chaps. 1 and 8.

3 Bruce Ward, "Americans Are Choosing to be Alone. Here's Why We Should Reverse That," *Washington Post*, November 23, 2022.

4 Henry Ford, *My Life and Work* (Garden City, NY: Doubleday, Page & Co., 1922), 73.

5 A classic text on American individualism is Philip Slater, *The Pursuit of Loneliness* (1970; repr., Boston: Beacon, 1990).

6 Robert and Helen Lynd, *Middletown in Transition* (New York: Harcourt, 1937), 244–46.

7 Kathleen Franz, *Tinkering: Consumers Reinvent the Automobile* (Philadelphia: University of Pennsylvania Press, 2005), chap. 3; John Rae, *The American Automobile: A Brief History* (Chicago: University of Chicago Press, 1965), 116; Gary Cross, *Machines of Youth: America's Car Obsession* (Chicago: University of Chicago Press, 2018), chap. 2.

8 Cotten Seiler, *Republic of Drivers: A Cultural History of Automobility in America* (Chicago: University of Chicago Press, 2008), 58–60, quotation at 43; Sarah Seo, *Policing the Open Road: How Cars Transformed American Freedom* (Cambridge, MA: Harvard University Press, 2019), 159, chap. 1, quotations at 10, 35; Virginia Scharff, *Taking the Wheel: Women and the Coming of the Motor Age* (Santa Fe: University of New Mexico Press, 1992), 13, 161.

9 Robert Fogelson, *Downtown: Its Rise and Fall, 1880–1950* (New Haven, CT: Yale University Press, 2001), chaps. 5 and 8; Ann Satterthwaite, *Going Shopping: Consumer Choice and Community Consequence* (New Haven, CT: Yale University Press, 2002), 95–98.

10 William Whyte, *The Organization Man* (New York: Anchor, 1957); K. T. Jackson, *Crabgrass Frontier* (New York: Oxford University Press, 1987), 281.

11 Warren Belasco, *Americans on the Road: From Autocamp to Motel, 1910–1945* (1979; repr., Baltimore: Johns Hopkins University Press, 1997); Robin Reid, "The History of the Drive-In Movie Theater," *Smithsonian Magazine*, May 27, 2008, www.smithsonianmag.com.

12 "Percentage of Households by Number of Vehicles, 1960–2017," The Geography of Transport Systems, website of Dr. Jean-Paul Rodrigue, Department of Global Studies and Geography, Hofstra University, accessed January 26, 2023, https://transportgeography.org; "Motorization Rate in Selected Countries as of 2018," Statista (website), 2023, www.statista.com; Robert Gordon, *The Rise and Fall of American Growth* (Princeton, NJ: Princeton University Press, 2016), 37, 60, 80.

13 Kris Lackey, *RoadFrames: The American Highway Narrative* (Omaha: University of Nebraska Press, 1997); David Laderman, *Driving Visions: Exploring the Road Movie* (Austin: University of Texas Press, 2002).

14 The classics are Susan Strasser, *Never Done: A History of American Housework* (1982; repr., New York: Holt Paperbacks, 2000), chap. 6; and Ruth Schwartz Cowan, *More Work for Mother: The Ironies of Household Technology from the Open Hearth to the Microwave* (1982; repr., New York: Holt, 2000), chap. 6. Note also Fred Schroeder, "More 'Small Things Forgotten': Domestic Electrical Plugs and Receptacles, 1881–1931," *Technology and Culture* 27 (1986): 525–43.

15 David Suisman, *Selling Sounds: The Commercial Revolution in American Music* (Cambridge, MA: Harvard University Press, 2012), chap. 3.

16 Suisman, *Selling Sounds*, 94–100; Q. David Bowers, *Put Another Nickel In: A History of Coin-Operated Pianos* (New York: Vestal, 1966).

17 Suisman, *Selling Sounds*, chap. 6; Roland Gelatt, *The Fabulous Phonograph 1877–1977* (New York: Macmillan, 1977), 178, 208–18; Evan Eisenberg, *The Recording Angel: Music, Records, and Culture from Aristotle to Zappa*, second edition (New Haven: Yale University Press, 2005), 18–22, 39.

18 Jacques Attali, *Noise: The Political Economy of Music* (Minneapolis: University of Minnesota Press, 1985), 89.

19 Edison Phonograph advertisement (circa 1900) in C. Fabrizio and George Paul, *Antique Phonograph Advertising* (Atglen, PA: Schiffer Publ. 2002), 91; Victor Talking Machine Company, Victor advertisement, *Ladies Home Journal*, August 1913, 460. For the phonograph and radio as a tool of sociability, see Luke Fernandez and Susan Matt, *Bored, Lonely, Angry, Stupid: Changing Feelings about Technology from the Telegraph to Twitter* (Cambridge, MA: Harvard University Press, 2019), 1, 103–18.

20 Among the many sources are Lenny Lipton, *The Cinema in Flux: The Evolution of Motion Picture Technology from the Magic Lantern to the Digital Era* (New York: Springer, 2021); André Gaudreault, ed., *American Cinema, 1890–1909* (New Brunswick, NJ: Rutgers University Press, 2009); Charles Musser, *The Emergence of Cinema: The American Screen to 1907* (New York: Scribner, 1990); Richard Abel, *Americanizing the Movies and "Movie-Mad" Audiences, 1910–1914* (Berkeley: University of California Press, 2002); Douglas Gomery, *Shared Pleasures: A History of Movie Presentation in the United States* (Madison: University of Wisconsin Press, 1992).

21 Richard Butsch, "The Imagined Audience in the Nickelodeon Era," in *The Wiley-Blackwell History of American Film*, eds. Cynthia Lucia, Roy Grundmann, and Art Simon, vol. 1 (Chichester, UK: Wiley Blackwell, 2012), 109–28; Tom Gunning, *D. W. Griffith and the Origins of American Narrative Film* (Urbana: University of Illinois Press, 1991), 56–65, 85–86.

22 Tom Gunning, "Motion Picture Patents Company," in *Encyclopedia of Early Cinema*, ed. Richard Abel (New York: Routledge, 2010), 447–48; David Robinson, *From Peep Show to Palace: The Birth of American Film* (New York: Columbia University Press, 1994), 101–10.

23 Gunning, *Narrative Film*, chap. 6; Robinson, *Peep Show to Palace*, 122–30; Tino Balio, ed., *The American Film Industry* (Madison: University of Wisconsin Press, 1985), 103–253.

24 Abel, *Americanizing the Movies*, 232–33; Susan Douglas and Andre McDonnell, *Celebrity: A History of Fame* (New York: New York University, 2019), chap. 3; Samantha Barbas, *Movie Crazy: Fans, Stars, and the Cult of Celebrity* (New York: Palgrave, 2002), 15–28, 35–57; Mark Anderson, "The Star System," in Lucia, Grundmann, and Simon, *Wiley-Blackwell History of American Film*, 349–70; Richard deCordova, *Picture Personalities: The Emergence of the Star System in America* (Urbana: University of Illinois Press, 1990), 85–90.

25 Jean-Gabriel Tarde, *Les Lois d'imitation* (Paris: Felix Alcan, 1890), 239, 322–44; Jean-Gabriel Tarde, *La Psychologie économique*, vol. 2 (Paris: Felix Alcan, 1902), 151–56, 256. For the system of film distribution in the early twentieth-century US, see Mike Walsh, Richard Maltby, and Dylan Walker, "Three Moments of Cinema Exhibition," in *The Routledge Companion to New Cinema History*, eds. Daniel Biltereyst, Richard Maltby, Philippe Meers (New York: Routledge, 2019), 217–31.

26 Shawn VanCour, *Making Radio: Early Radio Production and the Rise of Modern Sound Culture* (New York: Oxford University Press, 2018); Sungook Hong, *Wireless: From Marconi's Black-Box to the Audion* (Cambridge, MA: MIT Press, 2001); Steven Wurtzler, *Electric Sounds: Technological Change and the Rise of Corporate Mass Media* (New York: Columbia University Press, 2007); Susan Douglas, *Inventing American Broadcasting, 1899–1922* (Baltimore: Johns Hopkins University Press, 1987).

27 Douglas Gomery, *A History of Broadcasting in the United States* (Malden, MA: Blackwell, 2008), 11–105, quotation at 77.

28 Gomery, *Broadcasting in the United States*, 142–64; Michele Hilmes, *Radio Voices: American Broadcasting, 1922–1952* (Minneapolis: University of Minnesota Press 1997), chaps. 6 and 7; Susan Douglas, *Listening In: Radio and the American Imagination* (Minneapolis: University of Minnesota Press, 2004), chaps. 9–11.

29 Some sources include Gary Edgerton, *The Columbia History of American Television* (New York: Columbia University Press, 2007), chaps. 3 and 4; Harry Castleman and Walter J. Podrazik, *Watching TV: Eight Decades of American Television* (Syracuse, NY: Syracuse University Press, 2016), chaps. 13–15; Erik Barnouw, *Tube of Plenty: The Evolution of American Television* (New York: Oxford University Press, 1990), chap. 2; James Baughman, *Same Time, Same Station: Creating American Television, 1948–1961* (Baltimore: Johns Hopkins University Press, 2007), 300–302; Lynn Spigel, *Make Room for TV: Television and the Family Ideal in Postwar America* (Chicago: University of Chicago Press, 1992), chap. 1; Cecelia Tichi, *Electronic Hearth: Creating an American Television Culture* (New York: Oxford University Press, 1991).

30 Douglas, *Listening In*, chap. 9; Marc Fisher, *Something in the Air: Radio, Rock and the Revolution that Shaped a Generation* (New York: Random House, 2007), 5–15.

31 A classic is David Marc, *Demographic Vistas: Television in American Culture*, rev. ed. (Philadelphia: University of Pennsylvania Press, 1996).

32 Joshua Meyrowitz, *No Sense of Place: The Impact of Electronic Media on Social Behavior* (New York: Oxford University Press, 1985), 1–13, 88, 127–28; Marshall McLuhan, *Understanding Media: The Extensions of Man* (1964; repr., Cambridge, MA: MIT Press, 1994). For a critique of Meyrowitz, see Shaun Moores, *Media, Place and Mobility* (London: Palgrave, 2012), Chapter 1.

33 Tichi, *Electronic Hearth*, 63, 70, 78.

34 Gomery, *History of Broadcasting*, 299; Edgerton, *History of American Television*, 314, 320–22, 332–33, 350. A critique of media ownership convergence is Robert

McChesney, *Rich Media, Poor Democracy: Communication Politics in Dubious Times* (New York: New Press, 2016).

35 Leo Enticknap, *Moving Image Technology: From Zoetrope to Digital* (New York: Wallflower, 2005); Debra Geoghan, *Visualizing Technology*, 9th ed. (Boston: Pearson, 2021).

36 Bo Lojek, *History of Semiconductor Engineering* (New York: Springer, 2007); Eric Swedin and David Ferro, *The Computer: A Brief History of the Machine That Changed the World* (Santa Barbara, CA: Greenwood, 2021), chaps. 4 and 5.

37 Mark Coleman, *Playback: From the Victrola to MP3, 100 Years of Music, Machines, and Money* (New York: Da Capo, 2003), 159–63; Timothy Day, *A Century of Recorded Music* (New Haven, CT: Yale University Press, 2000), 213; Greg Milner, *Perfecting Sound Forever: An Aural History of Recorded Music* (New York: Faber and Faber, 2009), 191–94.

38 Recent sources are Thomas Haigh and Paul Ceruzzi, *A New History of Modern Computing* (Cambridge, MA: MIT Press, 2021); Martin Campbell-Kelly and Daniel Garcia-Swartz, *From Mainframes to Smart Phones: A History of the International Computer Industry* (Cambridge, MA: Harvard University Press, 2015); and Thomas Haigh, Mark Priestley, and Crispin Rope, *Eniac in Action: Making and Remaking the Modern Computer* (Cambridge, MA: MIT Press, 2016).

39 Janet Abbate, *Inventing the Internet* (Cambridge, MA: MIT Press, 1999); Martin Campbell-Kelly and Daniel Garcia-Swartz, *Mainframes to Smart Phones: A History of the International Computer Industry* (Cambridge, MA: Harvard University Press, 2015); Mark Graham and William H. Dutton, *Society and the Internet: How Networks of Information and Communication are Changing our Lives* (New York: Oxford University Press, 2014).

40 James Murray, *Wireless Nation: The Frenzied Launch of the Cellular Revolution in America* (Cambridge, MA: Perseus, 2001); Brian Merchant, *The One Device: The Secret History of the iPhone* (New York: Little Brown, 2017), 197–227; Steven Jones, *Cell Tower* (New York: Bloomsbury, 2020).

41 Lynne Kelly, Robert L. Duran, and Aimee E. Miller-Ott, "Helicopter Parenting and Cell-Phone Contact between Parents and Children in College," *Southern Communication Journal* 82, no. 2 (2017): 102–14.

42 Strong defenses of digital media are in Henry Jenkins, Sam Ford, and Joshua Green, *Spreadable Media: Creating Value and Meaning in a Networked Culture* (New York: New York University Press, 2013); and Henry Jenkins, *Participatory Culture: Interviews* (Medford, MA: Polity, 2019). An early celebration of the coming of a new age of individualism through the linked computer is in John Naisbitt, *Megatrends: Ten New Directions Transforming Our Lives* (New York: Warner, 1982). See also Daniel Rodgers, *Age of Fracture* (Cambridge, MA: Belknap Press of Harvard University, 2011), 108–11.

43 Cross, *Machines of Youth*, chap. 9; Joel Best and Kathleen Bogle, *Kids Gone Wild: From Rainbow Parties to Sexting, Understanding the Hype over Teen Sex* (New

York: New York University Press, 2014), 126–27; Katherina Boltholtz, "Americans Get Driver's Licenses Later in Life," Statista (website), January 6, 2020, www.statista.com.

44 Samuel Earle, "The Timeline We're on Is Even Darker Than 'The Matrix' Envisioned," *New York Times*, December 22, 2021, www.nytimes.com.

45 Sherry Turkle writes about the limits of digital connectedness in *Reclaiming Conversation: The Power of Talk in a Digital Age* (New York: Penguin, 2015); and *Alone Together: Why We Expect More from Technology and Less from Each Other* (New York: Basic, 2011). A balanced treatment of the narcissistic implications of digital media is in Fernandez and Matt, *Bored, Lonely*, 61–81. An interesting take on memory and the internet is in David Sisto, *Remember Me: Memory and Forgetting in the Digital Age* (Medford, MA: Polity, 2021).

46 Byung-Chul Han, *The Disappearance of Rituals* (Medford, MA: Polity, 2020), 1, 7.

47 Hayley Tsukayama, "Teens Spend Nearly Nine Hours Every Day Consuming Media," *Washington Post*, November 3, 2015, www.washingtonpost.com; Debashish Sengupta, *The Life of Z: Understanding the Digital Pre-Teen and Adolescent Generation* (Los Angeles: Sage, 2020), chaps. 4 and 5.

48 Setting off discussion was Stephen Marche, "Is Facebook Making Us Lonely," *Atlantic*, May 2012, www.theatlantic.com/; Fernandez and Matt, *Bored, Lonely*, 83–140, 172–87, quotation at 89; and William Cacioppo, *Loneliness: Human Nature and the Need for Social Connection* (New York: Norton, 2009).

49 Hartmut Rosa, *Social Acceleration: A New Theory of Modernity* (New York: Columbia University Press, 2015), 145–46, 228, 280, 306, 307.

50 John Beck, *The Kids are Alright: How the Gamer Generation is Changing the Workplace* (Cambridge, MA: Harvard Business School Press, 2006); Steve Johnson, *Everything Bad is Good for You: How Today's Popular Culture is Actually Making Us Smarter* (New York: Riverhead Books, 2005).

51 David Shenk, *Data Smog: Surviving the Information Age* (San Francisco: HarperOne, 1998); Erich Fromm, *Escape from Freedom* (1941; repr., New York: Avon, 1970), 155, 163–201. For a similar view, see Thomas Eriksen, *Tyranny of the Moment: Fast and Slow Time in the Information Age* (London: Pluto, 2001), 108–9, and his notion of how computer culture replaces the experience of "totalities" with "pieces."

52 Russell Belk, *Collecting in a Consumer Culture* (London: Routledge, 1995), 29–35; Simon Reynolds, *Retromania: Pop Culture's Addiction to its Own Past* (London: Farrar, Straus and Giroux, 2011), chap. 3.

53 Grace Hale, *Nation of Outsiders: How the White Middle Class Fell in Love with Rebellion in Postwar America* (New York: Oxford University Press, 2014), chap. 1; Fernandez and Matt, *Bored, Lonely*, 357–62; The classic sociology of recent American individualism is Robert Putnam, *Bowling Alone: The Collapse and Revival of American Community* (New York: Simon and Schuster, 2001).

Chapter 9. Making Time for Culture

1 Hartmut Rosa, *Resonance: A Sociology of Our Relationship to the World*, (Cambridge, UK: Polity Press, 2019).

2 Admittedly, I have not emphasized the topic of race. It clearly contributes to cultural divisions, as White and Black Americans still share relatively little free time together and many Whites continue to harbor disdain for and fear of the free-time activities of African Americans.

3 Barbara Ehrenreich, *Fear of Falling: The Inner Life of the Middle Class* (New York: Harper Perennial, 1985), 247.

4 Hartmut Rosa, *Social Acceleration* (New York: Columbia University Press, 2013), 220–21.

5 Gunnar Trumbull, "France's 35 Hour Work Week: Flexibility Through Regulation," *Brookings*, January 1, 2001, www.brookings.edu; Richard Venturi, "Busting the Myth of France's 35-hour workweek," *BBC Worklife*, March 12, 2014, www.bbc.com.

6 Erika Page, "Promises of a Shorter Workweek: Could it Be a Win-Win?," *Christian Science Monitor*, November 1, 2021, www.csmonitor.com. See also Bryce Covert, "8 Hours a Day, 5 Days a Week Is Not Working for Us," *New York Times*, July 20, 2021, www.nytimes.com; Christine Emba, "We're Making the Wrong Argument for a Four-Day Workweek," *Washington Post*, July 7, 2021, www.washingtonpost.com; Cassady Rosenblum, "Work Is a False Idol," *New York Times*, August 22, 2021, www.nytimes.com; and Claire Cain Miller, "Shorter Hours, No Promotions: How the Pandemic Stalled Some Parents' Careers," *New York Times*, July 21, 2021, www.nytimes.com.

7 Jennifer Liu, "U.S. Workers Are Among the Most Stressed in the World, New Gallup Report Finds," *CNBC*, June 15, 2021, www.cnbc.com. The issue of the symmetrical family was noted early by Peter Willmott and Michael Young in *The Symmetrical Family* (New York: Penguin, 1973), and subsequently this concept has been used to point out the continued asymmetry between the domestic work of men and women. See Arlie Hochschild and Anne Machung, *The Second Shift: Working Families and the Revolution at Home, rev. ed.* (New York: Penguin, 2012); and Jacqueline Scott, Shirley Dex, and Anke Plagno, eds., *Gendered Lives: Gender Inequalities in Production and Reproduction* (Northampton, MA: Edward Elgar Pub., 2012).

8 Spencer Bokat-Lindell, "Do We Need to Shrink the Economy to Stop Climate Change?" *New York Times*, September 16, 2021, www.nytimes.com; Kerryn Higgs, *Collusion Course: Endless Growth on a Finite Planet* (Cambridge, MA: MIT Press, 2014), 16, 26–27, 273–75, quotation at 282. See Herman Daley, *From Uneconomic Growth to a Steady-State Economy* (New York: Edward Elgar, 2016), for one of many arguments against growth economics. Note also, Naomi Klein, *This Changes Everything: Capitalism vs The Climate* (New York: Simon and Schuster, 2014).

9 Noah Smith, "People are Realizing that Degrowth is Bad," Noahpinion (blog), September 6, 2021, https://noahpinion.substack.com; Eric Levitz, "We'll Innovate Our Way Out of the Climate Crisis or Die Trying," *New York Magazine*, May 17, 2021, *https://nymag.com*; Kate Raworth, *Doughnut Economics: Seven Ways to Think Like a 21st-Century Economist* (London: Chelsea Green Publishing, 2017).

10 Daniel Hamermesh, *Spending Time: The Most Valuable Resource* (New York: Oxford University Press, 2018), 189–95.

11 For a defense of the experience economy and its potential for challenging consumer capitalism, see B. K. Hunnicutt, *Age of Experiences* (Philadelphia: Temple University Press, 2021); Joseph Pine and James Gilmore, *The Experience Economy* (Boston: Harvard Business Review Press, 2011); Martin Seligman, *Authentic Happiness: Using the New Positive Psychology to Realize Your Potential for Lasting Fulfilment* (New York: Free Press, 2002).

12 Rosa, *Social Acceleration*, 302–3; Tim Kasser, *The High Price of Materialism* (New York: Bedford Books, 2002), xiii, 113; Avner Offer, *The Challenge of Affluence: Self-Control and Well-Being in the United States and Britain since 1950* (New York: Oxford University Press, 2006), 367; Frank Trentmann, *Empire of Things* (New York: Penguin, 2016), 464–65.

13 Jennifer Rauch, *Slow Media: Why "Slow" is Satisfying, Sustainable, and Smart* (New York: Oxford University Press, 2018), 114–17.

14 Rosa, *Resonance*, part 2, 234–38, 331–51, 405.

15 Rosa, *Resonance*, 21–22, 26–27, 29, 41–42, 273, 370–71, 411, 438–39, quotations at 27, 344. Somewhat similar are the views of Eugene McCarraher, *The Enchantments of Mammon: How Capitalism Became the Religion of Modernity* (Cambridge, MA: Belknap Press of Harvard University, 2019), in his discussion of the decline of the sacramental in modern life as capitalism becomes the common religion.

16 Rosa, *Social Acceleration*, 302–3. See also the works of the popular cultural critic Byung-Chul Han, *The Disappearance of Ritual* (Medford, MA: Polity, 2020); *The Scent of Time: A Philosophical Essay on the Art of Lingering* (New York: Polity, 2020); *The Burnout Society* (Stanford, CA: Stanford University Press, 2015), among others.

17 The happiness literature begins with Richard Easterin, "Does Economic Growth Improve the Human Lot? Some Empirical Evidence," in *Nations and Households in Economic Growth*, eds. Paul David and Melvin Reder (New York: Elsevier, 1974), 89–125. Easterin observes that reported happiness did not increase with increased affluence. There is some evidence that it has not declined, though. For a summary of this issue, see Peter Stearns, *Satisfaction Not Guaranteed: Dilemmas of Progress in Modern Society* (New York: New York University, 2012), chap. 2.

18 Stearns, *Satisfaction* 5, 9.

19 Peter Whybrow, *American Mania: When More Is Not Enough* (New York: Norton, 2005), quotation 9, 93; Offer, *Challenge of Affluence*, 20, 74, 366, 369, 372. Also note Anna Lembke, *Dopamine Nation: Finding a Balance in an Age of Indulgence* (New York: Dutton, 2021).

20 Kasser, *Materialism*, 5–6; Mihalyi Csikszentmahalyi, *Finding Flow:* The Psychology of Engagement with Everyday Life (New York: Basic, 1997); Stearns, *Satisfaction*, 245.

21 Stephen Rosenberg, *Time for Things* (Cambridge, MA: Harvard University Press, 2021), 266–67.

22 Rosa, *Social Acceleration*, 220, 322; Rosa, *Resonance*; Higgs, *Collision Course*, 281.

Index

About the Author

Gary Cross is Distinguished Professor Emeritus of modern history in the Department of History at Pennsylvania State University and author of *Time and Money: The Making of Consumer Culture* and coauthor of *Packaged Pleasures: How Technology and Marketing Revolutionized Desire.*

Printed in the USA
CPSIA information can be obtained
at www.ICGtesting.com
LVHW090927210224
772430LV00010B/13/J